▲▲▲

# Linux Application Development

▼

▲▲▲

# Linux Application Development

▼

Michael K. Johnson

Erik W. Troan

**ADDISON–WESLEY**

**An Imprint of Addison Wesley Longman, Inc.**

Reading, Massachusetts • Harlow, England • Menlo Park, California
Berkeley, California • Don Mills, Ontario • Sydney
Bonn • Amsterdam • Tokyo • Mexico City

Many of the designations used by manufacturers and sellers to distinguish their products are claimed as trademarks. Where those designations appear in this book, and Addison-Wesley was aware of a trademark claim, the designations have been printed in initial capital letters or all capital letters.

The authors and publisher have taken care in preparation of this book, but make no expressed or implied warranty of any kind and assume no responsibility for errors or omissions. No liability is assumed for incidental or consequential damages in connection with or arising out of the use of the information or programs contained herein.

The publisher offers discounts of this book when ordered in quantity for special sales. For more information, please contact:

> Computer and Engineering Publishing Group
> Addison Wesley Longman, Inc.
> One Jacob Way
> Reading, Massachusetts 01867

*Library of Congress Cataloging-in-Publication Data*

Johnson, Michael K.
     Linux application development / Michael K. Johnson, Erik W. Troan
        p.   cm.
     Includes bibliographical references and index.
     ISBN 0-201-30821-5
     1. Linux. 2. Application software—Development.     I. Troan, Erik
W.
     QA76.76.O63J635     1998
     005.2′68—dc21

                                                         97–49039
                                                         CIP

Text design by Greg Johnson, Art Directions
Set in 11.5 Palatino by Erik Troan, using T$_{\!E}$X

ISBN 0-201-30821-5
1 2 3 4 5 6 7 8 9—MA—0201009998
*First printing, April 1998*

*To all of my parents, for giving constant support
despite ever-slipping schedules.*

*—Erik*

*To the memory of my grandmother, Eleanor Johnson,
who taught faith in God by example,
and who believed that I could write a book.*

*Soli Deo Gloria.*

*—Michael*

# Preface

We wrote this book for experienced (or not-so-experienced, but eager-to-learn) programmers who want to develop Linux software or to port software from other platforms to Linux. This is the book we wish we had when we were learning to program for Linux, and the book we now keep on our desks for reference. By the time we wrote our first three chapters, we were already using the drafts as reference material while we worked.

Linux is designed to be similar to Unix. This book gives you a good background in Unix programming basics and style. Linux is not fundamentally different from Unix—only different enough to repeatedly trip up a programmer who relies only on a Unix programming reference that ignores Linux. This book, therefore, is very much a Unix programming guide that is written from a Linux viewpoint.

Linux also has unique extensions, such as its direct screen access capabilities (see Chapter 20), and it has features that are used more often on it than on other systems, such as the S-Lang library (see Chapter 22). This book covers many of those extensions and features so that you can write programs that truly take advantage of Linux.

- If you are a C programmer, but you know neither Unix nor Linux, reading this book cover-to-cover and working with the examples should put you well on the road to being a competent Linux programmer. With the aid of other, system-specific documentation, you should find the transition to any version of Unix easy.

- If you are already a proficient Unix programmer, you will find that this book makes your transition to Linux easier. We have tried very hard to make it easy for you to find precisely the information you need to know. We also carefully and clearly cover topics that sometimes trip up even experienced Unix programmers, such as process and session groups, job control, and tty handling.

- If you are already a Linux programmer, this book covers confusing topics clearly and will make many of your programming tasks easier. Nearly every chapter will stand alone for you, because you already possess the minimal knowledge of Linux on which they are based. No matter how experienced you are, you will find material here that you will appreciate having at your elbow.

This book is different from usual Unix programming texts because it is unabashedly specific to a particular operating system. We have no need to confuse newcomers by saying *BSD does this this way, SVR4 does it another, HPUX has its own way of handling it, and SGI also has its way. We'll cover each of these and let you sort it all out.* We know from our own experience that once you learn how to program well for any Unix-like system, the others are easy to learn.

This book does not cover *all* the details of Linux programming. For example, it does not cover programming the X Window System, because such programming is the same on any Linux or Unix platform. Similarly, it does not explain the basic interface specified by ANSI C—other books do that quite well. Without extraordinary verbosity, we cover the information you need to know to go from being a C programmer for another system, such as DOS, Windows, or Macintosh, to being a C programmer for Linux. We do not cover the wealth of other programming languages available for Linux, and we do not cover the graphical programming libraries that are identical no matter what supported system you are using. Instead, we point you to books that specialize in those areas.

*Linux Application Development* is written in four parts.

- The first part introduces you to Linux—the operating system, license terms, documentation, and milieu.

- The second part covers the most important facets of the development environment—the compilers, linker and loader, and some debugging tools that are not widely used on other platforms.

- The third part is the heart of the book—it describes the interface to the kernel and to the system libraries, which are primarily meant as an interface to the kernel. Only the final three chapters of this section are very Linux-specific; most of this section covers general Unix programming from a Linux perspective.

- The fourth part rounds out your knowledge—it includes descriptions of some important libraries that provide interfaces that are more independent of the kernel. These libraries are, properly speaking, not Linux-specific, but several are used more often on Linux systems than on other systems.

If you are already familiar with Linux or Unix programming, you will be able to read the chapters in this book in any order. Do not feel compelled to read chapters that do not interest you. If you are not familiar with either Linux or Unix, most of the chapters will stand alone, but you will probably want to read Chapters 1, 2, 4, 5, 8, 9, 10, and 11 first, as they will give you most of what you need to know to read the other chapters. In particular, Chapters 9, 10, and 11 form the core of the Unix and Linux programming model.

The following books, although they may overlap a little here and there, mostly complement this book by being simpler, more advanced, or on related topics.

- *The C Programming Language, second edition* [Kernighan, 1988] concisely teaches ANSI standard C programming, with scant reference to the operating system. It recommends that readers have either some programming knowledge or "access to a more knowledgeable colleague."

- *Practical C Programming* [Oualline, 1993] teaches C programming and style in a step-by-step, easy-to-follow manner that is designed for people with no prior programming experience.

- *Programming with GNU Software* [Loukides, 1997] is an introduction to the GNU programming environment, including chapters on running the C compiler, the debugger, the make utility, and the RCS source code control system.

- *Advanced Programming in the UNIX Environment* [Stevens, 1992] covers most important Unix and Unix-like systems, although it predates

Linux. It covers similar material to the final two parts of *Linux Application Development*: system calls and shared libraries. It also provides many examples and explains the difference between various Unix versions.

- *UNIX Network Programming* [Stevens, 1990] thoroughly covers network programming, including legacy types of networking that are not available on Linux, at least as we write this. While reading this book, stick to the Berkeley socket interface (see Chapter 16) to maintain maximum portability. This book may be useful if you need to make a few slight changes to port your Linux network program to some brand of Unix.

See the bibliography on page 521 or at http://www.awl.com/cseng/books/lad/biblio.html for an extensive list of related titles.

All the source code in this book comes from working examples that we have tested while writing. All of the source code in this book is available in electronic format at http://www.awl.com/cseng/books/lad/src/ and ftp://ftp.awl.com/cseng/books/lad/src/. In the interest of clarity, some short source code segments check only for likely errors that document how the system works rather than check for all possible errors. However, in the full programs in the book and on our Web and FTP sites, we have made an attempt (we are not perfect) to check for all reasonable errors.

This book will teach you which functions to use and how they fit together; we encourage you to learn also how to use the reference documentation,[1] the great majority of which was included with your system.

We welcome your comments sent to lad-comments@awl.com. We will read your comments, although we cannot promise to respond to them individually.

Linux is a rapidly developing operating system, and by the time you read this book, some facts (though we hope little substance) will no doubt have changed. We wrote this book in reference to Linux 2.0.30 and the C library version 5.3.12 as distributed with Red Hat Software's Red Hat Linux 4.2. We have also tested our example source code with the C library version 6 (glibc 2.0.5) as distributed with Red Hat Linux 5.0.

---

1. Chapter 3 discusses how to find information on Linux-related topics.

With your help, we will maintain a list of errata and changes on the World Wide Web at http://www.awl.com/cseng/books/lad/errata.html and via FTP at ftp://ftp.awl.com/cseng/books/lad/errata/.

We would like to thank each of our technical reviewers for their time and careful thought. Their suggestions have made this book stronger. Particular thanks go to Linus Torvalds, Alan Cox, and Ted Ts'o, who took time to answer our questions.

Special thanks go out to Kim Johnson and Brigid Nogueira. Without their undying patience this book simply would not have been written.

# Contents

# List of Tables

*Part* 1

# Getting Started

# CHAPTER 1

# History of Linux Development

People use **Linux** to mean different things. The most technically accurate definition is this:

> Linux is a freely distributable, Unix-like operating system kernel.

However, most people use **Linux** to mean an entire operating system based on the Linux kernel.

> Linux is a freely distributable, Unix-like operating system that includes a kernel, system tools, applications, and a complete development environment.

In this book, we use the second definition, as you will be programming for the entire operating system, not just the kernel.

Linux (by the second definition) provides a good platform from which to port programs, because its recommended interfaces (the ones we discuss in this book) are supported by nearly every version of Unix available, as well as by most Unix clones. After you learn the contents of this book, you should be able to port your programs to nearly every Unix and Unix-like system, with little extra work.

On the other hand, after working with Linux, you may prefer to use only Linux and not bother porting.

Linux is not just another Unix. It is more than a good platform from which to port programs—it is also a good platform on which to build and run applications. Some of Linux's advantages include the following:

- Stable Linux kernel versions are clearly separated from experimental versions, and both are available to the general public. You can deploy known stable systems in a production environment. At the same time, experimental Linux versions are released on a frequent basis, allowing you to follow—and even participate in—the development of the operating system, if you want.

- Source code for the whole base operating system is available for your inspection, use, and even modification.

- Linux is controlled by a group of private individuals, not by a single corporation. Technical decisions are made on technical merits, not on marketing considerations, by people driven by technology. This means that Linux development moves very quickly, keeping pace with other complementary technology.

- The Linux developer and user communities are large and generally eager to help newcomers.

## 1.1 A Short History of Free Unix Software

If you are to understand what it means to develop software for Linux, you will need a short history lesson. The lesson we present is simplified and biased toward the most important elements in a Linux system. For longer, more even coverage, you can read an entire book, *A Quarter Century of Unix* [Salus, 1994].

In the early days of computing, software was seen as little more than a feature of the hardware. It was the hardware that people were trying to sell, so companies gave away the software with their systems. Enhancements, new algorithms, and new ideas flowed freely among students, professors, and corporate researchers.

It did not take long for companies to recognize the value of software as intellectual property. They began enforcing copyrights on their software technologies and restricting distribution of their source code. The innovations that had been seen as public property became fiercely protected corporate assets, and the culture of computer software development changed.

Richard Stallman at the Massachusetts Institute of Technology (MIT) did not want any part of a world in which software innovation was controlled by corporate ambitions. His answer to this development was to found the Free Software Foundation (FSF), in Cambridge, Massachusetts. The goal of the FSF is to encourage the development and use of freely redistributable software.

The use of the word *free* in this context has created great confusion, however. Richard Stallman meant *free* as in freedom, not *free* as in zero cost. He strongly believes that software and its associated documentation should be available with source code, with no restrictions placed on additional redistribution. To promote this ideal, he, with help from others, created the General Public License (GPL), a complete copy of which can be found in Appendix C of this book.

The GPL has three major points:

1.  Anyone who receives GPLed software has the right to obtain the source code to the software at no additional charge (beyond the cost of delivery).

2.  Any software derived from GPLed software must retain the GPL as its license terms for redistribution.

3.  Anyone in possession of GPLed software has the right to redistribute that software under terms that do not conflict with the GPL.

An important point to notice about these licensing terms is that they do not mention price (except that source is not allowed to be an extra-cost item). GPLed software may be sold to customers at any price. However, those customers then have the right to redistribute the software, including the source code, as they please. With the advent of the Internet, this right has the effect of keeping the cost of GPLed software low—even zero in many cases—while still allowing companies to sell GPLed software and services, such as support, designed to complement the software.

The part of the GPL that generates the most controversy is the second point: that software derived from GPLed software also must be GPLed. Although detractors refer to the GPL as a virus because of this clause, supporters insist that the clause is one of the GPL's greatest strengths. It prevents companies from taking GPLed software, adding features, and turning the result into a proprietary package.

The major project the FSF sponsors is the GNU's Not Unix (GNU) project, whose goal is to create a freely distributable Unix-like operating system. There was little high-quality freely distributable software available for the GNU project when it was started, so project contributors began by creating the applications and tools for the system rather than the operating system itself. As the GPL was also produced by the FSF, many of the key components of the GNU operating system are GPLed, but through the years the GNU project has adopted many software packages, such as the X Window System, the TEX typesetting system, and the Perl language, that are freely redistributable under other licenses.

Several major packages, and a multitude of minor ones, have been produced as a result of the GNU project. The major ones include the Emacs editor, gcc compiler, bash, and gawk (GNU's awk). The minor ones include the high-quality shell utilities and text-manipulation programs that users expect to find on a Unix system.

## 1.2 Development of Linux

In 1991, Linus Torvalds, a student at the University of Helsinki, initiated a project in order to teach himself about low-level 80386 programming. At the time, he was running the Minix operating system, designed by Andrew Tanenbaum, so keeping his system compatible with the Minix system calls and file-system structure made his work much easier. Although he released the first version of the Linux kernel to the Internet under a fairly restrictive license, he was soon convinced to change his license to the GPL.

The combination of the GPL license and the early functionality of the Linux kernel convinced other developers to help develop the kernel. A C-library implementation, derived from the then-dormant GNU C library project, was released, allowing native user applications to be built.  Native ports of gcc, Emacs, and bash quickly followed.  In early 1992, you could install and boot Linux 0.95 on most Intel machines without inordinate work.

The Linux project was closely associated with the GNU project from the beginning.  The GNU project's source base became an extremely important resource for the Linux community from which to build a complete system.  Although significant portions of Linux-based systems are derived from sources that include freely available Unix code from the University of California at Berkeley and the X Consortium, many important parts of a functional Linux system come directly from the GNU project.

As Linux matured, some individuals focused on easing the installation and usability of Linux systems for new users by creating packages, called **distributions,** of the Linux kernel and a reasonably complete set of utilities that together consituted a full operating system.  Manchester Computer Centre (of Manchester University in England) was one of the early leaders with the MCC distribution.  The SoftLanding Systems (SLS) distribution followed, from which the Slackware distribution descended.  Slackware was the first Linux distribution that users without significant Unix knowledge could install and maintain easily.  Its popularity gave rise to a flood of computer books devoted to the installation, use, and maintenance of Linux.  Red Hat Linux, a relative latecomer in the Linux distribution world, is now one of the most popular distributions, because of its concentration on making Linux stable, secure, and easy to install and use.

In addition to the Linux kernel, a Linux distribution contains development libraries, compilers, interpreters, shells, applications, utilities, and config-uration tools, along with many other components.  When a Linux system is built, distribution developers collect the tools from a variety of places to create a complete collection of all the software components that are neces-sary for a functional Linux system.  Most distributions also contain custom components that ease the installation and maintenance of Linux systems.

Many Linux distributions are available.  Each has its own advantages and disadvantages; however, they all share the common kernel and de-velopment libraries that distinguish Linux systems from other operating systems.  This book is intended to help developers build programs for any Linux system.  Because all Linux distributions use the same code to provide system services, program binaries and source code are highly compatible across distributions.

One project that has contributed to this compatibility is the **Linux Filesystem Standard** (FSSTND), which specifies where many files ought to be kept and explains, in general terms, how the rest of the file system ought to be organized. A new version of this document, the **Filesystem Hierarchy Standard** (FHS) is being drafted. Information on both standards is available from http://www.pathname.com/fhs/

# 1.3   Basic Lineage of Unix Systems

Although the major portions of Linux comprise code developed independent of traditional Unix source bases, the interfaces that Linux provides were influenced heavily by existing Unix systems.

In the early 1980s, Unix development split into two camps, one at the University of California at Berkeley, the other at AT&T's Bell Laboratories. Each institution developed and maintained Unix operating systems that were derived from the original Unix implementation done by Bell Laboratories.

The Berkeley version of Unix became known as the **Berkeley Software Distribution** (BSD) and was popular in academia. The BSD system was the first to include TCP/IP networking, which contributed to its success and helped to convince Sun Microsystems to base Sun's first operating system, SunOS, on BSD.

Bell Laboratories also worked on enhancing Unix, but, unfortunately, it did so in ways slightly different from those of the Berkeley group. The various releases from Bell Laboratories were denoted by the word *System* followed by a roman numeral. The final major release of Unix from Bell Laboratories was **System V** (SysV); **System V Release 4** (SVR4) provides the code base for most commercial Unix operating systems today.

This forked development of Unix caused major differentiation in the system calls, system libraries, and basic commands of Unix systems. One of the best examples of this split is in the networking interfaces that each operating system provided to applications. BSD systems used an interface known as **sockets** to allow programs to talk to one another over a network. By contrast, System V provided the **Transport Layer Interface** (TLI), which is completely incompatible with sockets but allows greater flexibility in many areas. This type of development greatly diminished the portability of programs across versions of Unix, increasing the cost and decreasing the availability of third-party products for all versions of Unix.

Another example of the incompatibilities among Unix systems is the `ps` command, which allows users to query the operating system's process information. On BSD systems, `ps aux` gives a complete listing of all the processes running on a machine; on System V, that command is invalid, and `ps -ef` can be used instead. Of course, the output formats are as incompatible as the command-line arguments.

In an attempt to standardize all the aspects of Unix that had diverged because of the split development in this period (which is affectionately known as the Unix Wars), the Unix industry sponsored a set of standards that would define the interfaces Unix provides. The portion of the standards that deals with programming and system-tool interfaces is known as **POSIX**, and is issued by the **Institute for Electrical and Electronic Engineers** (IEEE).

# 1.4 Linux Lineage

"The best thing about standards is that there are so many to choose from."[1] Linux developers had 20 years of history to examine when they designed Linux, and, more important, they had high-quality standards to reference. Linux was designed primarily according to POSIX; where POSIX left off, Linux generally follows System V practice, with a compatibility library that provides emulation of some BSD interfaces. Notable exceptions include: the networking interface, which is completely BSD and does not even provide emulation of the System V TLI interface; and several of the utilities, including networking utilities, which follow the BSD model.

System V provides the STREAMS interface, but Linux does not implement STREAMS because that interface has horrible performance, and its effects can be achieved in other ways. This missing misfeature has an effect on

---

1. Anonymous.

the rest of the programming environment; Linux uses BSD ptys instead of System V ptys (the only difference is in how they are allocated; they are used the same way) because the System V ptys are built on clone devices that require STREAMS.

The biggest difference between SVR4 and Linux, from a programming perspective, is that Linux does not provide as many duplicate programming interfaces. Even programmers coding exclusively for SVR4 systems generally prefer Berkeley sockets to TLI; Linux eschews the overhead of TLI and enforces sockets. Instead of the generic STREAMS interface, Linux provides stackable line disciplines and network drivers (in the kernel), removing the performance penalties of STREAMS while retaining its most-used and most-useful capabilities.

# CHAPTER 2

# Licenses and Copyright

Newcomers to the free-software world are often confused by the variety of licensing terms attached to free software. Some free-software devotees twist normal words into jargon and then expect you to understand every nuance they have attached to each piece of jargon.

To write and distribute software that runs on a free platform such as Linux, you must understand licenses and copyright. These matters are regularly confused by intelligent and informed people, free-software devotees among them. Whether you intend to write free or commercial software, you will be working with tools that come with a variety of license terms. A general understanding of the field of copyright and licensing will help you to avoid common errors.

In these litigious times, it is vitally important that we warn you that **we are not lawyers**. This chapter reflects our understanding of the matters that we discuss, but it does not offer legal advice. Before you make any decisions regarding your own or anyone else's intellectual property, you should study the subject further, and unless you think it unnecessary, consult an attorney.

## 2.1  Copyright

We deal with the simpler subject first. A **copyright** is the simple assertion of ownership of certain types of intellectual property. Under the latest international copyright conventions, you do not even need to claim copyright for material you create.  Unless you explicitly disclaim ownership, other people are allowed to use your intellectual property only in strictly defined ways, called **fair use**, unless you explicitly give them permission, called **license**, to do otherwise. So if you write a book or a piece of software, you do not need to put "Copyright © *year*" on it to own it.  However, if you do not put this phrase on your writing, you may find it much more difficult to claim ownership in court if someone violates either your copyright (by claiming that or acting as if you do not own the copyright) or your license terms.  The Berne copyright convention,[1] an international treaty covering international copyright conventions and enforcement, requires participating nations to enforce copyright only

> ...if from the time of the first publication all the copies of the work published with the authority of the author or other copyright proprietor bear the symbol of a lower case "c" inside of a circle accompanied by the name of the copyright proprietor and the year of first publication placed in such manner and location as to give reasonable notice of claim of copyright.

The sequence (c) has been generally used as a replacement for the lower case "c" inside of a circle, but courts have not upheld that.  Always use the word *Copyright*, in addition to the sequence (c), when asserting your copyright.

Copyright is not perpetual.  All intellectual property eventually passes into the **public domain**.  That is, the public eventually owns the copyright to the property, and any person can do anything with the property.  No license terms are binding once the property is in the public domain.  There is one twist:  If you create a **derived work** based on public-domain work, then you own the copyright to your **modifications**.  Therefore, although many old books are now **out of copyright**, their copyright having passed into the public domain, editors often make small changes here and there, correcting mistakes made in the original.  They often then claim copyright ownership of the derived work that includes their changes.  This copyright prevents you from legally copying the edited version, although you can freely copy the public-domain, out-of-copyright original.

Note that there are limits on what can be copyrighted.  You cannot publish a book containing only the word *the* and then attempt to extort license fees

---

1. http://www.wipo.org/

from everyone using the word *the* in their books. However, if you create a sufficiently stylized painting of the word *the*, you would own the copyright to that particular representation, as long as it was sufficiently identifiable for you to show that prior art did not exist with the same representation. Although we are free to use the word *the* in this sentence, we would not be allowed to sell reproductions of your work without getting a license from you.

These limitations apply to software as well. If you are licensed to alter someone else's software and you make a trivial, one-word change, it would be absurd for you to claim copyright to that change. You would not be able to defend a copyright claim to that change in court; your contribution would be as much in the public domain as the word *the* is. However, if you add significantly to the software, you would own the copyright to your modification, unless, for instance, the copyright owners of the original licensed the software for modification with the license restriction that copyright ownership of all modifications revert to them.

## 2.2 Licensing

Copyright owners have wide latitude in determining license terms. Common areas of restriction (or permission) include use, copying, distribution, and modification. As a concrete example, the GNU General Public License (GPL, commonly called the *copyleft*, see Appendix C) explicitly does not limit use. It limits only "copying, distribution, and modification."

Here is an example of free-software jargon with which you want to be familiar. In the free-software world, *public domain* is used almost exclusively in terms of **ownership**. In other circles, it is often applied to **use**, as well. Magazine articles that refer to the GPL as a "public-domain copyright" are clearly wrong because the GPL does not give ownership of the copyright to the public domain; articles that refer to it as a "public-domain license" are in one sense correct, because the GPL explicitly places no license restrictions on use. Free software fanatics, however, often cringe at this use of *public domain*, and many believe it to be completely incorrect.

Certain license restrictions may not be legal in certain localities. Most governing bodies prevent you from restricting what they consider **fair use** in a license agreement. For example, many European countries explicitly allow reverse engineering of software and hardware for certain purposes, license terms restricting such activities notwithstanding. For this reason, most license agreements include a **separability clause** something like the following one, from the GPL:

> If any portion of this section is held invalid or unenforceable under any particular circumstance, the balance of the section is intended to apply and the section as a whole is intended to apply in other circumstances.

Most license agreements use less comprehensible language to say the same thing.

Many people who attempt to write their own license terms without legal help write licenses with terms that have no legal force, and few of those licenses include a separability clause. If you wish to write your own license terms for your software, and if you care whether people comply with the license terms, have an intellectual-property lawyer vet your license terms.

## 2.3  Free Software Licenses

### 2.3.1 Combinations of Free and Commercial Software

Different free-software license terms allow various types of commercial use, modification, and distribution. It is often desirable to reuse existing code in your own projects. To some extent, it is inevitable that you do so—almost any program that you write will be linked with the C library, so you need to be aware of the licensing terms of the C library, as well as the terms of other libraries that you link with your program. You may often wish to include fragments of other programs' source code in your own programs, as well.

## 2.3.2 The GNU General Public License

The GPL is one of the more restrictive free-software licenses. If you include source code that is licensed under the terms of the GPL in another program, that program must also be licensed under the terms of the GPL.[2] The Free Software Foundation (FSF; author of the GPL) considers linking with a library to be "creating a derivative work"; some others believe it to be a "work of mere aggregation." Therefore, the FSF holds that you are not allowed to link with a library covered under the terms of the GPL unless the program being linked also is covered by the terms of the GPL.[3] However, some people hold that linking is "mere aggregation," and the GPL says:

> In addition, mere aggregation of another work not based on the Program with the Program (or with a work based on the Program) on a volume of a storage or distribution medium does not bring the other work under the scope of this License.

If you consider an executable to be a "volume of storage," you could consider linking mere aggregation.

To the best of our knowledge, this distinction has not yet been tested in court. In the fairly unlikely case that you wish to link a program not licensed under the terms of the GPL with a library that is, ask the authors of the library in question for their interpretation.[4]

## 2.3.3 The GNU Library General Public License

The GNU Library General Public License (LGPL) was designed to make libraries more generally useful. The point of the LGPL is to allow users to upgrade or improve their libraries without having to get new versions of programs linked against those libraries. To that end, the LGPL does not attempt to place any licensing restrictions on programs linked against the library, as long as those programs are linked against shared versions of libraries licensed under the LGPL or are provided with the object files

---

2. Some people call the GPL a virus for this reason.
3. Don't panic! See Section 2.3.3, next.
4. The only common library that is licensed under the terms of the GPL is the GNU Database Management library (gdbm). This book covers the Berkeley Database Library (db) instead, because db has less-restrictive license terms, as well as more capabilities than gdbm.

for the application, allowing the user to relink the application with new or altered versions of the library.

In practice, this restriction is not significant; it would be unreasonable not to link against shared libraries where they are available.

Few libraries are licensed under the terms of the GPL; most are licensed under the terms of the LGPL. Libraries licensed under the terms of the GPL are usually that way simply because the author did not know about or consider the LGPL. In response to a polite request, many will relicense their libraries under the terms of the LGPL.

## 2.3.4 MIT/X-Style Licenses

MIT/X-style licenses are much simpler than the GPL or LGPL; their only restrictions are (stated simply) to keep all existing copyright notices and license terms intact in source and binary distributions, and not to use the name of any author to endorse or promote derived works without prior written permission.

## 2.3.5 BSD-Style Licenses

BSD-style licenses essentially add to the conditions of the MIT/X-style licenses the restriction that advertising materials that mention features or use of the software include an acknowledgment.

## 2.3.6 Artistic License

The Perl language source code is distributed with a license that allows you to follow either the terms of the GPL or of an alternative license, whimsically called the **Artistic License.** The main goals of the Artistic License are to preserve redistribution rights and to prevent users from selling altered, proprietary modifications that masquerade as the official version. Other software authors have adopted Perl's convention of allowing users to follow the terms of either the GPL or the Artistic License; a few are licensed only under the terms of the Artistic License.

## 2.3.7 License Incompatibilities

Mixing code from software with different licenses can sometimes be a problem. The problem does not occur when linking with shared libraries, but it definitely applies to creating derived works. If you are modifying someone else's software, you have to understand their licensing terms. If you are trying to combine in one derived work two pieces of software that have different licenses, you have to determine if their licenses conflict. Again, this does not apply when you are writing your own code from scratch.

If you are working with code licensed under the terms of the GPL or LGPL, you cannot include in it code licensed under a BSD-style license, because the GPL and LGPL forbid "additional restrictions," and the BSD license contains additional restrictions (that is, beyond any in the GPL or LGPL) in regard to advertising and endorsement. Because of this conflict, many pieces of software are licensed under alternative terms—both the GPL and a BSD-style license terms are offered; you can choose with which licensing terms to comply.

If the code licensed under the GPL or LGPL is included in a work derived from an MIT/X-style license, the entire derived work (for all practical purposes) must be licensed under the terms of the GPL or LGPL, respectively.

There are many other potential incompatibilities. If you are in doubt about what you are allowed to do with particular pieces of free software, do not be shy—ask the copyright owners. Remember that they can give you license to use the software in any way they wish.

# CHAPTER 3

# More Information on Linux

Eventually, you will want to know something about Linux that this book does not cover. Finding Linux information is not hard unless you do not know where or how to look.

When you look for Linux information, you must realize that Linux was designed and created on the Internet, so most Linux documentation was designed for the Internet. Even if you have local sources of information, most of them will have been designed originally as online, Internet-available information sources. Your searches will be more successful if you keep this in mind, even if you limit yourself to printed documentation.

The *Linux Application Development* Web site, http://www.awl.com/cseng/ books/lad/, has updates to this book's text, detailed information beyond this book's scope, and pointers to more information all over the Internet. URLs given in this chapter may go out of date; when we are aware of dated URLs, we will post corrections on the *Linux Application Development* Web site.

## 3.1  Overview of Linux Documentation

One of the largest organized sources of information in the Linux world is the **Linux Documentation Project** (LDP). The LDP is primarily responsible for the standard online manual pages (man pages), a set of LDP books on a variety of topics, and a large collection of **HOWTO** documents that cover hundreds of topics, with varying degrees of detail. The HOWTO documents, in particular, are available in printed, hypertext, and plain-text formats.

The **Linux Usenet newsgroup hierarchy** (comp.os.linux.*) can also be a useful source of information for people generally familiar with gleaning information from Usenet. If you wish to keep up with Linux progress, glance through comp.os.linux.announce on at least a weekly basis.

Since the majority of the software you are likely to be running on a Linux system comes from the GNU project, the BSD project, or the X project, much of the documentation is similarly divided. The GNU project's main documentation format is Texinfo, which provides typeset and hypertext documentation from the same source, and also provides many man pages, although the Texinfo documentation is usually kept more up-to-date. The BSD project's documentation is mostly in man pages. The official X distribution includes man pages and books that you can typeset and print, but not easily view online. Most X programmers and users buy second-source documentation, including a well-known series of programming reference books published by O'Reilly.

The Linux Documentation Project maintains a large Web site that is as close to canonical as is anything in the Linux world. The project's home site is http://sunsite.unc.edu/LDP, and it is mirrored at hundreds of other sites around the globe, giving almost everyone quick, relatively local access.

The majority of the printable documentation issued by the Linux Documentation Project is made available on an irregular basis by various vendors under a variety of titles. In mid-1997, these books tend to be about 2,000 pages long. Linux Software Labs,[1] Red Hat Software,[2] and Yggdrasil[3] are currently the three largest vendors of these books.

Also, one vendor, Red Hat Software, sells a CD-ROM product called *Linux Library* that includes an indexed, browsable archive of various Linux documentation, including a snapshot of the entire LDP Web site.

---

1. http://www.lsl.com
2. http://www.redhat.com
3. http://www.yggdrasil.com

### 3.1.1 The HOWTOs and mini-HOWTOs

Documentation that originates on Usenet often takes the form of a **Frequently Asked Questions** (FAQ) document. These documents have a question-and-answer format that is appropriate to most of their subjects. However, the FAQ format is not suitable for many types of documentation, so the LDP has established a standard format for expository or narrative documentation. These documents are called HOWTO documents, since most of them explain how to do something. They are available in typeset, hypertext, and plain-text formats; they are written in SGML, which is designed to be translated into other formats.

Certain extremely simple documents, called **mini-HOWTOs**, are only a few pages long and generally describe one topic.

### 3.1.2 The LDP Books

One of the early projects of the LDP was to produce whole books about Linux. Most of these books are written for users and systems administrators; one is a guide to applications programming, and one is a guide to kernel programming. All are accessible in one form or another from the LDP home page.

### 3.1.3 The Linux Software Map

If you are having trouble finding a program you want, the **Linux Software Map** (LSM) at http://www.execpc.com/~lsm has thousands of records of software packages available for Linux. These records include names, descriptions, version numbers, and locations of the packages.

### 3.1.4 The man Pages

Access the system reference manual pages (man pages) through the `man` command. To read the reference page on the `man` command itself, run the command line `man man`. Man pages generally contain reference documentation, not tutorial information, and are renowned for being so succinct that they are barely understandable at times.  Nevertheless, when you need reference material, they can be exactly what you want.

Three programs provide access to man pages. The man program displays individual man pages, and the `apropos` and `whatis` commands search for a keyword in the set of man pages.  The `apropos` and `whatis` commands search the same database; the difference is that `whatis` displays only lines that match exactly the word you are searching for, and `apropos` displays any line that contains the word you are searching for.  That is, if you are looking for `man`, `apropos` matches `manager` and `manipulation`, whereas `whatis` matches only `man` separated from other letters by white space or by punctuation, as in `man.config`.  Try the commands `whatis man` and `apropos man` to see the difference.

Many of the man pages on a Linux system are part of a large package assembled by the LDP.  In particular, the section 2 (system calls), section 3 (libraries), section 4 (special, or device, files), and section 5 (file formats) pages are mainly from the LDP's man-pages collection and are generally the pages most useful for programming.  If you want to specify which section to look in, give the number of that section before the name of the man page you want to read.  For example, `man man` gives the man page for the `man` command from section 1; if you want to see the specification for how to write man pages, you need to specify section 7 with `man 7 man`.

While you are reading man pages, remember that many system calls and library functions use the same names.  In most cases, you want to know about the library functions to which you will be linking, not about the system calls that those library functions will eventually call.  Remember to use `man 3 function` to get the descriptions of library functions, because some library functions have the same names as system calls in section 2.

Also, be particularly aware that the C-library man pages are maintained separately from the C library itself.  Since the C library does not usually change behavior, that is not usually a problem.  All the Linux platforms are (as we write) in the process of moving to a unified C library: the GNU C library.  The GNU C library does come with full documentation, which is maintained with the library. This information is available in Texinfo form; see page 27 for information on finding and reading Texinfo documentation. Even when the GNU C library is used on all Linux platforms, the man pages will still be maintained separately; there will just be more documentation in Texinfo format.

## 3.2   Other Books

The LDP is not the only source of books on Linux. *A Practical Guide to Linux* [Sobell, 1997] is a 1,000-page tome that contains introductions to using Linux, shell programming, and system administration. It also contains a summary reference to many of the utilities that are included with a Linux system. *Linux in a Nutshell* [Heckman, 1997] is smaller and shorter and concentrates on a summary utility reference derived from O'Reilly's earlier nutshell references.

*Beginning Linux Programming* [Matthew, 1996] is a gentle and detailed introduction to Linux programming that includes important topics, such as shell programming. *Linux Multimedia Guide* [Tranter, 1996] includes information on multimedia solutions available for Linux, as well as information on programming the Linux sound interface. *Linux Device Drivers* [Rubini, 1998] teaches those who have never touched operating system code, as well as those who have, how to write Linux device drivers.

## 3.3   Source Code

Take advantage of free software—read the source code. If you purchase a Linux distribution, the vendor is legally obligated by the terms of the GPL to provide you with source code. Look at the source code for programs that do something similar to what you are trying to do. Your distribution should include instructions for finding the source code.

## 3.4   Linux (and Other) Newsgroups

Like other Usenet newsgroups, the Linux newsgroups have a lot of information hidden in an overwhelming amount of disinformation and misinformation. We will describe the newsgroups that we think might be useful to a programmer.

Furthermore, recognizing that Linux is a Unix-like operating system, we recommend several Unix newsgroups that are not specific to Linux, but may be worth reading.

- The moderated newsgroup **comp.os.linux.announce**, nicknamed *cola*, has low traffic, at least compared with other Linux newsgroups; there are perhaps 50 posts per week, on average. Most posts are given tags that distinguish their content; those whose content is of only local interest are designated LOCAL, those made for advertisement or commercial gain are designated COMMERCIAL, and so on.

  All the traffic on this newsgroup is archived in several places, including

  - http://www.cs.helsinki.fi/~wirzeniu/linux/cola.html

  - http://sunsite.unc.edu/pub/Linux/docs/
    linux-announce.archive/

  - the Red Hat Linux Library

- The moderated newsgroup **comp.os.linux.answers** contains FAQs, HOWTOs, READMEs, and so on, about Linux.

- The unmoderated newsgroup **comp.os.linux.development.apps** is intended for people who are writing Linux applications or porting old applications to Linux.

- The unmoderated newsgroup **comp.os.linux.development.system** is intended for people who are working on the Linux kernel, device drivers, modules, and particularly Linux-specific programs.

- The unmoderated newsgroup **comp.os.linux.hardware** is intended for people discussing hardware-related issues under Linux.

- The unmoderated newsgroup **comp.unix.programmer** is intended for people discussing general Unix programming. Most of it is relevant to Linux systems.

- The unmoderated newsgroup **comp.lang.c** is intended for people discussing the C programming language without considering the operating system being used.

## 3.5 Mailing Lists

**Mailing lists** are email addresses through which email is redistributed to multiple other addresses. In general, anyone on a mailing list can send messages, which will be distributed to everyone else. Moderated mailing lists, like moderated newsgroups, require an administrator to approve each message before it is redistributed.

Mailing lists are generally maintained with list-management software. Two of the most common list-management software packages are **smartlist** and **Majordomo**. In both cases, you mail requests to subscribe or unsubscribe to the automatic list-maintenance software. There are two major differences between smartlist and Majordomo: the address, and the request format. To subscribe to a Majordomo list, send a message to `majordomo@host.domain` with a body (not subject) of `subscribe listname you@yourdomain.com`. To subscribe to a smartlist list, send a message to `listname-request@host.domain` with a subject (or first body line) of `subscribe`. When you are told about a mailing list, you will generally be told either what software manages it or how to subscribe to it.

Usually, when you subscribe to a list, you are automatically sent a message that tells you how to post and how to unsubscribe. Save that message in a place where you can find it!

If you need help subscribing to a list or unsubscribing from a list, you can contact the list owner. Most lists have a `listname-owner` address that is read by the person who maintains the list; sometimes, the address is `owner-listname`.

The http://www.linuxhq.com/lnxlists/ site archives many mailing lists that have Linux-specific content. This site also has a how-to-subscribe page at http://www.linuxhq.com/lnxlists/subscribe.html which describes how to subscribe to the lists that the site archives.

The information on how to join these lists is current as we write it. Be aware that list managers occasionally change the software that runs a list, and that lists sometimes move. We keep up-to-date information on these lists on the LAD Web site at http://www.awl.com/cseng/books/lad/lists.html

### 3.5.1 vger

To the extent that anything related to Linux can be called "official," the mailing lists hosted by vger.rutgers.edu are the official Linux mailing lists. In particular, most of the major kernel developers read the linux-kernel@vger.rutgers.edu list.

The vger lists are run by Majordomo. You can get help with Majordomo commands by sending a message to majordomo@vger.rutgers.edu with a body containing the single word `help`. You can request a list of all the mailing lists currently available from vger with the word `lists`.

Most of the lists are related either to development of some particular part of Linux (such as the kernel, networking, or DOS emulator) or to some facet of administration.

### 3.5.2 Other Lists

People around the globe maintain mailing lists for one purpose or another. Most lists are mentioned in Web pages somewhere, and many are archived on the Web, so following links from Linux Web sites you know or searching a Web crawler, such as AltaVista, are useful ways to find mailing lists for a topic in which you are interested. Some lists are announced in the comp.os.linux.announce newsgroup; searching cola archives can sometimes be fruitful. Looking at the lists archived at linuxhq (see page 25) can also be useful.

Most Linux vendors contribute to Linux development by hosting mailing lists. They are rarely shy about this service; you can usually find out which lists they host by looking at their Web pages.

## 3.6 **Other Documentation**

There is certainly a wealth of Linux-specific and Linux-oriented documentation available, but there is also plenty of applicable documentation that was not written specifically for Linux.

### 3.6.1 GNU

The Free Software Foundation's GNU project has always emphasized documentation, and, like the LDP, it has an official format that is used for a large portion of its documentation. Texinfo was originally designed to produce two forms of output: typeset output and a simple hypertext format called **info**. You can now also use it to produce HTML.

Info files are read with an info reader. The GNU project includes a standalone info reader, appropriately called `info`; it has an interface similar to the info reader built into the Emacs editor. Several other editors, including jed, also include info readers. To learn how to use info, you can run `info info`. Alternatively, you can view a set of GNU documentation in HTML format on the LAD Web site at http://www.awl.com/cseng/books/lad/info/

### 3.6.2 BSD

Most BSD-derived documentation on a Linux system is in the form of man pages installed with programs originally written on BSD. The BSD 4.4lite source tree includes other **supplemental** documentation that is not in man page format; both the man pages and the supplemental documentation are available in printed form from O'Reilly [CSRG, 1994a] [CSRG, 1994b] [CSRG, 1994c] [CSRG, 1994d] [CSRG, 1994e].

# 3.7 Your Distribution Vendor

Most Linux distribution vendors maintain information resources for their users, such as mailing lists, Web pages, and ftp sites. Take time to get acquainted with what your vendor offers. At least, find out how you can be notified of bug fixes.

*Part* **2**

# Development Tools and Environment

# CHAPTER 4

# Development Tools

An amazing variety of development tools is available for Linux. Everyone should be familiar with a few of the important ones.

Linux distributions include many solid, proven development tools; most of the same tools have been included in Unix development systems for years. These tools are neither flashy nor fancy; most of them are command-line tools without a GUI. They have proved themselves through years of use, and it will be worth your while to learn them.

If you are already familiar with Emacs, vi, make, and gdb, you are not likely to learn anything new here. However, in the remainder of the book, we assume that you are comfortable with a text editor. Also, nearly all free Unix and Linux source code is built with make, and gdb is one of the most common debuggers available on Linux and Unix.

## 4.1 Editors

A few **integrated development environments** (IDEs) (for several different programming languages) are available for Linux, but they have not been as popular as have been IDEs on other platforms. Unix developers have traditionally held strong and diverse preferences, especially about editors.

Many programmers' editors are available for you to try; the two most common are vi and Emacs. Both have more power than they appear to have at first glance, both have a relatively steep learning curve—and they are radically different. Emacs is large;[1] it is really an operating environment of

---

1. Some people claim that Emacs stands for "Eighteen (or Eight, or Eighty) Megs And Constantly Swapping," rather than "Editor MACroS."

its own. vi is small and is designed to be one piece of the Unix environment. Many clones and alternative versions of each editor have been written, and each has its own following.

Tutorials on vi and Emacs would take far too much space to include in this book. The excellent *A Practical Guide to Linux* [Sobell, 1997] includes a detailed chapter on each editor. O'Reilly has published an entire book on each editor: *Learning GNU Emacs* [Cameron, 1996] and *Learning the vi Editor* [Lamb, 1990]. Here we will compare only Emacs and vi and tell you how to get online help for each.

Emacs includes a comprehensive set of manuals that explains not only how to use Emacs as an editor, but also how to use Emacs to read and send email and Usenet news, to play games (its gomoku game is not bad), and to run shell commands. In Emacs, you can always execute commands, even commands that are not bound to keys, by typing the entire name of the command.

In contrast, the documentation available for vi is less generous and less well known. It is exclusively an editor, and many powerful commands are bound to single keystrokes. You switch back and forth between a mode in which typing standard alphabetic characters causes them to be inserted in your document and a mode in which those alphabetic characters are commands; for example, you can use the h, j, k, and l keys as arrow keys to navigate your document.

Both editors allow you to create macros to make your work easier, but their macro languages could hardly be more different. Emacs has a complete programming language called elisp (Emacs Lisp), which is closely related to the Common Lisp programming language. vi has a more spartan, stack-based language. Most users merely map keys to simple, one-line vi commands, but those commands often execute programs outside vi to manipulate data within vi. Emacs Lisp is documented in a huge manual that includes a tutorial; documentation for vi's language is relatively sparse.

Some editors allow you to mix and match functionality. You can use Emacs in a vi mode (called **viper**) that allows you to use the standard vi commands, and one of the vi clones is called **vile**—"vi like Emacs."

## 4.1.1 Emacs

Emacs comes in several flavors. The original Emacs editor was written by Richard Stallman, of Free Software Foundation fame. For years, his **GNU Emacs** has been the most popular version. Recently, a more graphic-environment-aware variant of GNU Emacs, called XEmacs, has also become popular. XEmacs started life as Lucid Emacs, a set of enhancements to GNU Emacs managed by the now-defunct Lucid Technologies that was intended to be folded back into the official GNU Emacs. Technical differences prevented the teams from merging their code. The two editors remain highly compatible, however, and programmers on both teams regularly borrow code from each other. Because these versions are so similar, we refer to both of them as Emacs.

The best way to become comfortable with the Emacs editor is to follow its tutorial. Run emacs and type ^h t (think "control-help, tutorial"). Type ^x^c to exit Emacs. The tutorial will teach you how to get more information on Emacs. It will not teach you how to get at the Emacs manual that is distributed with Emacs. For that, use ^h i (control-help, info).

Although its user interface may not be as flashy as the IDEs available for some other systems, Emacs does have powerful features that many programmers want. When you use Emacs to edit C code, for example, Emacs recognizes the file type and enters "C mode," in which it recognizes C's syntax and helps you to recognize typos. When you run the compiler from within Emacs, it will recognize error and warning messages, and take you straight to the line at which each error was found when you type a single command, even if it has to read in a new file. It also provides a debugging mode that keeps the debugger in one window and follows the code you are debugging in another window.

## 4.1.2 vi

If you are a touch typist and like to keep your fingers on the home row,[2] you may appreciate vi, because its command set was designed to minimize finger movement for touch typists. It was also designed for Unix users; if you are familiar with sed or awk or other Unix programs that use standard

---

2. If you are a qwerty touch typist, that is. Dvorak touch typists who use vi generally use lots of vi macros to make vi comfortable for them.

**regular expressions**, using ^ to go to the beginning of a line and $ to go to the end of one will feel perfectly natural.

Unfortunately, vi can be harder to learn than Emacs because, although there are vi tutorials similar to the standard Emacs tutorial available, there is no standard way to execute the tutorial from any version of vi. However, most versions, including versions shipped with common Linux distributions, support the :help command.

# 4.2   Make

A mainstay of Unix development is make, a tool that makes it easy for you to describe how to compile programs. Although small programs may need only one command to compile their one source code file into one executable file, it is still easier to type make than to type gcc -O2 -ggdb -DSOME_DEFINE -o foo foo.c. Furthermore, when you have lots of files to compile, and you have changed only a few source files, make will create new object files only when the relevant source files have been modified.

For make to perform this magic, you will need to describe all the files in a **Makefile**. Here is an example.

```
 1: # Makefile
 2:
 3: OBJS = foo.o bar.o baz.o
 4: LDLIBS = -L/usr/local/lib/ -lbar
 5:
 6: foo: $(OBJS)
 7:         gcc -o foo $(OBJS) $(LDLIBS)
 8:
 9: install: foo
10:         install -m 644 foo /usr/bin
11: .PHONY: install
```

- Line 1 is a comment; make follows the common Unix tradition of delimiting comments with a # character.

- Line 3 defines a variable called OBJS as foo.o bar.o baz.o.

- Line 4 defines another variable, LDLIBS.

- Line 6 starts the definition of a **rule**, which states that the file foo depends on (in this case, is built from) the files whose names are contained in the variable OBJS. foo.c is called the **target**, and $(OBJS) is called the **dependency** list. Note the syntax for variable expansion: You wrap the variable name in $(...).

- Line 7 is a command line that tells you how to build the target from the dependency list. There may be multiple command lines, and the *first* character in the command line *must* be a tab.

- Line 9 is an interesting target. It does not actually try to make a file called install; instead (as you can see in line 10), it installs foo in /usr/bin using the standard install program. But this line brings up an ambiguity in make: What if a file named install exists and it is newer than foo? In that case, when you run the command make install, make will say, "'install' is up to date" and will quit.

- Line 11 tells make that install is not a file, and that it should ignore any file named "install" when computing the install dependency. Thus, if the install dependency is invoked (we shall see how to do that later), the command in line 10 will always be invoked. .PHONY is a **directive**, which alters make's operation; it tells make, in this case, that the install target is not the name of a file. PHONY targets are often used to take actions such as installation or making a single target name that relies on several other targets all being built, like this:

```
all: foo bar baz
.PHONY: all
```

Unfortunately, .PHONY is not supported by some versions of make. A less obvious, less efficient, but more portable way of doing the same things is

```
all: foo bar baz FORCE
FORCE:
```

This works only if there is no file named "FORCE".

Items in dependency lists may be file names, but, as far as make is concerned, they are other targets. The foo item in the install dependency list is a target. When make attempts to resolve the install dependency, it sees that it first has to resolve the foo dependency. To resolve the foo dependency, it has to resolve the foo.o, bar.o, and baz.o dependencies.

Note that there are no lines that explicitly tell make how to build foo.o, bar.o, or baz.o. You certainly do not create these files directly in your editor of choice! make provides implied dependencies that you do not have to write. If you have a dependency on a file that ends in .o and you have a file that has the same name except that it ends in .c, make assumes that the object file depends on the source file. Built-in **suffix rules** provided with make allow you to simplify many Makefiles greatly, and you can write your own suffix rules (explained on page 39) when the built-in rules do not meet your needs.

By default, make exits as soon as any command it runs fails (returns an error). There are two ways to get around this, if you wish to.

The -k argument causes make to build as much as possible, without stopping as soon as a command invocation returns an error. It is useful, for example, when porting; you can build as many object files as possible, then port the files that failed to build without having to wait for intermediary files to build in the meantime.

If you know that one command will always return an error, but you wish to ignore the error condition, you can use some shell magic. The /bin/false command always returns an error, so the command

```
/bin/false
```

will always cause make to abort its current run unless the -k option is in use. However,

```
any_command || /bin/true
```

will never cause make to abort its current run; if *any_command* returns false, then the shell will run /bin/true and return its exit code, which is guaranteed to be success.

Make interprets unrecognized command-line arguments that do not start with a dash (-)[3] as targets to build. So `make install` will cause make to try to satisfy the `install` target. If the `foo` target is not up to date, make will first satisfy the `foo` dependency by building it, and then it will install it. If you need to build a target that starts with a dash, you will need to precede the target name with a separate double-dash (`--`) argument.

## 4.2.1 Complex Command Lines

Each command line is executed in its own subshell, so `cd` commands in a command line affect only the line on which they are written. You can extend any line in a Makefile over multiple lines by using backslash extension: If you put a \ as the final character on a line, the line after it will be considered to be part of it, joined to it by a space. Command lines often look like this:

```
 1:        cd some_directory ; \
 2:          do this to file $(FOO); \
 3:          do that
 4:        cd another_directory ; \
 5:          if [ -f some_file ] ; then \
 6:            do something else ; \
 7:          done ; \
 8:          for i in * ; do \
 9:            echo $$i >> some_file ; \
10:          done
```

There are only two lines in that fragment, as far as make is concerned. The first command line starts on line 1 and continues through line 3; the second command line starts on line 4 and continues through line 10. There are several points to note here.

- *another_directory* is relative not to *some_directory*, but rather to the directory in which make was run, because they are executed in different subshells.

- The lines that constitute each command line are passed to the shell as a single line, so all the ; characters that the shell needs must be there, including the ones that are usually omitted in a shell script because

---

3. The combined minus and hyphen character is often called a dash.

the presence of newlines implies them. For more information on shell programming, see *Learning the bash Shell* [Newham, 1995].

- When you need to dereference a make variable, you can just dereference it normally (that is, $(VAR)), but when you need to dereference a shell variable, you need to escape the $ character by including it twice: $$i.

## 4.2.2 Variables

It often happens that you want to define a variable one component at a time. You might want to write something like this:

```
OBJS = foo.o
OBJS = $(OBJS) bar.o
OBJS = $(OBJS) baz.o
```

At this point, you expect OBJS to be defined as foo.o bar.o baz.o—but it is actually defined as $(OBJS) baz.o, because make does not expand variables until they are used.[4] If you do this, as soon as you reference OBJS in a rule, make will enter an infinite loop.[5] For this reason, many Makefiles have sections that look like this:

```
OBJS1 = foo.o
OBJS2 = bar.o
OBJS3 = baz.o
OBJS = $(OBJS1) $(OBJS1) $(OBJS1)
```

You will most often see variable declarations like the preceding one when a variable declaration would otherwise be too long for the programmer's comfort.

Variable expansion brings up a typical issue that a Linux programmer is called on to decide. The GNU tools distributed with Linux are generally more capable than the versions of the tools included with other systems,

---

4. Although this behavior may seem inconvenient, it is an important feature and not a bug. Not expanding variables is critically important for writing the generic suffix rules that create implied dependencies.
5. Most versions of make, including the GNU version, which is distributed with Linux, will detect that they are in an infinite loop and quit with an error message.

and GNU make is no exception. The authors of GNU make created another way to do variable assignment that avoids this problem, but not every version of make understands GNU make's alternative forms of variable assignment. Fortunately, GNU make can be built for any system to which you could easily port source code written on Linux, but do you want to force the people porting your code to other systems to use GNU make? If you do, you can use **simple variable assignment**:

```
OBJS := foo.o
OBJS := $(OBJS) bar.o
OBJS := $(OBJS) baz.o
```

The := operator causes GNU make to evaluate the variable expression at assignment time, rather than wait to evaluate the expression when it is used in a rule. With this code, OBJS does indeed contain foo.o bar.o baz.o.

Simple variable assignment is often useful, but GNU make also has another assignment syntax that deals specifically with this problem, one straight from the C language:

```
OBJS := foo.o
OBJS += bar.o
OBJS += baz.o
```

## 4.2.3 Suffix Rules

This is another context in which you have to decide whether to write standard Makefiles or to use useful GNU extensions. Standard suffix rules are more limited than are the GNU pattern rules, but most situations can be handled sufficiently well by the standard suffix rules, and pattern rules are not supported by many other versions of make.

Suffix rules look like this:

```
.c.o:
        $(CC) -c $(CFLAGS) $(CPPFLAGS) -o $@ $<
.SUFFIXES: .c .o
```

This rule says (we sweep the details under the carpet) that make should, *unless it is otherwise explicitly instructed*, turn a .c file into a .o file by running the attached command line. Each .c file will be treated as though it were explicitly listed as a dependency of the respective .o file in your Makefile.

That suffix rule introduces another of make's features: automatic variables. It is clear that you need a way to substitute the dependency and target into the command line. The automatic variable $@ stands for the target, $< stands for the first dependency, and $^ stands for all the dependencies.

Several other automatic variables are available and documented in the make manual. All automatic variables can be used in normal rules, as well as in suffix and pattern rules.

The final line of the example introduces another directive. .SUFFIXES tells make that .c and .o are suffixes that make should use to find a way to turn the existing source files into the desired targets.

Pattern rules are more powerful and, therefore, slightly more complex than suffix rules; it would take too long to cover them in detail here. The equivalent pattern rule to the preceding suffix rule is

```
%.o : %.c
        $(CC) -c $(CFLAGS) $(CPPFLAGS) -o $@ $<
```

If you want to know more about make, see *Managing Projects with make* [Oram, 1993]. GNU make also includes an excellent and easy-to-read manual in Texinfo format, which you can read online, print out, or order as a book from the Free Software Foundation.

# 4.3 The GNU Debugger

**Gdb** is the Free Software Foundation's debugger. It is a good command-line debugger, on which several tools have been built, including Emacs' gdb mode and the graphical **Data Display Debugger** (DDD).[6] We will cover only gdb in this section.

Start gdb by running gdb *progname*. Gdb will not search the PATH looking for the executable file. Gdb will load the executable's symbols and then prompt you for what to do next.

---

6. http://www.cs.tu-bs.de/softech/ddd/ddd.html

There are three ways to inspect a process with gdb:

- Use the `run` command to start the program normally.

- Use the `attach` command to start inspecting an already-running process. When you attach to a process, the process will be stopped.

- Inspect an existing core file to determine the state of the process when it was killed. To inspect a core file, start gdb with the command `gdb progname corefile`.

Before you run a program or attach to an already-running program, you can set breakpoints, list source code, and do anything else that does not necessarily involve a running process.

Gdb does not require that you type entire command names; `r` suffices for `run`, `n` for `next`, `s` for `step`. Furthermore, to repeat the most recent command, simply hit Return. This makes single-stepping easy.

A short selection of useful gdb commands is included here; gdb includes a comprehensive online manual in GNU info format (run `info gdb`) that explains all of gdb's options in detail in a tutorial format. *Programming with GNU Software* [Loukides, 1997] contains a good detailed tutorial on using gdb, and *Beginning Linux Programming* [Matthew, 1996] contains a short tutorial, as well. Gdb also includes extensive online help available from within gdb; access it with the `help` command. Specific help on each command is available with `help commandname` or `help topic`.

Just like shell commands, gdb commands may take arguments. We use "call `help` with an argument of *command*" to mean the same as "type `help command*".

Some gdb commands also take format identifiers to identify how to print values. Format identifiers immediately follow the command name and are separated from the command name by a slash. Once you have chosen a format, you do not have to use it each time you repeat the command; gdb will remember the format you chose as the default.

Format identifiers are separated from commands by a / character and are composed of three elements: a count, a format letter, and a size letter. The count and size letters are optional; count defaults to 1, and the size has reasonable defaults based on the format letter.

The format letters are o for octal, x for hexadecimal, d for decimal, u for unsigned decimal, t for binary, f for floating-point, a for address, i for instruction, c for character, and s for string.

The size letters are b for byte, h for half word (2 bytes), w for word (4 bytes), and g for giant (8 bytes).

attach, at    Attach to an already-running process. The only argument is the pid of the process to which to attach. This stops the processes to which you attach, interrupting any sleep or other interruptible system call in progress. See detach.

backtrace, bt, where, w
            Print a stack trace.

break, b      Set a breakpoint. You can specify a function name, a line number of the **current** file (the file containing the currently executing code), a *filename:linenumber* pair, or even an arbitrary address with *address. Gdb assigns and tells you a unique number for each breakpoint. See condition, clear, and delete.

clear         Clear a breakpoint. Takes the same arguments as break. See delete.

condition     Changes a breakpoint specified by number (see break) to break only if a condition is true. The condition is expressed as an arbitrary expression.

```
(gdb) b 664
Breakpoint 3 at 0x804a5c0: file ladsh4.c, line 664.
(gdb) condition 3 status == 0
```

delete        Clear a breakpoint by number.

detach        Detach from the currently attached process.

display

Display the value of an expression every time execution stops. Takes the same arguments (including format modifiers) as print. Prints a display number that can be used later to cancel the display. See undisplay.

help

Get help. Called with no argument, provides a summary of the help available. Called with another command as an argument, provides help on that command. Extensively cross-referenced.

jump

Jump to an arbitrary address and continue execution there. The address is the only argument, and it can be specified either as a line number or as an address specified as *address*.

list, l

With no argument, list first lists the 10 lines surrounding the current address. Subsequent calls to list list subsequent sections of 10 lines. With an argument of -, lists the previous 10 lines.

With a line number, lists the 10 lines surrounding that line. With a *filename:linenumber* pair, lists the 10 lines surrounding that line. With a function name, lists the 10 lines surrounding the beginning of the function. With an address specified as *address*, specifies the 10 lines surrounding the code found at that address.

With two line specifications separated by commas, lists all the lines between the two specified lines.

next, n

Step to the next line of source code in the current function; make function calls without stepping. See step.

nexti

Step to the next machine language instruction; make function calls without stepping. See stepi.

print, p

Print the value of an expression in a comprehensible representation. If you have a char *c, the command print c will print the address of the string, and print *c will print the string itself. Printing structures will expand the structures.

You can include casts in your expressions, and gdb will honor them. If the code was compiled with the -ggdb option, enumerated values and preprocessor definitions will be available for you to use in your expressions. See display.

The print command takes format identifiers, although with proper types and with typecasts, the format identifiers are rarely necessary. See x.

run, r — Run the current program from the beginning. The arguments to the run command are the arguments that would be used to run the program on the command line. Gdb will do shell-style globbing with * and [], and it will do shell-style redirection with >, >, and >>, but it will not do pipes or here documents.

With no arguments, run uses the arguments that were specified in the most recent run command, or in the most recent set args command. To run with no arguments after running with arguments, use the set args command with no extra arguments.

set — Gdb allows you to change the values of variables, like this:

```
(gdb) set a = argv[5]
```

Also, whenever you print an expression, gdb gives you a shorthand variable, like $1, that you can use to refer to it later. So if you had previously printed argv[5] and gdb had told you that it was $6, you could write the previous assignment as

```
(gdb) set a = $6
```

The set command also has many subcommands, far too numerous to list here. Use help set for more information.

step, s — Step the program instruction by instruction until it reaches a new line of source code. See next.

stepi        Execute exactly one machine language instruction; traces into function calls. See nexti.

undisplay        Without any argument, cancels all displays. Otherwise, cancels the displays whose numbers are given as arguments. See display.

whatis        Prints the data type of an expression given as its argument.

where, w        See backtrace.

x        The x command is like the print command, except that it is explicitly limited to printing the contents of an address in some arbitrary format. If you do not use a format identifier, gdb will use the most recently specified format identifier.

# gcc Options and Extensions

To use gcc, the standard C compiler used with Linux, you need to know the command-line options. Also, gcc extends the C language in several ways. Even if you intend to write only ANSI-C-compliant source code, you will need to know some of the extensions to understand the Linux header files.

Most of gcc's command-line options are normal, as C compilers go. For a few options, there do not appear to be any standards. We cover the most important options, options that are used on a day-to-day basis.

Standard—ANSI-standard—C is a useful goal, but as low-level as C is, there are situations in which it is not expressive enough. There are two areas in Linux in which gcc's extensions get particular use: interfacing with assembly-language code (covered in *Brennan's Guide to Inline Assembly*[1]) and building shared libraries (covered in Chapter 7). Because header files are parts of those shared libraries, some of the extensions show through in the system header files, as well.

Of course, there are also lots of extensions that are useful in all sorts of other everyday coding, as long as you do not mind being gratuitously nonstandard. For more documentation about these extensions, see the gcc Texinfo documentation.

---

1. http://www.rt66.com/~brennan/djgpp/djgpp_asm.html

# 5.1 gcc Options

gcc has a multitude of command-line options. Fortunately, the set you usually need to know about is much smaller, and we cover those options here. Most of the options are generally the same or similar on other compilers, as well. gcc has voluminous documentation on its options available with `info gcc`.[2]

`-o filename`     Specify the output file name. This is not usually needed if you are compiling to an object file because the default is to substitute filename.o for filename.c. However, if you are creating an executable, the default (for historical reasons) is to always create an executable named a.out. It is also useful if you wish to put output files in another directory.

`-c`     Compile, without linking, the source files specified on the command line, creating an object file for each source file. When using make, it is common to use one invocation of gcc per object file, because it is easy to see which file failed to compile if an error occurs. However, when you are typing commands by hand, it is commonly useful to specify many files in one invocation of gcc. In cases in which specifying many input files on the command line would be ambiguous, specify only one, or gcc may get confused. For instance, `gcc -c -o a.o a.c b.c` is equivalent to `gcc -c -o a.o b.c`.

`-Dfoo`     Define a preprocessor macro on the command line. You may need to escape characters that are special to the shell. For instance, if you want to define a string, you will have to escape the " characters that delimit the string. Two common ways to do this are `'-Dfoo="bar"'` and `-Dfoo=\"bar\"`. Note that the first works much better if there are any spaces in the string, because spaces are treated specially by the shell.

---

2. `man gcc` has them too, but the man page is not updated as often as the Texinfo documentation.

| | |
|---|---|
| -I*dir* | Prepend *dir* to the list of directories in which to search for include files. |
| -L*dir* | Prepend *dir* to the list of directories in which to search for libraries. Unless otherwise instructed, gcc uses shared libraries in preference to static libraries. |
| -l*foo* | Link against lib*foo*. Unless otherwise instructed, gcc links against shared libraries (lib*foo*.so) in preference to static libraries (lib*foo*.a). The linker searches for functions in all the libraries listed, in the order in which they are listed, until each function is found. |
| -static | Link against static libraries only. See Chapter 7 for details. |
| -g, -ggdb | Include debugging information. The -g option instructs gcc to include standard debugging information. The -ggdb option instructs gcc to include a large amount of information that only the gdb debugger is capable of understanding. Use -g if you have limited disk space, expect to use a debugger other than gdb, or are willing to trade away some functionality in gdb for linking speed. Use -ggdb if you need all the help you can get debugging, and gcc will pass more information to gdb. |
| | Note that unlike most compilers, gcc is willing to include debugging information in optimized code. However, following the debugger as it traces through optimized code can be challenging—the code path may jump around, and completely miss sections of code you expected to be executed. It can also give you a better understanding of your code, and of how optimizing compilers change the way your code executes. |
| -O, -O*n* | Instruct gcc to optimize your code. By default, gcc does a few optimizations; specifying a number (*n*) instructs gcc to optimize to a certain level. The most common optimization level is 2; with the standard version of gcc, 2 is currently the highest optimization level. Unless you wish to compile quickly at the expense of run-time speed, you expect to use a debugger on the output file, or you |

have found a bug in the optimizer, we recommend using -O2 when compiling.

gcc does not implement inline functions unless at least minimal optimization (-O) has been enabled.

-ansi   Support all standard ANSI C programs. Note that this does not enforce ANSI compliance! All it does is turn off gcc extensions that officially conflict with the ANSI standard. (Because many of these extensions are also supported by other C compilers, this is rarely a problem in practice.)

-pedantic   Give all warnings and errors *required* by the ANSI C standard. This does not enforce absolute ANSI compliance.

-Wall   Turn on all the *generally useful* warning messages that gcc can provide. It does not turn on options that are useful only in specific cases. This provides a similar level of detail to running the lint syntax checker on your source code. gcc allows you to turn each warning message on or off individually. The gcc manual lists all the warning messages.

## 5.2   Header Files

You may, from time to time, find yourself browsing the Linux header files. You are likely to find some constructs there that go beyond ANSI-compliant C code. A few, at least, are worth understanding. All of the constructs documented here are more fully documented in the gcc info documentation.

### **5.2.1** `long long`

The `long long` type denotes a storage unit at least as large as a `long`. On Intel i86 and other 32-bit platforms, `long` is 32 bits wide, and `long long` is 64 bits wide. On the Digital Alpha platform, `long long` and `long` are both 64 bits, as are pointers. The `long long` type is currently slated to be included in the next revision of the C language standard, so this will probably be ANSI-C-compliant at some future date.

## **5.2.2 Inline Functions**

In certain parts of the Linux header files (system-specific ones, in particular), inline functions are used pervasively. They are as fast as macros (no function call overhead is incurred) but provide all the type checking available with a normal function call. Code that calls inline functions must be compiled with at least minimal optimization on (`-0`).

## **5.2.3 Alternative Extended Keywords**

In gcc, every extended keyword (keywords not covered by the ANSI standard) has two versions: the keyword itself and the keyword surrounded by two underscore characters on each side. When the compiler is used in standard-compliant mode (usually, because the `-ansi` argument was used), the normal extended keywords are not recognized. So, for example, the `attribute` keyword is written as `__attribute__` in the header files.

## **5.2.4 Attributes**

The `attribute` extended keyword is used to tell gcc more about a function, variable, or declared type than is possible in ANSI-compliant C code. For example, the `aligned` attribute tells gcc exactly how to align a variable or type; the `packed` attribute specifies that padding not be used; and `noreturn` specifies that a function never returns, which allows gcc to optimize better and avoid spurious warnings.

Function attributes are declared by adding them to the function declaration, like this:

```
void die_die_die(int, char *) __attribute__ ((__noreturn__));
```

The attribute declaration is placed between the closing parenthesis and the semicolon of the declaration and consists of the attribute keyword followed by the attributes in double parentheses. If there are multiple attributes, use a comma-separated list.

```
int printm(char *, ...)
  __attribute__ ((const,
                  format (printf, 1, 2)))
  ;
```

This says that printm does not examine any values other than its arguments and has no side effects related to code generation (const), that gcc should check the arguments given to it as it checks the arguments to printf(), and that the first argument is the format string and the second argument is the first substituted parameter (format).

We cover some attributes in context (for instance, building shared libraries in Chapter 7), and you can find all the documentation on attributes in the gcc Texinfo documentation.

# CHAPTER 6

# Memory Debugging Tools

Although C is undisputedly the standard programming language on Linux systems, C has a number of features that lead programmers into writing code with subtle bugs that can be very hard to debug. Memory leaks (in which malloc()ed memory is never free()ed) and buffer overruns (writing past the end of an array, for example) are two of the most common and difficult-to-detect program bugs. This section presents a few debugging tools that greatly simplify the detection and isolation of such problems.

## 6.1   Buggy Code

```
1: #include <stdlib.h>
2: #include <stdio.h>
3:
4: char global[5];
5:
6: int main(void) {
7:     char * dyn;
8:     char local[5];
9:
10:     /* First, overwrite a buffer just a little bit */
11:     dyn = malloc(5);
12:     strcpy(dyn, "12345");
13:     printf("1: %s\n", dyn);
14:     free(dyn);
15:
16:     /* Now overwrite the buffer a lot */
```

```
17:     dyn = malloc(5);
18:     strcpy(dyn, "12345678");
19:     printf("2: %s\n", dyn);
20:
21:     /* Walk past the beginning of a malloced local buffer */
22:     *(dyn - 1) = '\0';
23:     printf("3: %s\n", dyn);
24:     /* note we didn't free the pointer! */
25:
26:     /* Now go after a local variable */
27:     strcpy(local, "12345");
28:     printf("4: %s\n", local);
29:     local[-1] = '\0';
30:     printf("5: %s\n", local);
31:
32:     /* Finally, attack global data space */
33:     strcpy(global, "12345");
34:     printf("6: %s\n", global);
35:
36:     /* And write over the space before the global buffer */
37:     global[-1] = '\0';
38:     printf("7: %s\n", global);
39:
40:     return 0;
41: }
```

Throughout this chapter, we shall be looking for the problems in this code segment. This code corrupts three types of memory regions: memory allocated from the dynamic memory pool via malloc(); local variables allocated on the program's stack; and global variables, which are stored in a separate area of memory. For each of these memory classes, this test program writes over the end of the reserved area of memory (usually, by a single byte) and stores a byte immediately before the allocated area as well. In addition, the code includes a memory leak to show how various tools can help track leaks down.

Although this code has many problems, it actually runs just fine. Does that mean these problems are not important? Not by any means. Buffer overruns tend to cause a program to misbehave long after the actual overrun, and memory leaks in programs that run for a length of time waste a computer's resources. For reference, here is what the program looks like when it is executed.

```
$ gcc -Wall -o broken broken.c
$ ./broken
1: 12345
2: 12345678
3: 12345678
4: 12345
5: 12345
6: 12345
7: 12345
```

# 6.2 Electric Fence

The first tool we shall look at is **Electric Fence**.[1] While it makes no attempt to find memory leaks, it does a nice job of helping programmers isolate buffer overruns. Every modern computer (including all the computers that Linux runs on) provides hardware memory protection. Linux takes advantage of this to isolate programs from each other (your vi session cannot access the memory of my gcc invocation, for example) and to safely share code among processes by making it read-only. Linux's mmap()[2] system call allows processes to take advantage of hardware memory protection, as well.

Electric Fence replaces the C library's normal malloc() function with a version that allocates the requested memory and (usually) allocates a section of memory immediately after this, which the process is not allowed to access! Although it may seem odd for a process to allocate memory that it is not allowed to access, doing so causes the kernel to immediately halt the process with a segmentation fault if the program tries to access the memory. By allocating the memory in this manner, Electric Fence has arranged things so that your program will be killed whenever it tries to read or write past the end of a malloc()ed buffer. For full details on using Electric Fence, consult its man page (man libefence), which is very complete.

---

1. Available from ftp://sunsite.unc.edu/pub/Linux/devel/lang/c as well as with many distributions.
2. See Chapter 12 for details on mmap().

## 6.2.1 Using Electric Fence

One of the nicest things about Electric Fence is that it is easy to use. Simply link a program against libefence.a by running the final link step with -lefence as the final argument, and the code is ready to be debugged. Let's see what happens when we run our test program against Electric Fence.

```
$ ./broken
  Electric Fence 2.0.5 Copyright (C) 1987-1995 Bruce Perens.
1: 12345
Segmentation fault (core dumped)
```

Although Electric Fence does not tell us exactly where the problem occurred, it does make the problem itself *much* more obvious. Pinpointing where the problem occurred is easily done by running the program under a debugger, such as gdb. To use gdb to pinpoint the problem, build the program with debugging information by using gcc's -g flag, run gdb and tell it the name of the executable to debug, and run the program. When the program is killed, gdb will show you exactly what line caused the problem. Here is what this procedure looks like:

```
$ gcc -ggdb -Wall -o broken broken.c -lefence
$ gdb broken
GDB is free software and you are welcome to distribute copies of it
under certain conditions; type "show copying" to see the conditions.
There is absolutely no warranty for GDB; type "show warranty" for details.
GDB 4.16 (i386-redhat-linux), Copyright 1996 Free Software Foundation, Inc.
(gdb) run
Starting program: /home/ewt/broken
  Electric Fence 2.0.5 Copyright (C) 1987-1995 Bruce Perens.
1: 12345
Program received signal SIGSEGV, Segmentation fault.
strcpy (dest="12345678", src="12345678") at strcpy.c:35
strcpy.c:35: No such file or directory.
(gdb) where
#0  strcpy (dest=0x40001ff8 "12345678", src=0x8053a75 "12345678")
    at strcpy.c:35
#1  0x8048190 in main () at broken.c:18
#2  0x80480eb in ___crt_dummy__ ()
(gdb)
```

Thanks to Electric Fence and gdb, we know there is a problem in file broken.c code at line 18, which is the second time `strcpy()` is called.

## 6.2.2 Memory Alignment

While Electric Fence did a fine job of finding the second problem in the code—namely, the `strcpy()` that overwrote its buffer by a large amount—it did not help us at all in finding the first buffer overflow.

The problem here has to do with memory alignment. Most modern CPUs require multibyte objects to start at particular offsets in the system's RAM. For example, Alpha processors require that an 8-byte long begin at an address that is evenly divisible by eight. This means that a long may appear at address 0x1000 or 0x1008, but not at 0x1005.[3]

Because of this consideration, `malloc()` implementations normally return memory whose first byte is aligned on the processor's word size (4 bytes on 32-bit processors and 8 bytes on 64-bit processors) to ensure the caller can store whatever data it likes into the memory. By default, Electric Fence attempts to mimic this behavior by providing a `malloc()` that returns only addresses that are an even multiple of `sizeof(int)`.

In most programs, such alignment is not all that important, because memory allocations are done in increments that are already based on the machine's word size, or of simple character strings, which do not have any alignment requirements (as each element is only one byte long).

In the case of our test program, the first `malloc()` call allocated five bytes. For Electric Fence to meet its alignment restrictions, it must treat the allocation as a request for eight bytes and set up the memory with an extra three bytes of accessible space after the `malloc()`ed region! Small buffer overruns in this region are not caught because of this.

As `malloc()` alignment concerns can normally be ignored and the alignment can allow buffer overruns to remain undetected, Electric Fence lets you control how alignment works through the `EF_ALIGNMENT` environment

---

3. Most traditional Unix systems deliver a bus error (`SIGBUS`) to a process that attempts to use misaligned data. The Linux kernel actually handles unaligned accesses so that the process can continue normally, but at a large performance penalty.

variable. If it is set, all `malloc()` results are aligned according to its value. For example, if it is set to 5, all `malloc()` results will be addresses evenly divisible by 5 (this probably is not a very useful value, though). To turn off memory alignment, set `EF_ALIGNMENT` to 1 before running your program. Under Linux, improperly aligned accesses are fixed in the kernel anyway, so although this may slow your program down substantially, it should function properly—well, unless it has slight buffer overflows!

Here is how our test program linked against Electric Fence behaved when we set `EF_ALIGNMENT` to 1.

```
$ export EF_ALIGNMENT=1
$ gdb broken
GDB is free software and you are welcome to distribute copies of it
under certain conditions; type "show copying" to see the conditions.
There is absolutely no warranty for GDB; type "show warranty" for details.
GDB 4.16 (i386-redhat-linux), Copyright 1996 Free Software Foundation, Inc.
(gdb) r
Starting program: /home/ewt/broken

  Electric Fence 2.0.5 Copyright (C) 1987-1995 Bruce Perens.
Program received signal SIGSEGV, Segmentation fault.
strcpy (dest=0x40001ffb "12345", src=0x8053a68 "12345") at strcpy.c:35
strcpy.c:35: No such file or directory.
(gdb) where
#0  strcpy (dest="12345", src=12345") at strcpy.c:35
#1  0x8048155 in main () at broken.c:12
#2  0x80480eb in ___crt_dummy__ ()
```

This time it found the first buffer overflow that occurred.

## 6.2.3 Other Features

Not only does Electric Fence help detect buffer overruns, but it can also detect buffer underruns (accessing the memory before the start of a `malloc()`ed buffer) and accesses to memory that has already been `free()`ed. If the `EF_PROTECT_BELOW` environment variable is set to 1, Electric Fence will trap buffer underruns. It does this by placing an inaccessible memory region immediately before the valid memory region returned by `malloc()`. When it does this, it can no longer detect overruns because of the memory paging layout of most processors. The memory alignment concerns that make overruns tricky do not affect underruns, however, as in this mode, Electric Fence's `malloc()` always returns a memory address at the beginning of a page, which is always aligned on a word boundary.

If `EF_PROTECT_FREE` is set to 1, `free()` will make the memory region passed to it inaccessible rather than return it to the free memory pool. If the program tries to access that memory at any point in the future, the kernel will detect the illegal access. Setting `EF_PROTECT_FREE` makes it easy to ensure that your code is not using `free()`ed memory at any point.

## 6.2.4 Limitations

While Electric Fence does a nice job of finding overflows of `malloc()`ed buffers, it does not help at all with tracking down problems with either global or locally allocated data. It also does not make any attempt to find memory leaks, so you will have to look elsewhere for help with those problems.

## 6.2.5 Resource Consumption

Although Electric Fence is powerful, easy to use, and fast (because all the access checks are done in hardware), it does exact a price. Most processors allow the system to control access to memory only in units of a **page** at a time. On Intel 80x86 processors, for example, each page is 4,096 bytes in size. Because Electric Fence wants `malloc()` to set up two different regions for each call (one allowing access, the other allowing no access), each call to `malloc()` consumes a page of memory, or 4K![4] If the code being tested allocates a lot of small areas, linking the code against Electric Fence can easily increase the program's memory usage by two or three orders of magnitude! Of course, using `EF_PROTECT_FREE` makes this even worse because that memory is never freed.

The moral is: If you find your system running out of memory when you debug a program with Electric Fence, do not be afraid to add more swap space!

---

4. On Linux/Intel and Linux/SPARC systems anyway. The page size depends on the underlying hardware architecture.

# 6.3 Checker

Checker[5] adds extra code to a program to help find overflows and memory leaks. Instead of compiling a program with gcc, use checkergcc everywhere and the resulting program will debug itself. To compile our test program, for example, the following command was used.

```
checkergcc -o broken broken.c
```

## 6.3.1 Finding Overruns

Once a program has been built with checkergcc, simply running the program yields a long report of the errors in it. Here is part of the output from our test program.

```
From Checker (pid:23136): (bvh) block bounds violation in the heap.
When Writing 1 byte(s) at address 0x08078fd9, inside the heap (sbrk).
0 bytes after a block (start: 0x8078fd4, length: 5, mdesc: 0x0).
The block was allocated from:
        pc=0x08051a50 in malloc() at ../l-malloc|malloc.c:251
        pc=0x080481d4 in main() at broken.c:11
        pc=0x0804810c in _start() at :0
Stack frames are:
        pc=0x08064980 in strcpy() at strcpy.c:35
        pc=0x08048209 in main() at broken.c:12
        pc=0x0804810c in _start() at :0
```

The first part of this output tells us that we wrote to part of the heap (the part of memory that malloc() is responsible for allocating) that was outside any allocated block. Checker tells us exactly where the block was allocated (broken.c line 11 in this case) and what function caused the overflow (the strcpy() function called from line 12 of broken.c). The final part of the output from this version of broken shows us another problem.

---

5. Available from ftp://sunsite.unc.edu/pub/Linux/devel/lang/c

```
From Checker (pid:23155): (nma) no memory addressed.
When Writing 1 byte(s) at address 0xbffffae7, inside the
    nothingness segment.
THIS SHOULD CAUSE A SEGMENTATION FAULT.
Known_stack_limit = 0xbffffae8
Stack frames are:
        pc=0x0804834e in main() at broken.c:29
        pc=0x0804810c in _start() at :0
```

This is warning us about writing off the end of our stack when we write too many bytes into a local variable. Although Checker did find this problem, you should not count on it to find writes past the end of local buffers. All it can find is writes past the end of the stack—if more variables had been allocated after local, Checker would not have helped us find this problem. Like Electric Fence, Checker does not help find problems with global variables.

## 6.3.2 Finding Memory Leaks

Checker is controlled through the CHECKEROPTS environment variable. You can get information on how to set CHECKEROPTS by reading the Checker Texinfo documentation or by setting CHECKEROPTS to --help before running a program built with checkergcc. One of the most useful things you can do with CHECKEROPTS is to set it to --detector=end, which tells Checker to run a memory-leak detector after the program has completed.

Here is what the memory-leak detection tells us about our test program.

```
From Checker (pid:23171): (gar) garbage detector results.
There is 1 leak and 0 potential leak(s).
Leaks consume 5 bytes (0 KB) / 131561 KB.
( 0.00% of memory is leaked.)
Found 1 block(s) of size 5.
Block at ptr=0x807a33c
        pc=0x08051a00 in malloc_1() at ../l-malloc|malloc.c:230
        pc=0x08048265 in main() at broken.c:17
        pc=0x0804810c in _start() at :0
```

With little effort, Checker just found exactly where the leaked memory was allocated.

# 6.4 **mpr and** `mcheck()`

A simple way to find all a program's memory leaks is to log all its calls to `malloc()` and `free()`. When the program has completed, it is straightforward to match each `malloc()`ed block with the point at which it was `free()`ed or report a leak if it was never freed. mpr[6] takes this approach to finding memory leaks. To help find memory corruption as well, mpr includes a replacement `malloc()` library from the GNU project that includes some support for memory allocation debugging, which is enabled by calling the `mcheck()` function. When an application is linked against `libmpr.a` with the `-lmpr` command-line option, `mcheck()` memory checking is automatically enabled as well.

## 6.4.1 Finding Memory Corruption with `mcheck`

Finding memory problems with mpr's `malloc()` library is as straightforward as it is with Electric Fence. Instead of trapping memory corruption in hardware, `malloc()` places known byte sequences before and after the returned memory region. `free()` looks for those signatures and calls `abort()` if they have been disturbed. Running a program linked against mpr through gdb shows you exactly which memory regions have been corrupted, as long as those regions are properly `free()`ed. However, the `mcheck()` method does not pinpoint exactly where the corruption occurred; it is up to the programmer to figure that out. Linking our test program against mpr and running it under gdb yields the following results.

```
$ gcc -ggdb -o broken broken.c -lmpr
$ gdb broken
GDB is free software and you are welcome to distribute copies of it
under certain conditions; type "show copying" to see the conditions.
There is absolutely no warranty for GDB; type "show warranty" for details.
GDB 4.16 (i386-redhat-linux), Copyright 1996 Free Software Foundation, Inc.
(gdb) r
Starting program: /home/ewt/lad/code/broken
1: 12345
mcheck: memory clobbered past end of allocated block
```

---

6. Available from ftp://sunsite.unc.edu/pub/Linux/devel/lang/c as well as with many Linux distributions.

```
Program received signal SIGABRT, Aborted.
0x8053b91 in kill ()
(gdb) where
#0  0x8053b91 in kill ()
#1  0x80537fa in raise (sig=6) at raise.c:27
#2  0x804ea43 in abort () at abort.c:61
#3  0x8049384 in mabort ()
#4  0x804915c in checkhdr ()
#5  0x8049181 in freehook ()
#6  0x8048d1b in free ()
#7  0x8048172 in main () at broken.c:14
#8  0x80480eb in ___crt_dummy__ ()
```

The important part of this is where it tells you that the problem was detected
in broken.c at line 14. That lets you see that the error was detected during
the first free() call, which indicates the problem was in the dyn memory
region.

Like Electric Fence and Checker, mpr does not help you to find overruns
in local or global variables, only in malloc()ed memory regions.

## 6.4.2 Finding Memory Leaks with mpr

Although mpr can make it easier to find memory corruption, it really excels
at finding memory leaks. The first step in using mpr for this (after building
the code with debug information enabled[7] and linking its code against mpr)
is to set two environment variables, MPRPC and MPRFI.

MPRPC contains values that the mpr library needs in order to properly walk
the function call chain when it writes to the log. The mprpc takes a program
name as its argument and writes the value for MPRPC to standard out, letting
you set it like this:

```
export MPRPC='mprpc program'
```

---

7. For portability, most of the mpr log analysis tools use gdb to relate addresses to their
   location in the source code. For this to work, the program must include debugging
   information.

The other environment variable, MPRFI, tells mpr what command it should pipe the log through (if it is not set, no log is generated). For small programs, MPRFI should be set to something like cat > mpr.log. For larger programs, it can save a significant amount of space to compress the log file while writing it by setting MPRFI to gzip > mpr.log.gz.

Before we can experiment with finding memory leaks, we need to remove the overruns of malloc()ed regions from our test program as mcheck() kept abort()ing the program. Here is what we did to create a log file for a fixed version of our test program:

```
$ gcc -ggdb -o broken-fixed broken-fixed.c -lmpr
$ export MPRPC='mprpc broken-fixed'
$ export MPRFI="cat > mpr.log"
$ ./broken-fixed
1: 12345
2: 12345678
3: 12345678
4: 12345
5: 12345
6: 12345
7: 12345
$ ls -l mpr.log
-rw-rw-r--   1 ewt        ewt             130 May 17 16:22 mpr.log
```

Once the log file has been created, there are a number of tools available for analyzing it. All of these programs expect an mpr log on standard input.

mpr *program*    This converts the program addresses in an mpr log into function names and source code locations. The executable file name that generated the log must be given as an argument. To see all the allocations that occurred in a program, along with the function call chain that led to the allocations, you could use mpr *program* < mpr.log. By default, this program displays the function name and the line number of the allocations within the function. Using the -f flag causes it to display the file names, as well, and -l displays the line number within the file.

The output of this program is considered a valid mpr log file, and as such it can be piped through any of the other mpr utility programs

mprcc

This converts the log into output grouped by call chain. A function call chain is a list of all the functions that are currently active at some point in a program. For example, if main() calls getargs(), which then calls parsearg(), the active call chain while parsearg() is running is displayed as main:getargs:parsearg. For each unique call chain that allocated memory during a program's execution, mprcc displays the number of allocations made by that chain[8] and the total bytes allocated by that chain.

mprlk

The log file is examined for all of the allocated regions that were never freed. A new log file, which consists of only those allocations that caused leaks, is generated on standard out.

mpr provides a few more log analyzers, but these are the most useful. Now that we know about them, it is easy to find the memory leak in our test program: Just use mprlk < mpr.log | mpr broken-fixed (which is equivalent to mpr broken-fixed < mpr.log | mprlk).

```
$ mprlk < mpr.log | mpr -f -l broken-fixed
m:main(broken-fixed.c,17):9:134615048
```

---

8. More specifically, it is the sum of all the allocations made by the final function in the chain when it was invoked through that particular chain.

# CHAPTER 7

# Creating and Using Libraries

Executable binaries can get functions from libraries in one of two ways: The functions can be copied from a static library directly into the executable binary image, or they can be indirectly referenced in a shared library file that is read when the executable is run. This chapter teaches you how to use and create both types of archives.

## 7.1  Static Libraries

Static libraries are simply collections of object files arranged by the **ar** (archiver) utility.  ar collects object files into one archive file and adds a table that tells which object files in the archive define what symbols. The linker, **ld**, then binds references to a symbol in one object file to the definition of that symbol in an object file in the archive. Static libraries use the suffix .a.

You can convert a group of object files into a static library with a command like

```
ar rcs libname.a foo.o bar.o baz.o
```

You can also add one object file at a time to an existing archive.

```
ar rcs libname.a foo.o
ar rcs libname.a bar.o
ar rcs libname.a baz.o
```

In either case, `libname.a` will be the same. The options used here are:

r           Includes the object files in the library, *replacing* any object files already in the archive that have the same names.

c           Silently create the library if it does not already exist.

s           Maintain the table mapping symbol names to object file names.

There is rarely any need to use other options when building static libraries. However, ar has other options and other capabilities; the ar man page describes them in detail.

# 7.2   Shared Libraries

Shared libraries have several advantages over static libraries:

- Linux shares the memory used for executable code among all the processes that use the shared library, so whenever you have more than one program using the same code, it is to your advantage, and to your users' advantage, to put the code in a shared library.

- Because shared libraries save system memory, they can make the whole system work faster, especially in situations in which memory is not plentiful.

- Because code in a shared library is not copied into the executable, only one copy of the library code resides on disk, saving both disk space and the computer's time spent copying the code from disk to memory when programs are run.

- When bugs are found in a library, a shared library can be replaced by a version that has the bugs fixed, instead of having to recompile every program that uses the library.

The cost exacted by these advantages is primarily complexity. The executable consists of several interdependent parts, and if you give a binary executable to someone who does not have a shared library that the executable requires, it will not run. A secondary cost is the time it takes when the program starts to find and load the shared libraries; this is generally negated because the shared libraries have usually already been loaded into memory for other processes, and so they do not have to be loaded from disk again when the new process is started.

Linux originally used a simplistic binary file format (actually, three variations on a simplistic binary file format) that made the process of creating shared libraries difficult and time-consuming. Once created, the libraries could not be easily extended in a backward-compatible way. The author of the library had to leave space for data structure expansion by hand-editing tables, and even that did not always work.

Now, the standard binary file format on almost every Linux platform is the modern, extensible ELF (Executable and Linking Format) file format.[1] This means that on practically all Linux platforms, the steps you take to create and use shared libraries are exactly the same.

# 7.3 **Designing Shared Libraries**

Building shared libraries is only marginally harder than building normal static libraries. There are a few constraints, all of which are easy to manage. There is also one major feature, designed to manage binary compatibility across library versions, that is unique to shared libraries.

Shared libraries are intended to preserve backward compatibility. That is, a binary built against an older version of the library still works when run against a newer version of the library. However, there needs to be a way to mark libraries as incompatible with each other for cases in which developers find it necessary to modify interfaces in a non-backward-compatible manner.

---

1. See *Understanding ELF Object Files and Debugging Tools* [Nohr, 1994] or ftp://tsx-11. mit.edu/pub/linux/packages/gcc/ELF.doc.tar.gz for detailed information on the ELF format. The document ftp://tsx-11.mit.edu/pub/linux/packages/gcc/elf. ps.gz covers Linux-specific details.

## 7.3.1 **Managing Compatibility**

Every Linux shared library is assigned a special name, called a **soname**, that includes the name of the library and a version number. When developers change interfaces, they increment the version number, altering the name. Some libraries do not have stable interfaces; developers may change their interface in an incompatible way when a new version is released that has changed only a minor number. Most library developers attempt to maintain stable interfaces that change in an incompatible manner only when they release a new major version of the library.

For example, the developers and maintainers of the Linux C library attempt to maintain backward compatibility for all releases of the C library with the same major number. Version 5 of the C library has gone through five minor revisions, and with few exceptions, programs that worked with the first minor revision work with the fifth. (The exceptions have been poorly coded programs that took advantage of C-library behavior that was not specified or that was buggy in older versions and fixed in newer versions.)

Because all version 5 C libraries are intended to be backward compatible with older versions, they all use the same soname—libc.so.5—which is related to the name of the file in which it is stored, /lib/libc.so.5.*m.r*, where *m* is the minor version number and *r* is the release number.

Applications that link against a shared library do not link directly against /lib/libc.so.5.3.12 (for instance), even though that file exists. The **ldconfig** program, a standard Linux system utility, creates a symbolic link from /lib/libc.so.5 (the soname) to /lib/libc.so.5.3.12, the real name of the library. This makes upgrading shared libraries easy. To upgrade from 5.2.18 to 5.3.12, it is necessary only to put the new libc.so.5.3.12 into the /lib directory and run ldconfig. The ldconfig looks at all the libraries that provide the libc.so.5 soname and makes the symbolic link from the soname to the latest library that provides the soname. Then all the applications linked against /lib/libc.so.5 automatically use the new library the next time they are run, and /lib/libc.so.5.2.18 can be removed immediately, since it is no longer in use.[2]

---

2. That is, you can use the rm command to remove it from the directory structure immediately; programs that are still using it keep it on the disk automatically until they exit. See page 178 for an explanation of how this works.

Unless you have a particular reason to do so, do not link against a specific version of a library. Always use the standard `-llibname` option to the C compiler or the linker, and you will never accidentally link against the wrong version. The linker will look for the file lib*libname*.so, which will be a symlink to the correct version of the library.

So, for linking against the C library, the linker finds /lib/libc.so, which is a link to /lib/libc.so.5.3.12. The application is linked against libc.so.5.3.12's soname, libc.so.5, so when the application is run, it finds /lib/libc.so.5 and links to libc.so.5.3.12, because libc.so.5 is a symlink to libc.so.5.3.12.

## 7.3.2 Incompatible Libraries

When a new version of a library needs to be incompatible with an old version, it should be given a different soname. For instance, to release a new version of the C library that is incompatible with the old one, developers use the soname libc.so.6 instead of libc.so.5, which shows that it is incompatible and also allows applications linked against either version to coexist on the same system. Applications linked against some version of libc.so.5 will continue to use the latest library version that provides the libc.so.5 soname, and applications linked against some version of libc.so.6 will use the latest library version that provides the libc.so.6 soname.

## 7.3.3 Designing Compatible Libraries

When you are designing your own libraries, you need to know what makes a library incompatible. There are three main things that cause incompatibilities.

1.  Changing or removing exported function interfaces.

2.  Changing exported data items, except adding optional items to the ends of structures that are allocated within the library.

3.  Changing the behavior of functions to something outside the original specification.

To keep new versions of your libraries compatible, you can:

- Add new functions with different names rather than change the definitions or interfaces of existing functions.

- When changing exported structure definitions, add items only to the end of the structures, and make the extra items optional or filled in by the library itself. Do not expand structures unless they are allocated within the library. Otherwise, applications will not allocate the right amount of data. Do not expand structures that are used in arrays.

## 7.4 Building Shared Libraries

Once you have grasped the concept of sonames, the rest is easy. Just follow a few simple rules.

- Build your sources with gcc's `-fPIC` flag. This generates position-independent code that can be linked and loaded at any address. Do not use the `-fpic` flag. If you do, your libraries *may* still work, but they will be less efficient.

- Do not use the `-fomit-frame-pointer` compiler option. The libraries will still work, but debuggers will be useless. When you need a user to provide you with a traceback because of a bug in your code (or a savvy user wants a traceback to do his or her own debugging), it will not work.

- When linking the library, use gcc rather than ld. The C compiler knows how to call the loader in order to link properly, and there is no guarantee that the interface to ld will remain constant.

- When linking the library, do not forget to provide the soname. You use a special compiler option: `-Wl` passes options on to ld, with commas replaced with spaces. Use

```
gcc -shared -Wl,-soname,soname -o libname filelist liblist
```

to build your library, where *soname* is the soname; *libname* is the name of the library, including the whole version number, such as `libc.so.5.3.12`; *filelist* is the list of object files that you want to put in the library; and *liblist* is the list of other libraries that provide symbols that will be accessed by this library. The last item is easy to overlook, because the library will still work without it on the system on which it was created, but it may not work in all other situations, such as when multiple libraries are available. For nearly every library, the C library should be included in that list, so explicitly place `-lc` at the end of this list.

So to create the file libfoo.so.1.0.1, with a soname of `libfoo.so.1`, from the object files foo.o and bar.o, use this invocation:

```
gcc -shared -Wl,-soname,libfoo.so.1 -o libfoo.so.1.0.1 foo.o bar.o -lc
```

- Do not strip the library unless you are in a particularly space-hungry environment. Shared libraries that have been stripped will still work, but they have the same general disadvantages as libraries built from object files compiled with `-fomit-frame-pointer`.

## 7.5   **Installing Shared Libraries**

All the hard work of installing a shared library is done by a program called ldconfig. You just need to put the files in place and run ldconfig. Follow these steps:

1.  Copy the shared library to the directory in which you want to keep it.

2.  If you want the linker to be able to find the library without giving it a `-Ldirectory` flag, install the library in /usr/lib, or make a symlink in /usr/lib named *libname*.so that points to the shared library file. Use a relative symlink (`/usr/lib/libc.so` points to `../../lib/libc.so.5.3.12`), not an absolute symlink (`/usr/lib/libc.so` does not point to `/lib/libc.so.5.3.12`).

3.  If you want the linker to be able to find the library without installing it on the system (or before installing it on the system), create a *libname*.so

link in the current directory just like the system-wide one. Then use -L. to tell gcc to look in the current directory for libraries.

4.  If the full pathname of the directory in which you installed the shared library file is not listed in /etc/ld.so.conf, add it, one directory path per line of the file.

5.  Run the ldconfig program, which will make another symlink in the directory in which you installed the shared library file from the soname to the file you installed. It will then make an entry in the dynamic loader cache so that the dynamic loader finds your library when you run programs linked with it, without having to search many directories in an attempt to find it.[3]

You need to create entries in /etc/ld.so.conf and run ldconfig only if you are installing the libraries as system libraries—if you expect that programs linked against the library will automatically work. Other ways to use shared libraries are explained in the next section.

## 7.5.1 Example

As an extremely simple, but still instructive, example, we have created a library that contains one short function. Here, in its entirety, is libhello.c.

```
1: /* libhello.c -- provides print_hello() function for libhello.so */
2: #include <stdio.h>
3:
4: void print_hello(void) {
5:    printf("Hello, library.\n");
6: }
```

Of course, we need a program that makes use of libhello.

```
1: /* usehello.c -- uses print_hello() function from libhello.so */
2: #include "libhello.h"
3:
4: int main (void) {
```

---

3. If you remove /etc/ld.so.cache, you may be able to detect the slowdown in your system. Run ldconfig to regenerate /etc/ld.so.cache.

```
5:    print_hello();
6:    return 0;
7: }
```

The contents of libhello.h are left as an excercise for the reader.

In order to compile and use this library without installing it in the system, we take the following steps:

1. Use `-fPIC` to build an object file for a shared library.

   ```
   gcc -fPIC -Wall -g -c libhello.c
   ```

2. Link libhello against the C library for best results on all systems.

   ```
   gcc -g -shared -Wl,-soname,libhello.so.0 -o libhello.so.0.0 libhello.o -lc
   ```

3. Create a pointer from the soname to the library.

   ```
   ln -sf libhello.so.0.0 libhello.so.0
   ```

4. Create a pointer for the linker to use when linking applications against `-lhello`.

   ```
   ln -sf libhello.so.0 libhello.so
   ```

5. Use `-L.` to cause the linker to look in the current directory for libraries, and use `-lhello` to tell it what library to link against. (This way, if you install the library on the system instead of leaving it in the current directory, your application will still link with the same command line.)

   ```
   gcc -Wall -g -c usehello.c -o usehello.o
   gcc -g -o usehello usehello.o -L. -lhello
   ```

6. Now run `usehello` like this:

   ```
   LD_LIBRARY_PATH='pwd' ./usehello
   ```

   The `LD_LIBRARY_PATH` environment variable tells the system where to look for libraries (see the next section for details). Of course, you can install `libhello.so.*` in the /usr/lib directory and avoid setting the `LD_LIBRARY_PATH` environment variable, if you like.

# 7.6 Using Shared Libraries

The easiest way to use a shared library is to ignore the fact that it is a shared library. The C compiler automatically uses shared libraries instead of static ones unless it is explicitly told to link with static libraries. However, there are three other ways to use shared libraries. One, explicitly loading and unloading them from within a program while the program runs, is called dynamic loading, and is described in Chapter 25. The other two are explained here.

## 7.6.1 Using Noninstalled Libraries

When you run a program, the dynamic loader usually looks in a cache (/etc/ld.so.cache, created by ldconfig) of libraries that are in directories mentioned in /etc/ld.so.conf to find libraries that the program needs. However, if the LD_LIBRARY_PATH environment variable is set, it will first dynamically scan the directories mentioned in LD_LIBRARY_PATH (which has the same format as the PATH environment variable) and load all the directories it finds in the path, before it looks in its cache.

This means that if you want to use an altered version of the C library when running one specific program, you can put that library in a directory somewhere and run the program with the appropriate LD_LIBRARY_PATH to access that library. As an example, a few versions of the Netscape browser that were linked against the 5.2.18 version of the C library would die with a segmentation fault when run with the standard 5.3.12 C library because of a more stringent enforcement of malloc() policies. Many people put a copy of the 5.2.18 C library in a separate directory, such as /usr/local/netscape/lib/, move the Netscape binary there, and replace /usr/local/bin/netscape with a shell script that looks something like this:

```
#!/bin/sh
export LD_LIBRARY_PATH=/usr/local/netscape/lib:$LD_LIBRARY_PATH
exec /usr/local/netscape/lib/netscape $*
```

## 7.6.2 Preloading Libraries

Sometimes, you do not want to replace an entire shared library, only a few functions. Because the dynamic loader searches for functions starting with the first loaded library and proceeds through the stack of libraries in order, it would be convenient to be able to tack an alternative library on top of the stack to replace only the functions you need.

An example is **zlibc**. This library replaces file functions in the C library with functions that deal with compressed files. When a file is opened, zlibc looks for both the requested file and a gzipped version of the file. If the requested file exists, zlibc mimics the C library functions exactly, but if it does not exist, and a gzipped version exists instead, it transparently uncompresses the gzipped file without the application knowing. There are limitations, which are described in the library's documentation, but it can trade off speed for a considerable amount of space.

There are two ways to preload a library. To affect only certain programs, you can set an environment variable for the cases you wish to affect:

```
LD_PRELOAD=/lib/libsomething.o exec /bin/someprogram $*
```

However, as with zlibc, you might want to preload a library for every program on the system. The easiest way to do that is to add a line to the /etc/ld.so.preload file specifying which library to preload. In the case of zlibc, it would look something like this:

```
/lib/uncompress.o
```

# CHAPTER 8

# Linux Development Environment

This chapter explains how to request system services, including low-level kernel facilities and higher-level library facilities.

## 8.1  Understanding System Calls

This book mentions **system calls** (syscalls, for short) repeatedly because they are fundamental to the programming environment.  At first glance, they look just like normal C function calls.  That is no accident; they are function calls, just a special variety. To understand the difference, you need to have a basic understanding of the structure of the operating system.

Although there are many pieces of code that make up the Linux operating system (utility programs, applications, programming libraries, device drivers, file systems, memory management, and so on), all those pieces run in one of two contexts: user mode or kernel mode.

When you write a program, the code that you write runs in user mode. Device drivers and file systems, by contrast, run in kernel mode.  In user mode, programs are strictly protected from damaging each other or the rest of the system.  Code that runs in kernel mode has full access to the machine to do, and break, anything.

For a device driver to manipulate the hardware device it is designed to control, it needs full access to it.  The device needs to be protected from arbitrary programs so that programs cannot damage themselves or each other by damaging or confusing the device. The memory it runs in is also protected from the ravages of arbitrary programs.

All this code running in kernel mode exists solely to provide services to code running in user mode. A system call is how application code running in user mode requests protected code running in kernel mode to provide a service.

Take allocating memory, for instance. It is protected, kernel-mode code that must allocate the physical memory for the process, but it is the process itself that must ask for the memory. Or file systems; they need to be protected to maintain coherent data on disk (or over the network), but it is your everyday, run-of-the-mill process that actually needs to read files from the file system.

The ugly details of calling through the user/kernel space barrier are mostly hidden in the C library. Calling through that barrier does not use normal function calls; it uses an ugly interface that is optimized for speed and has significant restrictions. The C library hides most of the interface from you by providing you with normal C functions wrapped around the system calls. However, you will be able to use the functions better if you have some idea what is going on underneath.

## 8.1.1 System Call Limitations

Kernel mode is protected from the rampages of user mode. One of those protections is that the kind of data that can be passed back and forth between kernel mode and user mode is limited to what can be easily verified, and it follows strict conventions.

- Each argument that is passed from user mode to kernel mode is the same length, which is almost always the native word size used by the machine for pointers. This size is big enough to pass long integer arguments, as well as pointers. `char` and `short` variables will be promoted to a larger type by C before being passed in.

- The return type is limited to a signed integer. The first few hundred small negative integers are reserved as error codes and have a common meaning across system calls. This means that system calls that return a pointer cannot return a few pointers to the top of available virtual memory. Fortunately, it turns out that those addresses are in reserved space and would never be returned anyway, so the signed integers that are returned can be cast to pointers without a problem.

Unlike the C calling convention, in which C structures can be passed by value on the stack, you cannot pass a structure by value from user mode to kernel mode, nor can the kernel return a structure to user mode. You can pass large data items only by reference. Pass pointers to structures, just as you always pass pointers to anything that may be modified.

## 8.1.2 System Call Return Codes

The return codes that are reserved across all system calls are universal error return codes, which are all small negative numbers. The C library checks for errors whenever a system call returns. If an error has occurred, the library stuffs the value of the error in the global variable errno.[1] Most of the time, to check for errors, all you have to do is see if the return code was negative. The error codes are defined in <errno.h>,[2] and you can compare errno to any error number defined there that you want to handle in a special way.

The errno variable has another use. The C library provides three ways to get at strings designed to describe the error you have just encountered:

perror()

> Prints an error message. Pass it a string with information about what the code in question was trying to do.
>
> ```
> if ( (file = open(DB_PATH, O_RDONLY)) < 0) {
>     perror("could not open database file");
> }
> ```

---

1. That is a white lie. If you are using threads, the library keeps the error where an errno() function that knows what thread is current can get at it, because different threads might have different current error return codes. But you can ignore that because it ends up working the same way as an errno variable.
2. Another white lie. By including <errno.h>, you will get the definitions. <errno.h> gets them (at least on Linux systems) from <asm/errno.h>, which is specific to each Linux port.

This will cause `perror()` to print an error describing the error that just occurred, along with the explanation of what it was trying to do, like this:

```
could not open database file: No such file or directory
```

It is generally a good idea to make your arguments to `perror()` unique throughout your program so that when you get bug reports with a report from `perror()`, you know exactly where to start looking. Note that there is no newline character in the string passed to `perror()`. You are passing it only one part of a line, and it prints the newline itself.

`strerror()`

Returns a statically allocated string describing the error passed as the only argument. Use this when building your own version of `perror()`, for instance. If you want to save a copy of the string, use `strdup()` to do so; the string returned by `strerror()` will be overwritten on the next call to `strerror()`.

```
if ( (file = open(DB_PATH, O_RDONLY)) < 0) {
    fprintf(stderr,
            "could not open database file %s, %s\n",
            DB_PATH, strerror(errno));
}
```

`sys_errlist`

A poor alternative to `strerror()`. `sys_errlist` is an array of size `sys_nerr` pointers to static, read-only character strings that describe errors. An attempt to write to those strings will cause a segmentation violation and a core dump.

```
if ( (file = open(DB_PATH, O_RDONLY)) < 0) {
    if (errno < sys_nerr) {
        fprintf(stderr, "could not open database file %s, %s\n",
                DB_PATH, sys_errlist[errno]);
    }
}
```

This is neither standard nor portable, and it is mentioned here only because you are likely to find code that relies on it. Convert each such instance to use `strerror()` and you will do the world a service.

If you are not going to use `errno` immediately after generating the error, you must save a copy. Any library function might reset it to any value, because it may make system calls that you do not know are being made, and some library functions may set `errno` without making any system calls.

## 8.1.3 Using System Calls

The interface that you as a programmer are expected to work with is the set of C library wrappers for the system calls. Therefore, we will use *system call* through the rest of this book to mean the C wrapper function that you call to perform a system call, rather than the ugly interface that the C library kindly hides from you.

Most, but not all, system calls are declared in ⟨unistd.h⟩. The ⟨unistd.h⟩ file is really a catch-all for system calls that do not seem to fit anywhere else. In order to determine which include files to use, you will generally need to use the system man pages. Although the function descriptions in the man pages are often terse, the man pages do accurately state, right at the top, which include files need to be included to use the function.

There is one snag here that is endemic on Unix systems. The system calls are documented in a separate manual page section from the library functions, and you will be using library functions to access system calls. Where the library functions differ from the system calls, there are separate man pages for the library functions and the system calls. This would not be so bad except that if there are two man pages for a function, you will nearly always want to read the one describing the library function with that name. But the system calls are documented in section 2, and the library functions in section 3, and because man gives lower numbers precedence, you will consistently be shown the wrong function.

You should not simply just specify the section number, however. System calls that use the most minimal wrappers in the C library are not documented as part of the C library, so `man 3 function` will not find them. In order to make sure you have read all the information you need, first look up the man page without specifying the section. If it is a section 2 man page, check to see if there is a section 3 man page by the same name. If, as happens with `open()`, you get a section 1 man page, look explicitly in sections 2 and 3.

There is, fortunately, another way around this problem. Many versions of the man program, including the one on most Linux systems, allow you to specify an alternate search path for man pages. Read the man man man page to determine if your version of man supports the MANSECT environment variable and the -S argument to the man command. If so, you can set MANSECT to something like 3:2:1:4:5:6:7:8:tcl:n:l:p:o. Look at your man configuration file (/etc/man.config on most Linux systems) to determine the current setting of MANSECT.

Most system calls return 0 to indicate success, and they return a negative value to indicate an error. Because of this, in many cases, a simple form of error handling is appropriate.

```
if (ioctl(fd, FN, data)) {
  /* error handling based on errno */
}
```

Also common is the following form.

```
if (ioctl(fd, FN, data) < 0) {
  /* error handling based on errno */
}
```

For the system calls that return 0 on success, these two cases are identical. In your own code, choose what suits you best. Be aware that you will see all sorts of conventions in others' code.

## 8.1.4 Common Error Return Codes

There are plenty of relatively commonly occurring error codes that you are likely to have seen error messages from before. Some of these explanations may seem confusing. Without knowing what you can do on a Linux system, it is hard to understand the errors you might get while you are working on one. Read this list now to get a sense of what errors exist, and then read it again after you have read this whole book, to gain a more thorough understanding.

For many of the error return codes, we give a sample system call or two likely to trigger the error message in common circumstances. This does not mean that those system calls are the only ones that trigger those errors. Consider them examples to elucidate the output of `perror()`, the brief descriptions in `<asm/errno.h>`, or `man 3 errno`.

Use the man pages to determine which errors to expect from a specific system call. In particular, use `man 3 errno` to get a list of error codes defined by POSIX. However, understand that this sometimes changes, and the man pages may not be completely up-to-date. If a system call returns an error code that you do not expect, presume that the man page is out of date rather than that the system call is broken. The Linux source code is maintained more carefully than the documentation.

EPERM                 The process has insufficient permissions to complete the operation. This error most commonly happens with file operations. See Chapter 10.

ENOENT                No such file or directory. See Chapter 11.

ESRCH                 No such process. See Chapter 9.

EINTR                 System call was interrupted. Interruptible system calls are explained in Chapter 13.

EIO                   I/O error. This is usually generated by a device driver to indicate a hardware error or unrecoverable problem communicating with the device.

ENXIO                 No such device or address. Usually generated by attempting to open a device special file that is associated with a piece of hardware that is not installed or configured.

E2BIG                 The argument list is too long. When trying to `exec()` a new process, there is a limit to the length of the argument list you can give. See Chapter 9.

ENOEXEC               Executable format error. This might happen if you attempt to run an (obsolete) a.out binary on a system without support for a.out binaries. It will also happen if you attempt to run an ELF binary built for another CPU architecture.

| | |
|---|---|
| EBADF | Bad file number. You have passed a file number that does not reference an open file to open(), close(), ioctl(), or another system call that takes a file number argument. |
| ECHILD | No child processes. Returned by the wait() family of system calls. See Chapter 9. |
| EAGAIN | Returned when you attempt to do nonblocking I/O and no input is available. EWOULDBLOCK is a synonym for EAGAIN. If you were doing blocking I/O, the system call would block and wait for input. |
| ENOMEM | Out of memory. Returned by the brk() and mmap() functions if they fail to allocate memory. |
| EACCES | Access *would be* denied. This is returned by the access() system call, explained in Chapter 10, and is more an informational return code than a true error condition. |
| EFAULT | A bad pointer (one that points to inaccessible memory) was passed as an argument to a system call. Accessing the same pointer from within the user-space program that made the system call would result in a segmentation fault. |
| ENOTBLK | The mount() system call returns this error if you attempt to mount as a file system a file that is not a block device special file. |
| EBUSY | The mount() system call returns this error if you attempt to mount a file system that is already mounted or unmount a file system that is currently in use. |
| EEXIST | Returned by creat(), mknod(), or mkdir() if the file already exists, or by open() in the same case if you specified O_CREAT and O_EXCL. |
| EXDEV | Returned by link() if the source and destination files are not on the same file system. |
| ENODEV | Returned by mount() if the requested file-system type is not available. Returned by open() if you attempt to open |

a special file for a device that does not have an associated device driver in the kernel.

ENOTDIR      An intermediate pathname component (that is, a directory name specified as part of a path) exists, but it is not a directory. Returned by any system call that takes a file name.

EISDIR      Returned by system calls that require a file name, such as unlink(), if the final pathname component is a directory rather than a file and the operation in question cannot be applied to a directory.

EINVAL      Returned if the system call received an invalid argument.

ENFILE      Returned if no more files can be opened by any process on the system.

EMFILE      Returned if no more files can be opened by the calling process.

ENOTTY      Generally occurs when an application that is attempting to do terminal control is run with its input or output set to a pipe, but it can happen whenever you try to perform an operation on the wrong type of device. The standard error message for this, "not a typewriter", is rather misleading.

ETXTBSY      Returned by open() if you attempt to open, with write mode enabled, an executable file or shared library that is currently being run. To work around this, rename the file, then make a new copy with the same name as the old one and work with the new copy. See Chapter 10 and its discussion of inodes for why this happens.

EFBIG      Returned by write() if you attempt to write a file longer than the file system can logically handle (this does not include simple physical space restrictions) or beyond your resource limits. See Chapter 9 for more information on resource limits.

ENOSPC              Returned by write() if you attempt to write a file longer
                    than the file system has space for.

ESPIPE              Returned by lseek() if you attempt to seek on a nonseek-
                    able file descriptor representing a pipe, FIFO, or socket.
                    See Chapter 10 and Chapter 16.

EROFS               Returned by write() if you attempt to write to a read-only
                    file system.

EMLINK              Returned by link() if the file being linked to already has
                    the maximum number of links for the file system it is on
                    (32,000 is currently the maximum on the standard Linux
                    file system).

EPIPE               Returned by write() if the reading end of the pipe is closed
                    and SIGPIPE is caught or ignored. See Chapter 13.

EDOM                Not really a system call error, EDOM is set by math functions
                    if an argument is out of range. (This is EINVAL for the
                    function's domain.) For example, the sqrt() function does
                    not know about complex numbers and therefore does not
                    approve of a negative argument.

ERANGE              Again, not really a system call error, ERANGE is set by math
                    functions if the result is not representable by its return
                    type. (This is EINVAL for the range.)

ENAMETOOLONG        A pathname was too long, either for the entire system or
                    for the file system you were trying to access.

ENOSYS              System call is not implemented. Usually caused by run-
                    ning a recent binary on an old kernel that does not imple-
                    ment the system call.

ENOTEMPTY           Returned by rmdir() if the directory you are trying to
                    remove is not empty.

ELOOP               Returned by system calls that take a path if too many
                    symbolic links in a row (that is, symbolic links pointing

to symbolic links pointing to symbolic links...) were encountered while parsing the path. The current limit is 16 symbolic links in a row.

A few other relatively common error return codes happen only in regard to networking; see page 319 for more information.

## 8.2 Finding Header and Library Files

Most header files that come with your Linux system are stored in the /usr/include hierarchy. There are two exceptions. Header files for the X Window System are available in /usr/include/X11, and many of the system header files stored in /usr/include depend on the header files included with the Linux kernel source. The compiler will search for include files only in /usr/include by default.

Linux distributions always put links from /usr/include to the header files that come with the Linux kernel source, so links called /usr/include/asm, /usr/include/linux, and /usr/include/scsi should all point to wherever those headers are kept, which keeps this transparent. You should never need to know it unless you start replacing the kernel sources that were included with your system with newer Linux sources that you download from the Internet.

Libraries are much the same way, with a twist. Libraries that are considered critical to booting the system (and repairing it, if necessary) are in /lib. Other system libraries are in /usr/lib, except for X11R6 libraries, which are in /usr/X11R6/lib. (There are no "kernel libraries" equivalent to the kernel header files. The kernel *is* a library that has special privileges and is accessed through system calls.) The compiler will search for libraries in /lib and /usr/lib by default.

In order to compile programs that use the standard X11R6 libraries, you will need to give gcc the `-I/usr/X11R6/include` option while compiling, and `-L/usr/X11R6/lib` while linking.

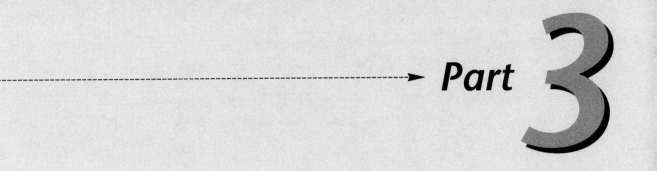

# Part 3

# System Programming

# CHAPTER 9

# The Process Model

One of Unix's hallmarks is its process model. It is the key to understanding access rights, the relationships among open files, signals, job control, and most other low-level topics in this book. Linux adopted most of Unix's process model and added new ideas of its own to allow a truly lightweight threads implementation.

## 9.1 Defining a Process

What exactly is a process? In the original Unix implementations, a process was any executing program. For each program, the kernel kept track of

- The current location of execution (such as waiting for a system call to return from the kernel), often called the program's **context**

- Which files the program had access to

- The program's **credentials** (which user and group owned the process, for example)

- The program's current directory

- Which memory space the program had access to and how it was laid out

A process was also the basic scheduling unit for the operating system. Only processes were allowed to run on the CPU.

## 9.1.1 Complicating Things with Threads

Although that may seem obvious, the concept of threads makes all of this less clear-cut. A thread allows a single program to run in multiple places at the same time. All the threads created (or spun off) by a single program share most of the characteristics that differentiate processes from each other. For example, multiple threads that originate from the same program share information on open files, credentials, current directory, and memory image. As soon as one of the threads modifies a global variable, all the threads see the new value rather than the old one.

Many Unix implementations (including AT&T's canonical System V release) were redesigned to make threads the fundamental scheduling unit for the kernel, and a process became a collection of threads that shared resources. As so many resources were shared among threads, the kernel could switch between threads in the same process more quickly than it could perform a full context switch between processes. This resulted in most Unix kernels having a two-tiered process model that differentiates between threads and processes.

## 9.1.2 The Linux Approach

Linux took another route, however. Linux context switches had always been extremely fast (on the same order of magnitude as the new "thread switches" introduced in the two-tiered approach), suggesting to the kernel developers that rather than change the scheduling approach Linux uses, they should allow processes to share resources more liberally.

Under Linux, a process is defined solely as a scheduling entity and the only thing unique to a process is its current execution context. It does not imply anything about shared resources, because a process creating a new child process has full control over which resources the two processes share (see the `clone()` system call described on page 138 for details on this). This model allows the traditional Unix process management approach to be retained while allowing a traditional thread interface to be built outside the kernel.

Luckily, the differences between the Linux process model and the two-tiered approach surface only rarely. In this book, we use the term **process** to refer to a scheduling entity that does not share fundamental resources with any other entity and **thread** to refer to a scheduling entity that shares many of its resources with other threads.To keep things simple, most of this chapter will ignore threads completely. Toward the end, we discuss the `clone()` system call, which is used to create threads (and can also create normal processes).

# 9.2 Process Attributes

## 9.2.1 The pid and Parentage

Two of the most basic attributes are its **process ID**, or **pid**, and the pid of its parent process. A pid is a positive integer that uniquely identifies a running process and is stored in a variable of type `pid_t`. When a new process is created, the original process is known as the **parent** of the new process and is notified when the new child process ends.

When a process dies, its exit code is stored until the parent process requests it. The exit status is kept in the kernel's process table, which forces the kernel to keep the process's entry active until it can safely discard its exit status. Processes that have exited and are kept around only to preserve their exit status are known as **zombies**. Once the zombie's exit status has been collected, the zombie is removed from the system's process table.

If a process's parent exits (making the child process an **orphan process**), that process becomes a child of the **init process**. The init process is the first process started when a machine is booted and is assigned a pid of 1. One of the primary jobs of the init process is to collect the exit statuses of processes whose parents have died, allowing the kernel to remove the child processes from the process table.

Processes can find their pid and their parent's pid through the `getpid()` and `getppid()` functions.

```
pid_t getpid(void)
```
Returns the pid of the current process.

```
pid_t getppid(void)
```
> Returns the parent process's pid

## 9.2.2 Credentials

Linux uses the traditional Unix security mechanisms of users and groups. User IDs (**uids**) and group IDs (**gids**) are integers[1] that are mapped to symbolic user names and group names through /etc/passwd and /etc/group, respectively (see Chapter 26 for more information on the user and group databases). However, the kernel knows nothing about the names—it is concerned only with the integer representation. The 0 uid is reserved for the system administrator, normally called **root**. All normal security checks are disabled for processes running as root (that is, with a uid of 0), giving the administrator complete control over the system.

In most cases, a process may be considered to have a single uid and gid associated with it. Those are the IDs that are used for most system security purposes (such as assigning ownerships to newly created files). The system calls that modify a process ownership are discussed later in this chapter.

As Unix developed, restricting processes to a single group turned out to create new difficulties. Users involved in multiple projects had to explicitly switch their gid when they wanted to access files whose access was restricted to members of different groups.

Supplemental groups were introduced in BSD 4.3 to eliminate this problem. Although every process still has its primary gid (which it uses as the gid for newly created files, for example), it also belongs to a set of supplemental groups. Security checks that used to ensure that a process belonged to a particular group (and only that group) now allow access as long as the group is one of the supplemental groups the process belongs to. The constant NGROUP, available from <sys/param.h>, specifies how many supplemental groups a process may belong to. Under Linux 2.0, NGROUP is 32.

---

1. uids and gids are normally positive integers, but negative ones will work. Using -1 as an ID is problematic, however, as many of the uid- and gid-related system calls use -1 as an indication not to modify a value (see setregid() on page 101 for an example of this).

Setting the list of groups for a process is done through the `setgroups()` system call and may be done only by processes running with root permissions.

```
int setgroups(size_t num, const gid_t * list);
```

The `list` parameter points to an array of `num` gids. The process's supplemental group list is set to the gids listed in the `list` array.

The `getgroups()` function lets a process get a list of the supplemental groups it belongs to.

```
int getgroups(size_t num, gid_t * list);
```

The `list` must point to an array of `gid_t`, which is filled in with the process's supplemental group list, and `num` specifies how many `gid_ts` `list` can hold. The `getgroups()` system call returns -1 on error (normally, if `list` is not large enough to hold the supplemental group list) or the number of supplemental groups. As a special case, if `num` is 0, `getgroups()` returns the number of supplemental groups for the process.

Here is an example of how to use `getgroups()`.

```
gid_t groupList[NGROUP];
int numGroups;

numGroups = getgroups(NGROUP, groupList);
```

A more complete example of `getgroups()` is in Chapter 26.

Thus a process has a uid, a primary gid, and a set of supplemental groups associated with it. Luckily, this is as much as most programmers ever have to worry about. There are two classes of programs that need very flexible management of uids and gids, however: setuid/setgid programs and system daemons.

System daemons are programs that are always running on a system and perform some action at the request of an external stimulus. For example, most World Wide Web (http) daemons are always running, waiting for a client to connect to it so that they can process the client's requests. Other daemons, such as the cron daemon (which runs requests periodically), sleep until a time when they need to perform actions. Most daemons need to run with root permissions but perform actions at the request of a user who may be trying to compromise system security through the daemon.

The ftp daemon is a good example of a daemon that needs flexible uid handling. It initially runs as root and then switches its uid to the uid of the user who logs into it (most systems start a new process to handle each ftp request, so this approach works quite well). This leaves the job of validating file accesses to the kernel where it belongs. Under some circumstances, however, the ftp daemon must open a network connection in a way that only root is allowed to do (see Chapter 16 for details on this). The ftp daemon cannot simply switch back to root, because user processes cannot give themselves superuser access (with good reason!), but keeping the root uid rather than switching to the user's uid would require the ftp daemon to check all file-system accesses itself. The solution to this dilemma has been applied symmetrically to both uids and primary gids, so we just talk about uids here.

A process actually has three uids: its *real uid*, *saved uid*, and *effective uid*.[2] The effective uid is used for all security checks and is the only uid of the process that normally has any effect.

The saved and real uids are checked only when a process attempts to change its effective uid. Any process may change its effective uid to the same value as either its saved or real uid. Only processes with an effective uid of 0 (processes running as root) may change their effective uid to an arbitrary value.

Normally, a process's effective, real, and saved uid are all the same. This mechanism solves the ftp daemon's dilemma quite nicely, though. When it starts, all its IDs are set to 0, giving it root permissions. When a user logs in, the daemon sets its effective uid to the uid of the user, leaving both the saved and real uids as 0. When the ftp daemon needs to perform an action restricted to root, it sets its effective uid to 0, performs the action, and then resets the effective uid to the uid of the user who is logged in.

Although the ftp daemon does not need the saved uid at all, the other class of programs that takes advantage of this mechanism, setuid and setgid binaries, does use it.

---

2. Linux processes also have a fourth uid and gid used for file-system accesses. This is discussed on page 100.

The passwd program is a simple example of why setuid and setgid functionality was introduced.  The passwd program allows users to change their passwords. User passwords are usually stored in /etc/passwd. Only the root user may write to this file, preventing other users from changing user information.  Users should be able to change their own passwords though, so some way is needed to give the passwd program permission to modify /etc/passwd.

To allow this flexibility, the owner of a program may set special bits in the program's permission bits (see pages 144–148 for more information), which tells the kernel that whenever the program is executed, it should run with the same effective uid (or gid) as the user who owns the program file, regardless of what user runs the program. These programs are called **setuid** (or **setgid**) executables.

Making the passwd program owned by the root user and setting the setuid bit in the program's permission bits lets all users change their passwords. When a user runs passwd, the passwd program is run with an effective user ID of 0, allowing it to modify /etc/passwd and change the user's password.  Of course, the passwd program has to be carefully written to prevent unintended side effects. Setuid programs are a popular target for system intruders, as poorly written setuid programs provide a simple way for users to gain unauthorized permissions.

There are many cases in which setuid programs need their special permissions only for short periods of time and would like to switch back to the uid of the actual user for the remainder of the time (like the ftp daemon). As setuid programs have only their effective uid set to the uid of the program's owner, they know the uid of the user who actually ran them (the saved uid), making switching back simple. In addition, they may set their real uid to the setuid value (without affecting the saved uid) and regain those special permissions as needed. In this situation, the effective, saved, and real uid work together to make system security as simple as possible.

Unfortunately, using this mechanism can be confusing because POSIX and BSD take slightly different approaches, and Linux supports both. The BSD solution is more full-featured than the POSIX method. It is accessed with the setreuid() function.

```
int setreuid(uid_t ruid, uid_t euid);
```

The real uid of the process is set to `ruid` and the effective uid of the process is set to `euid`. If either of the parameters is -1, that ID is not affected by this call.

If the effective uid of the process is 0, this call always succeeds. Otherwise, the IDs may be set to either the saved uid or the real uid of the process. Note this call never changes the saved uid of the current process; to do that, use POSIX's `setuid()` function, which can modify the saved uid.

```
int setuid(uid_t euid);
```

As in `setreuid()`, the effective uid of the process is set to `euid` as long as `euid` is the same as either the saved or real uids of the process, or as long as the process's effective uid at the time of the call is 0.

When `setuid()` is used by a process whose effective uid is 0, all the process's uids are changed to `uid`. Unfortunately, this makes it impossible for `setuid()` to be used in a setuid root program that needs to temporarily assume the permissions of another uid, because after calling `setuid()`, the process cannot recover its root privileges.

Although the ability to switch uids does make it easier to write code that cannot be tricked into compromising system security, it is not a panacea. There are many popular methods for tricking programs into executing arbitrary code [Lehey, 1995]. As long as either the saved or real uid of a process is 0, such attacks can easily set the effective uid of a process to 0. This makes switching uids insufficient to prevent serious vulnerabilities in system programs. However, if a process can give up any access to root privileges by setting its effective, real, and saved IDs to non-0 values, doing so limits the effectiveness of any attack against it.

## 9.2.3 The fsuid

In highly specialized circumstances, a program may want to keep its root permissions for everything but file-system access, for which it would rather use a user's uid. Linux's user-space NFS server illustrates the problem that can occur when a process assumes a user's uid. Although the NFS server used to use `setreuid()` to switch uids while accessing the file system, doing so allowed the user whose uid the NFS server was assuming to kill the NFS server. After all, for a moment that user owned the NFS server process.

To prevent this type of problem, Linux uses a separate uid for file-system access checks: the fsuid.

Whenever a process's effective uid is changed, the process's fsuid is set to the process's new effective user ID, making the fsuid transparent to most applications. Those applications that need the extra features provided by the separate fsuid must use the setfsuid() call to explicitly set the fsuid.

```
int setfsuid(uid_t uid);
```

The fsuid may be set to any of the current effective, saved, or real uids of the process. In addition, setfsuid() succeeds if the current fsuid is being retained or if the process's effective uid is 0.

### 9.2.4 User and Group ID Summary

Here is a summary of all the system calls that modify the access permissions of a running process. Most of the functions listed here that pertain to user IDs have been discussed in detail earlier in this chapter, but those related to group IDs have not. As those functions mirror similiar functions that modify user IDs, their behavior should be clear.

All of these functions return -1 on error and 0 on success, unless otherwise noted. Most of these prototypes are in ⟨unistd.h⟩. Those that are located elsewhere are noted below.

```
int setreuid(uid_t ruid, uid_t euid)
```
> Sets the real uid of the current process to ruid and the effective uid of the process to euid. If either of the parameters is -1, that uid remains unchanged.

```
int setregid(gid_t rgid, gid_t egid)
```
> Sets the real gid of the current process to rgid and the effective gid of the process to egid. If either of the parameters is -1, that gid remains unchanged.

```
int setuid(uid_t uid)
```
> If used by a normal user, sets the effective uid of the current process to uid. If used by a process with an effective gid of 0, it sets the real, effective, and saved uids to uid.

`int setgid(gid_t gid)`

> If used by a normal user, sets the effective gid of the current process to `gid`. If used by a process with an effective gid of 0, sets the real, effective, and saved gids to `gid`.

`int seteuid(uid_t uid)`

> Equivalent to `setreuid(-1, uid)`

`int setegid(gid_t gid)`

> Equivalent to `setregid(-1, gid)`

`int setfsuid(uid_t fsuid)`

> Sets the fsuid of the current process to `fsuid`. It is prototyped in `<sys/fsuid.h>`.

`int setfsgid(gid_t fsgid)`

> Sets the fsuid of the current process to `fsgid`. It is prototyped in `<sys/fsuid.h>`.

`int setgroups(size_t num, const gid_t * list)`

> Sets the supplemental groups for the current process to the groups specified in the array `list`, which must contain `num` items. The constant `NGROUP` tells how many groups may be in the list (currently 32). This function is prototyped in `<grp.h>`.

`uid_t getuid()`

> Returns the real uid of the process.

`uid_t geteuid()`

> Returns the effective uid of the process.

`gid_t getgid()`

> Returns the real group ID of the process.

`gid_t getegid()`

> Returns the effective group ID of the process.

`size_t getgroups(size_t size, gid_t list[])`

> Returns the current set of supplemental groups for the current process in the array `list`. `size` tells how many `gid_t`s the list can hold. If the list is not big enough to hold all of the groups, -1 is returned and

errno is set to EINVAL. Otherwise, the number of groups in the list is returned. If size is 0, the number of groups in the list is returned, but list is not affected. The getgroups() function is prototyped in <grp.h>.

# 9.3 Process Information

The kernel makes available quite a bit of information about each process, and some information is passed to new programs when they are loaded. All of this information forms the execution environment for a process.

## 9.3.1 Program Arguments

There are two types of values passed to new programs when they are run: command-line arguments and environment variables. Various conventions have been set for their usage, but the system itself does not enforce any of these conventions. It is a good idea to stay within the conventions, though, to help your program fit into the Unix world.

Command-line arguments are a set of strings passed to the program. Usually, these are the text typed after the command name in a shell (hence the name), with optional arguments beginning with a dash (-) character.

Environment variables are a set of name/value pairs. Each pair is represented as a single string of the form *NAME=VALUE*, and the set of these strings makes up the program's **environment**. For example, the current user's home directory is normally contained in the HOME environment variable, so programs Joe runs will often have HOME=/home/joe in their environment.

Both the command-line arguments and environment are made available to a program at startup. The command-line arguments are passed as parameters to the program's main() function, whereas a pointer to the environment is stored in the environ global variable, which is defined in <unistd.h>.[3]

---

3. Most systems pass the environment as a parameter to main(), as well, but this method is not standardized by POSIX. The environ variable is the POSIX-approved method.

Here is the complete prototype of `main()` in the Linux, Unix, and ANSI C world:

```
int main(int argc, char * argv[]);
```

You may be surprised to see that `main()` returns a value (other than `void`). The value `main()` returns is given to the process's parent after the process has exited. By convention, 0 indicates that the process completed successfully, and non-0 values indicate failure. Only the lower eight bits of a process's exit code are considered significant. The negative values between -1 and -128 are reserved for processes that are terminated abnormally by another process or by the kernel. An exit code of 0 indicates successful completion, and exit codes between 1 and 127 indicate the program exited because of an error.

The first parameter, `argc`, contains the number of command-line arguments passed to the program, whereas `argv` is an array of pointers to the argument strings. The first item in the array is `argv[0]`, which contains the name of the program being invoked (though not necessarily the complete path to the program). The next-to-last item in the array `argv[argc - 1]` points to the final command-line argument, and `argv[argc]` contains `NULL`.

To access the environment directly, use the following global variable.

```
extern char ** environ[];
```

This provides `environ` as an array of pointers to each element in the program's environment (remember, each element is a `NAME=VALUE` pair), and the final item in the array is `NULL`. This declaration appears in `<unistd.h>`, so you do not need to declare it yourself. The most common way of checking for elements in the environment is through `getenv`, which eliminates the need for directly accessing `environ`.

```
const char * getenv(const char * name);
```

The sole parameter to `getenv()` is the name of the environment variable whose value you are interested in. If the variable exists, `getenv()` returns a pointer to its value. If the variable does not exist in the current environment (the environment pointed to by `environ`), it returns `NULL`.

Linux provides two ways of adding strings to the program's environment, setenv() and putenv(). POSIX defines only putenv(), making it the more portable of the two.

```
int putenv(const char * string);
```

The string passed must be of the form *NAME=VALUE*. putenv() adds a variable named *NAME* to the current environment and gives it the value of *VALUE*. If the environment already contains a variable named *NAME*, its value is replaced with *VALUE*.

BSD defines setenv(), which Linux also provides, a more flexible and easier-to-use method for adding items to the environment.

```
int setenv(const char * name, const char * value, int overwrite);
```

Here the name and the new value of the environment variable to manipulate are passed separately, which is usually easier for a program to do. If overwrite is 0, the environment will not be modified if it already contains a variable called name. Otherwise, the variable's value will be modified, as in putenv().

Here is a short example of both of these functions. Both calls accomplish exactly the same thing, changing the current PATH environment variable for the running program.

```
putenv("PATH=/bin:/usr/bin");
setenv("PATH", "/bin:/usr/bin", 1);
```

## 9.3.2 Resource Usage

The Linux kernel tracks how many resources each process is using. Although only a few resources are tracked, their measurement can be useful for developers, administrators, and users. Table 9.1 lists the process resources usage currently tracked by the Linux kernel, as of version 2.0.30.

A process may examine the resource usage of itself, the accumulated usages of all its children, or the sum of the two. The getrusage() system call returns a struct rusage (which is defined in <sys/resource.h>) that contains the current resources used.

```
int getrusage(int who, struct rusage * usage);
```

The first parameter, who, tells which of the three available resource counts should be returned. RUSAGE_SELF returns the usage for the current process, RUSAGE_CHILDREN returns the total usage for all of the current process's children, and RUSAGE_BOTH yields the total resources used by this process and all its children. The second parameter to getrusage() is a pointer to a struct rusage, which gets filled in with the appropriate resource utilizations. Although struct rusage contains quite a few fields (the list is derived from BSD), most of those fields are not yet used by Linux. Here is the complete definition of struct rusage. Table 9.1 describes the fields currently used by Linux.

```
#include <sys/resource.h>
struct rusage
{
  struct timeval ru_utime;
  struct timeval ru_stime;
  long int ru_maxrss;
  long int ru_ixrss;
  long int ru_idrss;
  long int ru_isrss;
  long int ru_minflt;
  long int ru_majflt;
  long int ru_nswap;
  long int ru_inblock;
  long int ru_oublock;
  long int ru_msgsnd;
  long int ru_msgrcv;
  long int ru_nsignals;
  long int ru_nvcsw;
  long int ru_nivcsw;
};
```

**Table 9.1** Process Resources Tracked by Linux

| Type | Field | Description |
|------|-------|-------------|
| struct<br>timeval | ru_utime | Total time spent executing user mode code. This includes all the time spent running instructions in the application, but not the time the kernel spends fulfilling application requests. |
| struct<br>timeval | ru_stime | Total time the kernel spent executing requests from the process. This does not include time spent while the process was blocked inside a system call. |
| long | ru_minflt | The number of **minor faults** that this process caused. Minor faults are memory accesses that force the processor into kernel mode but do not result in a disk access. These occur when a process tries to write past the end of its stack, forcing the kernel to allocate more stack space before continuing the process, for example. |
| long | ru_majflt | The number of **major faults** that this process caused. Major faults are memory accesses that force the kernel to access the disk before the program can continue to run. One common cause of major faults is a process accessing a part of its executable memory that has not yet been loaded into RAM from the disk or has been swapped out at some point. |
| long | ru_nswap | The number of memory pages that have been paged in from disk due to memory accesses from the process. |

## 9.3.3 Establishing Usage Limits

To help prevent runaway processes from destroying a system's performance, Unix keeps track of many of the resources a process can use and allows the system administrator and the users themselves to place limits on the resources a process may consume.

There are two classes of limits available: hard limits and soft limits. Hard limits may be lowered by any process but may be raised only by the super user. Hard limits are usually set to RLIM_INFINITY on system startup, which

**Table 9.2** Resource Limits

| Value | Limit |
|-------|-------|
| RLIMIT_CPU | Total CPU time used (in seconds) |
| RLIMIT_FSIZE | Maximum size for an open file (checked on writes) |
| RLIMIT_DATA | Maximum size of data memory (in bytes) |
| RLIMIT_STACK | Maximum size of stack memory (in bytes) |
| RLIMIT_CORE | Maximum size of a core file generated by the kernel (if the core file would be too large, none is created) |
| RLIMIT_RSS | Maximum amount of RAM used at any time (any memory usage exceeding this causes paging). This is known as a process's **resident set size**. |
| RLIMIT_NPROC | Maximum number of child processes the process may spawn. This limits only how many children the process may have at one time. It does not limit how many descendants it may have—each child may have up to RLIMIT_NPROC children of its own. |
| RLIMIT_NOFILE | Maximum number of open files |
| RLIMIT_MEMLOCK | Maximum amount of memory that may be locked with mlock()[4] |

means no limit is enforced. The only exception to this is RLIMIT_CORE (the maximum size of a core dump), which Linux initializes to 0 to prevent unexpected core dumps. Many distributions reset this limit on startup, however, as most technical users expect core dumps under some conditions (see page 117 for information on what a core dump is). Soft limits are the limits that the kernel actually enforces. Any process may set the soft limit for a resource to any value less than or equal to that process's hard limit for the resource.

The various limits that may be set are listed in Table 9.2 and are defined in <sys/resource.h>. The getrlimit() and setrlimit() system calls get and set the limit for a single resource.

```
int getrlimit(int resource, struct rlimit *rlim);
int setrlimit(int resource, const struct rlimit *rlim);
```

---

4. mlock() allows a process to prevent a region of memory from being paged out. For more information on memory locking, see page 222.

Both of these functions use `struct rlimit`, which is defined as follows:

```
#include <sys/resource.h>

struct rlimit {
  long int rlim_cur;            /* the soft limit */
  long int rlim_max;            /* the hard limit */
};
```

The first field, `rlim_max`, indicates the hard limit for the limit indicated by the `resource` parameter, and `rlim_cur` contains the soft limit. These are the same sets of limits manipulated by the `ulimit` and `limit` commands, one or the other of which is built into most shells.

# 9.4 Process Primitives

Despite the relatively long discussion needed to describe a process, creating and destroying processes in Linux is straightforward.

## 9.4.1 Having Children

Linux has two system calls that create new processes: `fork()` and `clone()`. As mentioned earlier, `clone()` is used for creating threads and will be briefly discussed later in this chapter. For now, we shall focus on `fork()`, which is the most popular method of process creation.

```
pid_t fork(void);
```

This system call has the unusual property of not returning once per invocation, but twice: once in the parent and once in the child. Note that we did not say "first in the parent"—writing code that makes any assumptions about the two processes executing in a deterministic order is a very bad idea.

Each return from the `fork()` system call returns a different value. In the parent process, the system call returns the pid of the newly created child process; in the child process, the call returns 0.

The difference in return value is the only difference apparent to the processes. Both have the same memory image, credentials, open files,[5] and signal handlers. Here is a simple example of a program that creates a child.

```
#include <sys/types.h>
#include <stdio.h>
#include <unistd.h>

int main(void) {
    pid_t child;

    if (!(child = fork())) {
        printf("in child\n");
        exit(0);
    }
    printf("in parent -- child is %d\n", child);
    return 0;
}
```

## 9.4.2 Watching Your Children Die

Collecting the exit status of a child is called **waiting** on the process. There are four ways this can be done, although only one of the calls is provided by the kernel. The other three methods are implemented in the standard C library. As the kernel system call takes four arguments, it is called wait4().

```
pid_t wait4(pid_t pid, int *status, int options, struct rusage *rusage);
```

The first argument, pid, is the process whose exit code should be returned. It can take on a number of special values.

| | |
|---|---|
| < -1 | Waits for any child whose pgid is the same as the absolute value of pid. |
| = -1 | Waits for any child to terminate. |
| = 0 | Waits for a child in the same process group current process. |

---

5. For details on how the parent's and child's open files relate to each other, see page 182.

> 0                Waits for process `pid` to exit.

The second parameter is a pointer to an integer that gets set to the exit status of the process that caused the `wait4()` to return (which we will hereafter call the *examined* process). The format of the returned status is convoluted, and a set of macros is provided to make sense of it.

Three events cause `wait4()` to return the status of the examined process: The process could have exited, it could have been terminated by a `kill()` (sent a fatal signal), or it could have been stopped for some reason.[6] You can find out which of these occurred through the following macros, each of which takes the returned status from `wait4()` as the sole parameter:

`WIFEXITED(status)`

Returns true if the process exited normally. A process exits normally when its `main()` function returns or the program calls `exit()`. If `WIFEXITED()` is true, `WEXITSTATUS(status)` will return the process's exit code.

`WIFSIGNALED(status)`

Returns true if the process was terminated due to a signal (this is what happens for processes terminated with `kill()`). If this is the case, `WTERMSIG(status)` returns the signal number that terminated the process.

`WIFSTOPPED(status)`

If the process has been stopped by a signal, `WIFSTOPPED()` will return true and `WSTOPSIG(status)` returns the signal that stopped the process. `wait4()` returns information on stopped processes only if `WUNTRACED` was specified as an option.

The `options` argument controls how the call behaves. `WNOHANG` causes the call to return immediately. If no processes are ready to report their status, the call returns 0 rather than a valid pid. `WUNTRACED` causes `wait4()` to return if an appropriate child has been stopped. See Chapter 14 for more information on stopped processes. Both of these behaviors may be specified by logically OR'ing the two values together.

---

6. See Chapter 14 for reasons why this might happen.

The final parameter to wait4(), a pointer to a struct rusage, gets filled in with the resource usage of the examined process and all the examined process's children. See the discussion of getrusage() and RUSAGE_BOTH on pages 105–106 for more information on what this entails. If this parameter is NULL, no status information is returned.

There are three other interfaces to wait4(), all of which provide subsets of its functionality. Here is a summary of the alternative interfaces.

pid_t wait(int *status)

> The only parameter to wait() is a pointer to the location to store the terminated process's return code. This function always blocks until a child has terminated.

pid_t waitpid(pid_t pid, int *status, int options)

> The waitpid() function is similiar to wait4(); the only difference is that it does not return resource usage information on the terminated process.

pid_t wait3(int *status, int options, struct rusage *rusage)

> This function is also similiar to wait4(), but it does not allow the caller to specify which child should be checked.

## 9.4.3 Running New Programs

Although there are six ways to run one program from another, they all do about the same thing—replace the currently running program with another. Note the word *replace*—all traces of the currently running program disappear. If you want to have the original program stick around, you must create a new process with fork() and then execute the new program in the child process.

The six functions feature only slight differences in the interface. Only one of these functions, execve(), is actually a system call under Linux. The rest of the functions are implemented in user-space libraries and utilize execve() to execute the new program. Here are the prototypes of the exec() family of functions.

```
int execl(const char * path, const char * arg0, ...);
int execlp(const char * file, const char * arg0, ...);
int execle(const char * path, const char * arg0, ...);
int execv(const char * path, const char ** argv);
int execvp(const char * file, const char ** argv);
int execve(const char * file, const char ** argv, const char ** envp);
```

As mentioned, all of these programs try to replace the current program with a new program. If they succeed, they never return (as the program that called them is no longer running). If they fail, they return -1 and the error code is stored in errno, as with any other system call. When a new program is run (or exec()ed) it gets passed an array of arguments (argv) and an array of environment variables (envp). Each element in envp is of the form *VARIABLE=value*.[7]

The primary difference between the various exec() functions is how the command line arguments are passed to the child process. The execl family passes each element in argv (the command-line arguments) as a separate argument to the function, and NULL terminates the entire list. Traditionally, the first element in argv is the command used to invoke the new program. For example, the shell command /bin/cat /etc/passwd /etc/group normally results in the following exec call.

```
execl("/bin/cat", "/bin/cat", "/etc/passwd", "/etc/group", NULL);
```

The first argument is the full path to the program being executed and the rest of the arguments get passed to the program as argv. The final parameter to execl() must be NULL—it indicates the end of the parameter list. If you omit the NULL, the function call is likely to result in either a segmentation fault or return EINVAL. The environment passed to the new program is whatever is pointed to by the environ global variable.[8]

The execv functions pass the command-line argument as a C array of strings,[9] which is the same format used to pass argv to the new program.

---

7. This is the same format the command env uses to print the current environment variables settings, and the envp argument is of the same type as the environ global variable.
8. As mentioned on page 103.
9. Technically, a pointer to a NULL-terminated array of pointers to '\0' terminated arrays of characters. If this does not make sense, see [Kernighan, 1988].

The final entry in the `argv` array must be `NULL` to indicate the end of the array, and the first element (`argv[0]`) should contain the name of the program that was invoked. Our `./cat /etc/passwd /etc/group` example would be coded using `execv` like this.

```
char * argv[] = { "./cat", "/etc/passwd", "/etc/group", NULL };
execv("/bin/cat", argv);
```

If you need to pass a specific environment to the new program, `execle()` and `execve()` are available. They are exactly like `execl()` and `execv()` but they take a pointer to the environment as their final argument. The environment is set up just like `argv`.

For example, here is one way to execute `/usr/bin/env` (which prints out the environment it was passed) with a small environment.

```
char * newenv[] = { "PATH=/bin:/usr/bin",
                    "HOME=/home/sweethome", NULL };
execle("/usr/bin/env", "/usr/bin/env", NULL, newenv);
```

Here is the same idea implemented with `execve()`.

```
char * argv[] = { "/usr/bin/env", NULL };
char * newenv[] = { "PATH=/bin:/usr/bin",
                    "HOME=/home/sweethome", NULL };
execve("/usr/bin/env", argv, newenv);
```

The final two functions, `execlp()` and `execvp()`, differ from the first two by searching the current path (set by the `PATH` environment variable) for the program to execute. The arguments to the program are not modified though, so `argv[0]` does not contain the full path to the program being run. Here are modified versions of our first example that search for `cat` in the current `PATH`.

```
execlp("cat", "cat", "/etc/passwd", "/etc/group", NULL);

char * argv[] = { "cat", "/etc/passwd", "/etc/group", NULL };
execvp("cat", argv);
```

If `execl()` or `execv()` were used instead, those code fragments would fail unless `cat` was located in the current directory.

If you are trying to run a program with a specific environment while still searching the path, you need to search the path manually and use `execle()` or `execve()`, because none of the available `exec()` functions will do quite what you want.

### 9.4.4 A Bit of History: `vfork()`

Creating an entirely new execution environment can be quite expensive, especially on poor hardware that needs to make a copy of the entire addressable region. Linux, like most other modern Unix systems, copies pieces of the process's address space only when the need arises.[10]

As many of the `fork()` calls are immediately followed by the creation of a new virtual memory space through some flavor of `exec()`, some versions of Unix provide a version of `fork()` that does not copy the virtual memory region, providing a performance improvement. This variant is called `vfork()`; it leaves the memory mapping shared between the two processes. Its only additional semantic is not returning control to the parent process until after the child issues an `exec()` call to help prevent the processes from conflicting with each other. As Linux provides copy-on-write, which eliminates the need for this trick, it does not provide a `vfork()` system call. Instead, `vfork()` is implemented as a simple `fork()` call by the C library to provide backward compatibility. Although this works for many applications, it does not provide `vfork()`'s additional semantic, which forces the child process to run first.

### 9.4.5 Killing Yourself

Processes terminate themselves by calling either `exit()` or `_exit()`. When a process's `main()` function returns, the standard C library calls `exit()` with the value returned from `main()` as the parameter.

```
void exit(int exitCode)
void _exit(int exitCode)
```

---

10. This is known as **copy-on-write**, which is discussed in most operating system texts [Vahalia, 1997] [Bach, 1986] [McKusick, 1996].

The two forms, exit() and _exit(), differ in that exit() is a function in the C library, while _exit() is a system call. The _exit() system call terminates the program immediately, and the exitCode is stored as the exit code of the process. When exit() is used, functions registered by atexit() are called before the library calls _exit(exitCode). Among other things, this allows the ANSI standard I/O library to flush all its buffers.

Registering functions to be run when exit() is used is done through the atexit() function.

```
int atexit(void (*function)(void));
```

The only parameter passed to atexit() is a pointer to a function. When exit() is invoked, all the functions registered with atexit() are called in the opposite order from which they were registered. Note that if _exit() is used or the process is terminated due to a signal (see Chapter 13 for details on signals), functions registered via atexit() are not called.

## 9.4.6 Killing Others

Destroying other processes is almost as easy as creating a new one—just kill it:

```
int kill(pid_t pid, int sig);
```

pid should be the pid of the process to kill, and sig describes how to kill it. There are two choices[11] for how to kill a child. You can use SIGTERM to terminate the process gently. This means that the process can ask the kernel to tell it when someone is trying to kill it so that it can terminate gracefully (saving files, for example). The process may also ignore this type of request for it to terminate and, instead, continue running. Using SIGKILL for the sig parameter kills the process immediately, no questions asked.

The pid parameter can take on four types of values under Linux.

pid > 0      The signal is sent to the process whose pid is pid. If no process exists with that pid, ESRCH is returned.

---

11. This is a gross oversimplification. kill() actually sends a signal, and signals are a complicated topic in their own right. See Chapter 13 for a complete description of what signals are and how to use them.

pid < -1      The signal is sent to all the processes in the process group whose pgid is `-pid`. For example, `kill(-5316, SIGKILL)` immediately terminates all the processes in process group 5316. This ability is used by job control shells, as discussed in Chapter 14.

pid = 0       The signal is sent to all the processes in the current process's process group.

pid = -1      The signal is sent to all the processes on the system except the init process. This is used during system shutdown.

Processes can normally `kill()` only processes that share the same effective user ID as themselves. The only exception to this is processes with an effective uid of 0, which may `kill()` any process on the system.

### 9.4.7 Dumping Core

Although we just mentioned that passing `SIGTERM` and `SIGKILL` to `kill()` causes a process to terminate, you can use quite a few different values (Chapter 13 discusses all of them). Some of these, such as `SIGABRT`, cause the program to dump **core** before dying. A program's core dump contains a complete history of the state of the program when it died.[12] Most debuggers, including gdb, can analyze a core file and tell you what the program was doing when it died, as well as let you inspect the defunct process's memory image. Core dumps end up in the process's current working directory in a file called (simply enough) `core`.

When a process has violated some of the system's requirements (such as trying to access memory that it is not allowed to access) the kernel terminates the process by calling an internal version of `kill()` with a parameter that causes a core dump. The kernel will kill a process for several reasons,

---

12. A once-popular form of computer memory consists of small iron rings arranged in a matrix, with each ring held in place by two wires that are used to sense and set the magnetic polarity of the ring. Each of the rings is called a core, and the whole thing is core memory. So a core dump is a copy of the state of the system's memory (or core) at a given time.

including arithmetic violations, such as division by zero, the program running illegal instructions, and the program trying to access inaccessible regions of memory. This last case causes a **segmentation fault**, which results in the message `segmentation fault (core dumped)`. If you do any reasonable amount of Linux programming, you are sure to tire of this message!

If a process's resource limit for core files is 0 (see page 108 for details on the core resource limit), no core file is generated.

# 9.5   Simple Children

Although `fork()`, `exec()`, and `wait()` allow programs to make full use of the Linux process model, many applications do not need that much control over their children. There are two library functions that make it easier to use child processes: `system()` and `popen()`.

## 9.5.1 Running and Waiting with `system()`

Programs regularly want to run another program and wait for it to finish before continuing. The `system()` function allows a program to do this easily.

```
int system(const char * cmd);
```

`system()` forks a child process that `exec()`s `/bin/sh`, which then runs `cmd`. The original process waits for the child shell to exit and returns the same status code that `wait()` does. If you don't need the shell to hang around (which is rarely necessary), `cmd` should contain a preceding `"exec"`, which causes the shell to `exec()` `cmd` rather than run `cmd` as a subprocess.

As `cmd` is run through the `/bin/sh` shell, normal shell rules for command expansion apply. Here is an example of `system()` that displays all the C source files in the current directory.

```
#include <stdlib.h>
#include <sys/wait.h>

int main() {
    int result;

    result = system("exec ls *.c");

    if (!WIFEXITED(result))
        printf("(abnormal exit)\n");

    exit(0);
}
```

The system() command should be used very carefully in programs that run with special permissions. As the system shell provides many powerful features and is strongly influenced by environment variables, system() provides many potential security weaknesses for intruders to exploit. As long as the application is not a system daemon or a setuid/setgid program, however, system() is perfectly safe.

## 9.5.2 Reading or Writing from a Process

Although system() displays the command's output on standard output and allows the child to read from standard input, this is not always ideal. Often, a process wants to read the output from a process or send it text on standard input. popen() makes it easy for a process to do this.

```
FILE * popen(const char * cmd, const char * mode);
```

The cmd is run through the shell, just as with system(). The mode should be "r" if the parent wants to read the command's output and "w" to write to the child's standard input. Note that you cannot do both with popen(); two processes reading from and writing to each other is complex[13] and beyond

---

13. This type of processing often results in **deadlocks**, in which process A is waiting for process B to do something while process B is waiting for process A, resulting in nothing at all getting done.

popen()'s abilities.[14]

popen() returns a FILE * (as defined by the ANSI standard I/O library), which can be read from and written to just like any other stdio stream,[15] or NULL if the operation fails. When the parent process is finished, it should use pclose() to close the stream and terminate the child process if it is still running. Like system(), pclose() returns the child's status from wait4().

```
int pclose(FILE * stream);
```

Here is a simple calculator program that uses the **bc** program to do all of the real work. It is important to flush the popen()ed stream after writing to it to prevent stdio buffering from delaying output (see [Kernighan, 1988] for details on buffering in the ANSI C stdio library functions).

```
 1: /* calc.c - calculator front-end which uses bc for everything */
 2:
 3: /* This is a very simple calculator which uses the external bc
 4:    command to do everything. It opens a pipe to bc, reads a command
 5:    in, passes it to bc, and exits. */
 6: #include <stdio.h>
 7: #include <sys/wait.h>
 8: #include <unistd.h>
 9:
10: int main(void) {
11:     char buf[1024];
12:     FILE * bc;
13:     int result;
14:
15:     /* open a pipe to bc, and exit if we fail */
16:     bc = popen("bc", "w");
17:     if (!bc) {
18:         perror("popen");
19:         return 1;
20:     }
21:
```

---

14. If you find yourself needing to do this, start the child with fork() and exec() and use select() to read to and write from the child process. A program called **expect** is designed to do this.

15. For information on reading and writing from stdio streams, consult [Kernighan, 1988].

```
22:      /* prompt for an expression, and read it in */
23:      printf("expr: "); fflush(stdout);
24:      fgets(buf, sizeof(buf), stdin);
25:
26:      /* send the expression to bc for evaluation */
27:      fprintf(bc, "%s\n", buf);
28:      fflush(bc);
29:
30:      /* close the pipe to bc, and wait for it to exit */
31:      result = pclose(bc);
32:
33:      if (!WIFEXITED(result))
34:          printf("(abnormal exit)\n");
35:
36:      return 0;
37: }
```

Like `system()`, `popen()` runs commands through the system shell and should be used very cautiously by programs that run with root credentials.

## 9.6 Sessions and Process Groups

In Linux, as in other Unix systems, users normally interact with groups of related processes. Although they initially log into a single terminal and use a single process (their **shell**, which provides a command-line interface), users end up running many processes as a result of actions such as

- Running noninteractive tasks in the background

- Switching among interactive tasks via **job control**, which is discussed more fully in Chapter 14

- Starting multiple processes that work together through pipes

- Running a windowing system, such as the X Window System, which allows multiple terminal windows to be opened

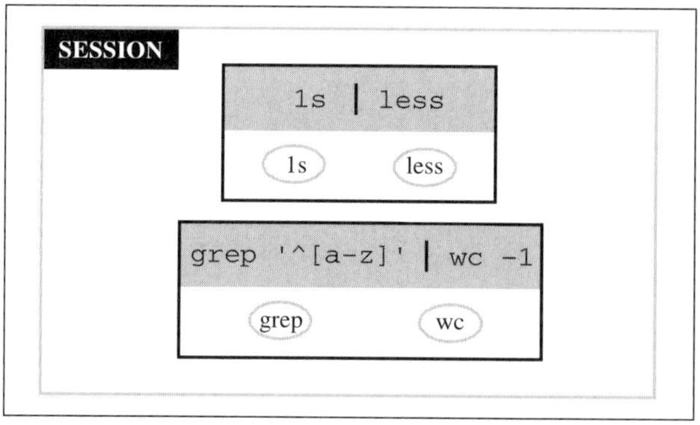

**Figure 9.1**   Sessions, Process Groups, and Processes

In order to manage all of these processes, the kernel needs to group the processes in ways more complicated than the simple parent/child relationship we have already discussed. These groupings are called **sessions** and **process groups**. Figure 9.1 shows the relationship between sessions, process groups, and processes.

## 9.6.1 Sessions

When a user logs out of a system, the kernel needs to terminate all the processes the user had running (otherwise, users would leave a slew of old processes sitting around waiting for input that can never arrive). To simplify this task, processes are organized into sets of **sessions**. The session's ID is the same as the pid of the process that created the session through the setsid() system call. That process is known as the **session leader** for that session group. All of that process's descendants are then members of that session unless they specifically remove themselves from it. The setsid() function does not take any arguments and returns the new session ID.

```
#include <unistd.h>

pid_t setsid(void);
```

## 9.6.2 Controlling Terminal

Every session is tied to a terminal from which processes in the session get their input and to which they send their output. That terminal may be the machine's local console, a terminal connected over a serial line, or a pseudo terminal that maps to an X window or across a network (see Chapter 15 for information on pseudo terminal devices). The terminal to which a session is related is called the **controlling terminal** (or **controlling tty**) of the session. A terminal can be the controlling terminal for only one session at a time.

Although the controlling terminal for a session can be changed, this is usually done only by processes that manage a user's initial logging into a system. Information on how to change a session's controlling tty is in Chapter 15, on pages 269–270.

## 9.6.3 Process Groups

One of the original design goals of Unix was to construct a set of simple tools that could be used together in complex ways (through mechanisms like pipes). Most Linux users have done something like the following, which is a practical example of this philosophy.

```
ls | grep "^[aA].*\.gz" | more
```

Another popular feature added to Unix fairly early was job control. Job control allows users to suspend the current task (known as the **foreground** task) while they go and do something else on their terminals. When the suspended task is a sequence of processes working together, the system needs to keep track of which processes should be suspended when the user wants to suspend "the" foreground task. Process groups allow the system to keep track of which processes are working together and hence should be managed together via job control.

Processes are added to a process group through setpgid().

```
int setpgid(pid_t pid, pid_t pgid);
```

pid is the process that is being placed in a new process group (0 may be used to indicate the current process). pgid is the process group ID the process pid should belong to, or 0 if the process should be in a new process group whose pgid is the same as that process's pid. Like sessions, a **process group leader** is the process whose pid is the same as its process group ID (or **pgid**).

The rules for how setpgid() may be used are a bit complicated.

1. A process may set the process group of itself or one of its children. It may not change the process group for any other process on the system, even if the process calling setpgid() has root privileges.

2. A session leader may not change its process group.

3. A process may not be moved into a process group whose leader is in a different session from itself. In other words, all the processes in a process group must belong to the same session.

setsid() call places the calling process into its own process group and its own session. This is necessary to ensure that two sessions do not contain processes in the same process group.

A full example of process groups is given when we discuss job control in Chapter 14.

When the connection to a terminal is lost, the kernel sends a signal (SIGHUP; see Chapter 13 for more information on signals) to the leader of the session containing the terminal's foreground process group, which is usually a shell. This allows the shell to terminate the user's processes uncondition- ally, notify the processes that the user has logged out (usually, through a SIGHUP), or take some other action (or inaction). Although this setup may seem complicated, it lets the session group leader decide how closed ter- minals should be handled rather than putting that decision in the kernel. This allows system administrators flexibile control over account policies.

Determining the process group is easily done through the getpgid() and getpgrp() functions.

```
pid_t getpgid(int pid)
```
Returns the pgid of process pid. If pid is 0, the pgid of the current process is returned. No special permissions are needed to use this

call; any process may determine the process group to which any other process belongs.

`pid_t getpgrp(void)`
> Returns the pgid of the current process (equivalent to `getpgid(0)`).

# 9.7   **Introduction to** `ladsh`

To help illustrate many ideas discussed in this book, we will develop a subset of a Unix command shell as the book progresses. At the end of the book, the shell will support

- Simple built-in commands

- Command execution

- I/O redirection (>, |, etc)

- Job control

The full source code of the final version of this shell, called `ladsh`, is in Appendix B. As new features are added to `ladsh`, the changes to the source code will be described in the text. To reduce the number of changes made between the versions, some early versions of the shell are a bit more complicated than they need to be. These extra complications make it easier to develop the shell later in the book though, so please be patient. Just take those pieces on faith for now; we explain them all to you later in the book.

## 9.7.1 **Running External Programs with** `ladsh`

Here is the first (and simplest) version of `ladsh`, called `ladsh1`:

```
1: /* ladsh1.c -- the beginning */
2:
3: #include <ctype.h>
4: #include <errno.h>
5: #include <fcntl.h>
```

```
 6: #include <signal.h>
 7: #include <stdio.h>
 8: #include <stdlib.h>
 9: #include <string.h>
10: #include <sys/ioctl.h>
11: #include <sys/wait.h>
12: #include <unistd.h>
13:
14: #define MAX_COMMAND_LEN 250     /* max length of a single command
15:                                       string */
16: #define JOB_STATUS_FORMAT "[%d] %-22s %.40s\n"
17:
18: struct jobSet {
19:     struct job * head;        /* head of list of running jobs */
20:     struct job * fg;          /* current foreground job */
21: };
22:
23: struct childProgram {
24:     pid_t pid;                /* 0 if exited */
25:     char ** argv;             /* program name and arguments */
26: };
27:
28: struct job {
29:     int jobId;                /* job number */
30:     int numProgs;             /* total number of programs in job */
31:     int runningProgs;         /* number of programs running */
32:     char * text;              /* name of job */
33:     char * cmdBuf;            /* buffer various argv's point into */
34:     pid_t pgrp;               /* process group ID for the job */
35:     struct childProgram * progs; /* array of programs in job */
36:     struct job * next;        /* to track background commands */
37: };
38:
39: void freeJob(struct job * cmd) {
40:     int i;
41:
42:     for (i = 0; i < cmd->numProgs; i++) {
43:         free(cmd->progs[i].argv);
44:     }
45:     free(cmd->progs);
46:     if (cmd->text) free(cmd->text);
```

```
47:        free(cmd->cmdBuf);
48: }
49:
50: int getCommand(FILE * source, char * command) {
51:        if (source == stdin) {
52:            printf("# ");
53:            fflush(stdout);
54:        }
55:
56:        if (!fgets(command, MAX_COMMAND_LEN, source)) {
57:            if (source == stdin) printf("\n");
58:            return 1;
59:        }
60:
61:        /* remove trailing newline */
62:        command[strlen(command) - 1] = '\0';
63:
64:        return 0;
65: }
66:
67: /* Return cmd->numProgs as 0 if no command is present (e.g. an empty
68:     line). If a valid command is found, commandPtr is set to point to
69:     the beginning of the next command (if the original command had more
70:     then one job associated with it) or NULL if no more commands are
71:     present. */
72: int parseCommand(char ** commandPtr, struct job * job, int * isBg) {
73:        char * command;
74:        char * returnCommand = NULL;
75:        char * src, * buf;
76:        int argc = 0;
77:        int done = 0;
78:        int argvAlloced;
79:        char quote = '\0';
80:        int count;
81:        struct childProgram * prog;
82:
83:        /* skip leading white space */
84:        while (**commandPtr && isspace(**commandPtr)) (*commandPtr)++;
85:
86:        /* this handles empty lines */
87:        if (!**commandPtr) {
```

```
 88:            job->numProgs = 0;
 89:            *commandPtr = NULL;
 90:            return 0;
 91:        }
 92:
 93:        *isBg = 0;
 94:        job->numProgs = 1;
 95:        job->progs = malloc(sizeof(*job->progs));
 96:
 97:        /* We set the argv elements to point inside of this string. The
 98:           memory is freed by freeJob().
 99:
100:           Getting clean memory relieves us of the task of NULL
101:           terminating things and makes the rest of this look a bit
102:           cleaner (though it is, admittedly, a tad less efficient) */
103:        job->cmdBuf = command = calloc(1, strlen(*commandPtr) + 1);
104:        job->text = NULL;
105:
106:        prog = job->progs;
107:
108:        argvAlloced = 5;
109:        prog->argv = malloc(sizeof(*prog->argv) * argvAlloced);
110:        prog->argv[0] = job->cmdBuf;
111:
112:        buf = command;
113:        src = *commandPtr;
114:        while (*src && !done) {
115:            if (quote == *src) {
116:                quote = '\0';
117:            } else if (quote) {
118:                if (*src == '\\') {
119:                    src++;
120:                    if (!*src) {
121:                        fprintf(stderr, "character expected after \\\n");
122:                        freeJob(job);
123:                        return 1;
124:                    }
125:
126:                    /* in shell, "\'" should yield \' */
127:                    if (*src != quote) *buf++ = '\\';
128:                }
```

```
129:                    *buf++ = *src;
130:                } else if (isspace(*src)) {
131:                    if (*prog->argv[argc]) {
132:                        buf++, argc++;
133:                        /* +1 here leaves room for the NULL which ends argv */
134:                        if ((argc + 1) == argvAlloced) {
135:                            argvAlloced += 5;
136:                            prog->argv = realloc(prog->argv,
137:                                        sizeof(*prog->argv) * argvAlloced);
138:                        }
139:                        prog->argv[argc] = buf;
140:                    }
141:                } else switch (*src) {
142:                  case '"':
143:                  case '\'':
144:                    quote = *src;
145:                    break;
146:
147:                  case '#':                     /* comment */
148:                    done = 1;
149:                    break;
150:
151:                  case '&':                     /* background */
152:                    *isBg = 1;
153:                  case ';':                     /* multiple commands */
154:                    done = 1;
155:                    returnCommand = *commandPtr + (src - *commandPtr) + 1;
156:                    break;
157:
158:                  case '\\':
159:                    src++;
160:                    if (!*src) {
161:                        freeJob(job);
162:                        fprintf(stderr, "character expected after \\\n");
163:                        return 1;
164:                    }
165:                    /* fallthrough */
166:                  default:
167:                    *buf++ = *src;
168:                }
169:
```

```
170:            src++;
171:        }
172:
173:        if (*prog->argv[argc]) {
174:            argc++;
175:        }
176:        if (!argc) {
177:            freeJob(job);
178:            return 0;
179:        }
180:        prog->argv[argc] = NULL;
181:
182:        if (!returnCommand) {
183:            job->text = malloc(strlen(*commandPtr) + 1);
184:            strcpy(job->text, *commandPtr);
185:        } else {
186:            /* This leaves any trailing spaces, which is a bit sloppy */
187:
188:            count = returnCommand - *commandPtr;
189:            job->text = malloc(count + 1);
190:            strncpy(job->text, *commandPtr, count);
191:            job->text[count] = '\0';
192:        }
193:
194:        *commandPtr = returnCommand;
195:
196:        return 0;
197: }
198:
199: int runCommand(struct job newJob, struct jobSet * jobList,
200:                int inBg) {
201:        struct job * job;
202:
203:        /* handle built-ins here -- we don't fork() so we can't background
204:           these very easily */
205:        if (!strcmp(newJob.progs[0].argv[0], "exit")) {
206:            /* this should return a real exit code */
207:            exit(0);
208:        } else if (!strcmp(newJob.progs[0].argv[0], "jobs")) {
209:            for (job = jobList->head; job; job = job->next)
210:                printf(JOB_STATUS_FORMAT, job->jobId, "Running",
```

```
211:                         job->text);
212:         return 0;
213:     }
214:
215:     /* we only have one program per child job right now, so this is
216:        easy */
217:     if (!(newJob.progs[0].pid = fork())) {
218:         execvp(newJob.progs[0].argv[0], newJob.progs[0].argv);
219:         fprintf(stderr, "exec() of %s failed: %s\n",
220:                 newJob.progs[0].argv[0],
221:                 strerror(errno));
222:         exit(1);
223:     }
224:
225:     /* put our child in its own process group */
226:     setpgid(newJob.progs[0].pid, newJob.progs[0].pid);
227:
228:     newJob.pgrp = newJob.progs[0].pid;
229:
230:     /* find the ID for the job to use */
231:     newJob.jobId = 1;
232:     for (job = jobList->head; job; job = job->next)
233:         if (job->jobId >= newJob.jobId)
234:             newJob.jobId = job->jobId + 1;
235:
236:     /* add the job to the list of running jobs */
237:     if (!jobList->head) {
238:         job = jobList->head = malloc(sizeof(*job));
239:     } else {
240:         for (job = jobList->head; job->next; job = job->next);
241:         job->next = malloc(sizeof(*job));
242:         job = job->next;
243:     }
244:
245:     *job = newJob;
246:     job->next = NULL;
247:     job->runningProgs = job->numProgs;
248:
249:     if (inBg) {
250:         /* we don't wait for background jobs to return -- append it
251:            to the list of backgrounded jobs and leave it alone */
```

```
252:
253:          printf("[%d] %d\n", job->jobId,
254:                  newJob.progs[newJob.numProgs - 1].pid);
255:      } else {
256:          jobList->fg = job;
257:
258:          /* move the new process group into the foreground */
259:
260:          if (tcsetpgrp(0, newJob.pgrp))
261:              perror("tcsetpgrp");
262:      }
263:
264:      return 0;
265: }
266:
267: void removeJob(struct jobSet * jobList, struct job * job) {
268:      struct job * prevJob;
269:
270:      freeJob(job);
271:      if (job == jobList->head) {
272:          jobList->head = job->next;
273:      } else {
274:          prevJob = jobList->head;
275:          while (prevJob->next != job) prevJob = prevJob->next;
276:          prevJob->next = job->next;
277:      }
278:
279:      free(job);
280: }
281:
282: /* Checks to see if any background processes have exited -- if they
283:    have, figure out why and see if a job has completed */
284: void checkJobs(struct jobSet * jobList) {
285:      struct job * job;
286:      pid_t childpid;
287:      int status;
288:      int progNum;
289:
290:      while ((childpid = waitpid(-1, &status, WNOHANG)) > 0) {
291:          for (job = jobList->head; job; job = job->next) {
292:              progNum = 0;
```

```
293:            while (progNum < job->numProgs &&
294:                        job->progs[progNum].pid != childpid)
295:                progNum++;
296:            if (progNum < job->numProgs) break;
297:        }
298:
299:        job->runningProgs--;
300:        job->progs[progNum].pid = 0;
301:
302:        if (!job->runningProgs) {
303:            printf(JOB_STATUS_FORMAT, job->jobId, "Done", job->text);
304:            removeJob(jobList, job);
305:        }
306:    }
307:
308:    if (childpid == -1 && errno != ECHILD)
309:        perror("waitpid");
310: }
311:
312: int main(int argc, char ** argv) {
313:    char command[MAX_COMMAND_LEN + 1];
314:    char * nextCommand = NULL;
315:    struct jobSet jobList = { NULL, NULL };
316:    struct job newJob;
317:    FILE * input = stdin;
318:    int i;
319:    int status;
320:    int inBg;
321:
322:    if (argc > 2) {
323:        fprintf(stderr, "unexpected arguments; usage: ladsh1 "
324:                        "<commands>\n");
325:        exit(1);
326:    } else if (argc == 2) {
327:        input = fopen(argv[1], "r");
328:        if (!input) {
329:            perror("fopen");
330:            exit(1);
331:        }
332:    }
333:
```

```
334:    /* don't pay any attention to this signal; it just confuses
335:       things and isn't really meant for shells anyway */
336:    signal(SIGTTOU, SIG_IGN);
337:
338:    while (1) {
339:        if (!jobList.fg) {
340:            /* no job is in the foreground */
341:
342:            /* see if any background processes have exited */
343:            checkJobs(&jobList);
344:
345:            if (!nextCommand) {
346:                if (getCommand(input, command)) break;
347:                nextCommand = command;
348:            }
349:
350:            if (!parseCommand(&nextCommand, &newJob, &inBg) &&
351:                              newJob.numProgs) {
352:                runCommand(newJob, &jobList, inBg);
353:            }
354:        } else {
355:            /* a job is running in the foreground; wait for it */
356:            i = 0;
357:            while (!jobList.fg->progs[i].pid) i++;
358:
359:            waitpid(jobList.fg->progs[i].pid, &status, 0);
360:
361:            jobList.fg->runningProgs--;
362:            jobList.fg->progs[i].pid = 0;
363:
364:            if (!jobList.fg->runningProgs) {
365:                /* child exited */
366:
367:                removeJob(&jobList, jobList.fg);
368:                jobList.fg = NULL;
369:
370:                /* move the shell to the foreground */
371:                if (tcsetpgrp(0, getpid()))
372:                    perror("tcsetpgrp");
373:            }
374:        }
```

```
375:      }
376:
377:      return 0;
378: }
```

This version does nothing more than run external programs with arguments, support # comments (everything after a # is ignored), and allow programs to be run in the background. It will work as a shell script interpreter for simple scripts written using the #! notation, but it will not do much else. It is designed to mimic the usual shell interpreter used on Linux systems, though it is necessarily simplified.

First of all, let's look at the data structures it uses. `struct jobSet` describes a set of jobs that are running. It contains a linked list of jobs and a pointer to the job that is currently running in the foreground. If there is no foreground job, the pointer is `NULL`. `ladsh1` uses `struct jobSet` to keep track of all the jobs that are currently running as background tasks.

`struct childProgram` describes a single program being executed. This is not quite the same as a job; eventually, we will allow each job to be multiple programs tied together with pipes. For each child program, `ladsh` keeps track of the child's pid, the program that was run, and the command-line arguments. The first element of `argv`, `argv[0]`, holds the name of the program that was run, which is also passed as the first argument to the child.

Multiple commands are tied into a single job by `struct job`. Each job has a job ID unique within the shell, an arbitrary number of programs that constitute the job (stored through `progs`, a pointer to an array of `struct childProgram`), and a pointer to another (next) job, which allows the jobs to be tied together in a linked list (which `struct jobSet` relies on). The job also keeps track of how many individual programs originally comprised the job and how many of those programs are still running (as all of a job's component processes may not quit at the same time). The remaining two fields, `text` and `cmdBuf`, are used as buffers that contain various strings used in the `struct childProgram` structures contained by the job.

Much of `struct jobSet` is made up of dynamically allocated memory that should be freed when the job is complete. The first function in `ladsh1`, `freeJob()`, frees the memory used by a job.

The next function, getCommand(), reads a command from the user and returns the string. If the commands are being read from a file, no prompting is done (which is why the code compares the input file stream against stdin).

parseCommand() breaks a command string into a struct job for ladsh to use. The first argument is a pointer to a pointer to the command. If there are multiple commands in the string, this pointer is advanced to the beginning of the second command. It is set to NULL once the final command from the string has been parsed. This allows parseCommand() to parse only a single command on each invocation and allows the caller to easily parse the entire string through multiple calls. Note that multiple programs piped together do not count as separate commands—only programs separated by ; or & are independent of each other. As parseCommand() is simply an exercise in string parsing, we shall not go over it in any detail.

The runCommand() function is responsible for running a single job. It takes a struct job describing the job to run, the list of jobs that are currently running, and a flag telling it whether the job should be run in the foreground or the background.

For now, ladsh does not support pipes, so each job may consist only of a single program (though much of the infrastructure for supporting pipes is already present in ladsh1). If the user runs exit, we exit the program immediately. This is an example of a **built-in** command that must be run by the shell itself to get the proper behavior. Another built-in, jobs, is also implemented here.

If the command is not a built-in, we need to execute a child command. As each job can consist only of a single program (until we implement pipes), this is pretty straightforward.

```
if (!(newJob.progs[0].pid = fork())) {
    execvp(newJob.progs[0].program, newJob.progs[0].argv);
    fprintf(stderr, "exec() of %s failed: %s\",
            newJob.progs[0].program,
            strerror(errno));
    exit(1);
}
```

First of all, we `fork()` off the child process. The parent stores the child's pid in `newJob.progs[0].pid`, whereas the child process places a 0 there (remember, the parent and child have different memory images, though they are initially filled with the same values). This results in the child going into the body of the `if` statement while the parent skips the body. The child immediately runs the new program via `execvp()`. If the `execvp()` call fails, the child prints an error message and then exits. That is all that is necessary for spawning a simple child process.

After forking the child, the parent places the child into its own process group and records the job in the list of running jobs. If the process is meant to run in the foreground, the parent makes the new process group the foreground process group for the shell's controlling terminal.

The next function, `checkJobs()`, looks for background jobs that have exited and cleans up the list of running jobs as appropriate. For each process that has exited (remember `waitpid()` returns only information on exited processes unless `WUNTRACED` is specified), the shell

1.   Finds the job the process was a part of

2.   Marks the program as completed (by setting the stored pid for the program to 0) and reduces the number of running programs for the job by one

If the job containing the deceased process has no more running processes, which is always the case in this version of `ladsh`, the shell prints a message telling the user the process completed and removes the job from the list of background processes.

The `main()` routine for `ladsh1` controls the shell's execution flow. If an argument was passed to the shell when it was invoked, it treats that as a file name and reads subsequent commands from that file. Otherwise, `stdin` is used as the source of commands. The program then ignores the `SIGTTOU` signal. This is a bit of job-control magic that keeps things going smoothly, and it will make sense once you get to Chapter 14. Job control is not fully implemented, however, and when you are experimenting with `ladsh1` do not try job-control activities (especially those activities that involve suspending programs `ladsh1` has run); they simply will not work. A complete job-control implementation will be added in Chapter 14; the current setup is only skeletal.

The remainder of `main()` is the main loop of the program. There is no exit condition for this loop; the program ends by calling `exit()` inside the `runCommand()` function.

The `nextCommand` variable points to the original (unparsed) string representation of the next command that should be run, or is `NULL` if the next command should be read from the input file, which is usually `stdin`. When no job is running in the foreground, `ladsh` calls `checkJobs()` to check for background jobs that have exited, reads the next command from the input file if `nextCommand` is `NULL`, and then parses and executes the next command.

When a foreground job is executing, `ladsh1` instead waits for one of the processes in the foreground job to terminate. Once all the processes in the foreground job have exited, the job is removed from the list of running jobs and `ladsh1` reads the next command as described previously.

# 9.8   Creating Clones

Although `fork()` is the traditional way of creating new processes in Unix, Linux also provides the `clone()` system call, which lets the process being duplicated specify what resources the parent process should share with its children.

```
int clone(int flags);
```

This is not much more than a `fork()`; the only difference is the `flags` parameter. It should be set to the signal that should be sent to the parent process when the child exits (usually, `SIGCHLD`), logically OR'ed with any number of the following flags, which are defined in `<sched.h>`:

`CLONE_VM`         The two processes share their virtual memory space (including the stack).

`CLONE_FS`         File-system information (such as the current directory) is shared.

CLONE_FILES          Open files are shared.

CLONE_SIGHAND        The signal handlers are shared for the two processes.

When two resources are shared, both processes see those resources identically. If the CLONE_SIGHAND is specified, when one of the processes changes the signal handler for a particular signal, both processes use the new handler (see Chapter 13 for details on signal handlers). When CLONE_FILES is used, not only is the set of open files shared, but the current location in each file is also shared. The return values for clone() are the same as for fork().

If a signal other than SIGCHLD is specified to be delivered to the parent on the death of a child process, the wait() family of functions will not, by default, return information on those processes. If you would like to get information on such processes, as well as on processes that use the normal SIGCHLD mechanism, the __WCLONE flag must be OR'ed with the flags parameter of the wait call. Although this behavior may seem odd, it allows greater flexibility. If wait() returned information on cloned processes, it would be more difficult to build standard thread libraries around clone(), because wait() would return information on other threads, as well as child processes.

Although it is not recommended that applications use clone() directly, numerous user-space libraries are available that use clone() and provide a fully POSIX-compatible thread implementation. Newer versions of the Linux C library (glibc 2) include such a library, providing standardized threading across all Linux platforms. Several good books on POSIX thread programming are available [Nichols, 1996] [Butenhof, 1997].

# CHAPTER 10

# Simple File Handling

Files are the most ubiquitous resource abstraction used in the Unix world. Resources such as memory, disk space, devices, and IPC channels are represented as files. By providing a uniform abstraction of these resources, Unix reduces the number of software interfaces programmers must master. The resources accessed through file operations are as follows:

**Regular files**   Regular files are the kind of files most computer users think of. They serve as data repositories that can grow arbitrarily large and allow random access. Unix files are byte-oriented—any other logical boundaries are purely application conventions; the kernel knows nothing about them.

**Pipes**   Pipes are Unix's simplest interprocess communication (IPC) mechanism. Usually, one process writes information into the pipe while another reads from it. Pipes are what shells use to provide I/O redirection (for example, `ls -lR | grep notes` or `ls | more`), and many programs use pipes to feed input to programs that run as their subprocesses. There are two types of pipes: unnamed and named. **Unnamed pipes** are created as they are needed and disappear once both the read and the write ends of the pipe are closed. Unnamed pipes are so called because they do not exist in the file system and, therefore, have no file name.[1] **Named pipes** do have file names, and

---

1. Under Linux, the /proc file system includes information on every file currently open on the system. Although this means that unnamed pipes can be found in a file system, they still do not have permanent file names, because they disappear when the processes using the pipe end.

the file name is used to allow two processes that do not share file descriptors to communicate through the pipe (similiar to the way Unix domain sockets work[2]). Pipes are also known as FIFOs because the data is ordered in a first-in/first-out manner.

**Directories**    Directories are special files that consist of a list of files they contain. Old Unix implementations allowed programs to read and write them in exactly the same manner as regular files. To allow better abstraction, a special set of system calls was implemented to provide directory manipulation, although the directories are still opened and closed like regular files. Those functions are presented in Chapter 11.

**Devices**    Most physical devices are represented as files. There are two types of device files: block devices and character devices. **Block device** files represent hardware devices that cannot be read from a byte at a time; they must be read from in multiples of some block size. Under Linux, block devices receive special handling from the kernel[3] and can contain file systems.[4] Disk drives, including CD-ROM drives and RAM disks, are the most common block devices. **Character devices** can be read from a single character at a time, and the kernel provides no caching or ordering facilities for them. Modems, terminals, printers, sound cards, and mice are all character devices. Traditionally, special directory entries kept in the /dev directory allow user-space processes to access device resources as files.

**Symbolic links**    A symbolic link (a symlink) is a special kind of file that contains the path to another file. When a symlink is opened, the system recognizes it as a symlink, reads its value, and opens the file it references instead of the symlink itself. When the value stored in the symbolic link is

---

2. See Chapter 16 for more information on Unix domain sockets.
3. Most notably, they are cached and access to them is ordered.
4. This is different from some systems that are capable of mounting file systems on character devices, as well as block devices.

used, the system is said to be **following the symlink**. Unless otherwise noted, system calls are assumed to follow symlinks that are passed to them.

**Sockets**    Sockets, like pipes, provide an IPC channel. They are more flexible than pipes, and can create IPC channels between processes running on different machines. Sockets are discussed in Chapter 16.

In many operating systems, there is a one-to-one correspondence between files and file names. Every file has a file name in a file system, and every file name maps to a single file. Unix divorces the two concepts, allowing for more flexibility.

The only unique identity a file has is its **inode** (an abbreviation of *information node*). A file's inode contains all the information about a file, including the access permissions associated with it, its current size, and how many file names it has (which could be zero, one, twenty, or more). There are two types of inodes. The **in-core inode** is the only type we normally care about; every open file on the system has one. The kernel keeps in-core inodes in memory, and they are the same for all file-system types. The other type of inodes are **on-disk inodes**. Every file on a file system has an on-disk inode, and their exact structure depends on the type of file system the file is stored on. When a process opens a file on a file system, the on-disk inode is loaded into memory and converted into an in-core inode. When the in-core inode has been modified, it is transformed back into an on-disk inode and stored in the file system.

On-disk and in-core inodes do not contain exactly the same information. Only the in-core inode, for example, keeps track of how many processes on the system are currently using the file associated with the inode.

As on-disk and in-core inodes are synchronized by the kernel, most system calls end up updating both inodes. When this is the case, we just refer to updating the inode; it is implied that both the in-core and on-disk are affected. Some files (such as unnamed pipes) do not have any on-disk inode. In these cases, only the in-core inode is updated.

A file name exists only in a directory that relates that file name to the on-disk inode. You can think of the file name as a pointer to the on-disk inode for the file associated with it. The on-disk inode contains the number of file names that refer to that inode, called the **link count**. When a file is removed, the link count is decremented and if the link count is 0 and no processes already have the file open, the space is freed. If other processes have the file open, the disk space is freed when the final process has closed the file.

All of this means that it is possible to

- Have multiple processes access a file that has never existed in a file system (such as a pipe)

- Create a file on the disk, remove its directory entry, and continue to read and write from the file

- Change /tmp/foo and see the changes immediately in /tmp/bar, if both file names refer to the same inode

Unix has always worked this way, but these operations can be disconcerting to new users and programmers. As long as you keep in mind that a file name is merely a pointer to a file's on-disk inode, and that the inode is the real resource, you should be fine.

## 10.1 The File Mode

Every file on a system has a file type (such as unnamed pipe or character device), as well as a set of access permissions that define what processes may access that file. A file's type and access permissions are combined in a 16-bit value (a C short) called the **file mode**.

The bottom 12 bits of a file's mode represent the access permissions that govern access to the file, as well as file permission modifiers. The file permission modifiers serve a variety of functions. The most important functions are allowing the effective user and group IDs to change when the file is executed.

The file mode is usually written in up to six octal (base 8) digits. When represented in octal, the low-order three digits are the access bits, the next digit contains the file permission modifiers, and the high-order two digits indicate the file type. For example, a file whose mode is 0041777 has a file type of 04, a file permission modifier of 1, and access bits 0777.[5] Similarly, a file of mode 0100755 is of type 010, has no file permission modifiers set, and has access permissions of 0755.

## 10.1.1  File Access Permissions

Each of the three access digits represents the permissions for a different class of users. The first digit represents the permissions for the file's owner, the second digit represents permissions for users in the file's group, and the final digit represents the permissions for all other users. Each octal digit is made up of three bits, which represent read permission, write permission, and execute permission, from most significant to least significant bit. **World permissions** is commonly used to refer to the permission given to all three classes of users.

Let's try to make the previous paragraph a little more concrete through some examples. Linux's chmod command allows the user to specify an access mode in octal and then applies that mode to one or more files. If we have a file, somefile, which we would like to allow only the owner to write but any user (including the owner) to read, we would use mode 0644 (remember, this is in octal). The leading 6 is 110 in binary, which indicates that the type of user to which it refers (in this case, the owner) is given both read and write permission; the 4s are 010 binary, giving the other types of users (group and other) only read permissions.

```
$ chmod 0644 somefile
$ ls -l somefile
-rw-r--r--   1 ewt      devel        31 Feb 15 15:12 somefile
```

If we wanted to allow any member of group devel to write the file, we would use mode 0664 instead.

```
$ chmod 0664 somefile
$ ls -l somefile
-rw-rw-r--   1 ewt      devel        31 Feb 15 15:12 somefile
```

---

5. This is the mode usually used for the /tmp directory.

If `somefile` is a shell script we want to execute, we must tell the system that the file is executable by turning on the execute bit—in this case, we are allowing the owner to read, write, and execute the file and members of group `devel` to read and execute the file. Other users may not manipulate the file in any way.

```
$ chmod 0750 somefile
$ ls -l somefile
-rwxr-x---  1 ewt      devel        31 Feb 15 15:12 somefile
```

Directories use the same set of access bits as normal files, but with slightly different semantics. Read permissions allow a process to access the directory itself, which lets a user list the contents of a directory. Write permissions allow a process to create new files in the directory and delete existing ones. The execute bit does not translate as nicely though (what does it mean to execute a directory?). It allows a process to **search** a directory, which means it can access a file in that directory, as long as it knows the name of that file.

Most system directories on Linux machines have 0755 permissions and are owned by the root user. This lets all users on the system list the files in a directory and access those files by name, but restricts writing in that directory to the root user. Anonymous ftp sites that allow any person to submit files but do not want to let people download them until an administrator has looked at the contents of the files normally set their incoming file directories to 0772. That allows all users to create new files in the directory without being allowed either to see the contents of the directory or access files in it.

More information on file access permissions may be found in any introductory Linux or Unix book [Sobell, 1997] [Welsh, 1996].

## 10.1.2 File Permission Modifiers

The file permission modifier digit is also a bitmask, whose values represent setuid, setgid, and the sticky bit. If the setuid bit is set for an executable file, the process's effective user ID is set to the owner of the file when the program is executed (see page 98 for information on why this is useful). The setgid bit behaves the same way, but sets the effective group ID to the file's group. The setuid bit has no meaning for files that are not executable, but if the setgid bit is set for a nonexecutable file, any locking done on the file is mandatory rather than advisory.[6] Under Linux, the setuid and setgid bits are ignored for scripts (programs that use #! at their beginning to specify a command interpreter) because setuid scripts tend to be insecure.

Neither setuid nor setgid bits have any obvious meaning for directories. The setuid bit actually has no semantics when it is set on a directory. If a directory's setgid bit is set, all new files created in that directory are owned by the same group that owns the directory itself. This makes it easier to use directories for collaborative work among users.

The sticky bit, the least significant bit in the file permission modifier digit, has an interesting history behind its name. Older Unix implementations had to load an entire program into memory before it could begin executing it. This meant big programs had long startup times, which could get quite annoying. If a program had the sticky bit set, the operating system would attempt to leave the program "stuck" in memory for as long as possible, even when the program was not running, reducing the startup time for those programs. Although this was a bit of a kludge, it worked reasonably well for commonly used programs, such as the C compiler. Modern Unix implementations, including Linux, use demand loading to run programs that load the program piece by piece, making the sticky bit unnecessary, and so Linux ignores the sticky bit for regular files.

The sticky bit is still used for directories. Usually, any user with write permissions to a directory can erase any file in that directory. If a directory's sticky bit is set, however, files may be removed only by the user who owns the file and the root user. This behavior is handy for directories that are repositories for files created by a wide variety of users, such as /tmp.

The final section of a file's mode specifies the file's type. It is contained in the high-order octal digits of the mode and is not a bitmask. Instead, the value of those digits equates to a specific file type (04 indicates a directory; 06 indicates a block device). A file's type is set when the file is created. It can never be changed except by removing the file.

The include file <sys/stat.h> provides symbolic constants for all of the access bits, which can make code more readable. Both Linux and Unix users

---

6. See Chapter 12 for more information on file locking.

**Table 10.1** File Permission Constants

| Name | Value | Description |
|------|-------|-------------|
| S_ISUID | 0004000 | The program is setuid. |
| S_ISGID | 0002000 | The program is setgid. |
| S_ISVTX | 0001000 | The sticky bit. |
| S_IRWXU | 00700 | The file's owner has read, write, and execute permissions. |
| S_IRUSR | 00400 | The file's owner has read permission. |
| S_IWUSR | 00200 | The file's owner has write permission. |
| S_IXUSR | 00100 | The file's owner has execute permission. |
| S_IRWXG | 00070 | The file's group has read, write, and execute permissions. |
| S_IRGRP | 00040 | The file's group has read permission. |
| S_IWGRP | 00020 | The file's group has write permission. |
| S_IXGRP | 00010 | The file's group has execute permission. |
| S_IRWXO | 00007 | Other users have read, write, and execute permissions. |
| S_IROTH | 00004 | Other users have read permission. |
| S_IWOTH | 00002 | Other users have write permission. |
| S_IXOTH | 00001 | Other users have execute permission. |

usually become comfortable with the octal representation of file modes, however, so it is common for programs to use the octal values directly. Table 10.1 lists the symbolic names used for both file access permissions and file permission modifiers.

## 10.1.3 File Types

The upper four bits of a file mode specify the file's type. Table 10.2 lists the constants that relate to the file's type, and Table 10.1 lists the constants that relate to access permissions. Logically AND'ing any of these constants with a file's mode yields non-0 if the bit is set.

The following macros take a file mode as an argument and return true or false.

S_ISLNK(m)    True if the file is a symbolic link

S_ISREG(m)    True if the file is a regular file

**Table 10.2**   File Type Constants

| Name | Value (Octal) | Description |
|------|---------------|-------------|
| S_IFMT | 00170000 | This value, logically ANDed with the mode, gives the file type (which equals one of the other S_IF values). |
| S_IFSOCK | 0140000 | The file is a socket. |
| S_IFLNK | 0120000 | The file is a symbolic link. |
| S_IFREG | 0100000 | The file is a regular file. |
| S_IFBLK | 0060000 | The file represents a block device. |
| S_IFDIR | 0040000 | The file is a directory. |
| S_IFCHR | 0020000 | The file represents a character device. |
| S_IFIFO | 0010000 | The file represents a first-in/first-out communications pipe. |

S_ISDIR(m)   True if the file is a directory

S_ISCHR(m)   True if the file represents a character device

S_ISBLK(m)   True if the file represents a block device

S_ISFIFO(m)   True if the file is a first-in/first-out pipe

S_ISSOCK(m)   True if the file is a socket

## 10.1.4 The Process's umask

The permissions given to newly created files depend on both a system's setup and an individual user's preferences. To relieve individual programs of the need to guess the permissions to use for a file, the system allows users to turn off particular permissions for newly created files (and directories, which are just special files). Every process has a **umask,** which specifies the permission bits to turn off when files are created. This allows a process to specify fairly liberal permissions (usually, world read and write permissions) and end up with the permissions the user would like. If the file is particularly sensitive, the creating process can specify more-restrictive permissions than normal, because the umask will never result in less-restrictive permissions, only in more-restrictive permissions.

The process's current umask is set by the umask system call.

```
#include <sys/stat.h>

int umask(int newmask);
```

The old umask is returned, and the process's umask is set to the new value. Only read, write, and execute permissions may be specified for the file—you cannot use the umask to prevent the setuid, setgid, or sticky bits from being set. The umask command present in most shells allows the user to set the umask for the shell itself and its subsequent child processes.

As an example, the touch command creates new files with 0666 (world read and write) permissions. Because the user rarely wants this, he could force the touch command to turn off world and group write permissions for a file with a umask of 022, as shown by this example.

```
$ umask 022
$ touch foo
$ ls -l foo
-rw-r--r--   1 ewt        ewt             0 Feb 24 21:24 foo
```

If he prefers group write permissions, he can use a umask of 002 instead.

```
$ umask 002
$ touch foo2
$ ls -l foo2
-rw-rw-r--   1 ewt        ewt             0 Feb 24 21:24 foo2
```

If he wants all his files to be accessible only by himself, a 077 umask will accomplish the task.

```
$ umask 077
$ touch foo3
$ ls -l foo3
-rw-------   1 ewt        ewt             0 Feb 24 21:26 foo3
```

The process's umask affects the open(), creat(), mknod(), and mkdir() system calls.

# 10.2   Basic File Operations

As a large proportion of Linux's system calls manipulate files, we begin by showing you the functions that are most widely used. We discuss the more specialized functions later in this chapter. The functions used to read through directories are presented in Chapter 11 to help keep this chapter a bit more concise.

## 10.2.1 File Descriptors

When a process gains access to a file (usually called *opening* the file), the kernel returns a **file descriptor** that the process uses to perform subsequent operations on the file. File descriptors are small, positive integers, which serve as indices into an array of open files the kernel maintains for each process.

The first three file descriptors for a process (0, 1, and 2) have standard usages. The first, 0, is known as standard input (**stdin**) and is where programs should take their interactive input from. File descriptor 1 is called standard output (**stdout**), and most output from the program should be directed there. Errors should be sent to standard error (**stderr**), which is file descriptor 2. The standard C library follows these rules, so gets() and printf() use stdin and stdout, respectively, and these conventions allow shells to properly redirect a process's input and output.

The <unistd.h> header file provides the STDIN_FILENO, STDOUT_FILENO, and STDERR_FILENO macros, which evaluate to the stdin, stdout, and stderr file descriptors, respectively. Using these symbolic names can make code slightly more readable.

Many of the file operations that manipulate a file's inode are available in two forms. The first form takes a file name as an argument. The kernel uses that argument to look up the file's inode and performs the appropriate operation on the inode (this usually includes following symlinks). The second form takes a file descriptor as an argument and performs the operation on the inode it refers to. The two sets of system calls use similiar names, with the system calls that expect a file descriptor argument prefixed with the letter *f*. For example, the chmod() system call changes the access permissions for the file referred to by the passed file name; `fchmod()` sets the access permissions for the file referred to by the specified file descriptor.

To make the rest of this discussion a bit less verbose, we present both versions of the system calls when they exist but discuss only the first version (which uses a file name).

## 10.2.2 Closing Files

One of the few operations that is the same for all types of files is closing the file. Here is how to close a file:

```
#include <unistd.h>

int close(int fd);
```

This is obviously a pretty basic operation. However, there is one important thing to remember about closing files—it could fail. Some systems (most notably, networked file systems such as NFS) do not try to store the final piece of written data in the file system until the file is closed. If that storage operation fails (the remote host may have crashed), then the `close()` will return an error. If your application is writing data but does not use synchronous writes (see the discussion of `O_SYNC` in the next section), you should always check the results of file closures. If `close()` fails, the updated file is corrupted in some unpredictable fashion! Luckily, this happens extremely rarely.

## 10.2.3 Opening Files in the File System

Although Linux provides many types of files, regular files are by far the most commonly used. Programs, configuration files, and data files all fall under that heading, and most applications do not (explicitly) use any other file type. There are two ways of opening files that have associated file names:

```
#include <fcntl.h>
#include <unistd.h>

int open(char * pathname, int flags, mode_t mode);
int creat(char * pathname, mode_t mode);
```

The open() function returns a file descriptor that references the file pathname. If the return value is less than 0, an error has occurred (as always, errno will contain the error code). The flags argument describes the type of access the calling process wants, and also controls various attributes of how the file is opened and manipulated. An access mode must always be provided, and is one of O_RDONLY, O_RDWR, and O_WRONLY, which request read-only, read-write, and write-only access, respectively. One or more of the following values may be logically OR'ed with the access mode to control other file semantics.

O_CREAT        If the file does not already exist, create it as a regular file.

O_EXCL         This flag should be used only with O_CREAT. When it is specified, open() fails if the file already exists. This flag allows a simple locking implementation, but it is unreliable across networked file systems like NFS.[7]

O_NOCTTY       The file being opened will not become the process's controlling terminal (see page 123 for more information on controlling terminals). This flag matters only when a process without any controlling terminal is opening a tty device. If it is specified any other time, it is ignored.

O_TRUNC        If the file already exists, the contents will be discarded and the file size set to 0.

O_APPEND       All writes to the file occur at the end of the file, although random access reads are still permitted.

O_NONBLOCK[8]   The file is opened in nonblocking mode. Operations on normal files always block because they are stored on local hard disks with predictable response times, but operations on certain file types have unpredictable completion times. For example, reading from a pipe that does not have any data in it will block the reading process until data becomes available. If O_NONBLOCK is specified, the read will return zero bytes rather than block. Files that

---

7. For more information on file locking, see Chapter 12.
8. O_NDELAY is the original name for O_NONBLOCK, but it is now obsolete.

may take an indeterminate amount of time to perform an operation are called **slow files**.

O_SYNC        Normally the kernel caches writes and records them to the hardware when it is convenient to do so. Although this implementation greatly increases performance, it is more likely to allow data loss than is immediately writing the data to disk. If O_SYNC is specified when a file is opened, all changes to the file are stored on the disk before the kernel returns control to the writing process. This is very important for some applications, such as database systems, in which write ordering is used to prevent data corruption in case of a system failure.

The mode parameter specifies the access permissions for the file if it is being created, and it is modified by the process's current umask. If O_CREAT is not specified, the mode is ignored.

The creat() function is exactly equivalent to

```
open(pathname, O_CREAT | O_WRONLY | O_TRUNC, mode)
```

We do not use creat() in this book because we find open() easier to read and to understand.[9]

## 10.2.4 Reading, Writing, and Moving Around

Although there are a few ways to read from and write to files, only the simplest is discussed here.[10] Reading and writing are nearly identical, so we discuss them simultaneously.

```
#include <unistd.h>

int read(int fd, void * buf, size_t length);
int write(int fd, const void * buf, size_t length);
```

---

9. creat() is misspelled, anyway.
10. readv(), writev(), and mmap() are discussed in Chapter 12; sendmsg() and recvmsg() are mentioned in Chapter 16.

Both functions take a file descriptor fd, a pointer to a buffer buf, and the length of that buffer. read() reads from the file descriptor and places the data read into the passed buffer; write() writes length bytes from the buffer to the file. Both functions return the number of bytes transferred, or -1 on an error (which implies no bytes were read or stored).

Now that we have covered these system calls, here is a simple example that creates the file hw in the current directory and writes Hello World! into it.

```
 1: /* hwwrite.c -- writes "Hello World!" to file hw in the current
 2:                 directory */
 3:
 4: #include <errno.h>
 5: #include <fcntl.h>
 6: #include <stdio.h>
 7: #include <stdlib.h>
 8: #include <unistd.h>
 9:
10: int main(void) {
11:     int fd;
12:
13:     /* open the file, creating it if it's not there, and removing
14:        its contents if it is there */
15:     if ((fd = open("hw", O_TRUNC | O_CREAT | O_WRONLY, 0644)) < 0) {
16:         perror("open"),
17:         exit(1);
18:     }
19:
20:     /* the magic number of 13 is the number of characters which will
21:        be written */
22:     if (write(fd, "Hello World!\n", 13) != 13) {
23:         perror("write");
24:         exit(1);
25:     }
26:
27:     close(fd);
28:
29:     return 0;
30: }
```

Here is what happens when we run `hwwrite`:

```
$ cat hw
cat: hw: No such file or directory
$ ./hwwrite
$ cat hw
Hello World!
$
```

Changing this function to read from a file is a simple matter of changing the `open()` to

```
open("hw", O_RDONLY);
```

and changing the `write()` of a static string to a `read()` into a buffer.

Unix files can be divided into two catgories: seekable and nonseekable.[11] Nonseekable files are first-in/first-out channels that do not support random reads or writes, and data cannot be reread or overwritten. Seekable files allow the reads and the writes to occur anywhere in the file. Pipes and sockets are nonseekable files; block devices and regular files are seekable.

As FIFOs are nonseekable files, it is obvious where `read()` reads from (the beginning of the file) and `write()` writes to (the end of the file). Seekable files, on the other hand, have no obvious place for the operations to occur. Instead, both happen at the "current" location in the file and advance the current location after the operation. When a seekable file is initially opened, the current location is at the beginning of the file, or offset 0. If 10 bytes are read, the current position is then at offset 10, and a write of 5 more bytes will overwrite the data, starting with the eleventh byte in the file (which is at offset 10, where the current position was). After such a write, the current position becomes offset 15, immediately after the overwritten data.

If the current position is the end of the file and the process tries to read from the file, `read()` returns 0 rather than an error. If more data is written at the end of the file, the file grows just enough to accommodate the extra data and the current position becomes the new end of the file. Each file

---

11. Although this division is almost clean, TCP sockets support out-of-band data, which makes it a bit dirtier. Out-of-band data is outside the scope of this book; [Stevens, 1990] provides a complete description.

descriptor keeps track of an independent current position[12] (it is not kept in the file's inode), so if a file is opened multiple times by multiple processes (or by the same process, for that matter), reads and writes through one of the file descriptors will not affect the location of reads and writes made through the other file descriptor. Of course, the multiple writes could corrupt the file in other ways, so some sort of locking may be needed in these situations.

Files opened with O_APPEND have a slightly different behavior. For such files, the current position is moved to the end of the file before the kernel writes any data. After the write, the current position is moved to the end of the newly written data, as normal. For append-only files, this guarantees that the file's current position is always at the end of the file immediately following a write().

Applications that want to read and write data from random locations in the file need to set the current position before reading and writing data, using lseek():

```
#include <unistd.h>

int lseek(int fd, off_t offset, int whence);
```

The current position for file fd is moved to offset bytes relative to whence, where whence is one of the following.

SEEK_SET[13]    The beginning of the file

SEEK_CUR        The current position in the file

SEEK_END        The end of the file

For both SEEK_CUR and SEEK_END the offset may be negative. In this case, the current position is moved toward the beginning of the file (from whence)

---

12. Almost independent; see the discussion of dup() on page 181 for the exceptions to this.
13. As most systems define SEEK_SET as 0, it is common to see lseek(fd, offset, 0) used instead of lseek(fd, offset, SEEK_SET). This is not as portable (or readable) as SEEK_SET, but it is fairly common in old code.

rather than toward the end of the file. For example, the following code moves the current position to five bytes from the end of the file:

```
lseek(fd, -5, SEEK_END);
```

The `lseek()` system call returns the new current position in the file relative to the beginning of the file, or -1 if an error occurred. Thus, `lseek(fd, 0, SEEK_END)` is a simple way of finding out how large a file is, but make sure you reset the current position before trying to read from `fd`.

Although the current position is not disturbed by other processes that access the file at the same time,[14] that does not mean multiple processes can safely write to a file simultaneously. Imagine the following sequence:

| Process A | Process B |
| --- | --- |
| `lseek(fd, 0, SEEK_END);` | |
| | `lseek(fd, 0, SEEK_END);` |
| | `write(fd, buf, 10);` |
| `write(fd, buf, 5);` | |

In this case process A would have overwritten the first five bytes of process B's data, which is probably not what was intended. If multiple processes need to write to append to a file simultaneously, the `O_APPEND` flag should be used, which makes the operation atomic.

Under most POSIX systems, processes are allowed to move the current position past the end of the file. The file is grown to the appropriate size, and the current position becomes the new end of the file. The only catch is that most systems do not actually allocate any disk space for the portion of the file that was never written to; they change only the logical size of the file.

Portions of files that are "created" in this manner are known as **holes**. Reading from a hole in a file returns a buffer full of zeros, and writing to them could fail with an out-of-disk space error. All of this means that `lseek()` should not be used to reserve disk space for later use because that space may not be allocated. If your application needs to allocate some disk space for later use, you must use `write()`. Files with holes in them are often

---

14. Well, not usually, anyway. The only exception to this is discussed on page 181.

used for files that have data sparsely spaced throughout them, such as files that represent hash tables.

For a simple, shell-based demonstration of file holes, look at the following example (note that /dev/zero is a character device that returns as many zeros as a process tries to read from it).

```
$ dd if=/dev/zero of=foo bs=1k count=10
10+0 records in
10+0 records out
$ ls -l foo
-rw-rw-r--  1 ewt      ewt        10240 Feb  6 21:50 foo
$ du foo
10      foo
$ dd if=/dev/zero of=bar bs=1k count=1 seek=9
1+0 records in
1+0 records out
$ ls -l bar
-rw-rw-r--  1 ewt      ewt        10240 Feb  6 21:50 bar
$ du bar
1       bar
$
```

Although both foo and bar are 10K in size, bar uses only 1K of disk space because the other 9K were seek()ed over when the file was created instead of written.

## 10.2.5 Partial Reads and Writes

Although both read() and write() take a parameter that specifies how many bytes to read or write, neither one is guaranteed to process the requested number of bytes, even if no error has occurred. The simplest example of this is trying to read from a regular file that is already positioned at the end of the file. The system cannot actually read any bytes, but it is not exactly an error condition either. Instead, the read() call will return 0 bytes. In the same vein, if the current position was 10 bytes from the end of the file and an attempt was made to read more than 10 bytes from the file, 10 bytes would be read and the read() call would return the value 10. Again, this is not considered an error condition.

The behavior of read() also depends on whether the file was opened with O_NONBLOCK. On many file types, O_NONBLOCK does not make any difference at all. Files for which the system can guarantee an operation's completion in a reasonable amount of time always block on reads and writes; they are sometimes referred to as **fast** files. This set of files includes devices and regular files. For other file types, such as pipes and such character devices as terminals, the process could be waiting for another process (or a human being) to either provide something for the process to read or free resources for the system to use when processing the write() request. In either case, the system has no way of knowing whether it will ever be able to complete the system call. When these files are opened with O_NONBLOCK, for each operation on the file, the system simply does as much as it is able to do immediately, and then returns to the calling process.

Nonblocking I/O is an important topic, and more examples of it will be presented in Chapter 12. With the standardization of the select() system call, however, the need for it (especially for reading) has diminished. If you find yourself using nonblocking I/O extensively, try to rethink your program in terms of select() to see if you can make it more efficient.

To show a concrete example of reading and writing files, here is a simple reimplementation of **cat**. It copies stdin to stdout until there is no more input to copy.

```
 1: /* cat.c -- simple version of cat */
 2: #include <stdio.h>
 3: #include <unistd.h>
 4:
 5: /* While there is data on standard in (fd 0), copy it to standard
 6:    out (fd 1). Exit once no more data is available. */
 7:
 8: int main(void) {
 9:     char buf[1024];
10:     int len;
11:
12:     /* len will be >= 0 while data is available, and read() is
13:        successful */
14:     while ((len = read(STDIN_FILENO, buf, sizeof(buf))) > 0) {
15:         if (write(1, buf, len) != len) {
16:             perror("write");
17:             return 1;
```

```
18:          }
19:      }
20:
21:      /* len was <= 0; If len = 0, no more data is available.
22:         Otherwise, an error occurred. */
23:      if (len < 0) {
24:          perror("read");
25:          return 1;
26:      }
27:
28:      return 0;
29: }
```

## 10.2.6  Shortening Files

Although regular files automatically grow when data is written to the end of them, there is no way for the system to automatically shrink files when the data at their end is no longer needed. After all, how would the system know when data becomes extraneous? It is a process's responsibility to notify the system when a file may be truncated at a certain point.

```
#include <unistd.h>

int truncate(const char * pathname, size_t length);
int ftruncate(int fd, size_t length);
```

The file's size is set to length, and any data in the file past the new end of the file is lost. If length is larger than the current size of the file, the file is actually grown to the indicated length (using holes if possible), though this behavior is not guaranteed by POSIX and should not be relied on in portable programs.

## 10.2.7  Other Operations

Linux's file model does a good job of standardizing most file operations through generic functions such as read() and write() (for example, writing to a pipe is the same as writing to a file on disk). However, some devices have operations that are poorly modeled by this abstraction. For example, terminal devices, represented as character devices, need to provide a method to change the speed of the terminal; and a CD-ROM drive, represented by a block device, needs to know when it should play an audio track to help increase a programmer's productivity.

All of these miscellaneous operations are accessed through a single system call, ioctl() (short for I/O control), which is prototyped like this:

```
#include <sys/ioctl.h>

int ioctl(int fd, int request, ...);
```

although it is almost always used like this:

```
int ioctl(int fd, int request, void * arg);
```

Whenever ioctl() is used, its first argument is the file being manipulated and the second argument specifies what operation is being requested. The final argument is usually a pointer to *something*, but what that something is, as well as the exact semantics of the return code, depends on what type of file fd refers to and what type of operation was requested. For some operations, arg is a long value instead of a pointer; in these instances, a typecast is normally used. There are many examples of ioctl() in this book, and you do not need to worry about using ioctl() until you come across them.

# 10.3 Querying and Changing Inode Information

## 10.3.1 Finding Inode Information

The beginning of this chapter introduced an inode as the data structure that tracks information about a file rather than just a single process's view of it. For example, a file's size is a constant at any given time—it does not change for different processes that have access to the file (compare this with the current position in the file, which is unique for the result of each open() rather than a property of the file itself). Linux provides three ways of reading a file's inode information.

```
#include <sys/stat.h>

int stat(const char * pathname, struct stat * statbuf);
int lstat(const char *pathname, struct stat * statbuf);
int fstat(int fd, struct stat * statbuf);
```

The first version, stat(), returns the inode information for the file referenced by pathname, following any symlinks that are present. If you do not want to follow symlinks (to check if a file name is a symlink, for example), use lstat() instead, which does not follow them. The final version, fstat(), returns the inode referred to by an open file descriptor. All three system calls fill in the struct stat referenced by statbuf with information from the file's inode. Table 10.3 describes the information available from struct stat.

## 10.3.2  A Simple Example of stat()

Here is a simple program that displays information from lstat() for each file name passed as an argument. It illustrates how to use the values returned by the stat() family of functions.

```
 1: /* statsamp.c -- display information returned by lstat() */
 2:
 3: /* For each file name passed on the command line, we display all of
 4:    the information lstat() returns on the file. */
 5:
 6: #include <errno.h>
 7: #include <stdio.h>
 8: #include <string.h>
 9: #include <sys/stat.h>
10: #include <sys/sysmacros.h>
11: #include <sys/types.h>
12: #include <time.h>
13: #include <unistd.h>
14:
15: #define TIME_STRING_BUF 50
16:
17: /* Make the user pass buf (of minimum length TIME_STRING_BUF) rather
18:    then using a static buf local to the function to avoid the use of
```

**Table 10.3** Members of `struct stat`

| Type | Field | Description |
|------|-------|-------------|
| dev_t | st_dev | The device number the file resides on. |
| ino_t | st_ino | The file's on-disk inode number. Each file has an on-disk inode number unique for the device it is on. Thus the (st_dev, st_ino) pair provides a unique identification of the file. |
| mode_t | st_mode | The mode of the file. This includes information on both the file permissions and the type of file. |
| nlink_t | st_nlink | The number of pathnames that reference this inode. This does not include symlinks, because symlinks reference other file names, not inodes. |
| uid_t | st_uid | The user ID that owns the file. |
| gid_t | st_gid | The group ID that owns the file. |
| dev_t | st_rdev | If the file is a character or block device, this gives the major and minor numbers of the file. See the discussion on mknod() on page 173 for more information on this field and the macros that manipulate its value. |
| off_t | st_size | The size of the file in bytes. This is defined only for regular files. |
| unsigned long | st_blksize | The block size for the file system storing the file. |
| unsigned long | st_blocks | The number of blocks allocated to the file. Normally, st_blksize * st_blocks is a little more than the st_size because some of the space in the final block is unused. However, for files with holes, st_blksize * st_blocks can be substantially smaller than st_size. |
| time_t | st_atime | The most recent access time of the file. This is updated whenever the file is opened or its inode is modified. |
| time_t | st_mtime | The most recent modification time of the file. It is updated whenever the file's data has changed |
| time_t | st_ctime | The most recent change time of the file or the inode, including owner, group, link count, etc. |

```
19:     static local variables and dynamic memory.  No error should ever occur,
20:     so we don't do any error checking. */
21: char * timeString(time_t t, char * buf) {
22:     struct tm * local;
23:
24:     local = localtime(&t);
25:     strftime(buf, TIME_STRING_BUF, "%c", local);
26:
27:     return buf;
28: }
29:
30: /* Display all of the information we get from lstat() on the file
31:    named as our sole parameter. */
32: int statFile(char * file) {
33:     struct stat statbuf;
34:     char timeBuf[TIME_STRING_BUF];
35:
36:     if (lstat(file, &statbuf)) {
37:         fprintf(stderr, "could not lstat %s: %s\n", file,
38:                 strerror(errno));
39:         return 1;
40:     }
41:
42:     printf("Filename : %s\n", file);
43:     printf("On device: major %d/minor %d     Inode number: %ld\n",
44:             major(statbuf.st_dev), minor(statbuf.st_dev), statbuf.st_ino);
45:     printf("Size     : %-10ld        Type: %07o         "
46:            "Permissions: %05o\n", statbuf.st_size,
47:             statbuf.st_mode & S_IFMT, statbuf.st_mode & ~(S_IFMT));
48:     printf("Owner    : %d              Group: %d"
49:            "            Number of links: %d\n",
50:             statbuf.st_uid, statbuf.st_gid, statbuf.st_nlink);;
51:     printf("Creation time: %s\n", timeString(statbuf.st_ctime, timeBuf));
52:     printf("Modified time: %s\n", timeString(statbuf.st_mtime, timeBuf));
53:     printf("Access time  : %s\n", timeString(statbuf.st_atime, timeBuf));
54:
55:     return 0;
56: }
57:
58: int main(int argc, char ** argv) {
59:     int i;
```

```
60:     int rc = 0;
61:
62:     /* Call statFile() for each file name passed on the command line. */
63:     for (i = 1; i < argc; i++) {
64:         /* If statFile() ever fails, rc will end up non-zero. */
65:         rc |= statFile(argv[i]);
66:
67:         /* this prints a blank line between entries, but not after
68:             the last entry */
69:         if ((argc - i) > 1) printf("\n");
70:     }
71:
72:     return rc;
73: }
```

## 10.3.3 Easily Determining Access Rights

Although the mode of a file provides all the information a program needs to determine whether it is allowed to access a file, testing the set of permissions is tricky and error prone. As the kernel already includes the code to validate access permissions, a simple system call is provided that lets programs determine whether they may access a file in a certain way.

```
#include <unistd.h>

int access(const char * pathname, int mode);
```

The mode is a mask that contains one or more of the following values.

F_OK            The file exists. This requires execute permissions on all the
                directories in the path being checked, so it could fail for a file
                that does exist.

R_OK            The process may read from the file.

W_OK            The process may write to the file.

X_OK            The process may execute the file (or search the directory).

access() returns 0 if the specified access modes are allowed, and an EACCES error otherwise.

### 10.3.4 Changing a File's Access Permissions

A file's access permissions and access permission modifiers are changed by the chmod() system call.

```
#include <sys/stat.h>

int chmod(const char * pathname, mode_t mode);
int fchmod(int fd, mode_t mode);
```

Although chmod() allows you to specify a path, remember that file permissions are based on the inode, not on the file name. If a file has multiple hard links to it, changing the permissions of one of the file's names changes the file's permissions everywhere it appears in the file system. The mode parameter may be any combination of the access and access modifier bits just discussed, logically OR'ed together. As there are normally quite a few of these values specified at a time, it is common for programs to specify the new permission value directly in octal. Only the root user and the owner of a file are allowed to change the access permissions for a file—all others who attempt to do so get EPERM.

### 10.3.5 Changing a File's Owner and Group

Just like a file's permissions, a file's owner and group are stored in the file's inode, so all hard links to a file have the same owner and group. The same system call is used to change both the owner and the group of a file.

```
#include <unistd.h>

int chown(const char * pathname, uid_t owner, gid_t group);
int fchown(int fd, uid_t owner, gid_t group);
```

The owner and group parameters specify the new owner and group for the file. If either is -1, that value is not changed. Only the root user may change the owner of a file. When a file's owner is changed or the file is written to, the setuid bit for that file is always cleared for security reasons. Both the owner of a file and the root user may change the group that owns a file, but the owner must be a member of the group to which he is changing the file. If the file has its group execute bit set, the setgid bit is cleared for security reasons. If the setgid bit is set but the group execute bit is not, the file has mandatory locking enabled and the mode is preserved.

## 10.3.6 Changing a File's Timestamps

A file's owner may change the mtime and atime of a file to any arbitrary value. This makes these timestamps useless as audit trails, but it allows archiving tools like tar and cpio to reset a file's timestamps to the same values they had when the file was archived. The ctime is changed when the mtime and atime are updated, so tar and cpio are unable to restore it.

There are two ways of changing these stamps: utime() and utimes(). utime() originated in System V and was adopted by POSIX, whereas utimes() is from BSD. Both functions are equivalent; they differ only in the way the new timestamps are specified.

```
#include <utime.h>
int utime(const char * pathname, struct utimbuf * buf);

#include <sys/time.h>
int utimes(const char * pathname, struct timeval * tvp);
```

The POSIX version, utime(), takes a struct utimbuf, which is defined in <utime.h> as

```
struct utimbuf {
    time_t actime;
    time_t modtime;
}
```

BSD's utimes() instead passes the new atime and mtime through a struct timeval, which is defined in <sys/time.h>.

```
struct timeval {
    long tv_sec;
    long tv_usec;
}
```

**Table 10.4**  Extended File Attributes

| Attribute | Definition |
|---|---|
| EXT2_APPEND_FL | If the file is opened for writing, O_APPEND must be specified. |
| EXT2_IMMUTABLE_FL | The file may not be modified or removed by any user, including root. |
| EXT2_NODUMP | The file should be ignored by the dump command. |
| EXT2_SYNC_FL | The file must be updated synchronously, as if O_SYNC had been specified on opening. |

The tv_sec element holds the new atime; tv_usec contains the new mtime for utimes().

If NULL is passed as the second argument to either function, both timestamps are set to the current time. The new atime and mtime are specified in elapsed seconds since the epoch (just like the value time() returns), as defined in Chapter 17.

## 10.3.7 Ext2 Extended Attributes

The primary file system used on Linux systems is the Second Extended file system,[15] commonly abbreviated as ext2. Although the ext2 file system supports all the traditional features of Unix file systems, such as the meanings of the various bits in each file's mode, it allows for other attributes for each file. Table 10.4 describes the extra attributes currently supported, along with the symbolic name for each attribute. These flags may be set and inspected through the chattr and lsattr programs.

As the ext2 extended attributes are outside the usual file system, they cannot be modified through chmod() like the file attributes. Instead, ioctl() is used. Recall that ioctl() is defined as

```
#include <sys/ioctl.h>
#include <linux/ext2_fs.h>

int ioctl(int fd, int request, void * arg);
```

---

15. So named because it was designed as a successor to the Linux extended file system, which was designed as a more complete file system than the Minix file system, the only file system Linux originally supported.

The file whose attributes are being changed must be open, just as for fchmod(). The request is EXT2_IOC_GETFLAGS to check the current flags for the file and EXT2_IOC_SETFLAGS to set them. In either case, arg must point to an int. If EXT2_IOC_GETFLAGS is used, the long is set to the current value of the program's flags. If EXT2_IOC_SETFLAGS is used, the new value of the file's flags is taken from the long pointed to by arg.

The append and immutable flags may be changed only by the root user, as they restrict the operations the root user is able to perform. The other flags may be modified by either the root user or the owner of the file whose flags are being modified.

Here is a small program that displays the flags for any files specified on the command line. It works only for files on an ext2 file system, however. The ioctl() fails for files on any other type of file system.

```
 1: /* checkflags.c - display info on ext2 extended attributes */
 2:
 3: /* For each file name passed on the command line, display information
 4:    on that file's ext2 attributes. */
 5:
 6: #include <errno.h>
 7: #include <fcntl.h>
 8: #include <linux/ext2_fs.h>
 9: #include <stdio.h>
10: #include <sys/ioctl.h>
11: #include <unistd.h>
12:
13: int main(int argc, char ** argv) {
14:     char ** filename = argv + 1;
15:     int fd;
16:     long flags;
17:
18:     /* Iterate over each file name on the command line. The last
19:        pointer in argv[] is NULL, so this while() loop is legal. */
20:     while (*filename) {
21:         /* Unlike normal attributes, ext2 attributes can only
22:            be queried if we have a file descriptor (a file name
23:            isn't sufficient). We don't need write access to query
24:            the ext2 attributes, so O_RDONLY is fine. */
25:         fd = open(*filename, O_RDONLY);
```

```
26:         if (fd < 0) {
27:             fprintf(stderr, "cannot open %s: %s\n", *filename,
28:                     strerror(errno));
29:             return 1;
30:         }
31:
32:         /* This gets the attributes, and puts them into flags */
33:         if (ioctl(fd, EXT2_IOC_GETFLAGS, &flags)) {
34:             fprintf(stderr, "ioctl failed on %s: %s\n", *filename,
35:                     strerror(errno));
36:             return 1;
37:         }
38:
39:         printf("%s:", *filename++);
40:
41:         /* Check for each attribute, and display a message for each
42:            one which is turned on. */
43:         if (flags & EXT2_APPEND_FL) printf(" Append");
44:         if (flags & EXT2_IMMUTABLE_FL) printf(" Immutable");
45:         if (flags & EXT2_SYNC_FL) printf(" Sync");
46:         if (flags & EXT2_NODUMP_FL) printf(" Nodump");
47:
48:         printf("\n");
49:         close(fd);
50:     }
51:
52:     return 0;
53: };
```

The following is a similiar program that sets the ext2 extended attributes for a given list of files. The first parameter must be a list of which flags should be set. Each flag is represented in the list by a single letter: A for append-only, I for immutable, S for sync, and N for the nodump flag. This program does not modify the current flags for the file; only the flags specified on the command line are set.

```
1: /* setflags.c - set the ext2 attributes for a set of files */
2:
3: /* The first parameter to this program is a string consisting of
4:    0 (an empty string is okay) or more of the letters I, A, S, and
5:    N. This string specifies which ext2 attributes should be turned
```

```
 6:     on for the files which are specified on the rest of the command
 7:     line -- the rest of the attributes are turned off. The letters
 8:     stand for immutable, append-only, sync, and nodump, respectively.
 9:
10:     For example, the command "setflags IN file1 file2" turns on the
11:     immutable and nodump flags for files file1 and file2, but turns
12:     off the sync and append-only flags for those files. */
13:
14: #include <errno.h>
15: #include <fcntl.h>
16: #include <linux/ext2_fs.h>
17: #include <stdio.h>
18: #include <string.h>
19: #include <sys/ioctl.h>
20: #include <unistd.h>
21:
22: int main(int argc, char ** argv) {
23:     char ** filename = argv + 1;
24:     int fd;
25:     int flags = 0;
26:
27:     /* make sure the flags to set were specified, along with
28:        some file names */
29:     if (argc < 3) {
30:         fprintf(stderr, "setflags usage: [I][A][S][N] <filenames>\n");
31:         return 1;
32:     }
33:
34:     /* each letter represents a flag; set the flags which are
35:        ·specified */
36:     if (strchr(argv[1], 'I')) flags |= EXT2_IMMUTABLE_FL;
37:     if (strchr(argv[1], 'A')) flags |= EXT2_APPEND_FL;
38:     if (strchr(argv[1], 'S')) flags |= EXT2_SYNC_FL;
39:     if (strchr(argv[1], 'N')) flags |= EXT2_NODUMP_FL;
40:
41:     /* iterate over all of the file names in argv[] */
42:     while (*(++filename)) {
43:         /* Unlike normal attributes, ext2 attributes can only
44:            be set if we have a file descriptor (a file name
45:            isn't sufficient). We don't need write access to set
46:            the ext2 attributes, so O_RDONLY is fine. */
```

```
47:         fd = open(*filename, O_RDONLY);
48:         if (fd < 0) {
49:             fprintf(stderr, "cannot open %s: %s\n", *filename,
50:                     strerror(errno));
51:             return 1;
52:         }
53:
54:         /* Sets the attributes as specified by the contents of
55:            flags. */
56:         if (ioctl(fd, EXT2_IOC_SETFLAGS, &flags)) {
57:             fprintf(stderr, "ioctl failed on %s: %s\n", *filename,
58:                     strerror(errno));
59:             return 1;
60:         }
61:         close(fd);
62:     }
63:
64:     return 0;
65: };
```

# 10.4  Manipulating Directory Entries

Remember that directory entries (file names) are nothing more than pointers to on-disk inodes; almost all the important information concerning a
file is stored in the inode. open() lets a process create directory entries that
are regular files, but other functions are needed to create other types of
files and to manipulate the entries themselves. The functions that allow
you to create, remove, and search directories are covered in Chapter 11;
socket files are introduced in Chapter 16. This section covers symbolic
links, device files, and FIFOs.

## 10.4.1 Creating Device and Named Pipe Entries

Processes create device file entries and named pipes in the file system
through mknod().

```
#include <fcntl.h>
#include <unistd.h>

int mknod(const char * pathname, mode_t mode, dev_t dev);
```

The pathname is the file name to create, mode is both the access mode of the new file (which gets modified by the current umask) and the new file type (S_IFIFO, S_IFBLK, or S_IFCHR). The final parameter, dev, contains the major and minor numbers of the device to create. The type of device (character or block) and the major number of the device tell the kernel which device driver is responsible for operations on that device file. The minor number is used internally by the device driver to differentiate among multiple devices it provides. Only the root user is allowed to create device files; all users may create named pipes.

The <sys/sysmacros.h> header file provides three macros for manipulating dev_t values. The makedev() macro takes a major number as its first argument and a minor number as its second, and it returns a dev_t suitable for mknod(). The major() and minor() macros take a dev_t value as their sole argument and return the device's major and minor numbers, respectively.

The mknod program available under Linux provides a user-level interface to the mknod() system call (see man 1 mknod for details). Here is a simple reimplementation of mknod to illustrate the mknod() system call. Notice that the program creates the file with mode 0666 (giving read and write access to all users), and it depends on the process's umask setting to get the permissions right.

```
 1: /* mknod.c - equivalent to standard /sbin/mknod command */
 2:
 3: /* Create the device or named pipe specified on the command line.
 4:    See the mknod(1) man page for details on the command line
 5:    parameters. */
 6:
 7: #include <errno.h>
 8: #include <stdio.h>
 9: #include <stdlib.h>
10: #include <string.h>
11: #include <sys/stat.h>
12: #include <sys/sysmacros.h>
```

```
13: #include <unistd.h>
14:
15: void usage(void) {
16:     fprintf(stderr, "usage: mknod <path> [b|c|u|p] <major> <minor>\n");
17:     exit(1);
18: }
19:
20: int main(int argc, char ** argv) {
21:     int major = 0, minor = 0;
22:     char * path;
23:     int mode = 0666;
24:     char *end;
25:     int args;
26:
27:     /* We always need at least the type of inode to create, and
28:        the path for it. */
29:     if (argc < 3) usage();
30:
31:     path = argv[1];
32:
33:     /* the second argument tells us the type of node to create */
34:     if (!strcmp(argv[2], "b")) {
35:         mode |= S_IFBLK;
36:         args = 5;
37:     } else if (!strcmp(argv[2], "c") || !strcmp(argv[2], "u")) {
38:         mode |= S_IFCHR;
39:         args = 5;
40:     } else if (!strcmp(argv[2], "p")) {
41:         mode |= S_IFIFO;
42:         args = 3;
43:     } else {
44:         fprintf(stderr, "unknown node type %s\n", argv[2]);
45:         return 1;
46:     }
47:
48:     /* args tells us how many parameters to expect, as we need more
49:        information to create device files then named pipes */
50:     if (argc != args) usage();
51:
52:     if (args == 5) {
53:         /* get the major and minor numbers for the device file to
```

```
54:                create */
55:            major = strtol(argv[3], &end, 0);
56:            if (*end) {
57:                fprintf(stderr, "bad major number %s\n", argv[3]);
58:                return 1;
59:            }
60:
61:            minor = strtol(argv[4], &end, 0);
62:            if (*end) {
63:                fprintf(stderr, "bad minor number %s\n", argv[4]);
64:                return 1;
65:            }
66:        }
67:
68:        /* if we're creating a named pipe, the final parameter is
69:           ignored */
70:        if (mknod(path, mode, makedev(major, minor))) {
71:            fprintf(stderr, "mknod failed: %s\n", strerror(errno));
72:            return 1;
73:        }
74:
75:        return 0;
76: }
```

## 10.4.2 Creating Hard Links

When multiple file names in the file system refer to a single inode, the files are called **hard links** to one other. All the file names must reside in the same physical file system (normally, this means they must all be on the same device). When a file has multiple hard links, each of those file names is an exact peer—there is no way to tell which file name was originally used. One nice benefit of this model is that removing one hard link does not remove the file from the device—it stays until all the links to it are removed. The link() system call links a new file name to an existing inode.

```
#include <unistd.h>

int link(const char * origpath, const char * newpath);
```

The `origpath` refers to a pathname that already exists; `newpath` is the path for the new hard link. Any user may create a link to a file he has read access to, as long as he has write access for the directory in which he is creating the link and execute permissions on the directory `origpath` is in. Only the root user is allowed to create hard links to directories, but doing so is generally a bad idea, because most file systems and several utilities do not handle it very well.

## 10.4.3 Using Symbolic Links

Symbolic links are a more flexible type of link than hard links, but they do not share the peer relationship that hard links enjoy. Whereas hard links share an inode, symbolic links point to other file names. If the destination file name is removed, the symbolic link then points to a file that does not exist, resulting in a **dangling link**. Using symbolic links between subdirectories is common, and symbolic links may also cross physical file system boundaries, which hard links cannot.

Almost all system calls that access files by their pathname automatically follow symbolic links to find the proper inode. The following calls do not follow symbolic links under Linux:

- `chown()`

- `lstat()`

- `readlink()`

- `rename()`

- `unlink()`

Creating symbolic links is just like creating hard links, but the `symlink()` system call is used instead.

```
#include <unistd.h>

int symlink(const char * origpath, const char * newpath);
```

If the call is successful, the file newpath gets created as a symbolic link pointing to origpath (often newpath is said to *contain* oldpath as its value).

Finding the value of the symbolic link is a bit more complicated.

```
int readlink(const char * pathname, char * buf,
             size_t bufsiz);
```

The buffer that buf points to is filled in by the contents of the pathname symlink as long as buf is long enough to hold the contents. bufsize should contain the length of buf in bytes. Usually, the PATH_MAX constant is used for the size of the buffer, as that should be big enough to hold the contents of any symlink.[16] One oddity of readlink() is that it does not end the string it writes to buf with a '\0' character, so buf is not a valid C string even if readlink() succeeds. It instead returns the number of bytes written to buf on success, and -1 on error. Thanks to this quirk, code that uses readlink() often looks like this:

```
char buf[PATH_MAX + 1];
int bytes;

if ((bytes = readlink(pathname, buf, sizeof(buf) - 1)) < 0) {
    perror("error in readlink");
} else {
    buf[bytes] = '\0';
}
```

## 10.4.4 Removing Files

Removing a file removes the pointer to its inode and removes the file's data if there are no other hard links to the file. If any processes have the file open, the file's inode is preserved until the final process closes the file, and then the inode and the file's data are both discarded. As there is no way of forcing a file to be removed immediately, this operation is called **unlinking** the file, since it removes a file name/inode link.

---

16. Although PATH_MAX is not guaranteed to be large enough, it is, for all practical purposes. If you are dealing with pathological cases, you should call readlink() iteratively, making the buffer bigger until readlink() returns a value smaller than bufsiz.

```
#include <unistd.h>

int unlink(char * pathname);
```

## 10.4.5 Renaming Files

A file name may be changed to any other file name as long as both names are on the same physical partition (this is the same limit that applies to creating hard links). If the new file name already references a file, that name will be unlinked before the move takes place. The rename() system call is guaranteed to be atomic. Other processes on the system will always see the file in existence under one name or the other; there is no point at which the file does not exist under either name, nor under both names. As open files are not related to file names (only to inodes), renaming a file that other processes have open does not affect those other processes in any way. Here is what the system call looks like.

```
#include <unistd.h>

int rename(const char * oldpath, const char * newpath);
```

After the call, the file referenced by oldpath may be refenced by newpath, but not by oldpath.

# 10.5  Manipulating File Descriptors

Nearly all the file-related system calls we have talked about, with the exception of lseek(), manipulate a file's inode, which causes their results to be shared among processes that have the file open. There are a few system calls that instead act on the file descriptor itself. The fcntl() system call can be used for numerous file descriptor manipulations. fcntl() looks like this:

```
#include <fcntl.h>

int fcntl(int fd, int command, long arg);
```

For many commands, `arg` is not used. We discuss most of `fcntl()`'s uses here. It is also used for file locking and asynchronous I/O, which are discussed in Chapter 12.

## 10.5.1 Changing the Access Mode for an Open File

Both append mode (as indicated by the `O_APPEND` flag when the file is opened) and nonblocking mode (the `O_NONBLOCK` attribute) may be turned on and off after a file has already been opened through the `fcntl()`'s `F_SETFL` command. The `arg` parameter should be the flags that should be set—if one of the flags is not specified, it is turned off for `fd`.

`F_GETFL` may be used to query the current flags for the file. It returns all the flags, including the read status of the file. `F_SETFL` ignores extra flags that have been set in `arg`. This means that the code fragment

```
fcntl(fd, F_SETFL, fcntl(fd, F_GETFL, 0) | O_RDONLY);
```

is perfectly legal, but it does not accomplish anything. Turning on append mode for a file descriptor looks like this:

```
fcntl(fd, F_SETFL, fcntl(fd, F_GETFL, 0) | O_APPEND);
```

Note that care was taken to preserve the `O_NONBLOCK` setting. Turning append mode off looks similiar:

```
fcntl(fd, F_SETFL, fcntl(fd, F_GETFL, 0) & ~O_APPEND);
```

## 10.5.2 Modifiying the close-on-exec Flag

During an `exec()` system call, file descriptors are normally left open for the new program to use. In certain cases, you may wish to have files closed when you call `exec()`. Rather than closing them by hand, you can ask the system to close a certain file descriptor when `exec()` is called through `fcntl()`'s `F_GETFD` and `F_SETFD` commands. If the close-on-exec flag is set when `F_GETFD` is used, `fcntl()` returns non-0; otherwise, it returns 0. The close-on-exec flag is set through `F_SETFD`; it is disabled if `arg` is 0 and enabled otherwise.

Here is how you would force fd to be closed when the process exec()s:

```
fcntl(fd, F_SETFD, 1);
```

### 10.5.3 Duplicating File Descriptors

Occasionally, a process will want to create a new file descriptor that references a file that is already open. Shells use this functionality to redirect standard input, output, and error at the user's request. If the process does not care what file descriptor is used for the new reference, it should use dup().

```
#include <unistd.h>

int dup(int oldfd);
```

dup() returns a file descriptor that references the same inode as oldfd, or -1 on an error. The oldfd is still a valid file descriptor and still references the original file. The new file descriptor will always be the smallest file descriptor currently available. If the process needs the new file descriptor to have a particular value (such as 0 to change its standard input), it should use dup2() instead.

```
#include <unistd.h>

int dup2(int oldfd, int newfd);
```

If newfd references an already open file descriptor, that file descriptor is closed. If the call succeeds, it returns the new file descriptor and newfd references the same file as oldfd. This call is identical to using the F_DUPFD functionality of fcntl(), and dup2() could be implemented as follows.

```
int dup2(int oldfd, int newfd) {
    return fcntl(oldfd, F_DUPFD, newfd);
}
```

Creating two duped file descriptors that reference the same file is not the same as opening a file twice. Nearly all duped file descriptors' attributes are shared; they share a common current position, access mode, and locks.[17] The only attribute that can be independently controlled for the two file descriptors is their close-on-exec status. After the process has fork()ed, the parent's open files are inherited by the child, and those pairs of file descriptors (one in the parent and one in the new child) behave exactly like a file descriptor that has been duped with the current position and most other attributes being shared.[18]

# 10.6 Creating Unnamed Pipes

Unnamed pipes are similiar to named pipes, but they do not exist in the file system. They have no pathnames associated with them, and they and all their remnants disappear after the final file descriptor that references them is closed. They are almost exclusively used for interprocess communication between a child and parent processes or between sibling processes.

Shells use unnamed pipes to execute commands such as ls | head. The ls process writes to the same pipe that head reads its input from, yielding the results the user intended.

Creating an unnamed pipe results in two file descriptors, one of which is read-only and the other one of which is write-only.

```
#include <unistd.h>

int pipe(int fds[2]);
```

The sole parameter is filled in with the two returned file descriptors, fds[0] for reading and fds[1] for writing.

---

17. These items are stored in a **file structure**, one of which is created each time the file is opened. A file descriptor refers to a file structure, and dup()ed file descriptors refer to a single file structure.
18. The file descriptor in each process refers to the same file structure.

# 10.7 Adding Redirection to ladsh

Now that we have covered the basics of file manipulation, we can teach ladsh to redirect input and output through files and pipes. ladsh2, which we present here, handles pipes (denoted by a | in ladsh commands, just as in most shells) and input and output redirection for arbitrary file descriptors. We show only the modified pieces of code here—full source to ladsh2 is available from http://www.awl.com/cseng/books/lad/src/. The changes to parseCommand() are a simple exercise in string parsing, so we do not bother discussing them here.

## 10.7.1 The Data Structures

Although ladsh1 included the concept of a job as multiple processes (presumably tied together by pipes), it did not provide a way of specifying which files to use for a child's input and output. To allow for this, new data structures are introduced and existing ones modified.

```
enum redirectionType { REDIRECT_INPUT,
                       REDIRECT_OVERWRITE,
                       REDIRECT_APPEND };

struct redirectionSpecifier {
    enum redirectionType type;   /* type of redirection */
    int fd;                      /* file descriptor being redirected */
    char * filename;             /* file to redirect fd to */
};

struct childProgram {
    pid_t pid;                   /* 0 if exited */
    char ** argv;                /* program name and arguments */
    int numRedirections;         /* elements in redirection array */
    struct redirectionSpecifier * redirections;  /* I/O redirections */
};
```

struct redirectionSpecifier tells ladsh2 how to set up a single file descriptor. It contains an enum redirectionType that tells us whether this redirection is an input redirection, an output redirection that should be appended to an already existing file, or an output redirection that replaces any existing file. It also includes the file descriptor that is being redirected, as well as the name of the file involved. Each child program (`struct childProgram`) now specifies an arbitrary number of redirections for itself.

These new data structures are not involved in setting up pipes between processes. As a job is defined as multiple child processes with pipes tying them together, there is no need for more-explicit information describing the pipes.

## 10.7.2 Changing the Code

Once `parseCommand()` has set up the data structures properly, running the commands in the proper sequence is easy enough, as long as you watch the details. First of all, we added a loop to `runCommand()` to start the child processes, because there could now be multiple children. Before entering the loop, we set up `nextin` and `nextout`, which are the file descriptors to use for the standard input and the standard output of the next process we start. To begin with, we use the same stdin and stdout as the shell.

Now we take a look at what happens inside the loop. The basic idea is as follows:

1. If this is the final process in the job, make sure `nextout` points at stdout. Otherwise, we need to connect the output of this job to the input side of an unnamed pipe.

2. Fork the new process. Inside the child, redirect stdin and stdout as specified by `nextout`, `nextin`, and any file redirections that were specified.

3. Back in the parent, we close the `nextin` and `nextout` used by the just-started child (unless they are the shell's own stdin or stdout).

4. Now set up the next process in the job to receive its input from output of the process we just created (through `nextin`).

Here is how these ideas translate into C.

```
nextin = 0, nextout = 1;
for (i = 0; i < newJob.numProgs; i++) {
    if ((i + 1) < newJob.numProgs) {
        pipe(pipefds);
        nextout = pipefds[1];
    } else {
        nextout = 1;
    }

    if (!(newJob.progs[i].pid = fork())) {
        if (nextin != 0) {
            dup2(nextin, 0);
            close(nextin);
        }

        if (nextout != 1) {
            dup2(nextout, 1);
            close(nextout);
        }

        /* explicit redirections override pipes */
        setupRedirections(newJob.progs + i);

        execvp(newJob.progs[i].argv[0], newJob.progs[i].argv);
        fprintf(stderr, "exec() of %s failed: %s\n",
         newJob.progs[i].argv[0], strerror(errno));
        exit(1);
    }

    /* put our child in the process group whose leader is the
       first process in this pipe */
    setpgid(newJob.progs[i].pid, newJob.progs[0].pid);

    if (nextin != 0) close(nextin);
    if (nextout != 1) close(nextout);

    /* If there is not another process; nextin is garbage
       but it does not matter */
    nextin = pipefds[0];
}
```

The only other code added to ladsh2 to allow redirection was setupRedirections(), the source of which appears unchanged in all subsequent versions of ladsh. Its job is to process the struct redirectionSpecifier specifiers for a child job and modify the child's file descriptors as appropriate. We recommend reading over the function as it appears in Appendix B to ensure you understand its implementation.

# CHAPTER 11

# Directory Operations

Linux, like many other operating systems, uses directories to organize files. Directories (which are just special types of files that contain lists of file names) contain files, as well as other directories, allowing a file hierarchy to be built. All Linux systems have a root directory, known as /, through which (directly or indirectly) you access all the files on the system.

## 11.1 The Current Working Directory

### 11.1.1 Finding the Current Working Directory

The getcwd() function allows a process to find the name of its current directory relative to the system's root directory.

```
#include <unistd.h>
char * getcwd(char * buf, size_t size);
```

The first parameter, buf, points to a buffer that is filled in with the path to the current working directory. If the current path is larger than size - 1 bytes long (the - 1 allows the path to be '\0' terminated), the function returns an error of ERANGE. If the call succeeds, buf is returned; NULL is returned if an error occurs. Although most modern shells maintain a PWD environment variable that contains the path to the current directory, it will not necessarily have the same value a call to getcwd() would return. PWD often includes path elements that are symbolic links to other directories, but getcwd() will always return a path free from symbolic links.

If the current path is unknown (such as at program startup), the buffer that holds the current directory must be dynamically allocated because the current path may be arbitrarily large. Code that reads the current path properly looks like this:

```
char * buf;
int len = 50;

buf = malloc(len);
while (!getcwd(buf, len)) {
    len += 50;
    buf = realloc(buf, len);
}
```

Linux, along with many other Unix systems, provides a useful extension to the POSIX getcwd() specification. If buf is NULL, the function allocates a buffer large enough to contain the current path through the normal malloc() mechanism. Although the caller must take care to properly free() the result, using this extension can make code look much cleaner than using a loop as was shown in the earlier example.

BSD's getwd() function is a commonly used alternative to getcwd(), but it suffers from certain defects that led to the development of getcwd().

```
#include <unistd.h>
char * getwd(char * buf);
```

Like getcwd(), getwd() fills in buf with the current path, although the function has no idea how large buf is. getwd() will never write more than PATH_MAX (defined through <unistd.h>) to the buffer, which allows programs to avoid buffer overruns, but does not give the program any mechanism for finding the correct path if it is longer than PATH_MAX bytes![1] This function is supported by Linux only for legacy applications and should not be used by new applications. Instead, use the correct and more portable getcwd() function.

If the current directory path is displayed to users, it is normally a good idea to check the PWD environment variable. If it is set, it contains the path the user thinks he is using (which may contain symbolic links for some of the elements in the path), which is generally what the user would like an

---

1. That is right; PATH_MAX is not an actual limit. POSIX considers it **indeterminate**, which is morally equivalent to "do not use this."

application to display. To make this easier, Linux's C library provides the get_current_dir_name() function, which is implemented like this:

```
char * get_current_dir_name() {
    char * env = getenv("PWD");

    if (env)
        return strdup(env);
    else
        return getcwd(NULL, 0);
}
```

## 11.1.2 The . and .. Special Files

Every directory, including the root directory, includes two special files, called . and .., which are useful in some circumstances. The first, ., is the same as the current directory. This means that the file names somefile and ./somefile are equivalent.

The other special file name, .., is the current directory's parent directory. For the root directory, .. refers to the root directory (because the root directory has no parent).

Both . and .. can be used wherever a directory name can be used. It is common to see symbolic links refer to paths such as ../local/include/mylib, and file names like /./foo/.././bar/./fubar/../../usr/bin/less are perfectly legal (although admittedly convoluted).[2]

## 11.1.3 Changing the Current Directory

Two system calls change a process's current directory: chdir() and fchdir().

```
#include <unistd.h>
int chdir(const char * pathname);
int fchdir(int fd);
```

The first of these takes the name of a directory as its sole argument; the second takes a file descriptor that is an open directory. In either case, the

---

2. For the curious, that pathname is equivalent to the much simpler /usr/bin/less.

specified directory is made the current working directory. These functions can fail if their arguments specify a file that is not a directory or if the process does not have proper permissions.

# 11.2  Changing the Root Directory

Although the system has a single root directory, the meaning of / may be changed for each process on the system. This is usually done to prevent suspect processes (such as ftp daemons handling requests from untrusted users) from accessing the complete file system. For example, if /home/ftp is specified as the process's root directory, running chdir("/") will make the process's current directory /home/ftp, and getcwd() will return / to keep things consistent for the process in question. To ensure security, if the process tries to chdir("/.."), it is left in its / directory (the system-wide /home/ftp directory), just as normal processes that chdir("/..") are left in the system-wide root directory. A process may easily change its current root directory through the chroot() system call. The process's new root directory path will be interpreted with the current root directory in place, so chroot("/") does not modify the process's current root directory.

```
#include <unistd.h>
int chroot(const char * path);
```

Here the path specifies the new root directory for the process. This system call does *not* change the current working directory of the process, however. The process can still access files in the current directory, as well as relative to it (that is, ../../directory/file). Most processes that chroot() themselves immediately change their current working directory to be inside the new root hierarchy with chdir("/"), or something similiar, and not doing so would be a security problem in some applications.

# 11.3  Creating and Removing Directories

## 11.3.1  Creating New Directories

Creating new directories is straightforward.

```
#include <fcntl.h>
#include <unistd.h>
int mkdir(const char * dirname, mode_t mode);
```

The path specified by `dirname` is created as a new directory with permissions `mode` (which is modified by the process's umask). If `dirname` specifies an existing file or if any of the elements of `dirname` are not a directory or a symbolic link to a directory, the system call fails.

### 11.3.2 Removing Directories

Removing a directory is almost exactly the same as removing a file; only the name of the system call is different.

```
#include <unistd.h>
int rmdir(char * pathname);
```

For `rmdir()` to succeed, the directory must be empty (other than the omnipresent . and .. entries); otherwise, `ENOTEMPTY` is returned.

## 11.4 Reading a Directory's Contents

It is common for a program to need a list of the files contained in a directory. Linux provides a set of functions that allow a directory to be handled as an abstract entity to avoid forcing programs to depend on the exact format of directories employed by a file system. Opening and closing directories is straightforward.

```
#include <dirent.h>
DIR * opendir(const char * pathname);
int closedir(DIR * dir);
```

`opendir()` returns a pointer to a `DIR` data type, which is abstract (just like stdio's `FILE` structure) and should not be manipulated outside the C library. As directories may be opened only for reading, it is not necessary to specify what mode the directory will be opened with. `opendir()` fails if the directory exists—it cannot be used to create new directories (use mkdir() for that). Closing a directory can fail only if the dir parameter is invalid.

Once the directory has been opened, directory entries are read sequentially until the end of the directory is reached.

readdir() returns the name of the next file in the directory. Directories are not ordered in any way, so do not assume the contents of the directory will be sorted. If you need a sorted list of files, you must sort the file names yourself. The readdir() function is defined like this:

```
#include <dirent.h>
struct dirent * readdir(DIR * dir);
```

A pointer to a struct dirent is returned to the caller. Although struct dirent contains multiple fields, the only one that is portable is d_name, which holds the file name of the directory entry. The rest of struct dirent's members are system specific. The only interesting one of these is d_ino, which contains the inode number of the file.

The only tricky part of this is determining when an error has occurred. Unfortunately, readdir() returns NULL if an error occurs or if there are no more entries in the directory. To differentiate between the two cases, you must check errno. This task is made more difficult by readdir() not changing errno unless an error occurs, which means errno must be set to a known value (normally, 0) before calling readdir() to allow proper error checking. Here is a simple program that writes the names of the files in the current directory to stdout:

```
 1: /* dircontents.c - display all of the files in the current directory */
 2:
 3: #include <errno.h>
 4: #include <dirent.h>
 5: #include <stdio.h>
 6:
 7: int main(void) {
 8:     DIR * dir;
 9:     struct dirent * ent;
10:
11:     /* "." is the current directory */
12:     if (!(dir = opendir("."))) {
```

```
13:            perror("opendir");
14:            return 1;
15:        }
16:
17:        /* set errno to 0, so we can tell when readdir() fails */
18:        errno = 0;
19:        while ((ent = readdir(dir))) {
20:            puts(ent->d_name);
21:            /* reset errno, as puts() could modify it */
22:            errno = 0;
23:        }
24:
25:        if (errno) {
26:            perror("readdir");
27:            return 1;
28:        }
29:
30:        closedir(dir);
31:
32:        return 0;
33: }
```

## 11.4.1 Starting Over

If you need to reread the contents of a directory that has already been opened with opendir(), rewinddir() resets the DIR structure so that the next call to readdir() will return the first file in the directory.

```
#include <dirent.h>
int rewinddir(DIR * dir);
```

# 11.5 File Name Globbing

Most Linux users take it for granted that running ls *.c will not tell them all about the file in the current directory called *.c. Instead, they expect to see a list of all the file names in the current directory whose names end with .c. This file-name expansion from *.c to ladsh.c dircontents.c (for example) is normally handled by the shell, which **globs** all the parameters to programs it runs. Programs that help users manipulate files often need to glob file names, as well. There are two common ways to glob file names from inside a program.

## 11.5.1 Use a Subprocess

The oldest method is simply to run a shell as a child process and let it glob the file names for you. The standard popen()[3] function makes this simple—just run the command ls *.c through popen() and read the results. Although this may seem simplistic, it is a simple solution to the globbing problem and is highly portable (which is why applications like Perl use this approach).

Here is a program that globs all its arguments and displays all of the matches:

```
 1: #include <stdio.h>
 2: #include <string.h>
 3: #include <sys/wait.h>
 4: #include <unistd.h>
 5:
 6: int main(int argc, char ** argv) {
 7:     char buf[1024];
 8:     FILE * ls;
 9:     int result;
10:     int i;
11:
12:     strcpy(buf, "ls ");
13:
14:     for (i = 1; i < argc; i++) {
15:         strcat(buf, argv[i]);
16:         strcat(buf, " ");
17:     }
18:
19:     ls = popen(buf, "r");
20:     if (!ls) {
21:         perror("popen");
22:         return 1;
```

---

3. See page 119 for information on popen().

```
23:    }
24:
25:    while (fgets(buf, sizeof(buf), ls))
26:        printf("%s", buf);
27:
28:    result = pclose(ls);
29:
30:    if (!WIFEXITED(result)) return 1;
31:
32:    return 0;
33: }
```

## 11.5.2 Internal Globbing

If you need to glob many file names, running many subshells through popen() may be too inefficient. The glob() function allows you to glob file names without running any subprocesses, at the price of increased complexity and reduced portability. Although glob() is specified by POSIX.2, many Unix variants do not yet support it.

```
#include <glob.h>
int glob(const char *pattern, int flags,
        int errfunc(const char * epath, int eerrno), glob_t * pglob);
```

The first parameter, pattern, specifies the pattern that file names must match. This function understands the *, ?, and [] globbing operators and treats them identically to the standard shells. The final parameter is a pointer to a structure that gets filled in with the results of the glob. The structure is defined like this:

```
#include <glob.h>
typedef struct
    int gl_pathc;     /* number of paths in gl_pathv */
    char **gl_pathv;  /* list of gl_pathc matched pathnames */
    int gl_offs;      /* slots to reserve in gl_pathv for GLOB_DOOFS */
 glob_t;
```

The flags are of one or more of the following values logically OR'ed together:

GLOB_ERR    Returned if an error occurs (if the function cannot read the contents of a directory due to permissions problems, for example).

GLOB_MARK    If the pattern matches a directory name, that directory name will have a / appended to it on return.

GLOB_NOSORT    Normally, the returned pathnames are sorted alphabetically. If this flag is specified, they are not sorted.

GLOB_DOOFS    If set, the first pglob->gl_offs strings in the returned list of pathnames are left empty. This allows glob() to be used while building a set of arguments that will be passed directly to execv().

GLOB_NOCHECK    If no file names match the pattern, the pattern itself is returned as the sole match (usually, no matches are returned). In either case, if the pattern does not contain any globbing operators, the pattern is returned.

GLOB_APPEND    pglob is assumed to be a valid result from a previous call to glob(), and any results from this invocation will be appended to the results from the previous call. This makes it easy to glob multiple patterns.

GLOB_NOESCAPE    Usually, if a backslash (\) precedes a globbing operator, the operator is taken as a normal character instead of being assigned its special meaning. For example, the pattern a\* usually will match only a file named a*. If GLOB_NOESCAPE is specified, \ loses this special meaning, and a\* will match any file name that begins with the characters a\. In this case, a\ and a\bcd would be matched, but arachnid would not because it does not contain a \.

GLOB_PERIOD    Most shells do not allow glob operators to match files whose names begin with a . (try ls * in your home directory and compare it with ls -a .). The glob() function generally behaves this way, but GLOB_PERIOD allows the globbing operators to match a leading . character.

Often, glob() will encounter directories to which the process does not have access, which causes an error. Although the error may need to be handled in some manner, if the glob() returns the error (thanks to GLOB_ERR), there is no way to restart the globbing operation where the previous globbing operation encountered the error. As this makes it difficult both to handle errors that occur during a glob() and also to complete the glob, glob() allows the errors to be reported to a function of the caller's choice, which is specified in the third parameter to glob(). It should be prototyped as follows:

```
int globerr(const char * pathname, int globerrno);
```

The function is passed the pathname that caused the error and the errno value that resulted from one of opendir(), readdir(), or stat(). If the error function returns non-0, glob() returns with an error. Otherwise, the globbing operation is continued.

The results of the glob are stored in the glob_t structure referenced by pglob. It includes the following fields, which allow the caller to find the matched file names:

gl_pathc       The number of pathnames that matched the pattern

gl_pathv       Array of pathnames that matched the pattern

After the returned glob_t has been used, the memory it uses should be freed by passing it to globfree().

```
void globfree(glob_t * pglob);
```

glob() returns GLOB_NOSPACE if it ran out of memory, GLOB_ABEND if a read error caused the function to fail, GLOB_NOMATCH if no matches were found, or 0 if the function succeeded and found matches.

To help illustrate glob(), here is a program called globit, which accepts multiple patterns as arguments, globs them all, and displays the result. If an error occurs, a message describing the error is displayed, but the glob operation is continued.

```
1: /* globit.c - globs all of its arguments, and displays the matches */
2: #include <errno.h>
```

```
 3: #include <glob.h>
 4: #include <stdio.h>
 5: #include <string.h>
 6: #include <unistd.h>
 7:
 8: /* This is the error function we pass to glob(). It just displays
 9:    an error and returns success, which allows the glob() to
10:    continue. */
11: int errfn(const char * pathname, int theerr) {
12:     fprintf(stderr, "error accessing %s: %s\n", pathname,
13:             strerror(theerr));
14:
15:     /* We want the glob operation to continue, so return 0 */
16:     return 0;
17: }
18:
19: int main(int argc, char ** argv) {
20:     glob_t result;
21:     int i, rc, flags;
22:
23:     if (argc < 2) {
24:         printf("at least one argument must be given\n");
25:         return 1;
26:     }
27:
28:     /* set flags to 0; it gets changed to GLOB_APPEND later */
29:     flags = 0;
30:
31:     /* iterate over all of the command-line arguments */
32:     for (i = 1; i < argc; i++) {
33:         rc = glob(argv[i], flags, errfn, &result);
34:
35:         /* GLOB_ABEND can't happen thanks to errfn */
36:         if (rc == GLOB_NOSPACE) {
37:             fprintf(stderr, "out of space during glob operation\n");
38:             return 1;
39:         }
40:
41:         flags |= GLOB_APPEND;
42:     }
43:
```

```
44:     if (!result.gl_pathc) {
45:         fprintf(stderr, "no matches\n");
46:         rc = 1;
47:     } else {
48:         for (i = 0; i < result.gl_pathc; i++)
49:             puts(result.gl_pathv[i]);
50:         rc = 0;
51:     }
52:
53:     /* the glob structure uses memory from the malloc() pool, which
54:        needs to be freed */
55:     globfree(&result);
56:
57:     return rc;
58: }
```

# 11.6  Adding Directories and Globbing to ladsh

The evolution of ladsh continues here by adding three new features to ladsh3.

1.  The cd built-in, to change directories

2.  The pwd built-in, to display the current directory

3.  File name globbing

## 11.6.1 Adding cd **and** pwd

Adding the built-in commands is a straightforward application of chdir() and getcwd(). The code fits into runProgram() right where all the other built-in commands are handled.  Here is how the built-in command-handling section looks in ladsh3.

```
if (!strcmp(newJob.progs[0].argv[0], "exit")) {
    /* this should return a real exit code */
    exit(0);
```

```
} else if (!strcmp(newJob.progs[0].argv[0], "pwd")) {
    len = 50;
    buf = malloc(len);
    while (!getcwd(buf, len)) {
        len += 50;
        buf = realloc(buf, len);
    }
    printf("%s\n", buf);
    free(buf);
    continue;
} else if (!strcmp(newJob.progs[0].argv[0], "cd")) {
    if (!newJob.progs[0].argv[1] == 1)
        newdir = getenv("HOME");
    else
        newdir = newJob.progs[0].argv[1];
    if (chdir(newdir))
        printf("failed to change current directory: %s\n",
                strerror(errno));
    continue;
} else if (!strcmp(newJob.progs[0].argv[0], "jobs")) {
    for (job = bgJobs->head; job; job = job->next)
        printf(JOB_STATUS_FORMAT, job->jobId, '-', "Running",
                job->text);
    continue;
}
```

## 11.6.2 Adding File Name Globbing

File name globbing, in which the shell expands the *, [], and ? characters into matching file names, is a bit tricky to implement because of the various quoting methods. The first modification to make is to build up each argument as a string suitable for passing to glob(). If a globbing character is quoted by a shell quoting sequence (enclosed in double quotes, for example), then the globbing character is prefixed by a \ to prevent glob() from expanding it. Although this sounds tricky, it is easy to do.

Two parts of parseCommand()'s command parsing need to be slightly modified. The " and ' sequences are handled near the top of the loop, which splits a command string into arguments. If we are in the middle of a quoted string and we encounter a globbing character, we quote the globbing character with a \ while parsing it, which looks like this:

```
} else if (quote) {
    if (*src == '\\') {
        src++;
        if (!*src) {
            fprintf(stderr, "character expected after \\\n");
            freeJob(job);
            return 1;
        }

        /* in shell, "\'" should yield \' */
        if (*src != quote) *buf++ = '\\';
    } else if (*src == '*' || *src == '?' || *src == '[' ||
            *src == ']')    /* check for quoted globbing characters */
        *buf++ = '\\';
    *buf++ = *src;
} else if (isspace(*src)) {
```

Only the middle `else if` and the assignment statement in its body were added to the code. Similar code needs to be added to the handling of \ characters that occur outside quoted strings. This case is handled at the end of `parseCommand()`'s main loop. Here is the modified code:

```
case '\\':
  src++;
  if (!*src) {
      freeJob(job);
      fprintf(stderr, "character expected after \\\n");
      return 1;
  }
  if (*src == '*' || *src == '[' || *src == ']' || *src == '?')
      *buf++ = '\\';
  /* fallthrough */
default:
  *buf++ = *src;
```

The same code was added here to quote the globbing characters.

Those two sequences of code ensure that each argument may be passed to `glob()` without finding unintended matches. Now we add a function, globLastArgument(), which globs the most recently found argument for a child program and replaces it with whatever matches it finds.

To help ease the memory management, a glob_t called globResult, which is used to hold the results of all glob operations, has been added to struct childProgram. We also added an integer, freeGlob, which is non-0 if freeJob() should free the globResult contained in the structure.

The first time globLastArgument() is run for a command string (when argc for the current child is 1), it initializes globResult. For the rest of the arguments, it takes advantage of GLOB_APPEND to add new matches to the end of the existing matches. This prevents us from having to allocate our own memory for globbing because our single glob_t is automatically expanded as necessary.

If globLastArgument() does not find any matches, the quoting \ characters are removed from the argument. Otherwise, all the new matches are copied into the list of arguments being constructed for the child program.

Here is the complete implementation of globLastArgument(). All the tricky parts are related to memory management; the actual globbing is similiar to the globit sample program presented earlier in this chapter.

```
void globLastArgument(struct childProgram * prog, int * argcPtr,
                      int * argcAllocedPtr) {
    int argc = *argcPtr;
    int argcAlloced = *argcAllocedPtr;
    int rc;
    int flags;
    int i;
    char * src, * dst;

    if (argc > 1) {          /* cmd->globResult is already initialized */
        flags = GLOB_APPEND;
        i = prog->globResult.gl_pathc;
    } else {
        prog->freeGlob = 1;
        flags = 0;
        i = 0;
    }
```

```
        rc = glob(prog->argv[argc - 1], flags, NULL, &prog->globResult);
        if (rc == GLOB_NOSPACE) {
            fprintf(stderr, "out of space during glob operation\n");
            return;
        } else if (rc == GLOB_NOMATCH ||
                    (!rc && (prog->globResult.gl_pathc - i) == 1 &&
                     !strcmp(prog->argv[argc - 1],
                            prog->globResult.gl_pathv[i]))) {
            /* we need to remove whatever \ quoting is still present */
            src = dst = prog->argv[argc - 1];
            while (*src) {
                if (*src != '\\') *dst++ = *src;
                src++;
            }
            *dst = '\0';
        } else if (!rc) {
            argcAlloced += (prog->globResult.gl_pathc - i);
            prog->argv = realloc(prog->argv,
                            argcAlloced * sizeof(*prog->argv));
            memcpy(prog->argv + (argc - 1), prog->globResult.gl_pathv + i,
                    sizeof(*(prog->argv)) * (prog->globResult.gl_pathc - i));
            argc += (prog->globResult.gl_pathc - i - 1);
        }

    *argcAllocedPtr = argcAlloced;
    *argcPtr = argc;
}
```

The final changes are the calls to `globLastArgument()` that need to be made once a new argument has been parsed. The calls are added in two places: when white space is found outside a quoted string and when the entire command string has been parsed. Both of the calls look like this:

```
globLastArgument(prog, &argc, &argvAlloced);
```

The complete source code for `ladsh3` is available on the LAD Web site at http://www.awl.com/cseng/books/lad/src/.

# CHAPTER 12

# Advanced File Handling

Files are used for a large number of tasks in the Linux world, such as persistent data storage in regular files, networking through sockets, and device access through device files. The variety of applications for files has led to the development of many specialized ways of manipulating files. Chapter 10 introduced the most common operations on files, and this chapter discusses some more specialized file operations. In this chapter, we cover using multiple files simultaneously, mapping files into system memory, file locking, and scatter/gather reads and writes.

## 12.1 Input and Output Multiplexing

Many client/server applications need to read input from or write output to multiple file descriptors at a time. For example, modern Web browsers open many simultaneous network connections to reduce the loading time for a Web page. This allows them to download the multiple images that appear on most Web pages more quickly than consecutive connections would allow. Along with the IPC channel that graphical browsers use to contact the X server they are displayed on, browsers have many file descriptors to keep track of.

The easiest way to handle all these files is for the browser to read from each file in turn and process whatever data that file delivers (a system call on a network connection, as on a pipe, returns whatever data is currently available and blocks only if no bytes are ready). This approach works fine, as long as all the connections are delivering data fairly regularly. If one of the network connections gets behind, problems start. When the browser next reads from that file, the browser stops running while the read() blocks, waiting for data to arrive. Needless to say, this is not the behavior the browser's user would prefer.

To help illustrate these problems, here is a short program that reads from two files: p1 and p2. To try it, open three X terminal sessions (or use three virtual consoles). Make named pipes named p1 and p2 (with the mknod command), then run cat > p1 and cat > p2 in two of the terminals while running mpx-blocks in the third. Once everything is running, type some text in each of the cat windows and watch how it appears. Remember that the two cat commands will not write any data into the pipes until the end of a line.

```
 1: /* mpx-blocks.c -- reads input from pipes p1, p2 alternately */
 2:
 3: #include <fcntl.h>
 4: #include <stdio.h>
 5: #include <unistd.h>
 6:
 7: int main(void) {
 8:     int fds[2];
 9:     char buf[4096];
10:     int i;
11:     int fd;
12:
13:     if ((fds[0] = open("p1", O_RDONLY)) < 0) {
14:         perror("open p1");
15:         return 1;
16:     }
17:
18:     if ((fds[1] = open("p2", O_RDONLY)) < 0) {
19:         perror("open p2");
20:         return 1;
21:     }
22:
23:     fd = 0;
24:     while (1) {
25:         /* if data is available read it and display it */
26:         i = read(fds[fd], buf, sizeof(buf) - 1);
27:         if (i < 0) {
```

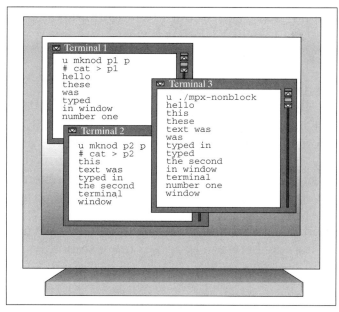

**Figure 12.1** Running Multiplex Examples

```
28:                    perror("read");
29:                    return 1;
30:            } else if (!i) {
31:                printf("pipe closed\n");
32:                return 0;
33:            }
34:
35:            buf[i] = '\0';
36:            printf("read: %s", buf);
37:
38:            /* read from the other file descriptor */
39:            fd = (fd + 1) % 2;
40:    }
41: }
```

Although mpx-blocks does read from both pipes, it does not do a very nice
job of it. It reads from only one pipe at a time. When it starts, it reads from
the first file until data becomes available on it; the second file is ignored
until the read() from the first file returns. Once that read does return, the
first file is ignored until data is read from the second file. This method does

not perform anything like smooth data multiplexing. Figure 12.1 shows what mpx-blocks looks like when it is run.

## 12.1.1 Nonblocking I/O

Recall from Chapter 10 that we may specify a file is nonblocking through the fcntl() system call. When a slow file is nonblocking, read() always returns immediately. If no data is available, it simply returns 0. Nonblocking I/O provides a simple solution to multiplexing by preventing operations on files from ever blocking.

Here is a modified version of mpx-blocks that takes advantage of nonblocking I/O to alternate between p1 and p2 more smoothly.

```
 1: /* mpx-nonblock.c -- reads input from pipes p1, p2 using
 2:    nonblocking i/o */
 3:
 4: #include <fcntl.h>
 5: #include <stdio.h>
 6: #include <unistd.h>
 7:
 8: int main(void) {
 9:     int fds[2];
10:     char buf[4096];
11:     int i;
12:     int fd;
13:
14:     /* open both pipes in nonblocking mode */
15:     if ((fds[0] = open("p1", O_RDONLY | O_NONBLOCK)) < 0) {
16:         perror("open p1");
17:         return 1;
18:     }
19:
20:     if ((fds[1] = open("p2", O_RDONLY | O_NONBLOCK)) < 0) {
21:         perror("open p2");
22:         return 1;
23:     }
24:
25:     fd = 0;
26:     while (1) {
```

```
27:          /* if data is available read it and display it */
28:          i = read(fds[fd], buf, sizeof(buf) - 1);
29:          if (i < 0) {
30:              perror("read");
31:              return 1;
32:          } else if (i) {
33:              buf[i] = '\0';
34:              printf("read: %s", buf);
35:          }
36:
37:          /* read from the other file descriptor */
38:          fd = (fd + 1) % 2;
39:      }
40: }
```

One important difference between `mpx-nonblock` and `mpx-blocks` is that `mpx-nonblock` does not exit when one of the pipes it is reading from is closed. Unfortunately, end-of-file on a pipe is indicated by a `read()` that returns 0 bytes, which is the same result nonblocking I/O gives on an empty pipe!

Although nonblocking I/O allows us to switch easily between file descriptors, it has a high price. The program is always polling the two file descriptors for input—it *never* blocks. As the program is constantly running, it inflicts a heavy performance penalty on the system as the operating system can never put the process to sleep (try running 10 copies of `mpx-nonblock` on your system and see how it affects system performance).

## 12.1.2 Multiplexing with `select()`

To allow efficient multiplexing, Unix provides the `select()` system call, which allows a process to block on multiple file descriptors simultaneously. Rather than constantly check each file descriptor it is interested in, a process makes a single system call that specifies which file descriptors the process would like to read from or write to. When one or more of those files have data available for reading or can accept data written to them, the `select()` returns and the application can read and write from those file descriptors without worrying about blocking. Once those files have been handled, the process makes another `select()` call, which blocks until a file is ready for more attention. Here is what the `select()` system call looks like:

```
#include <sys/time.h>
#include <sys/types.h>
#include <unistd.h>

int select(int numfds, fd_set * readfds, fd_set * writefds,
        fd_set * exceptfds, struct timeval * timeout);
```

The middle three parameters, readfds, writefds, and exceptfds, specify which file descriptors should be watched. Each parameter is a pointer to a fd_set, a data structure that allows a process to specify an arbitrary number of file descriptors.[1] It is manipulated through the following macros:

FD_ZERO(fd_set * fds);
> Clears fds—no file descriptors are contained in the set. This macro is used to initialize fd_set structures.

FD_SET(int fd, fd_set * fds);
> Adds fd to the fd_set.

FD_CLR(int fd, fd_set * fds);
> Removes fd from the fd_set.

FD_ISSET(int fd, fd_set * fds);
> Returns true if fd is contained in set fds.

The first of select()'s file descriptor sets, readfds, contains the set of file descriptors that will cause the select() call to return when they are ready to be read from[2] or (for pipes and sockets) when the process on the other end of the file has closed the file. When any of the file descriptors in writefds are ready to be written, select() returns. exceptfds contains the file descriptors to watch for exceptional conditions. Under Linux (as well as Unix), this occurs only when out-of-band data[3] has been received on a network connection. Any of these may be NULL if you are not interested in that type of event.

---

1. This is similiar to sigset_t used for signal masks.
2. When a network socket being listen()ed to is ready to be accept()ed, it is considered ready to be read from for select()'s purposes; information on sockets is in Chapter 16.
3. This is almost the only place in this book you will see out-of-band data mentioned. For more information, consult [Stevens, 1990].

The final parameter, `timeout`, specifies how long the `select()` call should wait for something to happen. It is a pointer to a `struct timeval`, which looks like this:

```
#include <sys/time.h>

struct timeval {
    int tv_sec;     /* seconds */
    int tv_usec;    /* microseconds */
};
```

The first element, `tv_sec`, is the number of seconds to wait, and `tv_usec` is the number of microseconds to wait. If the `timeout` value is `NULL`, `select()` will block until something happens. If it points to a `struct timeval` that contains zero in both its elements, `select()` will not block. It updates the file descriptor sets to indicate which file descriptors are currently ready for reading or writing, then returns immediately.

The first parameter, `numfds`, causes the most difficulty. It specifies how many of the file descriptors (starting from file descriptor 0) may be specified by the `fd_set`s. Another (and perhaps easier) way of thinking of `numfds` is as one greater than the maximum file descriptor `select()` is meant to consider. As Linux normally allows each process to have up to 1,024 file descriptors, `numfds` prevents the kernel from having to look through all 1,024 file descriptors each `fd_set` could contain, providing a performance increase.

On return, the three `fd_set` structures contain the file descriptors that have input pending, may be written to, or are in an exceptional condition. Linux's `select()` call returns the total number of items set in the three `fd_set` structures, 0 if the call timed out, or -1 if an error occurred. However, many Unix systems will count a particular file descriptor in the return value only once, even if it occurs in both `readfds` and `writefds`, so for portability, it is a good idea to check only whether the return value is greater than 0. If the return value is -1, do not assume the `fd_set` structures remain pristine. Linux updates them only if `select()` returns a value greater than 0, but some Unix systems behave differently.

Another portability concern is the `timeout` parameter. Linux kernels[4] update it to reflect the amount of time left before the `select()` call would have

---

4. Except for some experimental kernels in the 2.1 series.

timed out, but most other Unix systems do not update it.[5] However, other systems do not update the timeout, to conform to the more common implementation. For portability, do not depend on either behavior and explicitly set the timeout structure before calling select().

Now let's look at a couple of examples of using select(). First of all, we use select for something unrelated to files, constructing a subsecond sleep() call.

```
#include <sys/time.h>
#include <sys/types.h>
#include <unistd.h>

int usecsleep(int usecs) {
    struct timeval tv;

    tv.tv_sec = 0;
    tv.tv_usec = usecs;

    return select(0, NULL, NULL, NULL, &tv);
}
```

This code allows highly portable pauses of less than one second (which BSD's usleep() library function allows, as well, but select() is much more portable). For example, usecsleep(500000) causes a minimum of a half-second pause.

Now that we have seen a simple example of select(), let's look at a cleaner solution to the pipe multiplexing example we discussed earlier.

Rather than check each file descriptor in turn, the way we needed to when we used nonblocking I/O, we select() on both input pipes simultaneously. When the select() returns, we check the fd_set that was originally passed. After select() returns, the file descriptor set will include only file descriptors that are ready to be read from. Remembering that closed files are marked as ready to be read from, we check the pipes, possibly marking

---

5. When Linus Torvalds first implemented select(), the BSD man page for select() listed the BSD kernel's failure to update the timeout as a bug. Rather than write buggy code, Linus decided to "fix" this bug. Unfortunately, the standards commitees decided they liked BSD's behavior.

them as closed.  After checking them, we again select() on the open pipes.
Here is mpx-select.

```
 1: /* mpx-select.c -- reads input from pipes p1, p2 using
 2:    select() for multiplexing */
 3:
 4: #include <fcntl.h>
 5: #include <stdio.h>
 6: #include <sys/time.h>
 7: #include <sys/types.h>
 8: #include <unistd.h>
 9:
10: int main(void) {
11:     int fds[2];
12:     char buf[4096];
13:     int i, rc, maxfd;
14:     fd_set watchset;        /* fds to read from */
15:     fd_set inset;           /* updated by select() */
16:
17:     /* open both pipes */
18:     if ((fds[0] = open("p1", O_RDONLY | O_NONBLOCK)) < 0) {
19:         perror("open p1");
20:         return 1;
21:     }
22:
23:     if ((fds[1] = open("p2", O_RDONLY | O_NONBLOCK)) < 0) {
24:         perror("open p2");
25:         return 1;
26:     }
27:
28:     /* start off reading from both file descriptors */
29:     FD_ZERO(&watchset);
30:     FD_SET(fds[0], &watchset);
31:     FD_SET(fds[1], &watchset);
32:
33:     /* find the maximum file descriptor */
34:     maxfd = fds[0] > fds[1] ? fds[0] : fds[0];
35:
36:     /* while we're watching one of fds[0] or fds[1] */
37:     while (FD_ISSET(fds[0], &watchset) ||
38:            FD_ISSET(fds[1], &watchset)) {
39:         /* we copy watchset here because select() updates it */
```

```
40:          inset = watchset;
41:          if (select(maxfd + 1, &inset, NULL, NULL, NULL) < 0) {
42:              perror("select");
43:              return 1;
44:          }
45:
46:          /* check to see which file descriptors are ready to be
47:             read from */
48:          for (i = 0; i < 2; i++) {
49:              if (FD_ISSET(fds[i], &inset)) {
50:                  /* fds[i] is ready for reading, go ahead... */
51:                  rc = read(fds[i], buf, sizeof(buf) - 1);
52:                  if (rc < 0) {
53:                      perror("read");
54:                      return 1;
55:                  } else if (!rc) {
56:                      /* this pipe has been closed, don't try
57:                         to read from it again */
58:                      close(fds[i]);
59:                      FD_CLR(fds[i], &watchset);
60:                  } else {
61:                      buf[rc] = '\0';
62:                      printf("read: %s", buf);
63:                  }
64:              }
65:          }
66:      }
67:
68:      return 0;
69: }
```

Note that the core of this program consists of two nested loops rather than the single loop the previous examples used. This program gives the same result as the version that used nonblocking I/O, but it places substantially less load on the machine because it blocks on the select() call.

## 12.2  Memory Mapping

Linux allows a process to map files into its address space. Such a mapping creates a one-to-one correspondence between data in the file and data in the mapped memory region. Memory mapping has a number of applications.

1. High-speed file access. Normal I/O mechanisms, such as `read()` and `write()`, force the kernel to copy the data through a kernel buffer rather than directly between the file that holds the device and the user-space process. Memory maps eliminate this middle buffer, saving a memory copy.[6]

2. Executable files can be mapped into a program's memory, allowing a program to dynamically load new executable sections. This is how dynamic loading, described in Chapter 25, is implemented.

3. New memory can be allocated by mapping portions of /dev/zero, a special device that is full of zeros,[7] or through an anonymous mapping. Electric Fence, described in Chapter 6, uses this mechanism to allocate memory.

4. New memory allocated through memory maps can be made executable, allowing it to be filled with machine instructions, which are then executed. This feature is used by just-in-time compilers.

5. Files can be treated just like memory and read using pointers instead of system calls. This can greatly simplify programs by eliminating the need for `read()`, `write()`, and `lseek()` calls.

6. Memory mapping allows processes to share memory regions that persist across process creation and destruction. The memory contents are stored in the mapped file, making it independent of any process.

---

6. Although saving a memory copy may not seem that important, thanks to Linux's efficient caching mechanism, these copy latencies are the slowest part of writing to data files that do not have `O_SYNC` set.
7. Although most character devices do not allow themselves to be mapped, /dev/zero does so for exactly this type of application

## 12.2.1 Page Alignment

System memory is divided into chunks called **pages**. On Intel and SPARC machines, each page is 4,096 bytes (4K), whereas the Alpha has 8,192-byte (8K) pages. The getpagesize() function returns the size, in bytes, of each page on the system.

```
#include <unistd.h>

size_t getpagesize(void);
```

For each page on the system, the kernel tells the hardware how each process may access the page (such as write, execute, or not at all). When a process attempts to access a page in a manner that violates the kernel's restrictions, a segmentation fault (SIGSEGV) results, which normally terminates the process.

A memory address is said to be **page aligned** if it is the address of the beginning of a page. In other words, the address must be an integral multiple of the architecture's page size. On a system with 4K pages, 0, 4,096, 16,384, and 32,768 are all page-aligned addresses (of course, there are many more) because the first, second, fifth, and ninth pages in the system begin at those addresses.

## 12.2.2 Establishing Memory Mappings

New memory maps are created by the mmap() system call.

```
#include <sys/mman.h>

caddr_t mmap(caddr_t address, size_t length, int protection, int flags,
             int fd, off_t offset);
```

The address specifies where in memory the data should be mapped. Normally, address is NULL, which means the process does not care where the new mapping is, allowing the kernel to pick any address. If an address is specified, it must be page aligned and not already in use. If the requested mapping would conflict with another mapping or would not be page aligned, mmap() may fail.

**Table 12.1** `mmap()` Protections

| Flag | Description |
|---|---|
| PROT_READ | The mapped region may be read. |
| PROT_WRITE | The mapped region may be written. |
| PROT_EXEC | The mapped region may be executed. |

**Table 12.2** `mmap()` Flags

| Flag | POSIX? | Description |
|---|---|---|
| MAP_ANONYMOUS | yes | Ignore fd, create an anonymous mapping. |
| MAP_FIXED | yes | Fail if address is invalid. |
| MAP_PRIVATE | yes | Writes are private to process. |
| MAP_SHARED | yes | Writes are copied to the file. |
| MAP_DENYWRITE | no | Do not allow normal writes to the file. |
| MAP_GROWSDOWN | no | Grow the memory region downward. |
| MAP_LOCKED | no | Lock the pages into memory. |

The second parameter, `length`, tells the kernel how much of the file to map into memory. You can successfully map more memory than the file has data, but attempting to access it may result in a SIGSEGV.[8]

The process controls which types of access are allowed to the new memory region. It should be one or more of the values from Table 12.1 logically OR'ed together, or PROT_NONE if no access to the mapped region should be allowed. A file can be mapped only for access types that were also requested when the file was originally opened. For example, a file that was opened O_RDONLY cannot be mapped for writing with PROT_WRITE.

The enforcement of the specified protection is limited by the hardware plat-form on which the program is running. Many architectures cannot allow code to execute in a memory region while disallowing reading from that memory region. On such hardware, mapping a region with PROT_EXEC is equivalent to mapping it with PROC_EXEC | PROT_READ. The memory protec-tions passed to `mmap()` should be relied on only as minimal protections for this reason.

The `flags` specify other attributes of the mapped region. Table 12.2 summa-rizes all the flags. Many of the flags that Linux supports are not standard

---

8. A segmentation fault will result when you try to access an unallocated page.

but may be useful in special circumstances. Table 12.2 differentiates between the standard `mmap()` flags and Linux's extra flags. All calls to `mmap()` must specify one of `MAP_PRIVATE` or `MAP_SHARED`; the remainder of the flags are optional.

| | |
|---|---|
| MAP_ANONYMOUS | Rather than mapping a file, an **anonymous mapping** is returned. It behaves like a normal mapping, but no physical file is involved. Although this memory region cannot be shared with other processes, nor is it automatically saved to a file, anonymous mappings allow processes to allocate new memory for private use. Such mapping is often used by implementations of `malloc()`, as well as by more-specialized applications. The `fd` parameter is ignored if this flag is used. |
| MAP_FIXED | If the mapping cannot be placed at the requested `address`, `mmap()` fails. If this flag is not specified, the kernel will try to place the map at `address` but will map it at an alternate address if it cannot. |
| MAP_PRIVATE | Modifications to the memory region should be private to the process, neither shared with other processes that map the same file (other than related processes that are forked after the memory map is created) nor reflected in the file itself. Either `MAP_SHARED` or `MAP_PRIVATE` must be used. If the memory region is not writeable, it does not matter which is used. |
| MAP_SHARED | Changes that are made to the memory region are copied back to the file that was mapped and shared with other processes that are mapping the same file. `PROT_WRITE` must have been specified, or else the memory region will be immutable. Either `MAP_SHARED` or `MAP_PRIVATE` must be specified. |
| MAP_DENYWRITE | Usually, regular file calls (like `write()`) may modify a mapped file. If the region is being executed, this may not be a good idea, however. `MAP_DENYWRITE` causes writes to the file, other than those writes done through memory maps, to return `ETXTBSY`. |

MAP_GROWSDOWN  Trying to access the memory immediately before a mapped region normally causes a SIGSEGV. This flag tells the kernel to allocate a new anonymous region before this one if a process tries to access the memory there and continue the process as normal. This is used to allow the kernel to automatically grow processes' stacks.[9]

The only limit on MAP_GROWSDOWN is the stack-size resource limit, discussed on pages 107–109. If no limit is set, the kernel will grow the mapped segment whenever doing so would be beneficial. It will not grow the segment past other mapped regions, however.

MAP_LOCKED  The region is **locked** into memory, meaning it will never get swapped. This is important for real-time applications (mlock(), discussed on page 222, provides another method for memory locking). This may be specified only by the root user; normal users cannot lock pages into memory.

After the flags comes the file descriptor, fd, for the file that is to be mapped into memory. If MAP_ANONYMOUS was used, this value is ignored. The final parameter specifies where in the file the mapping should begin, and it must be an integral multiple of the page size. Most applications begin the mapping from the start of the file by specifying a 0 offset.

mmap() returns an address that should be stored in a pointer. If an error occurred, it returns the address that is equivalent to -1. To test for this, the -1 constant should be typecast to a caddr_t rather than typecasting the returned address to an int. This ensures you will get the right result no matter what the sizes of pointers and integers.

Here is a program that acts like cat and expects a single name as a command-line argument. It opens that file, maps it into memory, and writes the entire file to standard output through a single write() call. It may

---

9. Although it may seem odd that the kernel does not provide a MAP_GROWSUP for machines that have their stack growing in the opposite direction, the Linux kernel does not run on any machines on which the stack grows up. If Linux is ever ported to such a system, a MAP_GROWSUP flag will presumably be introduced.

be instructional to compare this example with the simple cat implementation on page 160. This example also illustrates that memory mappings stay in place after the mapped file is closed.

```
 1: /* map-cat.c - simple cat-like program which uses memory mapping */
 2:
 3: #include <errno.h>
 4: #include <fcntl.h>
 5: #include <sys/mman.h>
 6: #include <sys/stat.h>
 7: #include <sys/types.h>
 8: #include <stdio.h>
 9: #include <unistd.h>
10:
11: int main(int argc, char ** argv) {
12:     int fd;
13:     struct stat sb;
14:     void * region;
15:
16:     if ((fd = open(argv[1], O_RDONLY)) < 0) {
17:         perror("open");
18:         return 1;
19:     }
20:
21:     /* stat the file so we know how much of it to map into memory */
22:     if (fstat(fd, &sb)) {
23:         perror("fstat");
24:         return 1;
25:     }
26:
27:     /* we could just as well map it MAP_PRIVATE as we aren't writing
28:        to it anyway */
29:     region = mmap(NULL, sb.st_size, PROT_READ, MAP_SHARED, fd, 0);
30:     if (region == ((caddr_t) -1)) {
31:         perror("mmap");
32:         return 1;
33:     }
34:
35:     close(fd);
36:
37:     if (write(1, region, sb.st_size) != sb.st_size) {
```

```
38:        perror("write");
39:        return 1;
40:    }
41:
42:    return 0;
43: }
```

### 12.2.3 Unmapping Regions

After a process is finished with a memory mapping, it can unmap the memory region through munmap(). This causes future accesses to that adddress to cause a SIGSEGV (unless the memory is subsequently remapped) and saves some system resources. All memory regions are unmapped when a process terminates or begins a new program through an exec() system call.

```
#include <sys/mman.h>

int munmap(caddr_t addr, int length);
```

The addr is the address of the beginning of the memory region to unmap, and length specifies how much of the memory region should be unmapped. Normally, each mapped region is unmapped by a single munmap() call. Linux can fragment maps if only a portion of a mapped region is unmapped, but this is not a portable technique.

### 12.2.4 Syncing Memory Regions to Disk

If a memory map is being used to write to a file, the modified memory pages and the file will be different for a period of time. If a process wishes to immediately write the pages to disk, it may use msync().

```
#include <sys/mman.h>

int msync(caddr_t addr, size_t length, int flags);
```

The first two parameters, addr and length, specify the region to sync to disk. The flags parameter specifies how the memory and disk should be synchronized. It consists of one or more of the following flags logically OR'ed together:

MS_ASYNC            The modified portions of the memory region are sched-
                    uled to be synchronized "soon." Only one of MS_ASYNC
                    and MS_SYNC may be used.

MS_SYNC             The modified pages in the memory region are written to
                    disk before the msync() system call returns. Only one of
                    MS_ASYNC and MS_SYNC may be used.

MS_INVALIDATE       This option lets the kernel decide whether the changes
                    are ever written to disk. Although this does not ensure
                    they will not be written, it tells the kernel that it does not
                    have to save the changes. This flag is used only under
                    special circumstances.

## 12.2.5 Locking Memory Regions

Under Linux and most other modern operating systems, memory regions
may be paged to disk (or discarded if they can be replaced in some other
manner) when memory becomes scarce. Applications that are sensitive
to external timing constraints may be adversely affected by the delay that
results from the kernel paging memory back into RAM when the process
needs it. To make these applications more robust, Linux allows a process to
**lock** memory in RAM to make these timings more predictable. For security
reasons, only processes running with root permission may lock memory.[10]
If any process could lock regions of memory, a rogue process could lock
all the system's RAM, making the system unuseable. The total amount of
memory locked by a process cannot exceed its RLIMIT_MEMLOCK usage limit.[11]

The following calls are used to lock and unlock memory regions:

```
#include <sys/mman.h>

int mlock(caddr_t addr, size_t length);
int mlockall(int flags);
int munlock(caddr_t addr, size_t length);
int munlockall(void);
```

10. This may change in the future as finer-grained system permissions are imple-
    mented in the kernel.
11. See pages 105–106 for information on resource limits.

The first of these, mlock(), locks length bytes starting at address addr. An entire page of memory must be locked at a time, so mlock() actually locks all the pages between the page containing the first address and the page containing the final address to lock, inclusively. When mlock() returns, all the affected pages will be in RAM.

If a process wants to lock its entire address space, mlockall() should be used. The flags argument is one or both of the following flags logically OR'ed together:

MCL_CURRENT     All the pages currently in the process's address space are locked into RAM. They will all be in RAM when mlockall() returns.

MCL_FUTURE      All pages added to the process's address space will be locked into RAM.

Unlocking memory is nearly the same as locking it. If a process no longer needs any of its memory locked, munlockall() will unlock all the process's pages. munlock() takes the same arguments as mlock() and unlocks the pages containing the indicated region.

Locking a page multiple times is equivalent to locking it once. In either case, a single call to munlock() will unlock the affected pages.

# 12.3  **File Locking**

Although it is common for multiple processes to access a single file, doing so needs to be done carefully. Many files include complex data structures, and updating those data structures creates the same race conditions involved in signal handlers and shared memory regions.

There are two types of file locking. The most common, **advisory locking**, is not enforced by the kernel. It is purely a convention that all processes that access the file must follow. The other type, **mandatory** locking, is enforced by the kernel. When a process locks a file for writing, other processes that attempt to read or write to the file are suspended until the lock is released. Although this may seem like the more obvious method, mandatory locks force the kernel to check for locks on every read() and write(), substantially decreasing the performance of those system calls.

Linux provides two methods of locking files: lock files and record locking.

## 12.3.1 Lock Files

**Lock files** are the simplest method of file locking. Each data file that needs locking is associated with a lock file. When that lock file exists, the data file is considered locked and other processes do not access it. When the lock file does not exist, a process creates the lock file and then accesses the file. As long as the procedure for creating the lock file is atomic, ensuring that only one process at a time can "own" the lock file, this method guarantees that only one process will access the file at a time.

This idea is pretty simple. When a process wants to access a file, it locks the file as follows.

```
fd = open("somefile.lck", O_RDONLY, 0644);
if (fd >= 0) {
    close(fd);
    printf("the file is already locked");
    return 1;
} else {
    /* the lock file does not exist, we can lock it and access it */
    fd = open("somefile.lck", O_CREAT | O_WRONLY, 0644");
    if (fd < 0) {
        perror("error creating lock file");
        return 1;
    }
    /* we could write our pid to the file */
    close(fd);
}
```

When the process is done with the file, it calls unlink("somefile.lck"); to release the lock.

Although the above code segment may look correct, it would allow multiple processes to lock the same file under some circumstances, which is exactly what locking is supposed to avoid. If a process checks for the lock

file's existence, sees that the lock does not exist, and is then interrupted
by the kernel to let other processes run, another process could lock the file
before the original process creates the lock file! The O_EXCL flag to open()
is available to make lock file creation atomic, and hence immune to race
conditions. When O_EXCL is specified, open() fails if the file already exists.
This simplifies the creation of lock files, which is properly implemented as
follows.

```
fd = open("somefile.lck", O_WRONLY | O_CREAT | O_EXCL, 0644);
if (fd < 0 && errno == EEXIST) {
    printf("the file is already locked");
    return 1;
} else if (fd < 0) {
    perror("unexpected error checking lock %s");
    return 1;
}

/* we could write our pid to the file */
close(fd);
```

Lock files are used to lock a wide variety of standard Linux files, including
serial ports and the /etc/passwd file. Although they work well for many
applications, they do suffer from a number of serious drawbacks.

- Only one process may have the lock at a time, preventing multiple
  processes from reading a file simultaneously. If the file is updated
  atomically,[12] processes that read the file can ignore the locking issue,
  but atomic updates are difficult to guarantee for complex file structures.

- The O_EXCL flag is reliable only on local file systems. None of the
  network file systems supported by Linux preserve O_EXCL semantics
  between multiple machines that are locking a common file.[13]

- The locking is only advisory; processes can update the file despite the
  existence of a lock.

---

12. /etc/passwd is updated only by processes that create a new copy of the file with
    the modifications and then replace the original through a rename() system call. As
    this sequence provides an atomic update, processes may read from /etc/passwd
    at any time.
13. The Andrew Filesystem (AFS), which is available for Linux, does support O_EXCL
    across a network. However, it is available only as a binary-only client.

- If the process that holds the lock terminates abnormally, the lock file remains. If the pid of the locking process is stored in the lock file, other processes can check for the existence of the locking process and remove the lock if it has terminated. This is, however, a complex procedure that is no help if the pid is being reused by another process when the check is made.

## 12.3.2 Record Locking

To overcome the problems inherent with lock files, **record locking** was added to both System V and BSD 4.3 through the `lockf()` and `flock()` system calls, respectively. POSIX defined a third mechanism for record locking that uses the `fcntl()` system call. Although Linux supports all three interfaces, we discuss only the POSIX interface, as it is now supported by nearly all Unix platforms. The `lockf()` function is implemented as an interface to `fcntl()`, however, so the rest of this dicussion applies to both techniques.

There are two important distinctions between record locks and lock files. First of all, record locks lock an arbitrary portion of the file. For example, process A may lock bytes 50–200 of a file while another process locks bytes 2,500–3,000, without having the two locks conflict. Fine-grained locking is useful when multiple processes need to update a single file. The other advantage of record locking is that the locks are held by the kernel rather than the file system. When a process is terminated, all the locks it holds are released.

Like lock files, POSIX locks are also advisory. Linux, like System V, provides a mandatory variant of record locking that may be used but is not as portable. File locking may or may not work across networked file systems. Under current (2.0.x) versions of the Linux kernel, no locking technique is reliable across NFS. In future versions of Linux, NFS record locking will be implemented,[14] but many other network file systems will remain lockless.

Record locking provides two types of locks: **read locks** and **write locks**. Read locks are also known as **shared locks**, because multiple processes may simultaneously hold read locks over a single region. It is always safe for multiple processes to read a data structure that is not being updated.

---

14. NFS record locking is done via a lock daemon.

When a process needs to write to a file, it must get a write lock (or **exclusive lock**). Only one process may hold a write lock for a record, and no read locks may exist for the record while the write lock is in place. This ensures that a process will not interfere with readers while it is writing to a region.

Multiple locks from a single process never conflict. If a process has a read lock on bytes 200–250 and tries to get a write lock on the region 200–225, it will succeed. The original lock is moved and becomes a read lock on bytes 226–250, and the new write lock from 200–225 is granted.[15] This rule prevents a process from forcing itself into a deadlock (though multiple processes can still deadlock).

POSIX record locking is done through the fcntl() system call. Recall from Chapter 10 that fcntl() looks like this:

```
#include <fcntl.h>

int fcntl(int fd, int command, long arg);
```

For all of the locking operations, the third parameter (arg) is a pointer to a struct flock.

```
#include <fcntl.h>

struct flock {
        short l_type;       /* type of lock, F_RDLCK, F_WRLCK, F_UNLCK */
        short l_whence;     /* beginning of lock (i.e. SEEK_SET) */
        off_t l_start;      /* start of lock (relative to l_whence */
        off_t l_len;        /* number of bytes to lock, 0 is to EOF */
        pid_t l_pid;        /* process holding lock (for F_GETLK) */
};
```

The first element, l_type, tells what type of lock is being set. It is one of:

F_RDLCK        A read (shared) lock is being set.

F_WRLCK        A write (exclusive) lock is being set.

F_UNLCK        An existing lock is being removed.

---

15. This lock manipulation happens atomically—there is no point at which any part of the region is unlocked.

The next two elements, l_whence and l_start, specify where the region begins in the same manner file offsets are passed to lseek(). l_whence tells how l_start is to be interpreted and is one of SEEK_SET, SEEK_CUR, and SEEK_END; see page 157 for details on these values. The next entry, l_len, tells how long, in bytes, the lock is. If l_len is 0, the lock is considered to extend to the end of the file. The final entry, l_pid, is used only when locks are being queried. It is set to the pid of the process that owns the queried lock.

There are three fcntl() commands that pertain to locking the file. The operation is passed as the second argument to fcntl(). fcntl() returns -1 on error and 0 otherwise. The command argument should be set to one of:

F_SETLK        Sets the lock described by arg. If the lock cannot be granted because of a conflict with another process's locks, EAGAIN is returned. If the l_type is set to F_UNLCK, an existing lock is removed.

F_SETLKW      Similar to F_SETLK, but blocks until the lock is granted. If a signal occurs while the process is blocked, the fcntl() call returns EAGAIN.

F_GETLK        Checks to see if the described lock would be granted. If the lock would be granted, the struct flock is unchanged except for l_type, which is set to F_UNLCK. If the lock would not be granted, l_pid is set to the pid of the process that holds the conflicting lock. Success (0) is returned whether or not the lock would be granted.

Although F_GETLK allows a process to check if a lock would be granted, the following code sequence could still fail to get a lock.

```
fcntl(fd, F_GETLK, &lockinfo);
if (lockinfo.l_type != F_UNLCK) {
    fprintf(stderr, "lock conflict\n");
    return 1;
}
lockinfo.l_type = F_RDLCK;
fcntl(fd, F_SETLK, &lockinfo);
```

Another process could lock the region between the two fcntl() calls, causing the second fcntl() to fail to set the lock.

As a simple example of record locking, here is a program that opens a file, obtains a read lock on the file, frees the read lock, gets a write lock, and then exits. Between each step, the program waits for the user to press return. If it fails to get a lock, it prints the pid of a process that holds a conflicting lock and waits for the user to tell it to try. Running this sample program in two terminals makes it easy to experiment with POSIX locking rules.

```
 1: /* locks.c -- simple example of record locking */
 2:
 3: #include <errno.h>
 4: #include <fcntl.h>
 5: #include <stdio.h>
 6: #include <unistd.h>
 7:
 8: /* displays the message, and waits for the user to press
 9:    return */
10: void waitforuser(char * message) {
11:     char buf[10];
12:
13:     printf("%s", message);
14:     fflush(stdout);
15:
16:     fgets(buf, 9, stdin);
17: }
18:
19: /* Gets a lock of the indicated type on the fd which is passed.
20:    The type should be either F_UNLCK, F_RDLCK, or F_WRLCK */
21: void getlock(int fd, int type) {
22:     struct flock lockinfo;
23:     char message[80];
24:
25:     /* we'll lock the entire file */
26:     lockinfo.l_whence = SEEK_SET;
27:     lockinfo.l_start = 0;
28:     lockinfo.l_len = 0;
29:
30:     /* keep trying until we succeed */
31:     while (1) {
```

```
32:             lockinfo.l_type = type;
33:             /* if we get the lock, return immediately */
34:             if (!fcntl(fd, F_SETLK, &lockinfo)) return;
35:
36:             /* find out who holds the conflicting lock */
37:             fcntl(fd, F_GETLK, &lockinfo);
38:
39:             /* there's a chance the lock was freed between the F_SETLK
40:                and F_GETLK; make sure there's still a conflict before
41:                complaining about it */
42:             if (lockinfo.l_type != F_UNLCK) {
43:                 sprintf(message, "conflict with process %d... press "
44:                         "<return> to retry:", lockinfo.l_pid);
45:                 waitforuser(message);
46:             }
47:         }
48: }
49:
50: int main(void) {
51:     int fd;
52:
53:     /* set up a file to lock */
54:     fd = open("testlockfile", O_RDWR | O_CREAT, 0666);
55:     if (fd < 0) {
56:         perror("open");
57:         return 1;
58:     }
59:
60:     printf("getting read lock\n");
61:     getlock(fd, F_RDLCK);
62:     printf("got read lock\n");
63:
64:     waitforuser("\npress <return> to continue:");
65:
66:     printf("releasing lock\n");
67:     getlock(fd, F_UNLCK);
68:
69:     printf("getting write lock\n");
70:     getlock(fd, F_WRLCK);
71:     printf("got write lock\n");
72:
```

```
73:     waitforuser("\npress <return> to exit:");
74:
75:     /* locks are released when the file is closed */
76:
77:     return 0;
78: }
```

Locks are treated differently from other file attributes. Locks are associated with a *(pid, inode)* tuple, unlike most attributes of open files, which are associated with a file descriptor or file structure. This means that if a process

1. Opens a single file twice, resulting in two different file descriptors

2. Gets read locks on a single region in both file descriptors

3. Closes one of the file descriptors

then the file is no longer locked by the process. Only a single read lock was granted because only one *(pid, inode)* pair was involved (the second lock attempt succeeded because a process's locks can never conflict), and after one of the file descriptors is closed, the process does not have any locks on the file!

After a fork(), the parent process retains its file locks, but the child process does not. If child processes were to inherit locks, two processes would end up with a write lock on the same region of a file, which file locks are supposed to prevent.

File locks are inherited across an exec(), however. While POSIX does not define what happens to locks after an exec(), all variants of Unix preserve them.[16]

---

16. The effect of fork() and exec() calls on file locks is the biggest difference between POSIX file locking (and hence lockf() file locking) and BSD's flock() file locking.

### 12.3.3 Mandatory Locks

Both Linux and System V provide mandatory locking, as well as normal locking. Mandatory locks are established and released through the same fcntl() mechanism that is used for advisory record locking. The locks are mandatory if the locked file's setgid bit is set but its group execute bit is not set. If this is not the case, advisory locking is used.

When mandatory locking is enabled, the read() and write() system calls block when they conflict with locks that have been set. If a process tries to write() to a portion of a file that a different process has a read or write lock on, the process without the lock blocks until the lock is released. Similarly, read() calls block on regions that are included in mandatory write locks.

Mandatory record locking causes a larger performance loss than advisory locking, because every read() and write() call must be checked for conflicts with locks. It is also not as portable as POSIX advisory locks, so we do not recommend using mandatory locking in most applications.

## 12.4 Scatter/Gather Reads and Writes

Applications often want to read and write various types of data to consecutive areas of a file. Although this can be done fairly easily through multiple read() and write() calls, this solution is not atomic. Applications could instead move all the data into a consecutive memory region, but doing so results in many unnecessary memory operations.

Linux provides readv() and writev(), which implement scatter/gather reads and writes.[17] Instead of expecting a single pointer and buffer size to each of these functions, as is done with their standard siblings, they are passed an array of records, each record describing a buffer. The buffers get read from or written to in the order they are listed in the array. Each buffer is described by a struct iovec.

---

17. They are so named because the reads scatter data across memory, and the writes gather data from different memory regions. They are also known as vector reads and writes, which is the origin of the v at the end of readv() and writev().

```
#include <sys/uio.h>

struct iovec {
    void * iov_base;    /* buffer address */
    size_t iov_len;     /* buffer length */
};
```

The first element, iov_base, points to the buffer space. The iov_len item is the number of characters in the buffer. These items are the same as the second and third parameters passed to read() and write().

Here are the prototypes for readv() and writev():

```
#include <sys/uio.h>

int readv(int fd, const struct iovec * vector, size_t count);
int writev(int fd, const struct iovec * vector, size_t count);
```

The first argument is the file descriptor to be read from or written to. The second, vector, points to an array of count struct iovec items. Both functions return the total number of bytes read or written.

Here is a simple example program that uses writev() to display a simple message on standard output:

```
 1: /* gather.c -- sample of scatter/gather write */
 2: #include <sys/uio.h>
 3:
 4: int main(void) {
 5:     struct iovec buffers[3];
 6:
 7:     buffers[0].iov_base = "hello";
 8:     buffers[0].iov_len = 5;
 9:
10:     buffers[1].iov_base = " ";
11:     buffers[1].iov_len = 1;
12:
13:     buffers[2].iov_base = "world\n";
14:     buffers[2].iov_len = 6;
```

```
15:
16:     writev(1, buffers, 3);
17:
18:     return 0;
19: }
```

# CHAPTER 13

# Signal Processing

Signals are the simplest form of interprocess communication in the POSIX world. They allow a process to be asynchronously interrupted by another process (or by the kernel) to handle some event. Once the signal has been handled, the interrupted process resumes from the point of interruption. Signals are used for tasks such as terminating processes and telling daemons to reread their configuration file.

Signals have always been an integral part of Unix. The kernel uses them to inform a process of a variety of events, including:

- The death of one of the process's children

- An alarm set by the process has expired

- The size of the terminal window has changed

All of these messages share an important property: They are all asynchronous. The process has no control over when one of its children exits—it could happen at any point during the parent's execution. Each of these events causes a signal to be sent to the process. When a process is signaled, the process can do one of three things:

1. Ignore the signal.

2. Have the kernel run a special part of the process before allowing the process to continue (called **catching** the signal).

3. Let the kernel invoke its default action, which depends on the particular signal being sent.

Conceptually, this is fairly straightforward. However, the age of the signal feature shows when you compare the different signal interfaces that are supported by the various flavors of Unix. BSD, System V, and System 3 supported different and incompatible signal APIs. POSIX defined a standard that is now supported by nearly all versions of Unix (including Linux), and all new code should be written for the POSIX signal API. This chapter discusses the original implementation of Unix signals before explaining the POSIX API, as many of the features in the POSIX API were motivated by weaknesses in earlier signal implementations.

# 13.1 Signal Concepts

## 13.1.1 Simple Signals

Originally, setting signals was simple. The `signal()` system call is used to tell the kernel how to handle a particular signal:

```
#include <signal.h>

void * signal(int signumber, void * handler);
```

`signumber` is the signal to handle, and `handler` defines the action to perform when the signal is sent to the process. Normally, the handler is a pointer to a function that takes no parameters and returns no value. When the signal is sent to the process, the kernel executes the handler function as soon as possible. Once the function returns, the kernel resumes process execution wherever it was interrupted. System-level engineers will recognize this type of signal mechanism as analogous to hardware interrupt delivery; interrupts and signals are very similar and present many of the same problems.

There are many signal numbers available. Table 13.1 on page 248 lists all the signals Linux currently supports. They all have symbolic names that begin with SIG, and we use SIG*FOO* when we talk about signals in general.

The `handler` can take on two special values, SIG_IGN and SIG_DFL (both of which are defined through <signal.h>). If SIG_IGN is specified, the signal is ignored; SIG_DFL tells the kernel to perform the default action for the signal, usually killing the process or ignoring the signal. Two signals, SIGKILL and SIGSTOP, cannot be caught. The kernel always performs the default action for these two signals, killing the process and stopping the process, respectively.

The signal() function returns the previous signal handler (which could have been SIG_IGN or SIG_DFL). Processes use the same signal handlers as their parent, unless they reset it. When a new program is run by one of the exec() functions, all the signals that the original program was catching are set to SIG_DFL; the signals that the original program was ignoring continue to be ignored.

All this seems simple enough until you ask yourself: What will happen if SIGFOO is sent to a process that is already running a signal handler for SIGFOO? The obvious thing for the kernel to do is interrupt the process and run the signal handler again. This creates two problems. First, the signal handler must function properly if it is invoked while it is already running. Although this may be easy, signal handlers that manipulate program-wide resources, such as global data structures or files, need to be written extemely carefully. Functions that behave properly when they are called in this manner are called **reentrant**.[1]

The simple locking techniques that are sufficient to coordinate data access between concurrent processes do not allow reentrancy. For example, the file-locking techniques presented in Chapter 12 cannot be used to allow a signal handler that manipulates a data file to be reentrant. When the signal handler is called the first time, it can lock the data file just fine and begin writing to it. If the signal handler is then interrupted by another signal while it holds the lock, the second invocation of the signal handler cannot lock the file, because the first invocation holds the lock. Unfortunately, the invocation that holds the lock is suspended until the invocation that wants the lock finishes running.

The difficulty of writing reentrant signal handlers is a major reason for the kernel to not deliver signals that a process is already handling. Such a model also makes it difficult for processes to handle a large number of signals that are being sent to the process very rapidly. As each signal results in a new invocation of the signal handler, the process's stack could grow without bound, despite the program itself being well behaved.

---

1. The problem of writing reentrant functions is not limited to signal handlers. Multi-threaded applications must take great care to ensure proper reentrancy and locking.

The first solution to this problem was ill-conceived. Before the signal handler was invoked, the handler for that signal was reset to SIG_DFL and the signal handler was expected to set a more appropriate signal disposition as soon as it could. Although this did simplify writing signal handlers, it made it impossible for a developer to handle signals in a reliable fashion. If two occurrences of the same signal occurred quickly, the kernel handled the second signal in the default fashion. That meant that the second signal was ignored (and lost forever) or the process was terminated. This signal implementation is known as **unreliable signals** because it forces signal handling programs into this difficulty.

Unfortunately, this is exactly the signal model used in the ANSI C standard.[2] Although **reliable signal** APIs that fix these shortcomings are widespread, ANSI's unreliable standardization of the signal() function will probably be around forever.

## 13.1.2 POSIX Signals

The implementors of BSD realized that a solution to the multiple signals problem would be to simply wait to deliver the second signal until the process finishes handling the first one. This ensures that both signals are received and removes the risk of stack overflows. When the kernel is holding a signal for later delivery, the signal is said to be **pending**.

However, if a process is sent SIGFOO while a SIGFOO signal is already pending, only one of those SIGFOO signals is delivered to the process. There is no way for a process to know how many times a signal was sent to it, as multiple signals may have been coalesced into one. This is not normally much of a problem, though. As signals do not carry any information other than the signal number with them, sending a signal twice in a very short period of time is usually the same as sending it a single time, so if the program receives the signal only once, it does not matter much. This is different from performing the default action on the second signal (which is what occurs with unreliable signals).

---

2. Well, not *exactly*. The ANSI C signal handling model is not as well specified as the one we just presented. It does, however, mandate that signal handlers be reset to SIG_DFL before a signal is delivered, forcing all ANSI C signal() functions to be unreliable.

The concept of a signal being temporarily **blocked** has been extended to allow a process to explicitly block signals. This makes it easy to protect important pieces of code, while still handling all the signals that are sent. Such protection lets the signal handlers manipulate data structures that are maintained by other pieces of the code by providing simple synchronization.

Although BSD provided the basic signal model POSIX adopted, the POSIX standard committee made it simpler for system calls to modify the disposition of groups of signals by introducing new system calls that operate on sets of signals. A set of signals is represented by the data type sigset_t, and a set of macros are provided to manipulate it.[3]

## 13.1.3 Signals and System Calls

A process will often receive a signal while the process is waiting for an external event to occur. For instance, a networking daemon may be stuck in accept() waiting for another process to connect to a socket. When the system administrator sends the process a SIGTERM signal (the normal signal sent by the kill command, allowing a process to terminate cleanly), the process could handle it in a few ways.

1.  It could make no attempt to catch the signal and be terminated by the kernel (the default handling of SIGTERM).

2.  It could catch the signal and have the signal handler clean up everything the process was doing and then exit. Although this is appealing, in complex programs it is difficult to write a signal handler that knows enough about what the program was doing when it was interrupted to clean it up properly.

3.  It could catch the signal, set a flag indicating that the signal occurred, and somehow cause the blocked system call (in this case, accept()) to exit with an error indicating something unusual happened. The normal execution pathway could then check for the flag and handle it appropriately.

---

3. This is similar to the fdset_t type used by the select() system call.

As the final choice seems much cleaner and easier than the others, the original signal implementation caused **slow** system calls to return EINTR when they were interrupted by a signal, whereas **fast** system calls completed before the signal was delivered.

Slow system calls take an indeterminate amount of time to complete. System calls that wait for unpredictable resources, such as other processes or a *homo sapiens*, to perform some action are considered slow. The wait() family of system calls, for example, do not normally return until a child process exits. As there is no way to know how long that may take, wait() is a slow system call. File access system calls are considered slow if they access slow files, and fast if they access fast files.[4]

It was the process's job to handle EINTR and restart system calls as necessary. Although this provided all the functionality people needed, it made it more difficult to write code that handled signals. Every time read() was called on a slow file descriptor, the code had to be modified to check for EINTR and restart the call, or the code might not perform as expected.

To "simplify" things, 4.2BSD automatically restarted certain system calls (notably read() and write()). For the most common operations, programs no longer needed to worry about EINTR because the system call would continue after the process handled the signal. Later versions of Unix changed which system calls would be automatically restarted, and 4.3BSD allows you to choose whether to restart system calls. The POSIX signal standard does not specify which behavior should be used, but all popular systems agree on how to handle this case. By default, system calls are not restarted, but for each signal, the process can set a flag that indicates that it would like the system to automatically restart system calls interrupted by that signal.

# 13.2 The Linux (and POSIX) Signal API

### 13.2.1 Sending Signals

Sending signals from one process to another is done through the kill() system call. This system call is discussed in detail on page 116.

---

4. The difference between fast files and slow files is the same as the difference between fast and slow system calls and is discussed in more detail on page 153.

## 13.2.2 **Using** sigset_t

All the POSIX signal functions take a set of signals as one of the parameters (or part of one of the parameters in the case of sigaction()). The sigset_t data type is used to represent a signal set and it is defined in ⟨signal.h⟩. POSIX defines five functions for manipulating signal sets.

```
#include <signal.h>

int sigemptyset(sigset_t *set);
int sigfillset(sigset_t *set);
int sigaddset(sigset_t *set, int signum);
int sigdelset(sigset_t *set, int signum);
int sigismember(const sigset_t *set, int signum);
```

int sigemptyset(sigset_t *set);
> Makes the signal set pointed to by set empty (no signals are present in the set).

int sigfillset(sigset_t *set);
> Includes all available signals in set.

int sigaddset(sigset_t *set, int signum);
> Adds signal signum to set.

int sigdelset(sigset_t *set, int signum);
> Removes signal signum from set.

int sigismember(const sigset_t *set, int signum);
> Returns non-0 if signal signum is in set, 0 otherwise.

The only way any of these functions can return an error is if their signum parameter is an invalid signal. In that case, they will return EINVAL. Needless to say, this should never happen.

## 13.2.3 Catching Signals

Rather than use the signal() function (whose semantics were already irregular because of its evolution), POSIX programs register signal handlers through sigaction().

```
#include <signal.h>

int sigaction(int signum, struct sigaction * act,
              struct sigaction * oact);
```

This system call sets the handler for signal signum as defined by act. If oact is not NULL, it is set to describe the disposition of the signal before sigaction() was called. If act is NULL, the current signal disposition is left unchanged, allowing a program to discover the current disposition for a signal without modifying it. sigaction() returns 0 on success, non-0 on error. Errors occur only if one or more of the parameters passed to sigaction() are invalid.

The kernel's handling of a signal is fully described by struct sigaction.

```
#include <signal.h>

struct sigaction {
        sighandler_t sa_handler;
        sigset_t sa_mask;
        unsigned long sa_flags;
        void (*sa_restorer)(void);
};
```

sa_handler is a pointer to a function with the following prototype:

```
void handler(int signum);
```

where signum is set to the signal number that caused the function to be invoked. sa_handlers can point to a function of this type, or contain SIG_IGN or SIG_DFL.

A program also specifies a set of signals that should be blocked while the signal handler is being run. If a signal handler is designed to handle several different signals (which the signum parameter makes easy to do), this feature is essential to prevent race conditions. The sa_mask is a signal set that includes all the signals that should be blocked when the handler for the signal is invoked. However, the signal that is being delivered is blocked no matter what sa_mask contains—if you do not want it blocked, specify this through the sa_flags member of struct sigaction.

The sa_flags field lets the process modify various signal behaviors. It consists of one or more flags logically OR'ed together. The only flag specified by POSIX is SA_NOCLDSTOP—the remainder of these flags should not be used in portable applications.

SA_NOCLDSTOP     Normally, SIGCHLD is generated when one of a process's children has terminated or stopped (that is, whenever wait4() would return status information on the stopped process). If SA_NOCLDSTOP has been specified for the SIGCHLD signal, the signal is generated only when a child process has terminated; stopped children then do not cause any signal. SA_NOCLDSTOP has no effect on any other signal

SA_NOMASK        When the process's signal handler is invoked, the signal is not automatically blocked. Using this flag results in unreliable signals and should be used only to emulate unreliable signals for applications that depend on this behavior. It is identical to System V's SA_NODEFER flag.

SA_ONESHOT       When this signal is sent, the signal handler is reset to SIG_DFL. This flag allows the ANSI C signal() function to be emulated in a user-space library. This is identical to System V's SIG_RESETHAND flag.

SA_RESTART       When the signal is sent to the process while it is executing a slow system call, the system call is restarted after the signal handler returns. If this flag is not specified, the system call instead returns an error and sets errno to EINTR.

The final field of struct sigaction, sa_restore, is not part of the POSIX specification and is reserved for future use.[5] Applications may safely ignore it—there is no need to set its value to NULL.[6]

---

5. Future versions of the Linux kernel will use it to allow processes to specify an alternate piece of memory to use for the stack when signal handlers are being run.
6. If this value ever becomes defined, its value will still be ignored unless a new flag is set in the sa_flags field.

## 13.2.4 Manipulating a Process's Signal Mask

It is common for a signal handler to manipulate data structures that are used in other parts of the program. Unfortunately, the asynchronous nature of signals makes this dangerous unless it is done carefully. Manipulating all but the most simple of data structures subjects a program to race conditions.

An example should make this problem a bit more clear. Here is a simple SIGHUP handler that changes the value of a string pointed to by the global variable someString.

```
void handleHup(int signum) {
    free(someString);
    someString = strdup("a different string");
}
```

In real-world programs, the new value for someString would probably be read from an external source (such as a FIFO), but the same concepts apply. Now assume the main part of a program is copying a string (this code is similar to the code in a strcpy() implementation, though not very optimized) when a SIGHUP signal arrives.

```
src = someString;
while (*dest)
    *src++ = *dest;
```

When the the main part of the program resumes execution, dest will be pointing to memory that was freed by the signal handler. Needless to say, this is a very bad idea.[7]

To solve this type of problem, the POSIX signal API allows a process to block an arbitrary set of signals from being delivered to the process. The signals are not thrown away—their delivery is delayed until the process indicates it is willing to handle those signals by unblocking them. To make the string copy shown earlier legal, the program would have to block SIGHUP before the string copy and unblock it afterward. After discussing

---

7. Although referencing memory that has been freed will often work fine, it is not portable. Some malloc() implementations return memory to the operating system, which causes referencing the returned memory to cause a segmentation fault; others overwrite portions of the freed memory with bookkeeping information.

the interface for manipulating the signal mask, we will present a proper version of the code.

The set of signals that a process is currently blocking is often called the process's **signal mask**. The signal mask for a process is a sigset_t that contains the signals currently being blocked. The sigprocmask() function allows a process to control its current signal mask.

```
#include <signal.h>

int sigprocmask(int what, const sigset_t * set, sigset_t * oldset);
```

The first parameter, what, describes how the signal mask is to be manipulated. If set is NULL, what is ignored.

SIG_BLOCK      The signals in set are added to the current signal mask.

SIG_UNBLOCK    The signals in set are removed from the current signal mask.

SIG_SETMASK    Precisely the signals in set are blocked—the rest are unblocked.

In all three cases, the sigset_t pointed to by oldset is set to the original signal mask unless oldset is NULL, in which case oldset is ignored. The following finds the current signal mask for the running process:

```
sigprocmask(SIG_BLOCK, NULL, &currentSet);
```

The sigprocmask() system call allows us to fix the code presented earlier, which was afflicted by a race condition. All we need to do is block SIGHUP before we copy the string and unblock it afterward. The following change will render the code safe.

```
sigset_t hup;

sigemptyset(&hup);
sigaddset(&hup, SIGHUP);

sigprocmask(SIG_BLOCK, &hup, NULL);
src = someString;
while (*dest)
    *src++ = *dest;
sigprocmask(SIG_UNBLOCK, &hup, NULL);
```

The complexity of making signal handlers safe from race conditions should encourage you to keep your signal handlers as simple as possible.

## 13.2.5 Finding the Set of Pending Signals

It is easy to find out which signals are currently pending (signals that need to be delivered, but are currently blocked).

```
#include <signal.h>

int sigpending(sigset_t * set);
```

On return, the sigset_t pointed to by set will contain the signals currently pending.

## 13.2.6 Waiting for Signals

When a program is built primarily around signals, it is often designed to wait for a signal to occur before continuing. The pause() system call provides a simple way of doing this.

```
#include <unistd.h>

int pause(void);
```

pause() does not return until after a signal has been delivered to the process. If a signal handler is present for that signal, the signal handler is run before pause() returns. pause() always returns -1 and sets errno to EINTR.

The sigsuspend() system call provides an alternate method of waiting for a signal call.

```
#include <signal.h>

int sigsuspend(const sigset_t * mask);
```

Like pause(), sigsuspend() suspends the process until a signal has been received (and processed by a signal handler, if one is available), returning -1 and setting errno to EINTR.

Unlike pause(), sigsuspend() temporarily sets the process's signal mask to the value pointed to by the mask parameter before waiting for a signal to occur. Once the signal occurs, the signal mask is restored to the value it had before sigsuspend() was called. This allows a process to wait for a particular signal to occur by blocking all other signals.[8]

## 13.3  Available Signals

Linux has quite a few signals available for processes to use, all of which are summarized in Table 13.1. There are four default actions the kernel can take for a signal: ignore it, stop the process (it is still alive and can be restarted later), terminate the process, or terminate the process and generate a core dump.[9] The following are more detailed descriptions of each signal listed in Table 13.1.

SIGABRT     The abort() function sends this signal to the process that called it, terminating the process with a core file. Under Linux, the C library calls abort() whenever an assertion fails.[10]

SIGALRM     Sent when an alarm set by the alarm() system call has expired. Alarms are discussed in Chapter 17.

---

8. Using sigprocmask() and pause() to get this behavior presents a race condition if the signal that is being waited for occurs between the two system calls.
9. See page 117 for more information on core dumps.
10. Assertions are discussed in most introductory C books [Kernighan, 1988].

**Table 13.1** Signals

| Signal | Description | Default Action |
|---|---|---|
| SIGABRT | Delivered by abort() | Terminate, core |
| SIGALRM | An alarm() has expired | Ignored |
| SIGBUS | Hardware-dependent error | Terminate, core |
| SIGCHLD | Child process terminated | Ignored |
| SIGCONT | Process has been continued after being stopped | Ignored |
| SIGHUP | The process's controlling tty was closed | Ignored |
| SIGFPE | Arithmetic point exception | Terminate, core |
| SIGILL | An illegal instruction was encountered | Terminate, core |
| SIGINT | User sent the interrupt character (^C) | Ignored |
| SIGIO | Asynchronous I/O has been received | Ignored |
| SIGKILL | Uncatchable process termination | Terminate |
| SIGQUIT | User sent the quit character (^\) | Terminate, core |
| SIGPIPE | Process wrote to a pipe w/o any readers | Ignored |
| SIGPROF | Profiling segment ended | Ignored |
| SIGPWR | Power failure detected | Ignored |
| SIGSEGV | Memory violation | Terminate, core |
| SIGSTOP | Stops the process without terminating it | Process stopped |
| SIGTERM | Catchable termination request | Terminate |
| SIGTRAP | Breakpoint instruction encountered | Ignored |
| SIGTSTP | User sent suspend character (^Z) | Process stopped |
| SIGTTIN | Background process read from controlling tty | Process stopped |
| SIGTTOU | Background process wrote to controlling tty | Process stopped |
| SIGWINCH | Size of the controlling tty has changed | Process stopped |
| SIGURG | Urgent I/O condition | Ignored |
| SIGUSR1 | Process-defined signal | Ignored |
| SIGUSR2 | Process-defined signal | Ignored |
| SIGXCPU | CPU resource limit exceeded | Terminate, core |
| SIGXFSZ | File-size resource limit exceeded | Terminate, core |
| SIGVTALRM | setitimer() timer has expired | Terminate, core |

SIGBUS    When a process violates hardware constraints other than those related to memory protections, this signal is sent. This usually occurs on traditional Unix platforms when an unaligned access occurs, but the Linux kernel fixes unaligned access and continues the process. Memory alignment is discussed further on page 57.

SIGCHLD   This signal is sent to a process when one of that process's children has exited or stopped. This allows the process to avoid zombies by calling one of the wait() functions from the signal handler. If the parent always waits for its children to exit before continuing, this signal can be safely ignored. This signal is different from the SIGCLD signal provided by early releases of System V. SIGCLD is obsolete and should not be used anymore.

SIGCONT      This signal restarts a process that has been stopped. It may also be caught by a process, allowing it to take an action after being restarted. Most editors catch this signal and refresh the terminal when they are restarted. See Chapter 14 for more information on stopping and starting processes.

SIGHUP      When a terminal is disconnected, the session leader for the session associated with the terminal is sent a SIGHUP signal unless that terminal's CLOCAL flag has been set. If a session leader exits, SIGHUP is sent to the process group leader for each process group in the session. Most processes terminate when SIGHUP is received because it indicates the user is no longer present.

Many daemon processes interpret SIGHUP as a request to close and reopen log files and reread configuration files.

SIGFPE      This signal is sent when a process causes an arithmetic exception. All floating-point exceptions, such as overflows and underflows, cause this signal, as does integer division by 0.

SIGILL      The process attempted to run an illegal hardware instruction.

SIGINT      This signal is sent to all processes in the foreground process group when the user presses the interrupt character (normally, ^C).

SIGIO      An asynchronous I/O event has occurred. Asynchronous I/O is rarely used and is not documented in this book. We suggest consulting other books for information on using asynchronous I/O [Stevens, 1992].

SIGKILL      This signal is generated only by kill() and allows a user to unconditionally terminate a process.

SIGQUIT
: This signal is sent to all processes in the foreground process group when the user presses the quit character (usually, ^\).

SIGPIPE
: The process has written to a pipe that has no readers.

SIGPROF
: The profile timer has expired. This signal is usually used by profilers, which are programs that examine another process's run-time characteristics. Profilers are normally used to optimize a program's execution speed by helping programmers to find execution bottlenecks.[11]

SIGPWR
: The system detected an impending loss of power. It is usually sent to init by a daemon that is monitoring the machine's power source, allowing the machine to be cleanly shut down before power failure.

SIGSEGV
: This signal is sent when a process attempts to access memory it is not allowed to access. It is generated when a process tries to read from unmapped memory, execute a page of memory that has not been mapped with execute permissions, or write to memory it does not have write access to.

SIGSTOP
: This signal is generated only by kill() and allows a user to unconditionally stop a process. See Chapter 14 for more information on stopping processes.

SIGTERM
: This signal is generated only by kill() and allows a user to gracefully terminate a process. A process should exit as soon as possible after receiving this signal.

SIGTRAP
: When a process has crossed a breakpoint, this signal is sent to the process. It is usually intercepted by a debugger process that set the breakpoint.

SIGTSTP
: This signal is sent to all processes in the foreground process group when the user presses the suspend character (usually, ^Z). See Chapter 14 for more information on job control.

---

11. The gprof utility, included with all Linux distributions, is a simple profiler.

SIGTTIN      This signal is sent to a background process that has tried to read from its controlling terminal. See Chapter 14 for more information on job control.

SIGTTOU      This signal is sent to a background process that has tried to write to its controlling terminal. See Chapter 14 for more information on job control.

SIGWINCH     When a terminal window has changed size, such as when an xterm is resized, all processes in the foreground process group for that process are sent SIGWINCH. See page 295 for information on finding the current size of the controlling terminal.

SIGURG       This signal is sent when out-of-band data has been received on a socket. Out-of-band data is an advanced networking topic outside the scope of this book; [Stevens, 1990] covers it thoroughly, however.

SIGUSR1      There is no defined use for this signal; processes may use it for whatever purposes they like.

SIGUSR2      There is no defined use for this signal; processes may use it for whatever purposes they like.

SIGXCPU      The process has exceeded its CPU limit. For information on process resource limits, see pages 105–106.

SIGXFSZ      The process has exceeded its file size limit. For information on process resource limits, see pages 105–106.

SIGVTALRM    Sent when a timer set by setitimer() has expired. For information on using timers, see Chapter 17.

# 13.4 Writing Signal Handlers

Although a signal handler looks like a normal C function, it is not called like one. Rather than being run as part of a program's normal call sequence, signal handlers are called by the kernel. The key difference between the two cases is that a signal handler can be called at almost any time, even in the middle of a single C statement! There are only a few restrictions on when the system will call a signal handler on which you can rely:

1.  The semantics of some signals restrict when they will be sent. SIGCHLD, for example, will not normally be sent to a program that has no children.[12] Most signals are like SIGHUP, however, and are sent at unpredictable times.

2.  If the process is in the middle of handling a particular signal, the signal handler will not be reinvoked to handle the same signal unless the SA_NOMASK option was specified. The process can also block additional signals when a signal processor is running through the sa_mask field of struct sigaction.

3.  The process can block signals while running a part of code through use of sigprocmask(). Page 245 has an example of using this facility to allow atomic updates to data structures.

Because signal handlers can be run at almost any time, it is important to write them so that they do not make unwarranted assumptions about what the rest of the program is doing at the time and so that they do not rearrange things in a way that could confuse the rest of the program when it starts running again.

One of the most important things to watch is modifying global data. Unless this is done carefully, race conditions will result. The easiest way to keep updates of global data safe is simply to avoid them. The next best method is blocking all signal handlers that modify a particular data structure whenever the rest of the code is modifying it, ensuring that only one code segment is manipulating the data at a time.

---

12. Although users can send SIGCHLD to any processes they own, programs are not expected to respond reasonably to unexpected signals.

Although it is safe for the signal handler to read a data structure when it has interrupted another reader of that structure, all other combinations are unsafe. It is no more safe for the signal handler to modify a data structure that the rest of the program is reading than it is for the signal handler to read a data structure the rest of the program is writing. Some specialized data structures have been designed to allow concurrent access, but those data structures are well beyond the scope of this book.

If you must access global data from a signal handler (which most signal handlers end up doing), keep the data structure simple. Although it is pretty easy to safely modify a single data element, such as an `int`, more-complicated structures usually require blocking signals. Any global variables that a signal handler may modify should be declared with the `volatile` keyword. This tells the compiler that the variable may be changed outside the normal flow of the program and it should not try to optimize accesses to the variable.

The other thing to be careful of in signal handlers is calling other functions, as they may modify global data as well! The C stdio library tends to do this quite a bit and should never be used from a signal handler. Table 13.2 lists functions that are guaranteed to be safe to call from a signal handler; all other library functions should be avoided.

# 13.5 **Reopening Log Files**

Most system daemons keep log files indicating what they have been busy doing. As many Unix systems stay up for months without interruption, these log files can grow quite large. Simply removing (or renaming) the log files occasionally is not a good solution because the daemons would simply keep writing to the files despite their inaccessibility, and having to stop and start each daemon while the log files are cleaned up would result in system downtime (albeit not much). A common way for daemons to manage this situation is to catch `SIGHUP` and reopen their log files. This allows **log rotation** (periodically starting new log files while keeping the old ones) to happen with a simple shell script like

```
cd /var/log
mv messages messages.old
killall -HUP syslogd
```

**Table 13.2** Reentrant Functions

| | | | |
|---|---|---|---|
| access() | alarm() | cfgetispeed() | cfgetospeed() |
| cfsetispeed() | cfsetospeed() | chdir() | chmod() |
| chown() | close() | _exit() | abort() |
| access() | alarm() | cfgetispeed() | cfgetospeed() |
| cfsetispeed() | cfsetospeed() | chdir() | chmod() |
| chown() | close() | creat() | dup() |
| dup2() | execle() | execve() | fcntl() |
| fork() | fstat() | getegid() | geteuid() |
| getgid() | getgroups() | getpgrp() | getpid() |
| getppid() | getuid() | kill() | link() |
| longjmp() | lseek() | mkdir() | mkfifo() |
| open() | pathconf() | pause() | pipe() |
| read() | rename() | rmdir() | setgid() |
| setpgid() | setsid() | setuid() | sigaction() |
| sigaddset() | sigdelset() | sigemptyset() | sigfillset() |
| sigismember() | signal() | sigpending() | sigprocmask() |
| sigsuspend() | sleep() | stat() | sysconf() |
| tdcdrain() | tcflow() | tcflush() | tcgetattr() |
| tcgetpgrp() | tcsendbreak() | tcsetattr() | tcsetpgrp() |
| time() | times() | umask() | uname() |
| unlink() | ustat() | utime() | wait() |
| wait3() | wait4() | waitpid() | write() |

Logrotate[13] is one program that takes advantage of this feature to perform safe log rotation.

Including this ability in most daemons is straightforward. One of the easiest approaches is to include a global variable that indicates whether the logs need to be reopened. Then a SIGHUP signal handler sets this variable whenever it is invoked, and the main part of the program checks the variable as often as possible. The following is an example program that does this.

```
1: /* sighup.c -- sample program which illustrates how to use sighup to
2:    force a daemon to reopen its log files */
3:
4: #include <errno.h>
5: #include <signal.h>
6: #include <stdio.h>
7: #include <string.h>
```

---

13. ftp://ftp.redhat.com/pub/redhat/code/logrotate/

```
 8: #include <unistd.h>
 9:
10: volatile int reopenLog = 0;      /* volatile as it is modified by a signal
11:                                     handler */
12:
13: /* write a line to the log */
14: void logstring(int logfd, char * str) {
15:     write(logfd, str, strlen(str));
16: }
17:
18: /* When SIGHUP occurs, make a note of it and continue. */
19: void hupHandler(int signum) {
20:     reopenLog = 1;
21: }
22:
23: int main() {
24:     int done = 0;
25:     struct sigaction sa;
26:     int rc;
27:     int logfd;
28:
29:     logfd = STDOUT_FILENO;
30:
31:     /* Set up a signal handler for SIGHUP. Use memset() to initialize
32:        the struct sigaction to be sure we clear all of it. */
33:     memset(&sa, 0, sizeof(sa));
34:     sa.sa_handler = hupHandler;
35:
36:     if (sigaction(SIGHUP, &sa, NULL)) perror("sigaction");
37:
38:     /* Log a message every two seconds, and reopen the log file
39:        as requested by SIGHUP. */
40:     while (!done) {
41:         /* sleep() returns nonzero if it didn't sleep long enough */
42:         rc = sleep(2);
43:         if (rc) {
44:             if (reopenLog) {
45:                 logstring(logfd, "* reopening log files at SIGHUP's request\n");
46:                 reopenLog = 0;
47:             } else {
48:                 logstring(logfd, "* sleep interrupted by unknown signal "
```

```
49:                              "-- dying\n");
50:                   done = 1;
51:                }
52:          } else {
53:              logstring(logfd, "Periodic message\n");
54:          }
55:      }
56:
57:      return 0;
58: }
```

To test this program, run it in one xterm and send it SIGHUP from another. For each SIGHUP the program receives, it will print out a message where it would ordinarily rotate its logs. Remember that if a signal arrives while another instance of the signal is already pending, only one instance of the signal is delivered, so do not send the signals too quickly.

# CHAPTER 14

# Job Control

Job control, a feature standardized by POSIX.1 and mandated by many standards, allows a single terminal to run multiple jobs. Each job is a group of one or more processes, usually connected by pipes. Mechanisms are provided to move jobs between the foreground and the background and to prevent background jobs from accessing the terminal.

## 14.1  Job Control Basics

Recall from Chapter 9 that each active terminal runs a single group of processes, called a session. Each session is made up of process groups, and each process group contains one or more individual processes.

One of the process groups in a session is the foreground process group. The rest are background process groups. The foreground process group may be changed to any process group belonging to the session, allowing the user to switch among foreground process groups. Processes that are members of the foreground process group are often called foreground processes; processes that are not are called background processes.

### 14.1.1 Restarting Processes

Every process is in one of three states: running, stopped, or zombied. Running processes are terminated by calling the exit() system call or by being sent a fatal signal. Processes are moved between the running and stopped states exclusively through signals generated by another process, the kernel, or themselves.[1]

When a process receives SIGCONT, the kernel moves it from the stopped state to the running state; if the process is already running, the signal does not affect its state. The process may catch the signal, with the kernel moving the process to the running state before delivering the signal.

## 14.1.2 Stopping Processes

Four signals move a running process to the stopped state. SIGSTOP is never generated by the kernel. It is provided to allow users to stop arbitrary processes. It cannot be caught or ignored; it always stops the target process. The other three signals that stop processes, SIGTSTP, SIGTTIN, and SIGTTOU, may be generated by the terminal on which the process is running or by another process. Although these signals behave similarly, they are generated under different circumstances.

SIGTSTP      This signal is sent to every process in a terminal's foreground process group when a user presses the terminal's suspend key.[2]

SIGTTIN      When a background process attempts to read from the terminal, it is sent SIGTTIN.

SIGTTOU      This process is normally generated by a background process attempting to write to its terminal. The signal is generated only if the terminal's TOSTOP attribute is set, as discussed on page 307.

                 This signal is also generated by a background process calling one of tcflush(), tcflow(), tcsetattr(), tcsetpgrp(), tcdrain(), or tcsendbreak().

The default action of each of these three signals is to stop the process. They may all be caught or ignored. In both cases, the process will not be stopped.

---

1. Stopped processes cannot generate signals, however, so they cannot restart themselves either.
2. Normally, the suspend key is Ctrl-Z. The stty program allows users to change the suspend key for a terminal, and Chapter 15 details how a program can change it.

## 14.1.3 Handling Job Control Signals

Although many applications can be stopped and restarted with no ill effects, other processes need to handle process stops and starts. Most editors, for example, need to modify many of the terminal parameters while they are running. When users suspend the process, they expect their terminal to be restored to its default state.

When a process needs to perform actions before being suspended, it needs to provide a signal handler for SIGTSTP. This lets the kernel notify the process that it needs to suspend itself.

Upon receiving SIGTSTP, the process should immediately perform whatever actions it needs to take in order to allow suspension (such as restoring the terminal to its original state) and suspend itself. The simplest way for the process to suspend itself is by sending itself SIGSTOP. Most shells display messages that indicate which signal caused the process to stop, though, and if the process sent itself SIGSTOP, it would look different from most suspended processes. To avoid this nuisance, most applications reset their SIGTSTP handler to SIG_DFL and send themselves a SIGTSTP.

Processes that require special code for clean suspensions normally need to perform special actions when they are restarted. This is easily done by providing a signal handler for SIGCONT, which performs such actions. If the process suspended itself with SIGTSTP, such special actions will probably include setting a signal handler for SIGTSTP.

The following code provides a simple signal handler for both SIGCONT and SIGTSTP. When the user suspends or restarts the process, the process displays a message before stopping or continuing.

```
 1: /* monitor.c -- watch job control signals */
 2: #include <signal.h>
 3: #include <stdio.h>
 4: #include <string.h>
 5: #include <unistd.h>
 6:
 7: void catchSignal(int sigNum, int useDefault);
 8:
 9: void handler(int signum) {
10:     if (signum == SIGTSTP) {
```

```
11:            write(STDOUT_FILENO, "got SIGTSTP\n", 12);
12:            catchSignal(SIGTSTP, 1);
13:            kill(getpid(), SIGTSTP);
14:        } else {
15:            write(STDOUT_FILENO, "got SIGCONT\n", 12);
16:            catchSignal(SIGTSTP, 0);
17:        }
18: }
19:
20: void catchSignal(int sigNum, int useDefault) {
21:     struct sigaction sa;
22:
23:     memset(&sa, 0, sizeof(sa));
24:
25:     if (useDefault)
26:         sa.sa_handler = SIG_DFL;
27:     else
28:         sa.sa_handler = handler;
29:
30:     if (sigaction(sigNum, &sa, NULL)) perror("sigaction");
31: }
32:
33: int main() {
34:     catchSignal(SIGTSTP, 0);
35:     catchSignal(SIGCONT, 0);
36:
37:     while (1) ;
38:
39:     return 0;
40: }
```

# 14.2  **Job Control in** ladsh

Adding job control facilities to ladsh requires only system calls discussed
in previous chapters. The first step is to add a field to each of struct
childProgram, struct job, and struct jobSet. As ladsh has not been discussed
for a while, it may help to refer back to page 135, where these data structures
were first introduced. The following is how struct childProgram is now
defined.

```
struct childProgram {
    pid_t pid;                  /* 0 if exited */
    char ** argv;               /* program name and arguments */
    int numRedirections;        /* elements in redirection array */
    struct redirectionSpecifier * redirections;  /* I/O redirections */
    glob_t globResult;          /* result of parameter globbing */
    int freeGlob;               /* should we globfree(&globResult)? */
    int isStopped;              /* is the program currently running? */
};
```

We already differentiate between running children and terminated children through the `pid` member of `struct childProgram`—it is -1 if the child has terminated, and it contains a valid pid, otherwise. The new member, `isStopped`, is non-0 if the process has been stopped, and 0 otherwise. Note that its value is meaningless if the `pid` member is -1.

An analogous change needs to be made to `struct job`. It previously kept track of the number of programs in a job and how many of those processes were still running. Its new member, `stoppedProgs`, records how many of the job's processes are currently stopped. It could be calculated from the `isStopped` fields of the children that comprise the job, but it is simpler to track it separately. This change defines `struct job` as follows:

```
struct job {
    int jobId;                  /* job number */
    int numProgs;               /* total number of programs in job */
    int runningProgs;           /* number of programs running */
    char * text;                /* name of job */
    char * cmdBuf;              /* buffer various argv's point into */
    pid_t pgrp;                 /* process group ID for the job */
    struct childProgram * progs; /* linked list of programs in the job */
    struct job * next;          /* to track background commands */
    int stoppedProgs;           /* number of programs alive, but stopped */
};
```

Like previous versions of `ladsh`, `ladsh4` ignores `SIGTTOU`. It does this to allow `tcsetpgrp()` to be used even when the shell is not a foreground process. As the shell will have proper job control now, however, we do not want our children to ignore the signal. As soon as a new process is `fork()`ed by `runCommand()`, it sets the handler for `SIGTTOU` to `SIG_DFL`. This allows the terminal driver to suspend background processes that attempt to write to (or otherwise manipulate) the terminal. This is easily done by calling

```
signal(SIGTTOU, SIG_DFL);
```

immediately after the fork() that creates the child processes.

ladsh checks for terminated children in two places. The primary place is when it wait()s for processes in the foreground process group. When the foreground process has terminated or been stopped, ladsh checks for changes in the states of its background processes through the checkJobs() function. Both of these code paths need to be modified to handle stopped children, as well as terminated ones.

Adding the WUNTRACED flag to the waitpid() call, which waits on foreground processes, allows it to notice stopped processes, as well. When a process has been stopped rather than terminated, the child's isStopped flag is set and the job's stoppedProgs count is incremented. If all the programs in the job have been stopped, ladsh moves itself back to the foreground and waits for a user's command. Here is how the portion of ladsh's main loop that waits on the foreground process now looks:

```
/* a job is running in the foreground; wait for it */
i = 0;
while (!jobList.fg->progs[i].pid ||
       jobList.fg->progs[i].isStopped) i++;

waitpid(jobList.fg->progs[i].pid, &status, WUNTRACED);

if (WIFEXITED(status) || WIFSIGNALED(status)) {
    /* the child exited */
    jobList.fg->runningProgs--;
    jobList.fg->progs[i].pid = 0;

    if (!jobList.fg->runningProgs) {
        /* child exited */

        removeJob(&jobList, jobList.fg);
        jobList.fg = NULL;
```

```
            /* move the shell to the foreground */
            if (tcsetpgrp(0, getpid()))
                perror("tcsetpgrp");
        }
    } else {
        /* the child was stopped */
        jobList.fg->stoppedProgs++;
        jobList.fg->progs[i].isStopped = 1;

        if (jobList.fg->stoppedProgs == jobList.fg->runningProgs) {
            printf("\n" JOB_STATUS_FORMAT, jobList.fg->jobId,
                    "Stopped", jobList.fg->text);
            jobList.fg = NULL;
        }
    }

    if (!jobList.fg) {
        /* move the shell to the foreground */
        if (tcsetpgrp(0, getpid()))
            perror("tcsetpgrp");
    }
```

Similarly, background tasks may be stopped by signals. We again add WUN-TRACED to the waitpid(), which checks the states of background processes. When a background process has been stopped, the isStopped flag and stoppedProgs counter are updated, and if the entire job has been stopped, a message is printed.

The final ability that ladsh requires is to be able to move jobs between running in the foreground, running in the background, and being stopped. Two built-in commands allow this: fg and bg. They are limited versions of the normal shell commands that go by the same name. Both take a single parameter, which is a job number preceded by a % (for compatibility with standard shells). The fg command moves the specified job to the foreground; bg sets it running in the background.

Both chores are done by sending SIGCONT to every process in the process group being activated. Although it could send the signal to each process through separate kill() calls, it is slightly simpler to send it to the entire process group using a single kill(). Here is the implementation of the fg and bg built-in commands:

```
} else if (!strcmp(newJob.progs[0].argv[0], "fg") ||
        !strcmp(newJob.progs[0].argv[0], "bg")) {
    if (!newJob.progs[0].argv[1] || newJob.progs[0].argv[2]) {
        fprintf(stderr, "%s: exactly one argument is expected\n",
                newJob.progs[0].argv[0]);
        return 1;
    }

    if (sscanf(newJob.progs[0].argv[1], "%%%d", &jobNum) != 1) {
        fprintf(stderr, "%s: bad argument '%s'\n",
                newJob.progs[0].argv[0], newJob.progs[0].argv[1]);
        return 1;
    }

    for (job = jobList->head; job; job = job->next)
        if (job->jobId == jobNum) break;

    if (!job) {
        fprintf(stderr, "%s: unknown job %d\n",
                newJob.progs[0].argv[0], jobNum);
        return 1;
    }

    if (*newJob.progs[0].argv[0] == 'f') {
        /* Make this job the foreground job */

        if (tcsetpgrp(0, job->pgrp))
            perror("tcsetpgrp");
        jobList->fg = job;
    }

    /* Restart the processes in the job */
    for (i = 0; i < job->numProgs; i++)
        job->progs[i].isStopped = 0;

    kill(-job->pgrp, SIGCONT);
```

```
    job->stoppedProgs = 0;

    return 0;
}
```

Job control was the final ability that `ladsh` required in order to be useable. It is still missing many features present in regular shells, such as shell and environment variables, but it illustrates all the low-level tasks that shells perform.

The complete source code to the final version of `ladsh` is included in Appendix B for easy reference.

# CHAPTER 15

# Terminals and Pseudo Terminals

Devices designed for interactive use[1] all have a similar interface derived from the one created decades ago for serial TeleType paper-display terminals and thus dubbed the **tty** interface. The tty interface is used for accessing serial terminals, consoles, xterms, network logins, and more.

This tty interface is simple in conception but complex in implementation. It is flexible and powerful, which makes it possible to write applications that do not know much about how they get their input and output and can run over the network, on a local screen, or through a modem. Applications can even run under the control of another program without being aware of it.

Unfortunately, it took the Unix implementors several tries to get the interface right. They have left us with three distinct interfaces for connecting to tty devices. The BSD sgtty and System V **termio** interfaces have now been superceded by the POSIX **termios** interface, which is a superset of the termio interface. Because all current systems support the termios interface, and because it is the most powerful of the interfaces, we will document it only, not the earlier interfaces. (For the sake of supporting legacy source code, Linux supports termio, as well as termios. It also used to support the sgtty interface in a limited way, but that support is being removed because it was never perfect, and because there is no longer significant demand for it.)

Not only does the termios interface have to support interactive program use, but it must also support other kinds of data traffic. The same serial

---

1. That is, devices used both for input and for output.

line over which you log in using a modem you might also use for dialing out via a modem, to talk to a serial printer, or to talk to some specialized piece of hardware.

A tty device has two ends. The simplistic view is that one end is attached to the program and the other end is attached to the hardware device. This is true for a serial port; in this case, the serial device driver attaches the serial port (and thereby the terminal or modem) to a shell, editor, or other program. It is also true for the console; the console driver connects the keyboard and screen to the same types of programs. But in some cases, there is a program on each end; in these cases, one of the ends takes the place of hardware. For instance, with a network connection, one end of the tty device is connected to a program that provides the network connection, and the other end is connected to the shell, editor, or other potentially interactive program. When there is a program at each end, you need to keep a clear idea of which end is emulating hardware; in the case of network connections, the side that connects to the network is the hardware side.

tty devices that have software at both ends are called **pseudo ttys,** or, simply, **ptys.** For the first part of this chapter, you can pretend that they do not exist, because the "software" end of a pty is handled just like any tty device. Later on, we talk about programming the "hardware" end of a pty.

# 15.1 tty Operations

tty devices provide a large number of processing options; they are among the most complicated devices in the kernel. You can set input processing, output processing, and data flow processing options. You can also control a limited amount of data manipulation that occurs at the device driver level.

ttys operate in two basic modes: raw and cooked. **Raw mode** passes data to the application as it is received, with no changes made. **Cooked mode**, also known as **canonical** mode, provides a limited line editor inside the device driver and sends edited input to the application one line at a time. This mode is primarily derived from mainframe systems, in which dedicated input processing units provided cooked mode without interrupting the CPU at all.

Cooked mode processes certain control characters; for example, by default, ^U **kills** (erases) the current line, ^W erases the current word, backspace (^H) or delete erases the previous character, and ^R erases and then retypes the current line. Each of these control actions can be reassigned to a different character. For instance, on many terminals, DEL (character 127) is assigned the backspace action.

## 15.1.1 Controlling Terminals

Every session (see Chapter 9) is tied to a terminal from which processes in the session get their input and to which they send their output. That terminal may be the machine's local console, a terminal connected over a serial line, or a pseudo terminal that maps to an X window or across a network (see page 308 later in this chapter for more on pseudo terminals). The terminal to which a session is related is called the **controlling terminal** (or **controlling tty**) of the session. A terminal can be the controlling terminal for only one session at a time.

Normal processes cannot change their controlling terminal; only a session leader can do that. Under Linux, a change in the session leader's controlling terminal is not propagated to other processes in that session. Session leaders almost always set a controlling terminal when they initially start running, before they create any child processes, in order to ensure that all the processes in the session share a common controlling terminal.

There are two interfaces for changing a session group leader's controlling tty. The first is through the normal open() and close() system calls.

1.   Close all file descriptors that reference the current controlling terminal.

2.   Open a new terminal without specifying the O_NOCTTY flag.

The other method involves ioctl()s on separate file descriptors that reference the old and the new terminal devices.

1.   TIOCNOTTY on a file descriptor tied to the original controlling tty (usually, ioctl(0, TIOCNOTTY, NULL) works fine). This breaks the bond between the session and the tty.

2. `TIOCSCTTY` on the file descriptor tied to the new controlling tty. This sets a new controlling tty.

A terminal that is being used by a session keeps track of which process group is considered the **foreground process group**. Processes in that process group are allowed to read from and write to the terminal, whereas processes in other process groups are not (see Chapter 14 for details on what happens when background processes try to read and write from the controlling terminal). The `tcsetpgrp()` function allows a process running on a terminal to change the foreground process group for that terminal.[2]

```
int tcsetpgrp(int ttyfd, int pid_t pgrp);
```

The first parameter specifies the tty whose controlling process group is being changed, and `pgrp` is the process group that should be moved to the foreground. Processes may change the foreground process group only for their controlling terminal. If the process making the change is not in the foreground process group on that terminal, a `SIGTTOU` is generated, unless that signal is being ignored or is blocked.[3]

# 15.2 termios Overview

All tty manipulation is done through one structure, `struct termios`, and through several functions, all defined in the `<termios.h>` header file. Of those functions, only six are commonly used, and when you do not have to set line speeds, you are likely to use only two of them. The two most important functions are the `tcgetattr()` and `tcsetattr()` functions.

```
#include <termios.h>

struct termios {
    tcflag_t c_iflag;    /* input mode flags */
    tcflag_t c_oflag;    /* output mode flags */
```

---

2. Older implementations of Unix provided this functionality through the `TIOCSPGRP` `ioctl()`, which is still supported in Linux. For comparison, `tcsetpgrp()` could be implemented as `ioctl(ttyfd, TIOCSPGRP, &pgrp)`.
3. For more information on signals and their interaction with job control, see Chapter 13.

```
    tcflag_t c_cflag;    /* control mode flags */
    tcflag_t c_lflag;    /* local mode flags */
    cc_t c_line;         /* line discipline */
    cc_t c_cc[NCCS];     /* control characters */
};

int tcgetattr (int fd, struct termios *tp);
int tcsetattr (int fd, int oact, struct termios *tp);
```

In almost every situation, a program will use `tcgetattr()` to get a device's current settings, modify those settings, and then use `tcsetattr()` to make the modified settings active. Many programs will also save a copy of the original settings and restore them before terminating. In general, modify only the settings that you know you care about; changing other settings may make it difficult for users to work around unusual system configurations (or bugs in your code).

`tcsetattr()` may not honor all the settings you choose; it is allowed to ignore arbitrary settings. In particular, if the hardware simply does not support a setting, it will ignore it rather than return an error. If you care that a setting really takes effect, you will have to use `tcgetattr()` after `tcsetattr()` and test to make sure that your change took effect.

To get a tty device's settings, you have to open the device and use the file descriptor in the `tcgetattr()` call. This poses a problem with some tty devices; some may normally be opened only once, to prevent device contention. Fortunately, giving the `O_NONBLOCK` flag to `open()` will cause it to be opened immediately and not block on any operations. However, you may still prefer to block on `read()`; if so, use `fcntl()` to turn off `O_NONBLOCK` mode before you read or write to it:

```
    fcntl(fd, F_SETFL, fcntl(fd, F_GETFL, 0) & ~O_NONBLOCK);
```

The four termios flags control four distinct parts of managing input and output. The input flag, `c_iflag`, determines how received characters are interpreted and processed. The output flag, `c_oflag`, determines how characters your process writes to the tty are interpreted and processed. The control flag, `c_cflag`, determines serial protocol characteristics of the device and is useful only for physical devices. The local flag, `c_lflag`, determines how characters are collected and processed before they are sent to output

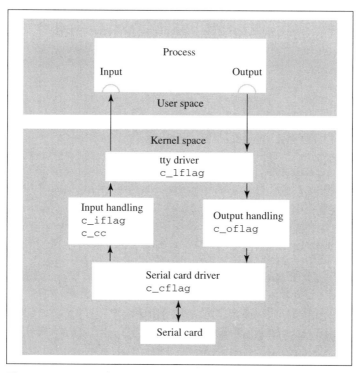

**Figure 15.1** Simplified View of tty Processing

processing. Figure 15.1 shows a simplified view of how each of these flags fits into the grand scheme of character processing.

We will first demonstrate ways to use termios, and then present a short reference to it.

## 15.3 termios Examples

### 15.3.1 Passwords

One common reason to modify termios settings is to read a password without echoing characters. To do this, you want to turn off local echo while reading the password. Your code will look like this:

```
struct termios ts, ots;
```

One structure keeps the original termios settings so that you can restore them, and the other one is a copy to modify.

```
tcgetattr(STDIN_FILENO, &ts);
```

Generally, you will be reading passwords from standard input.

```
ots = ts;
```

Keep a copy of the original termios settings to restore later.

```
ts.c_lflag &= ~ECHO;
ts.c_lflag |= ECHONL;
tcsetattr(STDIN_FILENO, TCSAFLUSH, &ots);
```

Turn off echoing characters except newlines, after all currently pending output is completed. (The first l in c_lflag stands for local processing.)

```
read_password();
```

Here, you read the password. This may be as simple as a single fgets() or read() call, or it may include more-complex processing, depending on whether the tty is in raw mode or cooked mode, and depending on the requirements of your program.

```
tcsetattr(STDIN_FILENO, TCSANOW, &ots);
```

This restores the original termios settings and does so immediately. (We explain other options later, in the reference section on page 290.)

A full example program, readpass, looks like this:

```
 1: /* readpass - read a password without echoing it */
 2: #include <stdio.h>
 3: #include <termios.h>
 4: #include <unistd.h>
 5:
 6: int main(void) {
 7:     struct termios ts, ots;
 8:     char passbuf[1024];
 9:
10:     /* get and save current termios settings */
```

```
11:     tcgetattr(STDIN_FILENO, &ts);
12:     ots = ts;
13:
14:     /* change and set new termios settings */
15:     ts.c_lflag &= ~ECHO;
16:     ts.c_lflag |= ECHONL;
17:     tcsetattr(STDIN_FILENO, TCSAFLUSH, &ts);
18:
19:     /* paranoia: check that the settings took effect */
20:     tcgetattr(STDIN_FILENO, &ts);
21:     if (ts.c_lflag & ECHO) {
22:         fprintf(stderr, "Failed to turn off echo\n");
23:         tcsetattr(STDIN_FILENO, TCSANOW, &ots);
24:         exit(1);
25:     }
26:
27:     /* get and print the password */
28:     printf("enter password: ");
29:     fflush(stdout);
30:     fgets(passbuf, 1024, stdin);
31:     printf("read password: %s", passbuf);
32:     /* there was a terminal \n in passbuf */
33:
34:     /* restore old termios settings */
35:     tcsetattr(STDIN_FILENO, TCSANOW, &ots);
36:
37:     exit(0);
38: }
```

## 15.3.2 Serial Communications

As an example of programming both ends of a tty, here is a program that connects the current terminal to a serial port. On one tty, the program, called **robin**, is talking to you as you type. On another tty, it is communicating with the serial port. In order to multiplex input to and output from the local tty and the serial port, the program uses the select() system call described in page 209.

Here is robin.c in its entirety, followed by an explanation.

```
 1: /* robin.c -- implements simple serial port interaction program */
 2: #include <sys/time.h>
 3: #include <sys/types.h>
 4: #include <errno.h>
 5: #include <fcntl.h>
 6: #include <popt.h>
 7: #include <stdio.h>
 8: #include <stdlib.h>
 9: #include <signal.h>
10: #include <string.h>                   /* for strerror() */
11: #include <termios.h>
12: #include <unistd.h>
13:
14: void usage(int exitcode, char *error, char *addl) {
15:     fprintf(stderr, "Usage: robin [options] <port>\n"
16:                     " [options] include:\n"
17:                     "     -H for this help\n"
18:                     "     -r for raw mode\n"
19:                     "     -c to add CR with NL on output\n"
20:                     "     -h for hardware flow control\n"
21:                     "     -s for software flow control\n"
22:                     "     -n for no flow control\n"
23:                     "     -b <bps> for signalling rate\n");
24:     if (error) fprintf(stderr, "%s: %s\n", error, addl);
25:     exit(exitcode);
26: }
27:
28: speed_t symbolic_speed(int speednum) {
29:     if (speednum >= 460800) return B460800;
30:     if (speednum >= 230400) return B230400;
31:     if (speednum >= 115200) return B115200;
32:     if (speednum >= 57600) return B57600;
33:     if (speednum >= 38400) return B38400;
34:     if (speednum >= 19200) return B19200;
35:     if (speednum >= 9600) return B9600;
36:     if (speednum >= 4800) return B4800;
37:     if (speednum >= 2400) return B2400;
38:     if (speednum >= 1800) return B1800;
39:     if (speednum >= 1200) return B1200;
40:     if (speednum >= 600) return B600;
41:     if (speednum >= 300) return B300;
```

```
42:    if (speednum >= 200) return B200;
43:    if (speednum >= 150) return B150;
44:    if (speednum >= 134) return B134;
45:    if (speednum >= 110) return B110;
46:    if (speednum >= 75) return B75;
47:    return B50;
48: }
49:
50: /* These need to have file scope so that we can use them in
51:  * signal handlers */
52: /* old port termios settings to restore */
53: static struct termios pots;
54: /* old stdout/in termios settings to restore */
55: static struct termios sots;
56: /* port file descriptor */
57: int    pf;
58:
59: /* restore original terminal settings on exit */
60: void cleanup_termios(int signal) {
61:    tcsetattr(pf, TCSANOW, &pots);
62:    tcsetattr(STDIN_FILENO, TCSANOW, &sots);
63:    exit(0);
64: }
65:
66: /* handle a single escape character */
67: void send_escape(int fd, char c) {
68:    switch (c) {
69:    case 'q':
70:       /* restore termios settings and exit */
71:       cleanup_termios(0);
72:       break;
73:    case 'b':
74:       /* send a break */
75:       tcsendbreak(fd, 0);
76:       break;
77:    default:
78:       /* pass the character through */
79:       /* "C-\ C-\" sends "C-\" */
80:       write(fd, &c, 1);
81:       break;
82:    }
```

```
83:     return;
84: }
85:
86: /* handle escape characters, writing to output */
87: void cook_buf(int fd, char *buf, int num) {
88:     int current = 0;
89:     static int in_escape = 0;
90:
91:     if (in_escape) {
92:         /* cook_buf last called with an incomplete escape sequence */
93:         send_escape(fd, buf[0]);
94:         num--;
95:         buf++;
96:         in_escape = 0;
97:     }
98:     while (current < num) {
99: #     define CTRLCHAR(c) ((c)-0x40)
100:        while ((current < num) && (buf[current] != CTRLCHAR('\\'))) current++;
101:        if (current) write (fd, buf, current);
102:        if (current < num) {
103:            /* found an escape character */
104:            current++;
105:            if (current >= num) {
106:                /* interpret first character of next sequence */
107:                in_escape = 1;
108:                return;
109:            }
110:            send_escape(fd, buf[current]);
111:        }
112:        num -= current;
113:        buf += current;
114:        current = 0;
115:     }
116:     return;
117: }
118:
119: int main(int argc, char *argv[]) {
120:     char    c;              /* used for argument parsing */
121:     struct  termios pts;    /* termios settings on port */
122:     struct  termios sts;    /* termios settings on stdout/in */
123:     char    *portname;
```

```
124:    int    speed = 0;    /* used in argument parsing to set speed */
125:    struct sigaction sact;/* used to initialize the signal handler */
126:    fd_set  ready;        /* used for select */
127:    int    raw = 0;       /* raw mode? */
128:    int    i = 0;         /* used in the multiplex loop */
129:    int    done = 0;
130: #  define BUFSIZE 1024
131:    char   buf[BUFSIZE];
132:    poptContext optCon;   /* context for parsing command-line options */
133:    struct poptOption optionsTable[] = {
134:            { "bps", 'b', POPT_ARG_INT, &speed, 0 },
135:            { "crnl", 'c', 0, 0, 'c' },
136:            { "help", 'H', 0, 0, 'H' },
137:            { "hwflow", 'h', 0, 0, 'h' },
138:            { "noflow", 'n', 0, 0, 0 },
139:            { "raw", 'r', 0, &raw, 0 },
140:            { "swflow", 's', 0, 0, 's' },
141:            { NULL, 0, 0, NULL, 0 }
142:    };
143:
144: #ifdef DSLEEP
145:    /* wait 10 minutes so we can attach a debugger */
146:    sleep(600);
147: #endif
148:
149:    if (argc < 2) usage(1, "Not enough arguments", "");
150:
151:    /* Normally, we'd let popt figure out which argument is the
152:       port name. Here we're forcing it to be the last one as it
153:       eases the rest of the option parsing. */
154:    portname = argv[argc - 1];
155:    pf = open(portname, O_RDWR);
156:    if (pf < 0)
157:       usage(1, strerror(errno), portname);
158:
159:    /* modify the port configuration */
160:    tcgetattr(pf, &pts);
161:    pots = pts;
162:    /* some things we want to set arbitrarily */
163:    pts.c_lflag &= ~ICANON;
164:    pts.c_lflag &= ~(ECHO | ECHOCTL | ECHONL);
```

```
165:       pts.c_cflag |= HUPCL;
166:       pts.c_cc[VMIN] = 1;
167:       pts.c_cc[VTIME] = 0;
168:
169:       /* Standard CR/LF handling: this is a dumb terminal.
170:        * Do no translation:
171:        *  no NL -> CR/NL mapping on output, and
172:        *  no CR -> NL mapping on input.
173:        */
174:       pts.c_oflag &= ~ONLCR;
175:       pts.c_iflag &= ~ICRNL;
176:
177:       /* Now deal with the local terminal side */
178:       tcgetattr(STDIN_FILENO, &sts);
179:       sots = sts;
180:       /* again, some arbitrary things */
181:       sts.c_iflag &= ~BRKINT;
182:       sts.c_iflag |= IGNBRK;
183:       sts.c_lflag &= ~ISIG;
184:       sts.c_cc[VMIN] = 1;
185:       sts.c_cc[VTIME] = 0;
186:       sts.c_lflag &= ~ICANON;
187:       /* no local echo: allow the other end to do the echoing */
188:       sts.c_lflag &= ~(ECHO | ECHOCTL | ECHONL);
189:
190:       optCon = poptGetContext("robin", argc, argv, optionsTable, 0);
191:
192:       /* option processing will now modify pts and sts */
193:       while ((c = poptGetNextOpt(optCon)) >= 0) {
194:          switch (c) {
195:             case 'H':
196:                 usage(0, NULL, NULL);
197:                 break;
198:             case 'c':
199:                 /* send CR with NL */
200:                 pts.c_oflag |= ONLCR;
201:                 break;
202:             case 'h':
203:                 /* hardware flow control */
204:                 pts.c_cflag |= CRTSCTS;
205:                 pts.c_iflag &= ~(IXON | IXOFF | IXANY);
```

```
206:            break;
207:         case 's':
208:            /* software flow control */
209:            pts.c_cflag &= ~CRTSCTS;
210:            pts.c_iflag |= IXON | IXOFF | IXANY;
211:            break;
212:         case 'n':
213:            /* no flow control */
214:            pts.c_cflag &= ~CRTSCTS;
215:            pts.c_iflag &= ~(IXON | IXOFF | IXANY);
216:            break;
217:      }
218:   }
219:
220:   if (c < -1) {
221:      /* an error occurred during option processing */
222:      fprintf(stderr, "%s: %s\n",
223:               poptBadOption(optCon, POPT_BADOPTION_NOALIAS),
224:               poptStrerror(c));
225:      return 1;
226:   }
227:
228:   /* speed is not modified unless -b is specified */
229:   if (speed) {
230:      cfsetospeed(&pts, symbolic_speed(speed));
231:      cfsetispeed(&pts, symbolic_speed(speed));
232:   }
233:
234:   /* set the signal handler to restore the old
235:    * termios handler */
236:   sact.sa_handler = cleanup_termios;
237:   sigaction(SIGHUP, &sact, NULL);
238:   sigaction(SIGINT, &sact, NULL);
239:   sigaction(SIGPIPE, &sact, NULL);
240:   sigaction(SIGTERM, &sact, NULL);
241:
242:   /* Now set the modified termios settings */
243:   tcsetattr(pf, TCSANOW, &pts);
244:   tcsetattr(STDIN_FILENO, TCSANOW, &sts);
245:
246:   do {
```

```
247:        FD_ZERO(&ready);
248:        FD_SET(STDIN_FILENO, &ready);
249:        FD_SET(pf, &ready);
250:        select(pf+1, &ready, NULL, NULL, NULL);
251:        if (FD_ISSET(pf, &ready)) {
252:            /* pf has characters for us */
253:            i = read(pf, buf, BUFSIZE);
254:            if (i >= 1) {
255:                write(STDOUT_FILENO, buf, i);
256:            } else {
257:                done = 1;
258:            }
259:        }
260:        if (FD_ISSET(STDIN_FILENO, &ready)) {
261:            /* standard input has characters for us */
262:            i = read(STDIN_FILENO, buf, BUFSIZE);
263:            if (i >= 1) {
264:                if (raw) {
265:                    write(pf, buf, i);
266:                } else {
267:                    cook_buf(pf, buf, i);
268:                }
269:            } else {
270:                done = 1;
271:            }
272:        }
273:    } while (!done);
274:
275:    /* restore original terminal settings and exit */
276:    tcsetattr(pf, TCSANOW, &pots);
277:    tcsetattr(STDIN_FILENO, TCSANOW, &sots);
278:    exit(0);
279: }
```

robin.c starts out by including a few header files (read the man page for each system call and library function to see which include files you need to include, as usual), then defines a few useful functions.

The symbolic_speed() function at line 28 converts an integer speed into a symbolic speed that termios can handle. Unfortunately, termios is not designed to handle arbitrary speeds, so each speed you wish to use must be part of the user-kernel interface.[4]

Note that it includes some rather high speeds. Not all serial ports support speeds as high as 230,400 or 460,800 bps; the POSIX standard defines speeds only up to 38,400 bps. To make this program portable, each line above the one that sets the speed to 38,400 bps would have to be expanded to three lines, like this:

```
#  ifdef B460800
    if (speednum >= 460800) return B460800;
#  endif
```

That will still allow users to specify speeds beyond what the serial ports may be able to handle, but the source code will now compile on any system with POSIX termios. (As discussed on page 271 and page 290, any serial port has the option of refusing to honor any termios setting it is incapable of handling, and that includes speed settings. So just because B460800 is defined does not mean you can set the port speed to 460,800 bits per second.)

Next, on lines 53 through 64, we see a few global variables for communicating some variables to a signal handler, and the signal handler itself. The signal handler is designed to restore termios settings on both tty interfaces when a signal is delivered, so it needs to be able to access the structures containing the old termios settings. It also needs to know the file descriptor of the serial port (the file descriptor for standard input does not change, so it is compiled into the binary). The code is identical to that in the normal exit path, which is described later. The signal handler is later attached to signals that would terminate the process if they were ignored.

The send_escape() and cook_buf() functions will be discussed later. They are used as part of the input processing in the I/O loop at the end of the main() function.

The conditionally compiled sleep(600) is there for debugging. In order to debug programs that modify termios settings for standard input or standard output, it is best to **attach** to the process from a different window or

---

4. See man setserial for a Linux-specific way to get around this limitation on a limited basis.

terminal session. However, that means that you cannot just set a breakpoint on the main function and step into the process one instruction at a time. You have to start the program running, find its pid, and attach to it from within the debugger. This process is described in more detail on page 289.

Therefore, if we are debugging and need to debug code that runs before the program waits for input, we will need the program to sleep for a while to give us time to attach. Once we attach, we will interrupt the sleep, so there is no harm in using a long sleep time. Compile robin.c with `-DDSLEEP` in order to activate this feature.

In real programs, you will generally want to use a more flexible option-processing scheme than the quick-and-dirty scheme used in robin.c. In robin, we grab the port name well before attempting other option processing, because the easiest way to write the option processing is to have the code open the port first, then modify it directly while processing the options. It is usually better to collect and verify all the command-line options before you act on any of them; we have taken this shortcut only because it makes the source code a bit shorter.

Next, we use the `tcgetattr()` function to get the existing termios configuration of the serial port, then we save a copy in `pots` so that we can restore it when we are through.

Starting with line 163, we modify settings for the serial port.

```
pts.c_lflag &= ~ICANON;
```

The first line turns off canonicalization in the serial port driver—that is, puts it in raw mode. In this mode, no characters are special—not newlines, not control characters.

```
pts.c_lflag &= ~(ECHO | ECHOCTL | ECHONL);
```

This turns off all local echoing on the serial port.

```
pts.c_cflag |= HUPCL;
```

If there is a modem connected, `HUPCL` arranges for it to be told to hang up when the final program closes the device.

```
pts.c_cc[VMIN] = 1;
pts.c_cc[VTIME] = 0;
```

When a tty is in raw mode, these two settings determine the read() system call's behavior. This particular setting says that when we call read(), we want read() to wait to return until one or more bytes have been read. We will never call read() unless we know that there is at least one byte to read, so this will be functionally equivalent to a nonblocking read(). The definition of VMIN and VTIME is complex, as we demonstrate on page 307.

The default termios settings include some end-of-line character translation. That is okay for dial-in lines and for terminal sessions, but when we are connecting two ttys, we do not want the translation to happen twice. We do not want to map newline characters to a carriage return/newline pair on output, and we do not want to map a received carriage return to a newline on input, because we are already receiving carriage return/newline pairs from the remote system:

```
pts.c_oflag &= ~ONLCR;
pts.c_iflag &= ~ICRNL;
```

Without these two lines, using robin to connect to another Linux or Unix computer will result in the remote system seeing you press Return twice each time you press it once, and each time it tries to display a new line on your screen, you will see two lines. So each time you press Return (assuming you manage to log in with these terminal settings), you will see two prompts echoed back to you, and if you run vi, you will see ~ characters on every other line rather than on every line.

At this point, we have made all the changes to the serial port's termios settings that we know we need to make before we process the command-line arguments. We will turn to modifying the settings for the tty that gives us standard input and output. Since it is one tty, we need to deal with only one of the two. By convention, we have chosen standard input, because the **stty** program does the same. We start out, again, by getting and saving attributes.

Then we modify some flags:

```
sts.c_iflag &= ~BRKINT;
sts.c_iflag |= IGNBRK;
sts.c_lflag &= ~ISIG;
```

Turning off BRKINT makes a difference only if robin is being called from a login session that is coming in over another serial port, where a break can be received. Turning it off means that the tty driver will not send a SIGINT to robin when a break condition occurs on robin's standard input, since robin does not have anything useful to do when it receives a break.

The IGNBRK function tells the tty driver to ignore breaks. Turning on IGNBRK is actually redundant here. If IGNBRK is set, then BRKINT is ignored. But it does not hurt to set both.

Those are input processing flags. We also modify a local processing flag: We turn off ISIG. This keeps the tty driver from sending SIGINTR, SIGQUIT, and SIGTSTP when the respective character (INTR, QUIT, or SUSP) is received. We do this because we want those characters to be sent to the remote system (or whatever is connected to the serial port) for processing there.

Next comes option processing, which is done with **popt**, discussed in Chapter 24. In some cases, the default modifications we made to the termios settings might not be sufficient, or they might be too much. In these cases, we provide some command-line options to modify the termios options.

When robin is being used as a helper program by another program, doing any special character processing (robin usually interprets a control-\ character specially) may get in the way, so we provide raw mode to sidestep all such processing. On line 127, we provide a variable that determines whether raw mode is enabled; the default is not to enable raw mode. On line 139, we tell popt how to inform us that the -r or --raw option was given on the command line, enabling raw mode.

Some systems require that you send them a carriage-return character to represent a newline. The word *systems* should be taken broadly here; as an example, this is true of many smart peripherals, such as UPSs, that have serial ports, because they were designed to function in the DOS world, where a carriage-return/newline pair is always used to denote a new line. Line 198 allows us to specify this DOS-oriented behavior.

```
case 'c':
    /* send CR with NL */
    pts.c_oflag |= ONLCR;
```

By default, we leave the serial port in whatever flow-control state we find it in. However, at line 202, there are options to do hardware flow control (which uses the CTS and RTS flow-control wires), software flow control (reserving ^S and ^Q for STOP and START, respectively), and no flow control at all.

```
case 'h':
    /* hardware flow control */
    pts.c_cflag |= CRTSCTS;
    pts.c_iflag &= ~(IXON | IXOFF | IXANY);
    break;
case 's':
    /* software flow control */
    pts.c_cflag &= ~CRTSCTS;
    pts.c_iflag |= IXON | IXOFF | IXANY;
    break;
case 'n':
    /* no flow control */
    pts.c_cflag &= ~CRTSCTS;
    pts.c_iflag &= ~(IXON | IXOFF | IXANY);
    break;
```

Note that software flow control involves three flags:

IXON   Stop sending output if a STOP character (usually, ^S) is received, and start again when a START character (usually, ^Q) is received.

IXOFF   Send a STOP character when there is too much data in the incoming buffer, and send a START character when enough of the data has been read.

IXANY   Allow any received character, not just START, to restart **output**. (This flag is commonly implemented on Unix systems, but it is not specified by POSIX.)

The final phrase in our `getopt` switch statement controls the **bits per second**[5] rate. Rather than include a large nested switch statement here, we call `symbolic_speed()`, already described, to get a `speed_t` that termios will understand, as shown on line 228.

```
/* speed is not modified unless -b is specified */
if (speed) {
   cfsetospeed(&pts, symbolic_speed(speed));
   cfsetispeed(&pts, symbolic_speed(speed));
}
```

Having determined the actual speed and gotten the symbolic value that represents it, we need to put that speed into the termios structure for the serial port. Since the termios structure supports asynchronous devices that can have different input and output speeds, we need to set both speeds to the same value here.

Before committing the changes we have made in our copies of the termios structures to the devices, on line 236 we register signal handlers for important signals that might otherwise kill us, causing us to leave the ttys in their raw state. For more information on signal handlers, see Chapter 13.

```
sact.sa_handler = cleanup_termios;
sigaction(SIGHUP, &sact, NULL);
sigaction(SIGINT, &sact, NULL);
sigaction(SIGPIPE, &sact, NULL);
sigaction(SIGTERM, &sact, NULL);
```

Once the signal handler is in place to restore the old termios settings if robin is killed, we can safely put the new termios settings in place.

```
tcsetattr(pf, TCSANOW, &pts);
tcsetattr(STDIN_FILENO, TCSANOW, &sts);
```

Note that we use the `TCSANOW` option when setting these options, indicating that we want them to take effect immediately. Sometimes, it is appropriate to use other options; they are covered later in the reference section.

---

5. Note: "bits per second" or "bps," not "baud." Bits per second indicates the rate at which information is sent. Baud is an engineering term that describes phase changes per second. Baud is irrelevant to termios, but the word *baud* has unfortunately made its way into some termios flags that are not covered in this book.

At this point, robin is ready to read and write characters. robin has two file descriptors to read from: data coming from the serial port and data coming from the keyboard. We use select() to multiplex I/O between the four file descriptors, as described in Chapter 12.

The select() loop makes the simplifying assumption that it can always write as much as it was able to read. This is almost always true and does not cause problems in practice, because blocking for short periods will not be noticeable in normal circumstances. The loop never reads from a file descriptor unless select() has already said that that file descriptor has data waiting to be read, so we know that we will not block while reading.

For data coming from the keyboard, we may need to process escape sequences before writing, if the user did not select raw mode when running robin. Rather than include that code in the middle of this loop, we call cook_buf() (line 87), which calls send_escape() (line 67) when necessary. Both of these functions are simple. The only tricks are that cook_buf() may be called once with the escape character, then a second time with the character to interpret, and that it is optimized to call the write() function as little as is reasonably possible.

cook_buf() calls the send_escape() function once for every character that is preceded by an unescaped control-\ character. A q character restores the original termios settings and quits by calling the signal handler (with a bogus signal number of 0), which restores the termios settings appropriately before exiting. A b character generates a break condition, which is a long string of continuous 0 bits. Any other character, including a second control-\ character, is passed through to the serial port verbatim.

If either input file descriptor returns an end-of-file condition, robin exits the select() loop and falls through to the exit processing, which is the same as the signal handler: It restores the old termios settings on both input file descriptors and exits. In raw mode, the only ways to get robin to quit are to close one of the file descriptors or to send it a signal.

# 15.4 termios Debugging

Debugging tty code is not always easy. The options overlap in meaning and affect each other in various ways, often in ways that you do not intend. But you cannot easily see what is happening with only a debugger, because the processing that you are trying to manage is happening in the kernel.

One effective way to debug code that communicates over a serial port is to use the script program. While developing robin, we connected two computers with a serial cable and verified that the connection worked by running the already-working kermit program. While still running kermit on the local computer, we ran the script program on the remote computer, which started keeping a log of all the characters in the file typescript. Then we quit kermit and ran script on the local computer, which put a typescript file in the current directory on the local computer. We then tried to run robin under script and compared the two typescript files at each end after each run to see the differences in characters. We thereby deciphered the effects of the processing options we had chosen.

Another debugging method takes advantage of the stty program. If, while you are testing a program, you think you recognize a mistake in the termios settings, you can use the stty program to make the change immediately rather than recompile your program first. If you are working on /dev/cua0, and you want to set the ECHOCTL flag, simply run the command

```
stty echoctl < /dev/cua0
```

while your program is running.

Similarly, you can view the current status of the port you are using with

```
stty -a < /dev/cua0
```

As we explained before, it is hard to use the same tty for running the debugger and for running the tty-mangling program you are debugging. Instead, you want to attach to the process. This is not difficult to do. In one X-terminal session (do this under X so that you can see both ttys at once), run the program you want to debug. If you need to, put a long sleep() in it at the point at which you wish to attach to it.

```
$ ./robin -b 38400 /dev/cua1
```

Now, from another X-terminal session, find the pid of the program you are trying to debug, in one of two ways:

```
$ ps | grep robin
30483  ?  S   0:00 ./robin -b 38400 /dev/cua1
30485  ?  S   0:00 grep robin
$ pidof robin
30483
```

pidof is more convenient, but may not be available on every system. Keep the number you found (here, 30483) in mind and start a debugging session the same way you normally would.

```
$ gdb robin 30483
GDB is free software...
...
Attaching to program '.../robin', process 30483
Reading symbols from ...
0x40075d88 in sigsuspend ()
```

From this point, you can set breakpoints and watchpoints, step through the program, or whatever you like.

# 15.5  termios Reference

The termios interface is composed of a structure, a set of functions that operate on it, and a multitude of flags that you can set individually.

```
#include <termios.h>

struct termios {
    tcflag_t c_iflag;    /* input mode flags */
    tcflag_t c_oflag;    /* output mode flags */
    tcflag_t c_cflag;    /* control mode flags */
    tcflag_t c_lflag;    /* local mode flags */
    cc_t c_line;         /* line discipline */
    cc_t c_cc[NCCS];     /* control characters */
};
```

The c_line member is used only in very system-specific applications[6] that are beyond the scope of this book. The other five members, however, are relevant in almost all situations that require you to manipulate terminal settings.

## 15.5.1 Functions

The termios interface defines several functions, all of which are declared in <termios.h>. Four of them are convenience functions for manipulating a struct termios in a portable way; the rest are system calls. Those that start with cf are convenience functions; those functions that start with tc are **terminal control** system calls. All of the terminal control system calls generate SIGTTOU if the process is currently running in the background and tries to manipulate its controlling terminal (see Chapter 14).

Except as noted, these functions return 0 to indicate success and -1 to indicate failure. The function calls you may use for terminal control are:

int tcgetattr(int fd, struct termios *t);
> Retrieves the current settings for the file descriptor fd and places them in the structure to which t points.

int tcsetattr(int fd, int options, struct termios *t);
> Sets the current terminal settings for the file descriptor fd to the settings specified in t. Always use tcgetattr() to fill in t, then modify it. Never fill in t by hand: Some systems require that flags

---

6. Such as setting up networking protocols that communicate through tty devices.

beyond the flags specified by POSIX be set or cleared, so filling in t by hand is nonportable.

The options argument determines when the change takes effect.

TCSANOW    The change takes effect immediately.

TCSADRAIN    The change takes effect after all the output that has already been written to fd has been transmitted; it drains the queue before taking effect. You should generally use this when you change output parameters.

TCSAFLUSH    The change takes effect after the output queue has been drained; the input queue is discarded (flushed) before the change takes effect.

If the system cannot handle some settings, such as data rate, it is allowed to silently **ignore** those settings without returning any error. The only way to see whether the settings were accepted is to use tcgetattr() and compare the contents of the structure it returns to the one you passed to tcsetattr().

Thus, most portable applications use code something like this:

```
#include <termios.h>

struct termios save;
struct termios set;
struct termios new;
int fd;
...
tcgetattr(fd, &save);
set = save;
cfsetospeed(&set, B2400);
cfsetispeed(&set, B2400);
tcsetattr(fd, &set);
tcgetattr(fd, &new);
if ((cfgetospeed(&set) != B2400) ||
    (cfgetispeed(&set) != B2400)) {
  /* complain */
}
```

Note that if you do not care if a termios setting sticks, it is fine to ignore the condition, as we do in robin.

```
speed_t cfgetospeed(struct termios *t);
speed_t cfgetispeed(struct termios *t);
```
Retrieve the output or input speed, respectively, from t. These functions return a symbolic speed, the same as is given to cfsetospeed() and cfsetispeed().

```
int cfsetospeed(struct termios *t, speed_t speed);
int cfsetispeed(struct termios *t, speed_t speed);
```
Set the output or input speed, respectively, in t to speed. Note that this function does not change the speed of the connection on any file descriptor; it merely sets the speed in the termios structure. The speed, like other characteristics, is applied to a file descriptor by tcsetattr().

These functions take a symbolic speed—that is, a number that matches the definition of one of the following macros whose names indicate the bits-per-second rate: B0 (0 bits per second indicates a disconnected state), B50, B75, B110, B134,[7] B150, B200, B300, B600, B1200, B1800, B2400, B4800, B9600, B19200, B38400, B57600, B115200, B230400, or B460800. B57600 and higher are not specified by POSIX; portable source code uses them only if they are protected by #ifdef statements.

More symbolic speeds will be added to the header file as Linux drivers are written for hardware that supports other data rates.

Currently, input speed is ignored. The termios interface specifies separate input and output speeds for some asynchronous hardware that allows split speeds, but little such hardware exists. Just call cfsetospeed() and cfsetispeed() in pairs so that your code will continue to work on systems that support split speeds.

Not all ttys support all rates. In particular, the serial ports on standard PCs do not support over 115,200 bps. As noted above, if you care whether this setting takes effect, you will need to use tcgetattr() to check after you attempt to set it with tcsetattr().

---

7. B134 is really 134.5 bps, a rate used by an obsolete IBM terminal.

Also, note that the rate you set is advisory. Some ttys, like local consoles, will cheerfully accept and ignore any rate you give them.

int tcsendbreak(int fd, int duration)

Sends a stream of 0 bits on fd for a specified duration. If duration is 0, the break is at least 250 milliseconds and no more than 500 milliseconds long. Unfortunately, POSIX did not bother to specify the unit in which the duration is measured, so the only portable value for duration is 0. Under Linux, duration multiplies the break; 0 or 1 specify between a quarter second and a half second; 2 specifies between a half second and a second, and so on.

int tcdrain(int fd)

Waits until all currently pending output on the file descriptor fd has been sent.

int tcflush(int fd, int queue_selector)

Discards some data on file descriptor fd, depending on the value of queue_selector:

| | |
|---|---|
| TCIFLUSH | Flush all data that the interface has received but that has not yet been read. |
| TCOFLUSH | Flush all data that has been written to the interface that has not yet been sent. |
| TCIOFLUSH | Flush all pending data, input and output. |

int tcflow(int fd, int action)

Suspend or resume output or input on the file descriptor fd. Exactly what to do is determined by action:

| | |
|---|---|
| TCOOFF | Suspend output. |
| TCOON | Resume output. |
| TCIOFF | Send a STOP character, requesting that the other end of the connection stop sending characters. |

TCION          Send a START character, requesting that the other end
               of the connection resume sending characters.

Note that TCIOFF and TCION are only advisory, and that even if the
other end of the connection does honor them, there may be a delay
before it does so.

## 15.5.2 Window Sizes

There are two ioctl() requests that, unfortunately, were not codified as part
of the termios interface, although they should have been. The size of the tty,
measured in rows and columns, ought to be managed with tcgetwinsize()
and tcsetwinsize(), but as they do not exist, you must use ioctl() instead.
For both requesting the current size and setting a new size, use a struct
winsize:

```
#include <termios.h>

struct winsize {
    unsigned short ws_row;      /* number of rows */
    unsigned short ws_col;      /* number of columns */
    unsigned short ws_xpixel;   /* unused */
    unsigned short ws_ypixel;   /* unused */
};
```

To request the current size, use

```
    struct winsize ws;

    ioctl(fd, TIOCGWINSZ, &ws);
```

To set a new size, fill in a struct winsize and call

```
    ioctl(fd, TIOCSWINSZ, &ws);
```

See page 308 for an example of the conditions in which you would want to
set a new window size.

When the window size changes, the signal SIGWINCH is sent to the foreground
process group leader on that tty. Your code can catch this signal, use

TIOCGWINSZ to query the new size and make any appropriate changes within your program.

### 15.5.3 Flags

The four flag variables, c_iflag, c_oflag, c_cflag, and c_lflag, hold flags that control various characteristics. The <termios.h> header file provides symbolic constant bitmasks that represent those flags. Set them with |= and unset them with &= ~, like this:

```
t.c_iflag |= BRKINT;
t.c_iflag &= ~IGNBRK;
```

A few of these symbolic defines are actually bitmasks that cover several related constants. They are used to extract parts of the structure for comparison:

```
if ((t.c_cflag & CSIZE) == CS7)
  character_size = 7;
```

The set of flags differs from system to system. The most important flags are specified by POSIX, but Linux follows System V in including several useful flags that POSIX does not define. This documentation is not complete; Linux supports some flags that you will probably never need. We cover the flags that you might possibly have a reason to use and refrain from confusing you with the rest.

In order to enable you to write portable software, we have labelled every flag that is not specified by the POSIX standard. For those flags, you should write code like this:

```
#ifdef IUCLC
   t.c_iflag |= IUCLC;
#endif
```

Also, some areas that present particular portability problems are mentioned, and we even break our rule of not confusing you with details from other implementations by presenting a few details about what other systems do.

## 15.5.4 Input Flags

The input mode flags affect input processing even though they sometimes have an effect on output. The flags that operate on `c_iflag` are as follows:

BRKINT and IGNBRK

> If IGNBRK is set, break conditions (see `tcsendbreak()`, mentioned earlier) are ignored.
>
> If IGNBRK is not set and BRKINT is set, break conditions cause the tty to flush all queued input and output data and send a SIGINT to processes in the foreground process group for the tty.
>
> If IGNBRK is not set and BRKINT is not set, break conditions are read as a 0-valued character ('\0'), except if PARMRK is set, in which case a framing error is detected and the three bytes '\377' '\0' '\0' are delivered to the application instead.

PARMRK and IGNPAR

> If IGNPAR is set, received bytes containing parity or framing errors are ignored (except as specified for break conditions earlier).
>
> If IGNPAR is not set and PARMRK is set, a received byte with a parity or framing error is reported to the application as the three-byte sequence '\377' '\0' '\n', where $n$ is the byte as it was received. In this case, if ISTRIP is not set, a valid '\377' character is reported to the application as the two-character sequence '\377' '\377'; if ISTRIP is set, a '\377' character will have its high bit stripped and will be reported as '\177'.
>
> If neither PARMRK nor IGNPAR is set, a received byte with a parity or framing error other than a break condition will be reported to the application as a single '\0' character.

INPCK

> If INPCK is set, parity checking is enabled. If it is not enabled, PARMRK and IGNPAR have no effect on received parity errors.

ISTRIP

> If ISTRIP is set, the high-order bit is stripped from all received bytes, limiting them to seven bits.

INLCR

If INLCR is set, received newline ('\n') characters are translated to carriage-return ('\r') characters.

IGNCR

If IGNCR is set, received carriage returns ('\r') are ignored (not reported to the application).

ICRNL

If ICRNL is set and IGNCR is not set, received carriage-return ('\r') characters are reported to the application as newline ('\n') characters.

IUCLC

If IUCLC and IEXTEN are set, received upper-case characters are reported to the application as lower-case characters. This flag is not specified by POSIX.

IXOFF

If IXOFF is set, the tty may send Control-S and Control-Q characters to the terminal to request that it stop and resume output (that is, sending data to the computer), respectively, to avoid overflowing the tty's input buffers. This is relevant only to serial terminals, as network and local terminals have more direct forms of flow control. Even serial terminals often have hardware flow control, which is controlled by the control flag (c_cflag) and which makes software flow control (Control-S and Control-Q) irrelevant.

IXON

If IXON is set, a received Control-S character will stop output to this tty and a received Control-Q character will restart output to this tty. This is relevant to any form of terminal I/O, as some users type literal Control-S and Control-Q characters to suspend and resume output.

IXANY

If IXANY is set, any received character (not just Control-Q) will restart output. This flag is not specified by POSIX.

IMAXBEL

> If IMAXBEL is set, the alert ('\a') character is sent whenever a character is received and the input buffer is already full. This flag is not specified by POSIX.

## 15.5.5 Output Flags

The output mode flags modify output processing *only if* OPOST *is set.* None of these flags are portable, because POSIX defines only OPOST and calls it "implementation defined." However, you will find that real terminal-handling applications often do need output processing, and the output flags available under Linux are generally available on most Unix systems, including SVR4.

The terminal code keeps track of the **current column**, which allows it to suppress extra carriage-return characters ('\r') and to convert tabs to spaces when appropriate. This current column is 0-based; the first column is column 0. The current column is set to 0 whenever a carriage return ('\r') is sent or implied, as it may be by a newline character ('\n') when ONLRET or ONLCR is set, or when the current column is set to 1 and a backspace character ('\b') is sent.

The flags that operate on c_oflag are as follows:

OPOST

> This is the only output flag specified by POSIX, which says that it turns on "implementation-defined" output processing. If OPOST is not set, none of the other output mode flags are consulted and no output processing is done.

OLCUC

> If OLCUC is set, lower-case characters are sent to the terminal as upper-case characters. This flag is not specified by POSIX.

ONLCR

> If ONLCR is set, when a newline character ('\n') is sent, a carriage-return ('\r') is sent before the newline. The current column is set to 0. This flag is not specified by POSIX.

ONOCR

> If ONOCR is set, carriage-return characters ('\r') are neither processed nor sent if the current column is 0. This flag is not specified by POSIX.

OCRNL

> If OCRNL is set, carriage-return characters ('\r') are translated into newline characters ('\n'). If, in addition, ONLRET is set, the current column is set to 0. This flag is not specified by POSIX.

ONLRET

> If ONLRET is set, when a newline character ('\n') or carriage return character ('\r') is sent, the current column is set to 0. This flag is not specified by POSIX.

OXTABS

> If OXTABS is set, tabs are expanded to spaces. Tab stops are assumed to be every eight characters, and the number of space characters that are sent is determined by the current column. This flag is not specified by POSIX.

In addition, there are delay flags that you never need to set; they are designed to compensate for old, badly designed, and, by now, mercifully rare hardware. The termcap and terminfo libraries are responsible for managing delay flags, which means that you should never have to modify them. *termcap & terminfo* [Strang, 1991B], which documents them, describes them as obsolete. The Linux kernel does not currently implement them, and as there has been no demand for this feature, they will likely never be implemented.

## 15.5.6 Control Flags

The control mode flags affect protocol parameters, such as parity and flow control. The flags that operate on c_cflag are as follows:[8]

---

8. Linux uses c_cflag to hold the speed, as well, but relying on that is completely nonportable. Use cfsetospeed() and cfsetispeed() instead.

CLOCAL

If CLOCAL is set, modem control lines are ignored. If it is not set, then open() will block until the modem announces an off-hook condition by asserting the carrier-detect line.

CREAD

Characters can be received only if CREAD is set. It cannot necessarily be unset.[9]

CSIZE

CSIZE is a mask for the codes that set the size of a transmitted character in bits. The character size should be set to:

CS5  for 5 bits per character
CS6  for 6 bits per character
CS7  for 7 bits per character
CS8  for 8 bits per character

CSTOPB

If CSTOPB is set, two stop bits are generated at the end of each transmitted character frame. If CSTOPB is not set, only one stop bit is generated. Obsolete equipment that requires two stop bits is rare.

HUPCL

If HUPCL is set, then when the final open file descriptor on the device is closed, the DTR and RTS lines on the serial port (if they exist) will be lowered to signal the modem to hang up. This means, for example, that when a user who logged in through a modem then logs out, the modem will be hung up. If a communications program has the device open for outbound calls and the process then closes the device (or exits), the modem will be hung up.

PARENB and PARODD

If PARENB is set, a parity bit is generated. If PARODD is not set, even parity will be generated. If PARODD is set, odd parity will be generated.

If PARENB is not set, PARODD is ignored.

---

9. Try running stty -cread!

CRTSCTS

Use hardware flow control (RTS and CTS lines). At high speeds (19,200 bps and higher) software flow control via the XON and XOFF characters becomes ineffective and hardware flow control must be used instead.

This flag is not specified by POSIX and is not available by this name on most other Unix systems. This is a particularly nonportable area of terminal control, despite the common need for hardware flow control on modern systems. SVR4 is particularly egregious in that it provides no way to enable hardware flow control through termios, only through a different interface called termiox.

## 15.5.7 Control Characters

Control characters are characters that have special meanings that may differ depending on whether the terminal is in canonical input mode or raw input mode and on the settings of various control flags. Each offset (except for VMIN and VTIME) in the c_cc array designates an action and holds the character code that is assigned that action. For example, set the interrupt character to Control-C with code like this:

```
ts.c_cc[VINTR] = CTRLCHAR('C');
```

CTRLCHAR() is a macro defined as

```
#define CTRLCHAR(ch) ((ch)&0x1F)
```

Some systems have a CTRL() macro defined in <termios.h>, but it is not defined on all systems, so defining our own version is more portable.

We will use the ^C notation to designate Control-C.

The character positions that are not specified by POSIX are active only if the IEXTEN local control (c_lflag) flag is set.

The control characters that you can use as subscripts to the c_cc array are:

VINTR

Offset VINTR is usually set to ^C. It normally flushes the input and output queues and sends SIGINT to the members of the foreground process group associated with the tty. Processes that do not explicitly handle SIGINT will exit immediately.

VQUIT

Offset VQUIT is usually set to ^\. It normally flushes the input and output queues and sends SIGQUIT to the members of the foreground process group associated with the tty. Processes that do not explicitly handle SIGQUIT will abort, dumping core if possible (see page 108).

VERASE

Offset VERASE is usually set to ^H or ^?. In canonical mode, it normally erases the previous character on the line. In raw mode, it is meaningless.

VKILL

Offset VKILL is usually set to ^U. In canonical mode, it normally erases the entire line. In raw mode, it is meaningless.

VEOF

Offset VEOF is usually set to ^D. In canonical mode, it causes read() on that file descriptor to return 0, signalling an end-of-file condition. On some systems, it may share space with the VMIN character, which is active only in raw mode. (This is not an issue if you save a struct termios with canonical mode settings to restore once you are done with raw mode, which is proper termios programming practice, anyway.)

VSTOP

Offset VSTOP is usually set to ^S. It causes the tty to pause output until the VSTART character is received, or, if IXANY is set, until any character is received.

VSTART

Offset VSTART is usually set to ^Q. It restarts paused tty output.

VSUSP

Offset VSUSP is usually set to ^Z. It causes the current foreground process group to be sent SIGTSTP; see Chapter 14 for details.

VEOL and VEOL2

In canonical mode, these characters, in addition to the newline character ('\n'), signal an end-of-line condition. This causes the collected buffer to be transmitted and a new buffer started. On some systems, VEOL may share space with the VTIME character, which is active only in raw mode, just as VEOF may share space with VMIN. The VEOL2 character is not specified by POSIX.

VREPRINT

Offset VREPRINT is usually set to ^R. In canonical mode, if the ECHO local flag is set, it causes the VREPRINT character to be echoed locally, a newline (and a carriage return, if appropriate) to be echoed locally, and the whole current buffer to be reprinted. This character is not specified by POSIX.

VWERASE

Offset VWERASE is usually set to ^W. In canonical mode, it erases any white space at the end of the buffer, then all adjacent non-white-space characters, which has the effect of erasing the previous word on the line. This character is not specified by POSIX.

VLNEXT

Offset VLNEXT is usually set to ^V. It is not itself entered into the buffer, but it causes the next character input to be put into the buffer literally, even if it is one of the control characters. Of course, to enter a single literal VLNEXT character, type it twice. This character is not specified by POSIX.

To disable any control character position, set its value to _POSIX_VDISABLE. This only works if _POSIX_VDISABLE is defined, and is defined as something other than -1. _POSIX_VDISABLE works on Linux, but a portable program will, unfortunately, not be able to depend on disabling control character positions on all systems.

## 15.5.8 Local Flags

The local mode flags affect local processing, which (roughly) refers to how characters are collected before they are output. When the device is in canonical (cooked) mode, characters are echoed locally without being sent to the remote system until a newline character is encountered. At that point, the whole line is sent, and the remote end processes it without echoing it again. In raw mode, each character is sent to the remote system as it is received. Sometimes the character is echoed only by the remote system; sometimes only by the local system; and sometimes, such as when reading a password, it is not echoed at all.

Some flags may act differently, depending on whether the terminal is in canonical mode or raw mode. Those that act differently in canonical and raw mode are marked.

The flags that operate on `c_lflag` are as follows:

ICANON

> If `ICANON` is set, canonical mode is enabled. If `ICANON` is not set, raw mode is enabled.

ECHO

> If `ECHO` is set, local echo is enabled. If `ECHO` is not set, all the other flags whose names start with `ECHO` will be effectively disabled and function as if they are not set, except for `ECHONL`.

ECHOCTL

> If `ECHOCTL` is set, control characters are printed as `^C`, where `C` is the character formed by adding octal 0100 to the control character, mod octal 0200. So Control-C is displayed as `^C`, and Control-? (octal 0177) is represented as `^?` (`?` is octal 77). This flag is not specified by POSIX.

ECHOE

> In canonical mode, if `ECHOE` is set, then when the `ERASE` character is received, the previous character on the display is erased if possible.

ECHOK and ECHOKE

> In canonical mode, when the `KILL` character is received, the entire current line is erased from the buffer.

If neither ECHOK, ECHOKE, nor ECHOE is set, the ECHOCTL representation of the KILL character (^U by default) will be printed to indicate that the line has been erased.

If ECHOE and ECHOK are set but ECHOKE is not set, the ECHOCTL representation of the KILL character will be printed, followed by a newline, which will be processed appropriately by OPOST handling if OPOST is set.

If ECHOE, ECHOK, and ECHOKE are all set, the line will be erased.

See the description of ECHOPRT for another variation on this theme.

The ECHOKE flag is not specified by POSIX. On systems without the ECHOKE flag, setting the ECHOK flag may be equivalent to setting both the ECHOK and ECHOKE flags under Linux.

ECHONL

In canonical mode, if ECHONL is set, newline ('\n') characters are echoed even if ECHO is not set.

ECHOPRT

In canonical mode, if ECHOPRT is set, characters will be printed as they are erased when the ERASE or WERASE (or KILL, if ECHOK and ECHOKE are set) characters are received. When the first erase character in a sequence is received, a \ will be printed, and when the final erased character is printed (the end of the line is reached or a nonerasing character is typed), a / will be printed. Every normal character you type will be merely echoed. So typing asdf, followed by two ERASE characters, followed by df, followed by a KILL character, would look like asdf\fd/df\fdsa/

This is useful for debugging and for using hardcopy terminals, such as the original teletype, where the characters are printed on paper, and is otherwise useless. This flag is not specified by POSIX.

ISIG

If ISIG is set, the INTR, QUIT, and SUSP control characters cause the corresponding signal (SIGINT, SIGQUIT, or SIGTSTP, respectively; see Chapter 13) to be sent to all the processes in the current foreground process group on that tty.

NOFLSH

Usually, when the INTR and QUIT characters are received, the input and output queues are flushed. When the SUSP character is received, only the input queue is flushed. If NOFLSH is set, neither queue is flushed.

TOSTOP

If TOSTOP is set, then when a process that is not in the current foreground process group attempts to write to its controlling terminal, SIGTTOU is sent to the entire process group of which the process is a member. By default, this signal stops a process, as if the SUSP character had been pressed.

IEXTEN

This flag is specified as implementation-dependent by POSIX. It enables implementation-defined processing of input characters. Although portable programs will not set this bit, the IUCLC and certain character-erasing facilities in Linux depend on it being set. Fortunately, it is generally enabled by default on Linux systems, because the kernel initially enables it when setting up ttys, so you should not normally need to set it for any reason.

### 15.5.9 **Controlling** read()

Two elements in the c_cc array are not control characters and are relevant only in raw mode: VTIME and VMIN. In raw mode only, these determine when read() returns. In canonical mode, read() returns only when lines have been assembled or end-of-file is reached, unless the O_NONBLOCK option is set.

In raw mode, it would not be efficient to read one byte at a time, and it is also inefficient to poll the port by reading in nonblocking mode. This leaves two complementary methods of reading efficiently.

The first is to use select(), as documented in Chapter 12 and demonstrated in robin.c. If select() says that a file descriptor is ready to read, you know that you can read() some number of bytes immediately. However, combining select() with the second method can make your code even more efficient by making it possible to read more bytes at a time.

The VTIME and VMIN "control characters" have a complex relationship. VTIME specifies an amount of time to wait in tenths of seconds (which cannot be larger than a cc_t, usually an 8-bit unsigned char), which may be 0. VMIN specifies the minimum number of bytes to wait for (not to read—read()'s third argument specifies the maximum number of bytes to read), which may also be 0.

- If VTIME is 0, VMIN specifies the number of bytes to wait for. A read() call will not return until at least VMIN bytes have been read or a signal has been received.

- If VMIN is 0, VTIME specifies the number of tenths of seconds for read() to wait before returning, even if no data is available. In this case, read() returning 0 does not necessarily indicate an end-of-file condition, as it usually does.

- If neither VTIME nor VMIN is 0, VTIME specifies the number of tenths of seconds for read() to wait after at least one byte is available. If data is available when read() is called, a timer starts immediately. If data is not available when read() is called, a timer is started when the first byte arrives. The read() call returns either when at least VMIN bytes have arrived or when the timer expires, whichever comes first. It will always return at least one byte because the timer does not start until at least one byte is available.

- If VTIME and VMIN are both 0, read() will always return immediately, even if no data is available. Again, 0 does not necessarily indicate an end-of-file condition.

## 15.6 Pseudo ttys

A pseudo tty, or pty, is a mechanism that allows a user-level program to take the place (logically speaking) of a tty driver for a piece of hardware. The pty has two distinct ends: The end that emulates hardware is called the **pty master**, and the end that provides programs with a normal tty interface is called the **pty slave**. The slave looks like a normal tty; the master is like a standard character device and is not a tty.

A serial port driver is generally implemented as an interrupt-driven piece of code in the kernel, to which programs talk through a specific device file. That does not have to be the case, however. For example, at least one SCSI-based terminal server exists that uses a generic interface to the SCSI protocol to have a user-level program that talks to the terminal server and provides access to the serial ports via ptys.

Network terminal sessions are done in the same manner; the rlogind and telnetd programs connect a network socket to a pty master and run a shell on a pty slave to make network connections act like ttys, allowing you to run interactive programs over a non-tty network connection. The screen program multiplexes several pty connections onto one tty, which may or may not itself be a pty, connected to the user. The expect program allows programs that insist on being run in interactive mode on a tty to be run on a pty slave under the control of another program connected to a pty master.

## 15.6.1 Opening Pseudo ttys

Unfortunately, the process of opening pseudo ttys varies on different platforms. Linux follows the BSD model, rather than the SysV model. 256 pty devices are available, and to find the first open device, programs normally search through the devices in order by minor number. They do this by searching in the peculiar lexicographic manner demonstrated in the ptypair program included in this section.

If 256 devices were always available, it might make programs faster if each program searched through the devices in a different order. Unfortunately, old versions of Linux, as well as many Unix variants and clones, provide only the first 64 devices. Therefore, searching in order is a simple way to search correctly on all systems, however configured.

The example `get_master_pty()` function on line 19 of ptypair.c opens a master pty and returns the file descriptor to the parent. The corresponding `get_slave_pty()` function on line 61 can be used after a `fork()` to open the corresponding slave pty device.

```
 1: #include <errno.h>
 2: #include <fcntl.h>
 3: #include <grp.h>
 4: #include <stdlib.h>
```

```
 5: #include <string.h>
 6: #include <sys/types.h>
 7: #include <sys/stat.h>
 8: #include <unistd.h>
 9:
10:
11: /* get_master_pty() takes a double-indirect character pointer in which
12:  * to put a slave name, and returns an integer file descriptor.
13:  * If it returns < 0, an error has occurred.
14:  * Otherwise, it has returned the master pty file descriptor, and fills
15:  * in *name with the name of the corresponding slave pty.
16:  * Once the slave pty has been opened, you are responsible to free *name.
17:  */
18:
19: int get_master_pty(char **name) {
20:     int i, j;
21:     /* default to returning error */
22:     int master = -1;
23:
24:     /* create a dummy name to fill in */
25:     *name = strdup("/dev/ptyXX");
26:
27:     /* search for an unused pty */
28:     for (i=0; i<16 && master <= 0; i++) {
29:         for (j=0; j<16 && master <= 0; j++) {
30:             (*name)[8] = "pqrstuvwxyzPQRST"[i];
31:             (*name)[9] = "0123456789abcdef"[j];
32:             /* open the master pty */
33:             if ((master = open(*name, O_RDWR)) < 0) {
34:                 if (errno == ENOENT) {
35:                     /* we are out of pty devices */
36:                     free (*name);
37:                     return (master);
38:                 }
39:             }
40:         }
41:     }
42:     if ((master < 0) && (i == 16) && (j == 16)) {
43:         /* must have tried every pty unsuccessfully */
44:         free (*name);
45:         return (master);
```

```
46:    }
47:
48:    /* By substituting a letter, we change the master pty
49:     * name into the slave pty name.
50:     */
51:    (*name)[5] = 't';
52:
53:    return (master);
54: }
55:
56: /* get_slave_pty() returns an integer file descriptor.
57:  * If it returns < 0, an error has occurred.
58:  * Otherwise, it has returned the slave file descriptor.
59:  */
60:
61: int get_slave_pty(char *name) {
62:    struct group *gptr;
63:    gid_t gid;
64:    int slave = -1;
65:
66:    /* chown/chmod the corresponding pty, if possible.
67:     * This will only work if the process has root permissions.
68:     * Alternatively, write and exec a small setuid program that
69:     * does just this.
70:     */
71:    if ((gptr = getgrnam("tty")) != 0) {
72:       gid = gptr->gr_gid;
73:    } else {
74:       /* if the tty group does not exist, don't change the
75:        * group on the slave pty, only the owner
76:        */
77:       gid = -1;
78:    }
79:
80:    /* Note that we do not check for errors here.  If this is code
81:     * where these actions are critical, check for errors!
82:     */
83:    chown(name, getuid(), gid);
84:    /* This code only makes the slave read/writeable for the user.
85:     * If this is for an interactive shell that will want to
86:     * receive "write" and "wall" messages, OR S_IWGRP into the
```

```
87:     * second argument below.
88:     */
89:    chmod(name, S_IRUSR|S_IWUSR);
90:
91:    /* open the corresponding slave pty */
92:    slave = open(name, O_RDWR);
93:
94:    return (slave);
95: }
```

The get_slave_pty() function does nothing new. Every function in it is described elsewhere in this book, so we will not explain it here.

## 15.6.2 Pseudo tty Example

Perhaps one of the simplest programs that can be written to use ptys is a program that opens a pty pair and runs a shell on the slave pty, connecting it to the master pty. Having written that program, you can expand it in any way that you wish. ptytest.c is an example that uses the functions defined in ptypair.c.

```
 1: #include <errno.h>
 2: #include <fcntl.h>
 3: #include <grp.h>
 4: #include <signal.h>
 5: #include <stdio.h>
 6: #include <stdlib.h>
 7: #include <string.h>
 8: #include <sys/ioctl.h>
 9: #include <sys/time.h>
10: #include <sys/types.h>
11: #include <sys/stat.h>
12: #include <termios.h>
13: #include <unistd.h>
14: #include "ptypair.h"
15:
16:
17: volatile int propagate_sigwinch = 0;
18:
19: /* sigwinch_handler
```

```
20:   * propagate window size changes from input file descriptor to
21:   * master side of pty.
22:   */
23: void sigwinch_handler(int signal) {
24:     propagate_sigwinch = 1;
25: }
26:
27:
28: /* ptytest tries to open a pty pair with a shell running
29:  * underneath the slave pty.
30:  */
31: int main (void) {
32:     int master;
33:     int pid;
34:     char *name;
35:     fd_set ready;
36:     int i;
37: #define BUFSIZE 1024
38:     char buf[1024];
39:     struct termios ot, t;
40:     struct winsize ws;
41:     int done = 0;
42:     struct sigaction act;
43:
44:     if ((master = get_master_pty(&name)) < 0) {
45:         perror("ptypair: could not open master pty");
46:         exit(1);
47:     }
48:
49:     /* set up SIGWINCH handler */
50:     act.sa_handler = sigwinch_handler;
51:     sigemptyset(&(act.sa_mask));
52:     act.sa_flags = 0;
53:     if (sigaction(SIGWINCH, &act, NULL) < 0) {
54:         perror("ptypair: could not handle SIGWINCH ");
55:         exit(1);
56:     }
57:
58:     if (ioctl(STDIN_FILENO, TIOCGWINSZ, &ws) < 0) {
59:         perror("ptypair: could not get window size");
60:         exit(1);
```

```
61:    }
62:
63:    if ((pid = fork()) < 0) {
64:       perror("ptypair");
65:       exit(1);
66:    }
67:
68:    if (pid == 0) {
69:       int slave;  /* file descriptor for slave pty */
70:
71:       /* We are in the child process */
72:       close(master);
73:
74:       if ((slave = get_slave_pty(name)) < 0) {
75:          perror("ptypair: could not open slave pty");
76:          exit(1);
77:       }
78:       free(name);
79:
80:       /* We need to make this process a session group leader, because
81:        * it is on a new PTY, and things like job control simply will
82:        * not work correctly unless there is a session group leader
83:        * and process group leader (which a session group leader
84:        * automatically is). This also disassociates us from our old
85:        * controlling tty.
86:        */
87:       if (setsid() < 0) {
88:          perror("could not set session leader");
89:       }
90:
91:       /* Tie us to our new controlling tty. */
92:       if (ioctl(slave, TIOCSCTTY, NULL)) {
93:          perror("could not set new controlling tty");
94:       }
95:
96:       /* make slave pty be standard in, out, and error */
97:       dup2(slave, STDIN_FILENO);
98:       dup2(slave, STDOUT_FILENO);
99:       dup2(slave, STDERR_FILENO);
100:
101:       /* at this point the slave pty should be standard input */
```

```
102:        if (slave > 2) {
103:            close(slave);
104:        }
105:
106:
107:        /* Try to restore window size; failure isn't critical */
108:        if (ioctl(STDOUT_FILENO, TIOCSWINSZ, &ws) < 0) {
109:            perror("could not restore window size");
110:        }
111:
112:        /* now start the shell */
113:        execl("/bin/sh", "/bin/sh", 0);
114:
115:        /* should never be reached */
116:        exit(1);
117:    }
118:
119:    /* parent */
120:    free(name);
121:
122:    /* Note that we only set termios settings for standard input;
123:     * the master side of a pty is NOT a tty.
124:     */
125:    tcgetattr(STDIN_FILENO, &ot);
126:    t = ot;
127:    t.c_lflag &= ~(ICANON | ISIG | ECHO | ECHOCTL | ECHOE | \
128:                   ECHOK | ECHOKE | ECHONL | ECHOPRT );
129:    t.c_iflag |= IGNBRK;
130:    t.c_cc[VMIN] = 1;
131:    t.c_cc[VTIME] = 0;
132:    tcsetattr(STDIN_FILENO, TCSANOW, &t);
133:
134:    /* This code comes nearly verbatim from robin.c
135:     * If the child exits, reading master will return -1 and we exit.
136:     */
137:    do {
138:        FD_ZERO(&ready);
139:        FD_SET(STDIN_FILENO, &ready);
140:        FD_SET(master, &ready);
141:        select(master+1, &ready, NULL, NULL, NULL);
142:
```

```
143:        if (propagate_sigwinch) {
144:            /* signal handler has asked for SIGWINCH propagation */
145:            if (ioctl(STDIN_FILENO, TIOCGWINSZ, &ws) < 0) {
146:                perror("ptypair: could not get window size");
147:            }
148:            if (ioctl(master, TIOCSWINSZ, &ws) < 0) {
149:                perror("could not restore window size");
150:            }
151:
152:            /* now do not do this again until next SIGWINCH */
153:            propagate_sigwinch = 0;
154:
155:            /* select may have been interrupted by SIGWINCH,
156:             * so try again. */
157:            continue;
158:        }
159:
160:        if (FD_ISSET(master, &ready)) {
161:            i = read(master, buf, BUFSIZE);
162:            if (i >= 1) {
163:                write(STDOUT_FILENO, buf, i);
164:            } else {
165:                done = 1;
166:            }
167:        }
168:
169:        if (FD_ISSET(STDIN_FILENO, &ready)) {
170:            i = read(STDIN_FILENO, buf, BUFSIZE);
171:            if (i >= 1) {
172:                write(master, buf, i);
173:            } else {
174:                done = 1;
175:            }
176:        }
177:
178:    } while (!done);
179:
180:    /* this really doesn't matter because each time a master pty is
181:     * opened, the corresponding slave pty has its termios settings
182:     * reset
183:     */
```

```
184:        tcsetattr(STDIN_FILENO, TCSANOW, &ot);
185:        exit(0);
186: }
```

ptytest.c does very little that we have not seen before. Creating a child process is introduced in Chapter 9, signal handling in Chapter 13, and the select loop is almost exactly straight from robin.c on page 274 (minus the escape-character processing), as is modifying termios settings.

This leaves propagating window-size changes to be explained here.

On line 143, after select() exits, we check to see if the reason that select() exited was the SIGWINCH signal being delivered to the sigwinch_handler function on line 23. If it was, we need to get the new current window size from standard input and propagate it to the slave's pty. By setting the window size, SIGWINCH will *automatically* be sent to the process running on the pty; we should not explicitly send a SIGWINCH to that process.

# CHAPTER 16

# Networking with Sockets

As the computer world becomes more networked, network-aware applications are increasingly important. Linux provides the Berkeley socket API, which has become the standard networking API. We discuss the basics of using Berkeley sockets for both TCP/IP networking and simple **inter-process communication** (IPC) through Unix-domain sockets.

This chapter is not intended to be a complete guide to network programming. Network programming is a complicated topic, and we recommend dedicated network programming books for programmers who intend to do serious work with sockets [Stevens, 1990]. This chapter should be sufficient to allow you to write simple networked applications, however.

## 16.1 Protocol Support

The Berkeley socket API was designed as a gateway to multiple protocols. Although this does necessitate extra complexity in the interface, it is much easier than inventing (or learning) a new interface for every new protocol you encounter. Linux already supports many protocols (including TCP/IP, AppleTalk, and IPX) through the socket API, proving the value of this abstraction.

We discuss using sockets for two of the protocols available through Linux's socket implementation. The most important protocol that Linux supports is

TCP/IP,[1] which is the protocol that drives the Internet. We also cover Unix domain sockets, which are an IPC mechanism restricted to a single machine. Although they do not work across networks, Unix domain sockets are widely used for other applications.

Protocols normally come in groups, or **protocol families**. The popular TCP/IP protocol suite includes the TCP and UDP protocols (among others). Making sense of the various protocols requires you to know a few networking terms.

## 16.1.1 Nice Networking

Most users consider networking protocols to provide the equivalent of Unix pipes between machines. If a byte (or sequence of bytes) goes in one end of the connection, it is guaranteed to come out the other end. Not only is it guaranteed to come out the other end, but it also will come out right after the byte that was sent before it and immediately before the byte that was sent after it. Of course, all of these bytes should be received exactly as they were sent; no bytes should change. Also, no other process should be able to interject extra bytes into the conversation; it should be restricted to the original two parties.

A good visualization of this idea is the telephone. When you speak to your friends, you expect them to hear the same words you speak, and in the order you speak them.[2] Not only that, you do not expect your mother to pick up her phone (assuming she is not in the same house as you) and start chatting away happily to you and your friend.

---

1. The 2.0.x kernels covered by this book support only version 4 of the TCP/IP protocol suite, the version in widespread use at press time. A newer version of TCP/IP, version 6, is expected to eventually supersede version 4, and the newer versions of the Linux kernel (2.1.x and later) will fully support it.
2. Well, this depends on the character of the friends and how late they were out the night before the conversation.

## 16.1.2 Real Networking

Although this may seem pretty basic, it is not at all how underlying computer networks work. Networks tend to be chaotic and random. Imagine a first grade class at recess, except they are not allowed to speak to each other and they have to stay at least five feet apart. Now, chances are those kids are going to find some way to communicate—perhaps even by paper airplanes!

Imagine that whenever students want to send letters to one another, they simply write the letters on pieces of paper, fold them into airplanes, write the name of the intended recipient on the outside, and hurl them toward someone who is closer to the final recipient than the sender is. This intermediate looks at the airplane, sees who the intended target is, and sends it toward the next closest person. Eventually, the intended recipient will (well, *may*) get the airplane and unfold it to read the message.

Believe it or not, this is almost exactly how computer networks operate.[3] The intermediaries are called **routers** and the airplanes are called **packets**, but the rest is the same. Just as in the first grade class, some of those airplanes (or packets) are going to get lost. If a message is too long to fit in a single packet, it must be split across multiple ones (each of which may be lost). All the students in between can read the packets if they like[4] and may simply throw the message away rather than try to deliver it. Also, anyone can interrupt your conversation by sending new packets into the middle of it.

## 16.1.3 Making Reality Play Nice

Confronted with the reality of millions of paper airplanes, protocol designers endeavor to present a view of the network more on par with the telephone than the first grade class. Various terms have evolved to describe networking protocols.

---

3. This is how **packet-switched** networks work, anyway. An alternative design, **circuit-switched** networks, acts more like telephone connections. They are not widely used in computer networking, however.
4. This is why cryptography has gained so much importance since the advent of the Internet.

- **Connection-oriented** protocols have two endpoints, like a telephone conversation. The connection must be established before any communication takes place, just as you answer the phone by saying "hello" rather than just talking immediately. Other users cannot (or should not be able to) intrude into the connection. Protocols that do not have these characteristics are known as **connectionless**.

- Protocols provide **sequencing** if they ensure the data arrives in the same order it was sent.

- Protocols provide **error control** if they automatically discard messages that have been corrupted and arrange to retransmit the data.

- **Streaming** protocols recognize only byte boundaries. Sequences of bytes may be split up and are delivered to the recipient as the data arrives. **Packet-based** protocols handle packets of data, preserving the packet boundaries and delivering complete packets to the receiver. Packet-based protocols normally enforce a maximum packet size.

Although each of these attributes is independent of the others, two major types of protocols are commonly used by applications. **Datagram** protocols are packet-oriented transports that provide neither sequencing nor error control; UDP, part of the TCP/IP protocol family, is a widely used datagram protocol. **Stream** protocols, such as the TCP portion of TCP/IP, are streaming protocols that provide both sequencing and error control.

Although datagram protocols, such as UDP, can be useful,[5] we focus on using stream protocols, because they are easier to use for most applications. More information on protocol design and the differences between various protocols is available from many books [Stevens, 1990] [Stevens, 1994].

---

5. Many higher-level protocols, such as BOOTP and NFS, are built on top of UDP.

### 16.1.4 Addresses

As every protocol has its own definition of a network address, the sockets API must abstract addresses. It uses a `struct sockaddr` as the basic form of an address; its contents are defined differently for each protocol family. Whenever a `struct sockaddr` is passed to a system call, the process also passes the size of the address that is being passed.

All `struct sockaddr` types conform to the following definition:

```
#include <sys/socket.h>

struct sockaddr {
    unsigned short sa_family;
    char sa_data[MAXSOCKADDRDATA];
}
```

The first two bytes (the size of a `short`) specifies the **address family** this address belongs to. A list of the common address families that Linux applications use is in Table 16.1, on page 325.

## 16.2 Utility Functions

All of the examples in this section use two functions, `copyData()` and `die()`. `copyData()` reads data from a file descriptor and writes it to another as long as data is left to be read. `die()` calls `perror()` and exits the program. We put both of these functions in the file sockutil.c to keep the example programs a bit cleaner. For reference, here is the implementation of these two functions.

```
1: /* sockutil.c - simple utility functions */
2:
3: #include <stdio.h>
4: #include <unistd.h>
5:
6: #include "sockutil.h"
7:
8: /* issue an error message via perror() and terminate the program */
9: void die(char * message) {
```

```
10:        perror(message);
11:        exit(1);
12: }
13:
14: /* Copies data from file descriptor 'from' to file descriptor 'to'
15:    until nothing is left to be copied. Exits if an error occurs.   */
16: void copyData(int from, int to) {
17:        char buf[1024];
18:        int amount;
19:
20:        while ((amount = read(from, buf, sizeof(buf))) > 0) {
21:            if (write(to, buf, amount) != amount) {
22:                die("write");
23:                return;
24:            }
25:        }
26:        if (amount < 0)
27:            die("read");
28: }
```

# 16.3  Basic Socket Operations

Like most other Linux resources, sockets are implemented through the
file abstraction. They are created through the socket() system call, which
returns a file descriptor. Once the socket has been properly initialized,
that file descriptor may be used for read() and write() requests, like any
other file descriptor. When a process is finished with a socket, it should be
close()ed to free the resources associated with it.

## 16.3.1 Creating a Socket

New sockets are created by the socket() system call, which returns a file
descriptor for the *uninitialized* socket. The socket is tied to a particular
protocol when it is created, but it is not connected to anything. As it is not
connected, it cannot yet be read from or written to.

**Table 16.1** Protocol and Address Families

| Address | Protocol | Protocol Description |
|---|---|---|
| AF_UNIX | PF_UNIX | Unix domain |
| AF_INET | PF_INET | TCP/IP (version 4) |
| AF_AX25 | PF_AX25 | AX.25, used by amateur radio |
| AF_IPX | PF_IPX | Novell IPX |
| AF_APPLETALK | PF_APPLETALK | AppleTalk DDS |
| AF_NETROM | PF_NETROM | NetROM, used by amateur radio |

```
#include <sys/socket.h>

int socket(int domain, int type, int protocol);
```

Like open(), socket() returns a value less than 0 on error and a file descriptor, which is greater than or equal to 0, on success.

The three parameters specify the protocol to use. The first parameter specifies the protocol family that should be used and is usually one of the values specified in Table 16.1.

The next parameter, type, is SOCK_STREAM or SOCK_DGRAM.[6] SOCK_STREAM specifies a protocol from the specified family that provides a streaming connection, whereas SOCK_DGRAM specifies a datagram protocol from the same family.

The final parameter specifies which protocol is to be used, subject to the constraints specified by the first two parameters. Usually, this parameter is 0, letting the kernel use the default protocol of the specified type and family. For the PF_INET protocol family, TCP is the default stream protocol and UDP is the default datagram protocol.

---

6. A couple of other values are available, but they are not usually used by application code.

## 16.3.2 Establishing Connections

After you create a stream socket, it needs to be connected to something before it is of much use. Establishing socket connections is an inherently asymmetric task; each side of the connection does it differently.

One side gets its socket ready to be connected to something and then waits for someone to connect to it. This is usually done by server applications that are started and continuously run, waiting for other processes to connect to them.

Client processes instead create a socket, tell the system which address they want to connect it to, and then try to establish the connection. Once the server (which has been waiting for a client) accepts the connection attempt, the connection is established between the two sockets. After this happens, the socket may be used for bidirectional communication.

## 16.3.3 Binding an Address to a Socket

Both server and client processes need to tell the system which address to use for the socket. Attaching an address to the local side of a socket is called **binding** the socket and is done through the bind() system call.

```
#include <sys/socket.h>

int bind(int sock, struct sockaddr * my_addr, int addrlen);
```

The first parameter is the socket being bound, and the other parameters specify the address to use for the local endpoint.

## 16.3.4 Waiting for Connections

After creating a socket, server processes bind() the socket to the address they are listening to. After the socket is bound to an address, the process tells the system it is willing to let other processes establish connections to that socket (at the specified address) by calling listen(). Once a socket is bound to an address, the kernel is able to handle processes' attempts to connect to that address. However, the connection is not immediately established. The listen()ing process must first accept the connection at-tempt through the accept() system call. New connection attempts that have been made to addresses that have been listen()ed to are called **pending connections** until the connections has been accept()ed.

Normally, accept() blocks until a client process tries to connect to it. If the socket has been marked as nonblocking through fcntl(), accept() instead returns an error if no client process is available. The select() system call may also be used to determine whether a connection to a socket is pending. If a connection is pending, the socket is considered ready to be read from for select()'s purposes.

Here are the prototypes of listen() and accept():

```
#include <sys/socket.h>

int listen(int sock, int backlog);
int accept(int sock, struct sockaddr * addr, int * addrlen);
```

Both of these functions expect the socket's file descriptor as the first pa-rameter. listen()'s other parameter, backlog, specifies how many connec-tions may be pending on the socket before further connection attempts are refused. Network connections are not established until the server has accept()ed the connection; until the accept(), the incoming connection is considered pending. By providing a small queue of pending connections, the kernel relaxes the need for server processes to be constantly prepared to accept() connections. Applications have historically set the maximum backlog to 5, though a larger value may sometimes be necessary. listen() returns 0 on success and non-0 on failure.

The accept() call changes a pending connection to an established connec-tion. The established connection is given a new file descriptor, which accept() returns. The new file descriptor inherits its attributes from the socket that was listen()ed to.

The addr and addrlen parameters point to data that the kernel fills in with the address of the remote (client) end of the connection. Initially, addrlen should point to an integer containing the size of the buffer addr points to. accept() returns a file descriptor, or less-than-0 if an error occurs, just like open().

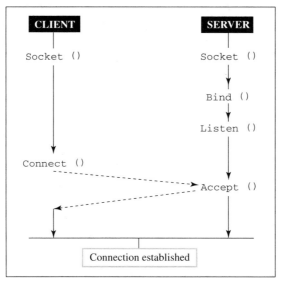

**Figure 16.1**    Establishing Socket Connections

## 16.3.5 Connecting to a Server

Like servers, clients may `bind()` the local address to the socket immediately after creating it. Usually, the client does not care what the local address is and skips this step, allowing the kernel to assign it any convienent local address.

After the `bind()` step (which may be omitted), the client `connect()`s to a server.

```
#include <sys/socket.h>

int connect(int sock, struct sockaddr * servaddr, int addrlen);
```

The process passes to `connect()` the socket that is being connected, followed by the address to which the socket should be connected.

Figure 16.1 shows the system calls usually used to establish socket connections, and the order in which they occur.

# 16.4  Unix Domain Sockets

**Unix domain sockets** are the simplest protocol family available through the sockets API. They do not actually represent a network protocol; they can connect only to sockets on the same machine. Although this restricts their usefulness, they are used by many applications because they provide a flexible IPC mechanism. Their addresses are pathnames, which are created in the file system when a socket is bound to the pathname. Socket files, which represent Unix domain addresses, can be stat()ed but cannot be opened through open(); the socket API must be used instead.

The Unix domain provides both datagram and stream interfaces. The datagram interface is rarely used and is not discussed here. The stream interface, which is discussed here, is similiar to named pipes. Unix domain sockets are not identical to named pipes, however.

When multiple processes open a named pipe, any of the processes may read a message sent through the pipe by another process. Each named pipe is like a bulletin board. When a process posts a message to the board, any other process (with sufficient permission) may take the message from the board.

Unix domain sockets are connection-oriented; each connection to the socket results in a new communication channel. The server, which may be handling many simultaneous connections, has a different file descriptor for each. This property makes Unix domain sockets much better suited to many IPC tasks than are named pipes; this is the primary reason they are used by many standard Linux services, including the X Window System and the system logger.

## 16.4.1 Unix Domain Addresses

Addresses for Unix domain sockets are pathnames in the file system. If the file does not already exist, it is created as a socket-type file when a socket is bound to the pathname through bind(). If a file (even a socket) exists with the pathname being bound, bind() fails and returns EADDRINUSE. bind() sets the permissions of newly created socket files to 0666, as modified by the current umask.

To connect() to an existing socket, the process must have read and write permissions for the socket file.[7]

Unix domain socket addresses are passed through a struct sockaddr_un structure.

```
#include <sys/socket.h>
#include <sys/un.h>

struct sockaddr_un {
    unsigned short sun_family;      /* AF_UNIX */
    char sun_path[UNIX_PATH_MAX];   /* pathname */
};
```

In the Linux 2.0.x kernel, UNIX_PATH_MAX is 108, but that may change in future versions of the Linux kernel.

The first element, sun_family, must contain AF_UNIX to indicate that the structure contains a Unix domain address. The sun_path holds the pathname to use for the connection. When the size of the address is passed to and from the socket-related system calls, the passed length should be the number of characters in the pathname plus the size of the sun_family member. The sun_path does not need to be '\0' terminated, though it usually is.

## 16.4.2 Waiting for a Connection

Listening for a connection to be established on a Unix domain socket follows the procedure we described earlier: Create the socket, bind() an address to the socket, tell the system to listen() for connection attempts, and then accept() the connection.

Here is a simple server that repeatedly accepts connections on a Unix domain socket (the file sample-socket in the current directory) and reads all the data available from the socket, displaying it on standard output.

```
1: /* userver.c - simple server for Unix domain sockets */
2:
```

---

7. For both bind() and connect(), the process must have execute permission for the directories traversed during the pathname lookup, just as with opening normal files.

```
 3: /* Waits for a connection on the ./sample-socket Unix domain
 4:    socket. Once a connection has been established, copy data
 5:    from the socket to stdout until the other end closes the
 6:    connection, and then wait for another connection to the socket. */
 7:
 8: #include <stdio.h>
 9: #include <sys/socket.h>
10: #include <sys/un.h>
11: #include <unistd.h>
12:
13: #include "sockutil.h"           /* some utility functions */
14:
15: int main(void) {
16:     struct sockaddr_un address;
17:     int sock, conn;
18:     size_t addrLength;
19:
20:     if ((sock = socket(PF_UNIX, SOCK_STREAM, 0)) < 0)
21:         die("socket");
22:
23:     /* Remove any preexisting socket (or other file) */
24:     unlink("./sample-socket");
25:
26:     address.sun_family = AF_UNIX;       /* Unix domain socket */
27:     strcpy(address.sun_path, "./sample-socket");
28:
29:     /* The total length of the address includes the sun_family
30:        element */
31:     addrLength = sizeof(address.sun_family) +
32:                  strlen(address.sun_path);
33:
34:     if (bind(sock, (struct sockaddr *) &address, addrLength))
35:         die("bind");
36:
37:     if (listen(sock, 5))
38:         die("listen");
39:
40:     while ((conn = accept(sock, (struct sockaddr *) &address,
41:                           &addrLength)) >= 0) {
42:         printf("---- getting data\n");
43:         copyData(conn, 1);
```

```
44:        printf("---- done\n");
45:        close(conn);
46:    }
47:
48:    if (conn < 0)
49:        die("accept");
50:
51:    close(sock);
52:    return 0;
53: }
```

Although this program is small, it illustrates how to write a simple server process. This server is an **iterative server** because it handles one client at a time. Servers may also be written as **concurrent servers,** which handle multiple clients simultaneously.

Notice the unlink() call before the socket is bound. Because bind() fails if the socket file already exists, this allows the program to be run more than once without requiring that the socket file be manually removed.

The server code typecasts the struct sockaddr_un pointer passed to both bind() and accept() to a (struct sockaddr *). All the various socket-related system calls are prototyped as taking a pointer to struct sockaddr; the typecast keeps the compiler from complaining about pointer type mismatches.

## 16.4.3 Connecting to a Server

Connecting to a server through a Unix domain socket consists of creating a socket and connect()ing to the desired address. Once the socket is connected, it may be treated like any other file descriptor.

The following program connects to the same socket that the example server uses and copies its standard input to the server.

```
1: /* uclient.c - simple client for Unix domain sockets */
2:
3: /* Connect to the ./sample-socket Unix domain socket, copy stdin
4:    into the socket, and then exit. */
5:
6: #include <sys/socket.h>
```

```
 7: #include <sys/un.h>
 8: #include <unistd.h>
 9:
10: #include "sockutil.h"          /* some utility functions */
11:
12: int main(void) {
13:     struct sockaddr_un address;
14:     int sock;
15:     size_t addrLength;
16:
17:     if ((sock = socket(PF_UNIX, SOCK_STREAM, 0)) < 0)
18:         die("socket");
19:
20:     address.sun_family = AF_UNIX;    /* Unix domain socket */
21:     strcpy(address.sun_path, "./sample-socket");
22:
23:     /* The total length of the address includes the sun_family
24:        element */
25:     addrLength = sizeof(address.sun_family) +
26:                  strlen(address.sun_path);
27:
28:     if (connect(sock, (struct sockaddr *) &address, addrLength))
29:         die("connect");
30:
31:     copyData(0, sock);
32:
33:     close(sock);
34:
35:     return 0;
36: }
```

The client is not much different than the server. The only changes were replacing the bind(), listen(), accept() sequence with a single connect() call and copying a slightly different set of data.

## 16.4.4 Running the Unix Domain Examples

The previous two example programs, one a server and the other a client, are designed to work together. Run the server from one terminal, then run the client from another terminal (but in the same directory). As you type lines into the client, they will be sent through the socket to the server. When you exit the client, the server will wait for another connection. You can transmit files through the socket by redirecting the input to the client program.

## 16.4.5 Unnamed Unix Domain Sockets

Because Unix domain sockets have some advantages over pipes (such as being full duplex), they are often used as an IPC mechanism. To facilitate this, the `socketpair()` system call was introduced.

```
#include <sys/socket.h>

int socketpair(int domain, int type, int protocol, int sockfds[2]);
```

The first three parameters are the same as the parameters passed to `socket()`. The final parameter, `sockfds()`, is filled in by `socketpair()` with two file descriptors, one for each end of the socket. A sample application of `socketpair()` is shown on page 336.

## 16.4.6 Passing File Descriptors

Unix domain sockets have a unique ability: File descriptors can be passed through them. No other IPC mechanism supports this facility. It allows a process to open a file and pass the file descriptor to another—possibly unrelated—process. All the access checks are done when the file is opened, so the receiving process gains the same access rights to the file as the original process.

File descriptors are passed as part of a more complicated message that is sent using the `sendmsg()` system call and received using `recvmsg()`.

```
#include <sys/socket.h>

int sendmsg(int fd, const struct msghdr * msg, unsigned int flags);
int recvmsg(int fd, const struct msghdr * msg, unsigned int flags);
```

The fd parameter is the file descriptor through which the message is transmitted; the second parameter is a pointer to a structure describing the message. The flags are not usually used and should be set to 0 for most applications. More advanced network programming books discuss the available flags [Stevens, 1990].

A message is described by the following structure:

```
#include <sys/socket.h>
#include <sys/un.h>

struct msghdr {
    void * msg_name;              /* optional address */
    unsigned int msg_namelen;     /* size of msg_name */
    struct iovec * msg_iov;       /* scatter/gather array */
    unsigned int msg_iovlen;      /* number of elements in msg_iov */
    void * msg_control;           /* ancillary data */
    unsigned int msg_controllen;  /* ancillary data buffer len */
    int msg_flags;                /* flags on received message */
};
```

The first two elements, msg_name and msg_namelen, are not used with stream protocols. Applications that send messages across stream sockets should set msg_name to NULL and msg_namelen to 0.

msg_iov and msg_iovlen describe a set of buffers that are sent or received. Scatter/gather reads and writes, as well as struct iovec, are discussed on pages 232–234. The final element of the structure, msg_flags, is not currently used and should be set to 0.

The two elements we skipped over, msg_control and msg_controllen, provide the file descriptor passing ability. The msg_control element points to an array of control message headers; msg_controllen specifies how many bytes the array contains. Each control message consists of a struct cmsghdr followed by extra data.

```
#include <sys/socket.h>

struct cmsghdr {
    unsigned int cmsg_len;       /* length of control message */
    int cmsg_level;              /* SOL_SOCKET */
    int cmsg_type;               /* SCM_RIGHTS */
    int cmsg_data[0];            /* file descriptor goes here */
};
```

The size of the control message, including the header, is stored in cmsg_len. The only type of control message currently defined is SCM_RIGHTS, which passes file descriptors.[8] For this message type, cmsg_level and cmsg_type must be set to SOL_SOCKET and SCM_RIGHTS, respectively. The final element, cmsg_data, is an array of size 0. This is a gcc extension that allows an application to copy data to the end of the structure (see the following program for an example of this).

Receiving a file descriptor is similiar. Enough buffer space must be left for the control message, and a new file descriptor follows each struct cmsghdr that arrives.

To illustrate the use of these nested structures, we wrote an example program that is a fancy cat. It takes a file name as its sole argument, opens the specified file in a child process, and passes the resulting file descriptor to the parent through a Unix domain socket. The parent then copies the file to standard output. The file name is sent along with the file descriptor for illustrative purposes.

```
 1: /* passfd.c -- sample program which passes a file descriptor */
 2:
 3: /* We behave like a simple /bin/cat, which only handles one
 4:    argument (a file name). We create Unix domain sockets through
 5:    socketpair(), and then fork(). The child opens the file whose
 6:    name is passed on the command line, passes the file descriptor
 7:    and file name back to the parent, and then exits. The parent waits
 8:    for the file descriptor from the child, then copies data from that
 9:    file descriptor to stdout until no data is left. The parent then
10:    exits. */
11:
```

---

8. This is sometimes called passing access rights.

```
12: #include <alloca.h>
13: #include <fcntl.h>
14: #include <stdio.h>
15: #include <string.h>
16: #include <sys/socket.h>
17: #include <sys/uio.h>
18: #include <sys/un.h>
19: #include <sys/wait.h>
20: #include <unistd.h>
21:
22: #include "sockutil.h"          /* simple utility functions */
23:
24: /* The parent process. This sends the file descriptor. */
25: int childProcess(char * filename, int sock) {
26:     int fd;
27:     struct iovec vector;        /* some data to pass w/ the fd */
28:     struct msghdr msg;          /* the complete message */
29:     struct cmsghdr * cmsg;      /* the control message, which will */
30:                                 /* include the fd */
31:
32:     /* Open the file whose descriptor will be passed. */
33:     if ((fd = open(filename, O_RDONLY)) < 0) {
34:         perror("open");
35:         return 1;
36:     }
37:
38:     /* Send the file name down the socket, including the trailing
39:        '\0' */
40:     vector.iov_base = filename;
41:     vector.iov_len = strlen(filename) + 1;
42:
43:     /* Put together the first part of the message. Include the
44:        file name iovec */
45:     msg.msg_name = NULL;
46:     msg.msg_namelen = 0;
47:     msg.msg_iov = &vector;
48:     msg.msg_iovlen = 1;
49:
50:     /* Now for the control message. We have to allocate room for
51:        the file descriptor. */
52:     cmsg = alloca(sizeof(struct cmsghdr) + sizeof(fd));
```

```
53:        cmsg->cmsg_len = sizeof(struct cmsghdr) + sizeof(fd);
54:        cmsg->cmsg_level = SOL_SOCKET;
55:        cmsg->cmsg_type = SCM_RIGHTS;
56:
57:        /* copy the file descriptor onto the end of the control
58:           message */
59:        memcpy(cmsg->cmsg_data, &fd, sizeof(fd));
60:
61:        msg.msg_control = cmsg;
62:        msg.msg_controllen = cmsg->cmsg_len;
63:
64:        if (sendmsg(sock, &msg, 0) != vector.iov_len)
65:            die("sendmsg");
66:
67:        return 0;
68: }
69:
70: /* The parent process. This receives the file descriptor. */
71: int parentProcess(int sock) {
72:        char buf[80];                /* space to read file name into */
73:        struct iovec vector;         /* file name from the child */
74:        struct msghdr msg;           /* full message */
75:        struct cmsghdr * cmsg;       /* control message with the fd */
76:        int fd;
77:
78:        /* set up the iovec for the file name */
79:        vector.iov_base = buf;
80:        vector.iov_len = 80;
81:
82:        /* the message we're expecting to receive */
83:
84:        msg.msg_name = NULL;
85:        msg.msg_namelen = 0;
86:        msg.msg_iov = &vector;
87:        msg.msg_iovlen = 1;
88:
89:        /* dynamically allocate so we can leave room for the file
90:           descriptor */
91:        cmsg = alloca(sizeof(struct cmsghdr) + sizeof(fd));
92:        cmsg->cmsg_len = sizeof(struct cmsghdr) + sizeof(fd);
93:        msg.msg_control = cmsg;
```

```
 94:        msg.msg_controllen = cmsg->cmsg_len;
 95:
 96:        if (!recvmsg(sock, &msg, 0))
 97:            return 1;
 98:
 99:        printf("got file descriptor for '%s'\n",
100:               (char *) vector.iov_base);
101:
102:        /* grab the file descriptor from the control structure */
103:        memcpy(&fd, cmsg->cmsg_data, sizeof(fd));
104:
105:        copyData(fd, 1);
106:
107:        return 0;
108: }
109:
110: int main(int argc, char ** argv) {
111:        int socks[2];
112:        int status;
113:
114:        if (argc != 2) {
115:            fprintf(stderr, "only a single argument is supported\n");
116:            return 1;
117:        }
118:
119:        /* Create the sockets. The first is for the parent and the
120:           second is for the child (though we could reverse that
121:           if we liked. */
122:        if (socketpair(PF_UNIX, SOCK_STREAM, 0, socks))
123:            die("socketpair");
124:
125:        if (!fork()) {
126:            /* child */
127:            close(socks[0]);
128:            return childProcess(argv[1], socks[1]);
129:        }
130:
131:        /* parent */
132:        close(socks[1]);
133:        parentProcess(socks[0]);
134:
```

```
135:      /* reap the child */
136:      wait(&status);
137:
138:      if (WEXITSTATUS(status))
139:          fprintf(stderr, "child failed\n");
140:
141:      return 0;
142: }
```

# 16.5 Networking Machines with TCP/IP

The primary use for sockets is to allow applications running on different machines to talk to one another. The TCP/IP protocol family [Stevens, 1994] is the protocol used on the Internet, the largest set of networked computers in the world. Linux provides a complete, robust TCP/IP implementation that allows it to act as both a TCP/IP server and client.

The current version of TCP/IP is version 4 (IPv4). The rapid growth of the Internet has shown a few shortcomings of this version, and at the time of this writing, work has begun on TCP/IP version 6 (IPv6). This version is carefully designed to allow a slow migration to it from IPv4, and most Internet hosts are expected to convert to IPv6 over time.

The socket interface for IPv4 and the proposed interface for IPv6 are a bit different. We will cover only IPv4 sockets; if you need to develop IPv6 applications, keep in mind that the remainder of this chapter may not be completely applicable, though the concepts are the same.

## 16.5.1 Byte Ordering

TCP/IP networks are usually heterogenous; they include a wide variety of machines and architectures. One of the most common differences between architectures is how they store numbers.

Computer numbers are made up of a sequence of bytes. C integers are commonly 4 bytes (32 bits), for example. There are quite a few ways of storing those four bytes in memory. **Big-endian** architectures store the most significant byte at the lowest hardware address, and the other bytes follow in order from most significant to least significant. **Little-endian** machines store multibyte values in exactly the opposite order: The least significant byte is stored at the smallest memory address. Other machines store bytes in different orders yet.

Because multiple byte quantities are needed as part of the TCP/IP protocol, the protocol designers adopted a single standard for how multibyte values are sent across the network.[9] TCP/IP mandates that *big-endian* byte order be used for transmitting protocol information and suggests that it be used for application data, as well (though no attempt is made to enforce the format of an application's data stream). The ordering used for multibyte values sent across the network is known as the **network byte order**.

Four functions are available for converting between host byte order and network byte order.

```
#include <netinet/in.h>

unsigned int htonl(unsigned int hostlong);
unsigned short htons(unsigned short hostshort);
unsigned int ntohl(unsigned int netlong);
unsigned short ntohs(unsigned short netshort);
```

Although each of these functions is prototyped for unsigned quantities, they all work fine for signed quantities, as well.

The first two functions, htonl() and htons(), convert longs and shorts, respectively, from host order to network order. The final two, ntohl() and ntohs(), convert longs and shorts to network order from the host byte ordering.

Although we use the term *long* in the descriptions, that is a misnomer. htonl() and ntohl() both expect 32-bit quantities, not values that are C longs. We prototype both functions as manipulating int values as all Linux platforms currently use 32-bit integers.

---

9. Although it may seem like this is an obvious thing to do, some protocols allow the sender to use any byte order and depend on the recipient to convert the information to the proper (native) order. This gives a performance boost when like machines communicate, at the expense of algorithmic complexity.

## 16.5.2 IPv4 Addressing

IPv4 connections are a 4-tuple of (*local host, local port, remote host, remote port*). Each part of the connection must be determined before a connection can be established. *Local host* and *remote host* are each IP addresses. IP addresses are 32-bit (4-byte) numbers unique across the entire connected network. Usually, they are written as *aaa.bbb.ccc.ddd*, with each element in the address being the decimal representation of one of the bytes in the machine's address. The left-most number in the address corresponds to the most significant byte in the address. This format for IP addresses is known as **dotted-decimal notation**.

As most machines need to run multiple concurrent TCP/IP applications, an IP number does not provide a unique identification for a connection on a single machine. **Port numbers** are 16-bit numbers that uniquely identify one endpoint of a connection on a single host. The combination of an IP address and a port number identifies a connection endpoint anywhere on a single TCP/IP network (the Internet is a single TCP/IP network). Two connection endpoints form a TCP connection, so two IP number/port number pairs uniquely identify a TCP/IP connection on a network.

Although the port numbers range from 0 to 65,535, Linux divides them into two classes. The **reserved ports**, numbering from 0 to 1,024, may be used only by processes running as root. This allows client programs to trust that a program running on a server is not a Trojan horse started by a user.[10]

## 16.5.3 IP Socket Addresses

IP addresses are stored in a `struct sockaddr_in`, which is defined as follows:

```
#include <sys/socket.h>
#include <netinet.h/in.h>

struct sockaddr_in {
  short int            sin_family; /* AF_INET */
  unsigned short int   sin_port;   /* port number */
  struct in_addr       sin_addr;   /* IP address */
}
```

---

10. It may still be a Trojan horse started by the superuser, however.

The first element must be AF_INET, indicating that this is an IP address. The next element is the port number in network byte order. The final element is the IP number of the machine for this TCP address. The IP number, stored in sin_addr, should be treated as an opaque type and not accessed directly.

If either sin_port or sin_addr is filled with 0 bytes (normally, by memset()), that indicates a "don't care" condition. Server processes usually do not care what IP address is used for the local connection, for example, as they are willing to accept connections to any address the machine has. If an application wishes to listen for connections only on a single interface, however, it would specify the address.

## 16.5.4 Manipulating IP Addresses

Applications often need to convert IP addresses between dotted-decimal notation and struct in_addr's binary representation. inet_ntoa() takes a binary IP address and returns a pointer to a string containing the dotted-decimal form.[11]

```
#include <netinet/in.h>
#include <arpa/inet.h>

char * inet_ntoa(struct in_addr address);
```

The resulting string is stored in a static area of memory and will be destroyed on the next call to inet_ntoa().

Originally, inet_addr() provided the inverse, converting a dotted-decimal string to a binary IP address. This function had two problems, both caused by it returning a long. Not returning a struct in_addr, which is what the rest of the standard functions expect, forced programmers into ugly casts. In addition, if a long was 32 bits, programs could not differentiate between a return of -1 (indicating an error, such as a malformed address) and the binary representation of 255.255.255.255. For the sake of legacy applications, here is what inet_addr() looks like:

---

11. The *ntoa* is a mnemonic for *network-to-ascii*.

```
#include <netinet/in.h>
#include <arpa/inet.h>

unsigned long int inet_addr(const char * ddaddress);
```

The function takes the passed string, which should contain a dotted-decimal IP address, and converts it to a binary IP address.

Rather than use the broken interface of `inet_addr()`, new programs should instead use `inet_aton()`.

```
#include <netinet/in.h>
#include <arpa/inet.h>

int inet_aton(const char * ddaddress, struct in_addr * address);
```

This function expects a string containing a dotted-decimal IP address and fills in the `struct in_addr` pointed to by `address` with the binary representation of the address. Unlike most library functions, `inet_aton()` returns 0 if an error occurred and non-0 if the conversion was successful.

## 16.5.5 Using Hostnames

Although 32-bit numbers are a perfectly reasonable identification method for computers to use for recognizing each other, people tend to get dismayed at the idea of dealing with strings of digits. To allow humans to use alphabetic names for computers instead of numeric ones, the TCP/IP protocol suite includes a distributed database for converting between hostnames and IP addresses. This database is called the **Domain Name System** (DNS) and is covered in depth by many books [Stevens, 1994] [Albitz, 1996].

DNS provides many features, but the only one we are interested in here is its ability to convert between IP addresses and hostnames. Although it may seem like this should be a one-to-one mapping, it is actually a many-to-many mapping: Every IP address corresponds to 0 or more hostnames and every hostname corresponds to 0 or more IP addresses.

Although using a many-to-many mapping between hostnames and IP addresses may seem strange, many Internet sites use a single machine for their ftp site and Web site. They would like `www.some.org` and `ftp.some.org` to refer to a single machine, and they have no need for two IP addresses for the machine. Similarly, Internet routers almost always have multiple hardware interfaces they route between. Some sites prefer that a single hostname refer to all the interfaces on the router, although many other sites name each interface independently.

To handle all of this complexity, `struct hostent` was defined. It contains all the hostnames and addresses for a single host.

```
#include <netdb.h>

struct hostent {
    char * h_name;          /* canonical hostname            */
    char ** h_aliases;      /* aliases (NULL terminated)     */
    int h_addrtype;         /* host address type             */
    int h_length;           /* length of address             */
    char ** h_addr_list;    /* list of addresses (NULL term) */
};
```

The `h_name` is the canonical (official) name for the host. The `h_aliases` array contains any aliases for the host. The final entry in `h_aliases` is a `NULL` pointer, signalling the end of the array.

`h_aliases` tells the type of address the host has. For the purposes of this chapter, it is always `AF_INET`. Applications that are written to support IPv6 will see other address types. The next element, `h_length`, specifies the length of the binary addresses for this host. For `AF_INET` addresses, it is equal to `sizeof(struct in_addr)`. The final element, `h_addr_list`, is an array of pointers to the addresses for this host, with the final pointer being `NULL` to signify the end of the list. When `h_addrtype` is `AF_INET`, each pointer in this list points to a `struct inaddr`.

Two library functions convert between IP numbers and hostnames. The first, `gethostbyname()`, returns a `struct hostent` for a hostname; the other, `gethostbyaddr()`, returns information on a machine with a particular IP address.

```
#include <netdb.h>

struct hostent * gethostbyname(const char * name);
struct hostent * gethostbyaddr(const char * addr, int len, int type);
```

Both functions return a pointer to a struct hostent. The structure may be overwritten by the next call to either function, so the program should save any values it will need later. gethostbyname() takes a single parameter, a string containing a hostname. gethostbyaddr() takes three parameters, which together specify an address. The first, addr, should point to a struct in_addr. The next, len, specifies how long the information pointed to by addr is. The final parameter, type, specifies the type of address that should be converted to a hostname—AF_INET for IPv4 addresses.

When errors occur during hostname lookup, an error code is set in h_errno. The herror() function call prints a description of the error, behaving almost identically to the standard perror() function.

The only error code that most programs explicitly test for is NETDB_INTERNAL, which indicates a failed system call. When this error is returned, errno contains the error that led to the failure.

## 16.5.6 Host Information Lookup Example

Here is a sample program that makes use of inet_aton(), inet_ntoa(), gethostbyname(), and gethostbyaddr(). It takes a single argument that may be either a hostname or an IP address in dotted-decimal notation. It looks up the host and prints all the hostnames and IP addresses associated with it.

Any argument that is a valid dotted-decimal address is assumed to be an IP number, not a hostname. Although the rules of hostname formation allow hostnames to be purely numeric (and confused with IP numbers), the regulations that govern hostname assignments prevent this. All top-level domains, such as .com, .edu, and .org, are alphabetic, preventing hostnames from looking like IP numbers.

```
1: /* lookup.c -- print basic DNS information on an Internet host */
2:
3: /* Given either a hostname or IP address on the command line, print
4:    the canonical hostname for that host and all of the IP numbers
5:    and hostnames associated with it. */
6:
7: #include <netdb.h>              /* for gethostby* */
8: #include <sys/socket.h>
```

```
 9: #include <netinet/in.h>        /* for address structures */
10: #include <arpa/inet.h>         /* for inet_ntoa() */
11: #include <stdio.h>
12:
13: int main(int argc, char ** argv) {
14:     struct hostent * answer;
15:     struct in_addr address, ** addrptr;
16:     char ** next;
17:
18:     if (argc != 2) {
19:         fprintf(stderr, "only a single argument is supported\n");
20:         return 1;
21:     }
22:
23:     /* If the argument looks like an IP, assume it was one */
24:     if (inet_aton(argv[1], &address))
25:         answer = gethostbyaddr((char *) &address, sizeof(address),
26:                             AF_INET);
27:     else
28:         answer = gethostbyname(argv[1]);
29:
30:     /* the hostname lookup failed :-( */
31:     if (!answer) {
32:         herror("error looking up host");
33:         return 1;
34:     }
35:
36:     printf("Canonical hostname: %s\n", answer->h_name);
37:
38:     /* if there are any aliases, print them all out */
39:     if (answer->h_aliases[0]) {
40:         printf("Aliases:");
41:         for (next = answer->h_aliases; *next; next++)
42:             printf(" %s", *next);
43:         printf("\n");
44:     }
45:
46:     /* display all of the IP addresses for this machine */
47:     printf("Addresses:");
48:     for (addrptr = (struct in_addr **) answer->h_addr_list;
49:                 *addrptr; addrptr++)
```

```
50:         printf(" %s", inet_ntoa(**addrptr));
51:     printf("\n");
52:
53:     return 0;
54: }
```

Here is what this program looks like when it is run:

```
$ ./lookup ftp.netscape.com
Canonical hostname: ftp25.netscape.com
Aliases: ftp.netscape.com anonftp10.netscape.com
Addresses: 207.200.74.21
```

## 16.5.7 Looking Up Port Numbers

Part of the Internet standards are a set of **well-known port numbers** maintained by the **Internet Assigned Numbers Authority** (IANA).[12] Common Internet protocols, such as ftp, telnet, and http, are each assigned a port number. Most servers provide those services at the assigned numbers, making them easy to find. Some servers are run at alternate port numbers, usually to allow multiple services to be provided by a single machine.

Linux systems include the file /etc/services, which maps protocols to port numbers. The most common way to access this file is through the getservbyname() function, which returns information on a particular service.

```
#include <netdb.h>

struct servent * getservbyname(const char * name,
                               const char * protocol);
```

The first parameter, name, is the service name about which the application needs information. The protocol parameter specifies the protocol that will be used. The services database contains information on other protocols (especially UDP); specifying the protocol allows the function to ignore information on other protocols. The protocol is usually the string "tcp", though other protocol names, such as "udp", may be used.

---

12. See http://www.iana.org for information on the IANA.

getservbyname() returns a pointer to a structure that contains information
on the queried service. The information may be overwritten by the next
call to getservbyname(), so any important information should be saved by
the application. Here is the information returned by getservbyname():

```
#include <netdb.h>

struct servent {
    char * s_name;      /* service name */
    char ** s_aliases;  /* service aliases */
    int s_port;         /* port number */
    char * s_proto;     /* protocol to use */
}
```

Each service may have multiple names associated with it but only one
port number. s_name lists the canonical name of the service, s_port contains
the well-known port number for the service (in network byte order), and
s_proto is the protocol for the service (such as "tcp"). The s_aliases element
is an array of pointers to aliases for the service, with a NULL pointer marking
the end of the list.

If the function fails, it returns NULL and sets h_errno.

Here is an example program that looks up a TCP service specified on the
command line and displays the service's canonical name, port number, and
all of its aliases:

```
 1: #include <netdb.h>
 2: #include <netinet/in.h>
 3: #include <stdio.h>
 4:
 5: /* display the TCP port number and any aliases for the service
 6:    which is named on the command line */
 7:
 8: /* services.c - finds the port number for a service */
 9: int main(int argc, char ** argv) {
10:     struct servent * service;
11:     char ** ptr;
12:
13:     if (argc != 2) {
14:         fprintf(stderr, "only a single argument is supported\n");
15:         return 1;
```

```
16:    }
17:
18:    /* look up the service in /etc/services, give an error if
19:       we fail */
20:    service = getservbyname(argv[1], "tcp");
21:    if (!service) {
22:        herror("getservbyname failed");
23:        return 1;
24:    }
25:
26:    printf("service: %s\n", service->s_name);
27:    printf("tcp port: %d\n", ntohs(service->s_port));
28:
29:    /* display any aliases this service has */
30:    if (*service->s_aliases) {
31:        printf("aliases:");
32:        for (ptr = service->s_aliases; *ptr; ptr++)
33:            printf(" %s", *ptr);
34:        printf("\n");
35:    }
36:
37:    return 0;
38: }
```

Here is an example of running the program; notice it can look up services by either their canonical name or an alias.

```
$ ./services http
service: http
tcp port: 80
$ ./services source
service: chargen
tcp port: 19
aliases: ttytst source
```

## 16.5.8 Listening for TCP Connections

Listening for TCP connections is nearly identical to listening for Unix domain connections. The only differences are the protocol and address families. Here is a version of the example Unix domain server that works over TCP sockets instead:

```
 1: /* tserver.c - simple server for TCP/IP sockets */
 2:
 3: /* Waits for a connection on port 1234. Once a connection has been
 4:    established, copy data from the socket to stdout until the other
 5:    end closes the connection, and then wait for another connection to
 6:    the socket. */
 7:
 8: #include <arpa/inet.h>
 9: #include <netinet/in.h>
10: #include <stdio.h>
11: #include <string.h>
12: #include <sys/socket.h>
13: #include <unistd.h>
14:
15: #include "sockutil.h"          /* some utility functions */
16:
17: int main(void) {
18:     struct sockaddr_in address;
19:     int sock, conn, i;
20:     size_t addrLength;
21:
22:     if ((sock = socket(PF_INET, SOCK_STREAM, 0)) < 0)
23:         die("socket");
24:
25:     /* Let the kernel reuse the socket address. This lets us run
26:        twice in a row, without waiting for the (ip, port) tuple
27:        to time out. */
28:     i = 1;
29:     setsockopt(sock, SOL_SOCKET, SO_REUSEADDR, &i, sizeof(i));
30:
31:     address.sin_family = AF_INET;
32:     address.sin_port = htons(1234);
33:     memset(&address.sin_addr, 0, sizeof(address.sin_addr));
34:
35:     if (bind(sock, (struct sockaddr *) &address, sizeof(address)))
```

```
36:          die("bind");
37:
38:      if (listen(sock, 5))
39:          die("listen");
40:
41:      while ((conn = accept(sock, (struct sockaddr *) &address,
42:                            &addrLength)) >= 0) {
43:          printf("---- getting data\n");
44:          copyData(conn, 1);
45:          printf("---- done\n");
46:          close(conn);
47:      }
48:
49:      if (conn < 0)
50:          die("accept");
51:
52:      close(sock);
53:      return 0;
54: }
```

Notice that the IP address bound to the socket specifies a port number, 1234, but not an IP address. This leaves the kernel free to use whatever local IP address it likes.

The other thing that needs some explaining is this code sequence on lines 28–29:

```
i = 1;
setsockopt(sock, SOL_SOCKET, SO_REUSEADDR, &i, sizeof(i));
```

Linux's TCP implementation, like that of most Unix systems, restricts how soon a (*local host*, *local port*) can be reused.[13] This code sets an option on the socket that bypasses this restriction and allows the server to be run twice in a short period of time. This is similiar to the reason the Unix domain socket example server removed any preexisting socket file before calling bind().

The setsockopt() allows you to set many socket- and protocol-specific options.

---

13. For TCP ports, the combination may not be used within a two-minute period.

```
#include <sys/socket.h>

int setsockopt(int sock, int level, int option,
               const void * valptr, int vallength);
```

The first argument is the socket whose option is being set. The second argument, level, specifies what type of option is being set. In our server, we used SOL_SOCKET, which specifies that a generic socket option is being set. The option parameter specifies the option to be changed. A pointer to the new value of the option is passed through valptr and the size of the value pointed to by valptr is passed as vallength. For our server, we use a pointer to a non-0 integer, which turns on the SO_REUSEADDR option.

## 16.5.9 TCP Client Applications

TCP clients are similiar to Unix domain clients. Usually, a socket is created and immediately connect()ed to the server. The only differences are in how the address passed to connect() is set. Rather than use a file name, most TCP clients look up the hostname to connect to through gethostbyname(), then copy the address they find into a struct sockaddr_in, which they then pass to connect().

Here is a simple TCP client that talks to the server presented in the previous section. It takes a single argument, which is the name or IP number (in dotted-decimal notation) of the host the server is running on. It otherwise behaves like the sample Unix domain socket client presented on page 332.

```
 1: /* tclient.c - simple client for TCP/IP sockets */
 2:
 3: /* Connect to the server whose hostname or IP is given as an
 4:    argument, at port 1234. Once connected, copy everything on
 5:    stdin to the socket, then exit. */
 6:
 7: #include <arpa/inet.h>
 8: #include <netdb.h>
 9: #include <netinet/in.h>
10: #include <stdio.h>
11: #include <sys/socket.h>
12: #include <unistd.h>
```

```
13:
14: #include "sockutil.h"          /* some utility functions */
15:
16: int main(int argc, char ** argv) {
17:     struct sockaddr_in address;
18:     struct in_addr inaddr;
19:     struct hostent * host;
20:     int sock;
21:
22:     if (argc != 2) {
23:         fprintf(stderr, "only a single argument is supported\n");
24:         return 1;
25:     }
26:
27:     /* If the argument can be converted to an IP, do so. If not, try
28:        to look it up in DNS. */
29:     if (inet_aton(argv[1], &inaddr))
30:         host = gethostbyaddr((char *) &inaddr, sizeof(inaddr),
31:                             AF_INET);
32:     else
33:         host = gethostbyname(argv[1]);
34:
35:     if (!host) {
36:         /* We can't find an IP number */
37:         herror("error looking up host");
38:         exit(1);
39:     }
40:
41:     if ((sock = socket(PF_INET, SOCK_STREAM, 0)) < 0)
42:         die("socket");
43:
44:     address.sin_family = AF_INET;
45:     address.sin_port = htons(1234);
46:
47:     /* Take the first IP address associated with this hostname */
48:     memcpy(&address.sin_addr, host->h_addr_list[0],
49:         sizeof(address.sin_addr));
50:
51:     if (connect(sock, (struct sockaddr *) &address, sizeof(address)))
52:         die("connect");
53:
```

```
54:     copyData(0, sock);
55:
56:     close(sock);
57:
58:     return 0;
59: }
```

# 16.6  Socket Errors

A number of `errno` values occur only with sockets. Here is a list of socket-specific errors and a short description of each:

ENOTSOCK
> A socket-specific operation was attempted on a file descriptor that references a file other than a socket.

EDESTADDRREQ
> An attempt was made to send data over a socket without providing the destination address. This can occur only for datagram sockets.

EPROTOTYPE
> An inappropriate protocol type was specified for the socket.

ENOPROTOOPT
> An attempt to set an invalid option was made.

EPROTONOSUPPORT
> A request was made for an unsupported protocol.

ESOCKTNOSUPPORT
> An attempt was made to create an unsupported socket type.

EPFNOSUPPORT
> An unsupported protocol family was specified.

EAFNOSUPPORT
> An unsupported address family was specified.

EADDRINUSE

> A requested address is already in use and cannot be reassigned.

EADDRNOTAVAIL

> An unavailable address was requested.

ENETDOWN

> The network connection is down.

ENETUNREACH

> The specified network cannot be reached.

ENETRESET

> The network was reset, causing the connection to be dropped.

ECONNABORTED

> The connection was aborted by software.

ECONNRESET

> The connection was reset by the remote end. This usually indicates that the remote machine was restarted.

ENOBUFS

> Not enough buffer space is available to handle the request.

EISCONN

> A connection is already established for the socket.

ENOTCONN

> A connection must be established before the operation can succeed.

ETIMEDOUT

> The connection timed out.

ECONNREFUSED

> The remote machine refused the connection attempt.

EHOSTDOWN

> The remote host is not on the network.

EHOSTUNREAD

> The remote host cannot be reached.

# CHAPTER 17

# Time

## 17.1 Telling Time and Dates

### 17.1.1 Representing Time

Unix and Linux keep track of time in seconds before or after the **epoch**, which is defined as midnight, January 1, 1970 UTC.[1] Positive time values are after the epoch; negative time values are before the epoch. In order to provide processes with the current time, Linux, like all versions of Unix, provides a system call called `time()`:

```
#include <time.h>
time_t time(time_t *t);
```

`time()` returns the number of seconds since epoch, and if `t` is non-null, it also fills in `t` with the number of seconds since epoch.

Some problems require higher resolution. Linux provides another system call, `gettimeofday()`, which provides more information:

---

1. UTC: Universal Coordinated Time, also known as UCT; roughly equivalent to Greenwich Mean Time (GMT) and Zulu. Time zone designations involve technical detail far beyond the scope of this book.

```
#include <sys/time.h>
#include <unistd.h>

int gettimeofday(struct timeval *tv, struct timezone *tz);

struct timeval {
    int tv_sec;         /* seconds */
    int tv_usec;        /* microseconds */
};

struct timezone {
    int tz_minuteswest; /* minutes west of Greenwich */
    int tz_dsttime;     /* type of dst correction */
};
```

On many platforms, including the i386 platform, Linux is able to provide very accurate time measurements. Industry-standard PCs have a hardware clock that provides microsecond-accurate time information. Alpha and SPARC hardware also provides a high-resolution timer. On some other platforms, however, Linux can keep track of time only within the resolution of the system timer, which is generally set to 100Hz, so the tv_usec member of the timeval structure may be less accurate on those systems.

Three macros are provided in sys/time.h for operating on timeval structures:

timerclear(struct timeval)
> This clears a timeval structure.

timerisset(struct timeval)
> This checks to see if a timeval structure has been filled in (that is, if either element is non-0).

timercmp(struct timeval t0, struct timeval t1, operator)
> This allows you to compare two timeval structures in the time domain. It evaluates the logical equivalent of t0 operator t1, if t0 and g1 were arithmetic types. Note that timercmp() does not work for the <= and >= operators. Use !timercmp(t1, t2, >) and !timercmp(t1, t2, <) instead.

A third representation of time, struct tm, puts the time in terms that are more human-oriented:

```
struct tm
{
    int tm_sec;
    int tm_min;
    int tm_hour;
    int tm_mday;
    int tm_mon;
    int tm_year;
    int tm_wday;
    int tm_yday;
    int tm_isdst;
    long int tm_gmtoff;
    const char *tm_zone;
};
```

The first nine elements are standard; the final two are nonstandard but useful when they exist, as they do on Linux systems.

| | |
|---|---|
| tm_sec | The number of elapsed seconds in the minute. Will be between 0 and 61 (two extra seconds are allocated to deal with leap seconds). |
| tm_min | The number of elapsed minutes in the hour. Will be between 0 and 59. |
| tm_hour | The number of elapsed hours in the day. Will be between 0 and 23. |
| tm_mday | The number of the day of the month. Will be between 1 and 31. This is the only field that will never be 0. |
| tm_mon | The number of elapsed months in the year. Will be between 0 and 11. |
| tm_year | The number of elapsed years since 1900. |
| tm_wday | The number of elapsed days in the week (since Sunday). Will be between 0 and 6. |

| tm_yday | The number of elapsed days in the year. Will be between 0 and 365. |
|---|---|
| tm_isdst | Whether some sort of daylight savings time is in effect in the expressed time value in the current time zone, if applicable. tm_isdst will be positive if daylight savings time is in effect, 0 if it is not in effect, and -1 if the system does not know. |
| tm_gmtoff | This is not portable as it does not exist on all systems. If it exists, it may also be named __tm_gmtoff. It specifies seconds east of UTC or negative seconds west of UTC for time zones east of the date line. |
| tm_zone | This is not portable as it does not exist on all systems. If it exists, it may also be named __tm_zone. It holds a name for the current time zone (some time zones may have several names). |

Finally, the POSIX.1b real-time processing standard allows even higher resolution than the microsecond resolution available in struct timeval. struct timespec uses nanoseconds instead and provides larger places to put the numbers:

```
struct timespec
{
    long int tv_sec;   /* seconds     */
    long int tv_nsec;  /* nanoseconds */
};
```

## 17.1.2 Converting, Formatting, and Parsing Times

Four functions are available for converting among times expressed in terms of time_t and times expressed in terms of struct tm. Three are standard and are available on all Linux and Unix systems. The fourth, though useful, is not universally available, although it is available on all current Linux systems. A fifth function, which is standard, calculates the difference in seconds between time_t times. (Notice that even the time_t arguments are passed as pointers, not just the struct tm arguments.)

`struct tm * gmtime(const time_t *t)`
> Short for Greenwich Mean Time, `gmtime()` converts a `time_t` value into a `struct tm` that expresses that time in UTC.

`struct tm * localtime(const time_t *t)`
> `localtime()` acts like `gmtime()` except that it creates the `struct tm` expressed in terms of local time. Local time is defined for the whole system by the settings of the zoneinfo files, and that can be overridden by a `TZ` environment variable by users who are working from a different time zone than the one the computer is in.

`time_t mktime(struct tm *tp);`
> `mktime()` converts a `struct tm` to a `time_t`, assuming that the `struct tm` is expressed in terms of local time.

`time_t timegm(struct tm *tp);`
> `timegm()` acts like `mktime()` except that it assumes that the `struct tm` is expressed in terms of UTC. It is not a standard function.

`double difftime(time_t time1, time_t time0);`
> `difftime()` returns a floating-point number representing the difference in time in seconds between two `time_t` values. Although `time_t` is guaranteed to be an arithmetic type, the unit is not specified by ANSI C; `difftime()` returns the difference in seconds, regardless of the units of `time_t`.

Four more functions are available to convert time between computer-friendly numbers and human-friendly textual representations. Again, the final one is not standard, despite its obvious general usefulness.

`char *asctime(struct tm *tp);`
`char *ctime(time_t *t);`
> `asctime()` and `ctime()` both convert a time value into a standard Unix date string that looks something like this:

> `Tue Jun 17 23:17:29 1997`

> In both cases, the string is 26 characters long and includes a final newline character and the terminating `'\0'`.

The length of the string may not be guaranteed to be 26 characters in all locales, as it is in the default C locale.

ctime() expresses this date in local time. asctime() expresses this date in whatever time zone the struct tm specifies; if it was created with gmtime(), it is in UTC, but if it was created with localtime(), it is in local time.

size_t strftime(char *s, size_t max, char *fmt, struct tm *tp);

strftime() is like sprintf() for time. It formats a struct tm according to the format fmt and places the result in no more than max bytes (including the terminating '\0') of the string s.

Like sprintf(), strftime() uses the % character to introduce escape sequences into which data is substituted. All of the substituted strings are expressed in terms of the current locale. However, the escape sequences are completely different. In several cases, lower-case letters are used for abbreviations and upper-case letters are used for full names. Unlike sprintf(), you do not have the option of using numbers in the middle of an escape sequence to limit the length of the substituted string; %.6A is invalid. Like sprintf(), strftime() returns the number of characters printed into the s buffer. If it is equal to max, the buffer is not large enough for the current locale; allocate a larger buffer and try again.

strftime() uses the same substitutions used by the date program. These definitions of the substitutions are for the default locale and are here to help you identify the type of information they provide; they may be somewhat different in other locales.

%a    The three-character abbreviation for the name of the weekday.

%A    The full name of the weekday.

%b    The three-character abbreviation for the name of the month.

%B    The full name of the month.

%c    The preferred local expression of the date and time, as returned by ctime() and asctime().

`%d`    The numeric day of the month, counting from zero.

`%H`    The hour of the day, in 24-hour time, counting from zero.

`%I`    The hour of the day, in 12-hour time, counting from zero.

`%j`    The day of the year, counting from one.

`%m`    The month of the year, counting from one.

`%M`    The minute of the hour, counting from zero.

`%p`    The correct string for the local equivalent of AM or PM.

`%S`    The second of the minute, counting from zero.

`%U`    The numeric week of the year, where week one starts on the first Sunday of the year.

`%W`    The numeric week of the year, where week one starts on the first Monday of the year.

`%w`    The numeric day of the week, counting from zero.

`%x`    The preferred local expression of the date only, without the time.

`%X`    The preferred local expression of the time only, without the date.

`%y`    The two-digit representation of the year, without the century. (Do not use this—it is a potent source of year-2000 problems.)

`%Y`    The full four-digit numeric representation of the year.

`%Z`    The name or standard abbreviation of the time zone.

`%%`    The literal character %.

`char *strptime(char *s, char *fmt, struct tm *tp);`
Like `scanf()`, `strptime()` converts a string to a parsed format. It tries to be liberal in interpreting the `s` input string according to the `fmt`

format string. It takes the same escape sequences that strftime() takes, but for each type of input, it will accept both abbreviations and full names. It does not distinguish between upper and lower case, and it does not recognize %U and %W.

strptime() also provides a few extra escape sequences and interprets a few sequences slightly differently than does strftime(). Only the significantly different escape sequences (that is, beyond the changes already mentioned) are documented in this list. Numbers may have leading zeros, but they are not required.

%h    Equivalent to %b and %B.

%c    Reads the date and time as printed by strftime() with the format string %x %X.

%C    Reads the date and time as printed by strftime() with the format string %c.

%e    Equivalent to %d.

%D    Reads the date as printed by strftime() with the format string %m/%d/%y.

%k    Equivalent to %H.

%l    Equivalent to %I.

%r    Reads the time as printed by strftime() with the format string %I:%M:%S %p.

%R    Reads the time as printed by strftime() with the format string %H:%M.

%T    Reads the time as printed by strftime() with the format string %H:%M:%S.

%y    Reads the year within the 20th century. 1900 will be added to the value, and only values of 0–99 are allowed.

%Y    Reads the full year. Use this instead of %y if you possibly can, to avoid year-2000 problems.

strptime() returns a pointer to the character in s one character beyond the final character that it reads while parsing.

The strptime() function is, unfortunately, specified neither by ANSI nor POSIX, which limits its portability.

## 17.1.3 The Limits of Time

On 32-bit Linux systems, like most Unix systems, time_t is a signed integer 32 bits long. This means that it will overflow Monday, January 18, 2038, at 10:14:07 PM. So Monday, January 18, 2038, 10:14:08 PM will be represented as Friday, December 13th, 3:45:52 PM, 1901. As you can see, Linux does not have a year-2000 problem (as far as the native time libraries are concerned), but it does have a year-2038 problem.

On the Digital Alpha platform (and probably other 64-bit platforms Linux is ported to), time_t is instead a 64-bit signed long. This is effectively forever; signed 64-bit time is truly astronomical, as it will not overflow until well after the sun is predicted to envelope the Earth as it becomes a red giant.

To find the beginning of time, the current time, and the end of time for the system you are using, you can build and run this program, daytime.c:

```
 1: #include <stdio.h>
 2: #include <sys/time.h>
 3: #include <unistd.h>
 4:
 5: int main() {
 6:    struct timeval tv;
 7:    struct timezone tz;
 8:    time_t now;
 9:    /* beginning_of_time is smallest time_t-sized value */
10:    time_t beginning_of_time = 1L<<(sizeof(time_t)*8 - 1);
11:    /* end_of_time is largest time_t-sized value */
12:    time_t end_of_time = ~beginning_of_time;
13:
```

```
14:     printf("time_t is %d bits long\n\n", sizeof(time_t)*8);
15:
16:     gettimeofday(&tv, &tz);
17:     now = tv.tv_sec;
18:     printf("Current time of day represented as a struct timeval:\n"
19:             "tv.tv_sec = 0x%08x, tv.tv_usec = 0x%08x\n"
20:             "tz.tz_minuteswest = 0x%08x, tz.tz_dsttime = 0x%08x\n\n",
21:             tv.tv_sec, tv.tv_usec, tz.tz_minuteswest, tz.tz_dsttime);
22:
23:     printf("Demonstrating ctime()%s:\n", sizeof(time_t)*8 <= 32 ? "" :
24:             " (may hang after printing first line; press control-C)");
25:     printf("time is now %s", ctime(&now));
26:     printf("time begins %s", ctime(&beginning_of_time));
27:     printf("time ends %s", ctime(&end_of_time));
28:
29:     exit (0);
30: }
```

Unfortunately, the ctime() function is iterative, which means that it (for all practical purposes) never terminates on the Alpha system for astronomical dates like the 64-bit beginning and end of time.

# 17.2  Using Timers

A timer is simply a way of scheduling an event to happen at some point in the future. Instead of looping around, looking at the current time, and wasting CPU cycles, a program can ask the kernel to notify it when at least a certain amount of time has passed.

There are two ways to use timers: synchronously and asynchronously. The only way to use a timer synchronously is to wait for the timer to expire—sleeping. Using a timer asynchronously, like every other asynchronous facility, involves signals. What may be suprising is that using a timer synchronously may also involve signals.

## 17.2.1 Sleeping

Sleeping is when a process requests that it not be scheduled for at least a certain amount of time. Four functions are available for sleeping; each measures time in different units. They also have slightly different behavior and interact with other parts of the system differently.

`unsigned int sleep(unsigned int seconds);`

> `sleep()` causes the current process to sleep at least `seconds` seconds *or* until a signal that the process does not ignore is received by the process. On most platforms, `sleep()` is implemented in terms of the `SIGALRM` signal, and therefore it does not mix well with using the `alarm()` system call, creating a `SIGALRM` handler, ignoring the `SIGALRM` signal, or using `ITIMER_REAL` interval timers (described later), which share the same timer and signal.
>
> If `sleep()` does not sleep for the full time allotted, it returns the number of seconds left to sleep. If it has slept at least as long as requested, it returns 0.

`void usleep(unsigned long usec);`

> `usleep()` causes the current process to sleep at least `usec` microseconds. No signals are used. On most platforms, `usleep()` is implemented via `select()`.

`int select(0, NULL, NULL, NULL, struct timeval tv);`

> `select()`, documented in Chapter 12, provides a portable way to sleep for a precise amount of time. Simply fill in the `struct timeval` with the amount of time you wish to wait, and do not wait for any events to occur.

`int nanosleep(struct timespec *req, struct timespec *rem);`

> `nanosleep()` causes the current process to sleep at least the amount of time specified in `req` (see page 360 for `timespec`), unless a signal is received by the process. If `nanosleep()` terminates early due to a received signal, it returns -1 and sets `errno` to `EINTR` and, if `rem` is not `NULL`, sets `rem` to represent the amount of time remaining in the sleep period.
>
> `nanosleep()` is currently the least portable of these functions, because it is specified as part of the POSIX.1b (previously called POSIX.4)

real-time functions, which are not implemented on all versions of Unix. However, in time, it may become one of the most portable because it is more stringently specified than the others, POSIX.1b functionality is becoming more common, and it does not interact with other sleeping functions the way sleep() does with interval timers.

Not all platforms that provide the nanosleep() function provide high accuracy, but Linux, like other real-time operating systems, will attempt to honor short waits with extreme accuracy for real-time processes. See *Programming for the Real World* [Gallmeister, 1995] for more information on real-time programming.

## 17.2.2 Interval Timers

Interval timers, once enabled, continually deliver signals to a process on a regular basis. Exactly what *regular* means depends on which interval timer you use. Each process has three interval timers associated with it.

ITIMER_REAL

Tracks time in terms of the clock on the wall—real time, regardless of whether the process is executing—and delivers a SIGALRM signal. It conflicts with the alarm() system call, which is used by the sleep() function. Use neither alarm() nor sleep() if you have a real itimer active.

ITIMER_VIRTUAL

Counts time only when the process is executing—excluding any system calls the process makes—and delivers a SIGVTALRM signal.

ITIMER_PROF

Counts time when the process is executing—including the time the kernel spends executing system calls on the behalf of the process, but not including any time spent processing interrupts on behalf of the process—and delivers a SIGPROF signal. Accounting for time spent processing interrupts would be so expensive that it would change the timings.

The combination of ITIMER_VIRTUAL and ITIMER_PROF is often used for profiling code.

Each of these timers will generate its associated signal within one system clock tick (10 milliseconds on most Linux systems, 1 millisecond on Linux/Alpha) of the timer expiring. If the process is currently running when the signal is generated, it will be delivered immediately; otherwise, it will be delivered soon after, depending on system load. Since ITIMER_VIRTUAL is tracked only when the process is running, it will always be delivered immediately.

Use a struct itimerval to query and set itimers.

```
struct itimerval {
    struct timeval it_interval;
    struct timeval it_value;
};
```

The it_value member is the amount of time left until the next signal is sent. The it_interval member is the amount of time between signals; it_value is set to this value each time the timer goes off.

There are two system calls for dealing with interval timers. Both take a which argument that specifies which timer to manipulate.

int getitimer(int which, struct itimerval *val);
> Fills in val with the current state of the which timer.

int setitimer(int which, struct itimerval *new,
                struct itimerval *old);
> Sets the which timer to new and fills in old with the previous setting if it is non-NULL.

Setting a timer's it_value to zero immmediately disables it. Setting a timer's it_interval to zero disables it after the next time the timer triggers.

# CHAPTER 18

# Random Numbers

The word *random* means different things to different programmers at different times. For most applications, the pseudo-random numbers provided by the C library are quite sufficient. Because they allow you to reproduce conditions if necessary (perhaps for debugging purposes), they are preferable to truly random numbers.

But certain applications, including cryptography, require truly random numbers for best results. The Linux kernel samples events from the unpredictable outside world to provide cryptographically strong random numbers.

Computers are predictable. Most of the tasks that we want computers to do are tasks in which predictability is the most important thing. Even when bugs appear in your program, you want them to appear predictably so that you can find them and squash them.

## 18.1 Pseudo-Random Numbers

Sometimes you want to provide the appearance of unpredictability, however. The C library contains functions for generating a well-respected series of pseudo-random numbers. These functions are easy to use and are the same on every Unix platform. Here is an example of how these functions are typically used:

```
#include <stdlib.h>
#include <time.h>...
   srand(time() + getpid());
   for (...; ...; ...) {
     do_something(rand());
   }
```

It is common to **seed** the pseudo-random number generator with the current date, as returned by the time() function. time() returns the number of seconds since January 1, 1970, so the seed changes once per second and is therefore unique over a long time span (approximately 49,710 days on a 32-bit computer). If you want to keep a program from acting the same for two people who start it in the same second, add the current process ID to the time.

The numbers subsequently returned by the rand() function satisfy the mathematical property of random distribution but not of high entropy: For large enough samples, they are relatively well distributed within the space of possible 32-bit numbers, but it is possible to infer other numbers given one number. This means that these kinds of pseudo-random numbers are useful for almost every application that requests a random distribution of numbers. This includes games, Monte Carlo methods (here it is important to save the seed so that you or others can verify your results), and protocols that handle collision by inserting random delays.

Note that for debugging purposes, you may want to save the seed you used when you called srand() so that if a bug occurs that relies on data produced by the rand() function, you can use the same seed to produce the same stream of random numbers to reproduce the bug.

## 18.2 Cryptography and Random Numbers

The authors of this book are not cryptography experts. Writing cryptographic software is a particularly subtle pursuit, and anyone who attempts it without proper research will fail to write robust and secure cryptographic applications. This chapter has two, and only two, purposes:

- To convince people who are not experts in cryptography that this is an area best left to experts.

- To let experts in cryptography know that a particularly useful tool is available for their use.

If you are not an expert in cryptography, but need to use it, we suggest *Applied Cryptography* [Schneier, 1996] as an excellent overview and introduction to the topic.

Cryptography is generally no different from other software in its predictability requirements; when you give a program the key to decrypt data, you want it to decrypt the data the same way every time. There is one exception: choosing a truly random key. No matter how sophisticated an encryption algorithm is, it is worthless if an attacker can guess what key was used to generate the data. For example, many encrypted messages include some sort of timestamp that tells approximately when they were created. If you then use the current time to seed a common pseudo-random number generator, it would not take long for the attacker to decrypt the data by simply using the time when the message was created to seed common pseudo-random number generators and try keys based on those numbers.

It does not work much better to ask a human to provide a key. In general, people pick keys that are hardly random. Their keys are generally related to natural language text, which is highly predictable in terms of information theory. Natural language is said to have **low entropy**; a truly random key has **high entropy**.

If every computer had a small radiation source, the unpredictable amount of time between the particles emitted by decaying atoms could be used to produce truly random numbers, numbers that could not be predicted based on any other information. No other known data would be sufficient to predict which numbers might have been created by the emission of radiation.

Since most computers are not equipped with such devices, Linux improvises. Ted Ts'o wrote code that examines timings of external events (mouse clicks, keyboard keypresses, and so on) and extracts information from them, storing it in an **entropy pool**. There are components of human (and other external) interaction with the computer that are essentially random. The code that fills the entropy pool attempts to distinguish the amount of entropy that is being added, which allows the programmer to determine the amount of entropy used to generate random information.

Programmers who need random numbers based on unpredictable events can take random numbers from the entropy pool through one of two similar devices: /dev/random and /dev/urandom. The /dev/random device will return only as many bytes of random data as the device currently estimates are in the entropy pool. The /dev/urandom device does not try to offer any guarantees about the amount of entropy in the information it returns; it generates as much random data as you want, based on the entropy pool. Whenever either device is read, it subtracts the number of bytes read from the entropy count.

When you read data from either device, it does not simply return the data that is in the entropy pool. It returns data stirred by a one-way hash algorithm that does not reveal the state of the pool in its output.

- Use neither /dev/random nor /dev/urandom for data you want to replicate. They are particularly useless sources of data for Monte Carlo methods; even 1,2...*n-1,n* would be better; it is at least a repeatable series.

- If you need only a certain amount of entropy, but need more raw data than entropy, you can read a small amount of data from one of the random devices (depending on what quality you need guaranteed) and then extend it with a hash function such as MD5 or SHA.

The source code to the random driver, drivers/char/random.c, includes considerable documentation on the details. If you do intend to write cryptographic code that uses the data provided by one of the interfaces, we recommend that you read that documentation first.

# CHAPTER 19

# Programming Virtual Consoles

The Linux virtual console programming interface is modelled on the one provided with some versions of UNIX. It is not a complete reimplementation (though it is complete enough for source code compatibility with almost all programs), and it provides several valuable extensions.

Linux can multiplex multiple terminal sessions over one screen and one keyboard. Special key sequences allow the user to control which terminal session is currently being displayed. Each of these login sessions has its own keyboard settings (such as whether the Caps Lock key is engaged), terminal settings (such as what the terminal size is, whether the screen is in graphics mode, and what the fonts are), and device entries (such as /dev/tty1, /dev/vcs1, and /dev/vcsa1).

The keyboard and terminal settings together make up **virtual consoles** (VCs),[1] so called because of their similarity to virtual memory, in which the system uses disk space to provide more usable memory than is physically present in the machine.

Unless you wish to manage or manipulate VCs, you can skip this chapter. A few programming libraries manage VCs for you, but you may still need to know what they are doing behind your back, so that you work with them rather than against them.

For instance, svgalib, a library for using graphics on several types of graphics controllers, has functions that do most of the basic VC manipulation for

---

1. Linux users, as a group, do not seem to care about venture capitalists, so we have overloaded their acronym.

you. It still requires that you avoid writing random bits to the graphics controller while it is in text mode; doing so would scramble the screen. The current lack of documentation for svgalib makes it even more important that you know what is going on underneath.[2]

VCs provide users with many options, but the majority of users ignore the options and simply use the X Window System. Those users who do use VCs can

- Choose a separate font for each VC

- Choose a separate terminal size for each VC

- Choose key mappings (more on these later) for *all* VCs

- Choose a different keystroke encoding for *all* VCs

- Switch VCs on command with user-specifiable keystrokes

The Linux Documentation Project (LDP) has documents explaining how the user can use programs that already exist in order to take advantage of these capabilities. Your goal is different—you wish to program VCs, not just use them. Although font setting and keyboard settings are well encapsulated in utilities[3] that you can simply call from within your programs, there are cases in which those external programs are insufficient.

# 19.1 Getting Started

Here is a list of some of the things that you can do with VCs. Some are specific to an individual VC (usually, the currently active VC); some apply to all VCs in use:

---

2. We do not recommend using svgalib to do graphics programming. Many books document programming for the X Window System, and X provides a far saner, safer, and portable method of graphics programming. On the other hand, if you actually want to program the X Window server, you may need to program VCs. You have then come full circle and still need to read this chapter.
3. Read the man pages for the loadkeys, dumpkeys, keytables, setfont, and mapscrn utilities.

- Find the current VC

- Initiate a VC switch

- Refuse or allow a switch to or from a VC

- Disable VC switching completely

- Find an unused VC

- Allocate and deallocate VCs dynamically in the kernel

- Make simple sounds

In all cases, the same preparation is needed. You will use `ioctl()` commands on /dev/tty—so you need to start out by including the header files that define the `ioctl()` arguments:

```
#include <signal.h>
#include <sys/ioctl.h>
#include <sys/vt.h>
#include <sys/kd.h>
#include <sys/param.h>
```

Then open /dev/tty:

```
if ((fd = open("/dev/tty", O_RDWR)) < 0) {
    perror("myapp: could not open /dev/tty");
    exit (1);
}
```

If you find that you cannot open /dev/tty, you probably have a permission problem: /dev/tty should be readable and writable by everyone.

Note that in addition to ioctl.h, there are two main header files that define the `ioctl()` calls that manipulate VCs. vt.h defines calls that start with `VT` and control the virtual terminal, or screen, part of the virtual consoles. kd.h defines calls that start with `KD` and that control the keyboard and fonts. You can ignore most of the contents of kd.h because the functionality it covers is so nicely encapsulated in utility programs, but it is useful for making the console beep at controlled frequencies.

Those two main header files also define structures that are used with the ioctl()s.

You use the vt_mode structure to find and change the current VC:

```
struct vt_mode {
    char mode;
    char waitv;
    short relsig;
    short acqsig;
    short frsig;
};
```

- mode is either VT_AUTO, which tells the kernel to switch VCs automatically when keys are pressed or when a program sends a request to the kernel to change VCs, or VT_PROCESS, which tells the kernel to ask before switching.

- waitv is unused, but should be set to 1 for SVR4 compatibility.

- relsig names a signal that the kernel should raise to request that the process release the VC.

- acqsig names a signal that the kernel should raise to alert the process that it has acquired the VC.

- frsig is unused and should be set to 0 for SVR4 compatibility.

```
struct vt_stat {
    unsigned short v_active;
    unsigned short v_signal;
    unsigned short v_state;
};
```

- v_active holds the number of the currently active VC.

- v_signal is not implemented.

- v_state holds a bitmask telling which of the *first 16* VCs are currently open (Linux supports up to 63). There is rarely any reason to consult this bitmask under Linux; you should probably ignore it because it is not sufficiently large to contain complete information, and because in most cases you need to know only the number of some open VC, which you can get with VT_OPENQRY (see page 380).

# 19.2  Beeping

Last things first: Causing the console to beep for a certain amount of time at a certain frequency is fairly simple. There are two ways to make the console beep. The first is to turn on or off a constant tone. KIOCSOUND turns off the sound if its argument is 0; if its argument is non-0, it specifies the frequency in a rather bizarre way, as this code shows.

```
void turn_tone_on(int fd, int hertz) {
    ioctl(fd, KIOCSOUND, 1193180/hertz)
}
void turn_tone_off(int fd) {
    ioctl(fd, KIOCSOUND, 0)
}
```

The second way to cause the console to beep is to use the KDMKTONE ioctl to turn on a tone for a period specified in **jiffies**, which are ticks of the system clock. Unfortunately, the time per tick varies from architecture to architecture; the HZ macro defined by sys/param.h gives ticks per second. The tone() function below shows how to derive the number of ticks from hundredths of a second and the value of HZ.

```
#include <sys/param.h>
void tone(int fd, int hertz, int hundredths) {
    unsigned int ticks = hundredths * HZ / 100;

    /* ticks & 0xffff will not work if ticks == 0xf0000
     * need to round off to highest legal value instead */
    if (ticks > 0xffff) ticks = 0xffff;
    /* now the other rounding error */
    if (hundredths && ticks == 0) ticks = 1;
    ioctl(fd, KDMKTONE, ((1193180/hertz)<<16 | ticks)
}
```

## 19.3    Determining Whether the Terminal Is a VC

To find out whether the current terminal is a VC, you can open /dev/tty and use VT_GETMODE to query the mode.

```
struct vt_mode vtmode;

fd = open("/dev/tty", O_RDWR);
retval = ioctl(fd, VT_GETMODE, &vtmode);
if (retval < 0) {
    /* This terminal is not a VC; take appropriate action */
}
```

## 19.4    Finding the Current VC

To find the number of the current VC, use the VT_GETSTATE ioctl, which takes a pointer to a struct vt_stat and returns the number of the current VC in the v_active element.

```
unsigned short get_current_vc(int fd) {
    struct vt_stat vs;

    ioctl(fd, VT_GETSTATE, &vs);
    return (vs.v_active);
}
```

To locate the correct device entry for the current VC, use

```
sprintf(ttyname, "/dev/tty%d", get_current_vc(fd));
```

## 19.5    Managing VC Switching

To find an unused VC (that is, a VC currently referenced by no processes' open file descriptors) to activate, use the VT_OPENQRY ioctl.

```
retcode = ioctl(fd, VT_OPENQRY, &vtnum);
if ((retcode < 0) || (vtnum == -1)) {
    perror("myapp: no available virtual terminals");
    /* take appropriate action /*
}
```

If fewer than 63 VCs are in use and all the currently allocated VCs are in use, a new VC will be allocated dynamically by the kernel.[4]

To trigger a switch to another VC (perhaps the available one that you just found), use the VT_ACTIVATE ioctl. Use the VT_WAITACTIVE ioctl if you wish to wait for the VC to become active. Changing VCs can take some time—possibly several seconds—because the console to which you are switching may be in graphical mode and the contents of the screen may have to be reconstructed from memory, fetched from swap, or rebuilt in some other time-consuming manner.[5]

```
ioctl(fd, VT_ACTIVATE, vtnum);
ioctl(fd, VT_WAITACTIVE, vtnum);
```

To exercise control over when VC switches take place, or simply to be notified of such switches, you must provide reliable signal handlers with sigaction, as discussed in Chapter 13. We use SIGUSR1 and SIGUSR2 here; if you prefer, you can reuse almost any other two signals that you do not intend to use otherwise, such as SIGPROF or SIGURG. Just make sure that the signals you choose meet the following criteria:

- They are not needed for other system functions, especially signals that cannot be trapped or ignored.

- They are not used elsewhere in your application for other purposes.

- They are not the same signal number with two different names, such as SIGPOLL and SIGIO (see the relevant definitions in /usr/include/asm/ signal.h).

---

4. Most other systems with virtual consoles or virtual terminals do not dynamically allocate them.
5. Certain systems (but not Linux) will initiate a switch automatically if one is not in progress and VT_WAITACTIVE is called.

```
void relsig (int signo) {
   /* take appropriate action to release VC */
}
void acqsig (int signo) {
   /* take appropriate action to acquire VC */
}

void setup_signals(void) {
   struct sigaction sact;

   /* Do not mask any signals while these
    * handlers are being called. */
   sigemptyset(&sact.sa_mask);
   /* You may wish to add calls to sigaddset()
    * here if there are signals that you wish to mask
    * during VC switching. */
   sact.flags = 0;
   sact.sa_handler = relsig;
   sigaction(SIGUSR1, &sact, NULL);
   sact.sa_handler = acqsig;
   sigaction(SIGUSR2, &sact, NULL);
}
```

You then need to change the VC mode from VT_AUTO (the default) to VT_PROCESS, while telling the VC about your signal handlers by setting relsig and acqsig:

```
void control_vc_switching(int fd) {
   struct vt_mode vtmode;

   vtmode.mode = VT_PROCESS;
   vtmode.waitv = 1;
   vtmode.relsig = SIGUSR1;
   vtmode.acqsig = SIGUSR2;
   vtmode.frsig = 0;
   ioctl(fd, VT_SETMODE, &vtmode);
}
```

The signal handlers that are called when a VC is in VT_PROCESS mode do not have to agree to the switch. More precisely, the relsig handler may refuse to allow the VC switch to take place. The acqsig handler usually manages the process of taking over the console, but it could conceivably initiate a switch to yet another VC. Be careful in coding your signal handlers not to call any nonreentrant library functions that cannot be called from a signal handler. POSIX.1 specifies that the functions listed in Table 13.2 are reentrant; you should consider all others nonreentrant, especially if you wish to write a portable program. Note in particular that malloc() and printf() are nonreentrant.

Here are examples of relsig() and acqsig() functions that do useful work. Note that, for the relsig() function, calling VT_RELDISP is required, but for the acqsig() function, calling VT_RELDISP is recommended only for the sake of portability.

```
void relsig (int signo) {
   if (change_vc_ok()) {
      /* VC switch allowed */
      save_state();
      ioctl(fd, VT_RELDISP, 1);
   } else {
      /* VC switch disallowed */
      ioctl(fd, VT_RELDISP, 0);
   }
}

void acqsig (int signo) {
   restore_state();
   ioctl(fd, VT_RELDISP, VT_ACKACQ);
}
```

It is up to you to implement the change_vc_ok(), save_state(), and restore_state() code.

VCs are allocated dynamically when they are opened, but they are *not* reaped automatically when they are closed. To reap the kernel memory used to store the state of a VC, you need to call an ioctl.

```
ioctl(fd, VT_DISALLOCATE, vtnum);
```

You can disable and reenable VC switching completely with a few simple ioctls.

```
void disallow_vc_switch(int fd) {
   ioctl(fd, VT_LOCKSWITCH, 0);
}
void allow_vc_switch(int fd) {
   ioctl(fd, VT_UNLOCKSWITCH, 0);
}
```

# 19.6 Example: The open Command

Here is sample code to find an unused VC, to run a shell on it, to wait for the shell to exit, and to switch back and deallocate the VC when the program exits. The open program, which is distributed with Linux, does the same, but it has more options and error checking, and is thus more robust. Although this version works, it is hardly friendly, robust, or secure.

```
 1: #include <stdio.h>
 2: #include <unistd.h>
 3: #include <stdlib.h>
 4: #include <signal.h>
 5: #include <fcntl.h>
 6: #include <sys/ioctl.h>
 7: #include <sys/vt.h>
 8: #include <sys/stat.h>
 9: #include <sys/types.h>
10: #include <sys/wait.h>
11:
12: int main (int argc, char **argv) {
13:     int vtnum;
14:     int vtfd;
15:     struct vt_stat vtstat;
16:     char device[32];
17:     int child;
18:
19:     vtfd = open("/dev/tty", O_RDWR, 0);
20:     if (vtfd < 0) {
21:        perror("minopen: could not open /dev/tty");
22:        exit (1);
23:     }
```

```
24:     if (ioctl(vtfd, VT_GETSTATE, &vtstat) < 0) {
25:         perror("minopen: tty is not virtual console");
26:         exit (1);
27:     }
28:     if (ioctl(vtfd, VT_OPENQRY, &vtnum) < 0) {
29:         perror("minopen: no free virtual consoles");
30:         exit (1);
31:     }
32:     sprintf(device, "/dev/tty%d", vtnum);
33:     if (access(device, (W_OK|R_OK)) < 0) {
34:         perror("minopen: insufficient permission on tty");
35:         exit (1);
36:     }
37:     child = fork();
38:     if (child == 0) {
39:         ioctl(vtfd, VT_ACTIVATE, vtnum);
40:         ioctl(vtfd, VT_WAITACTIVE, vtnum);
41:         setsid();
42:         close (0); close (1); close (2);
43:         close (vtfd);
44:         vtfd = open(device, O_RDWR, 0); dup(vtfd); dup(vtfd);
45:         execlp("/bin/bash", "bash", NULL);
46:     }
47:     wait (&child);
48:     ioctl(vtfd, VT_ACTIVATE, vtstat.v_active);
49:     ioctl(vtfd, VT_WAITACTIVE, vtstat.v_active);
50:     ioctl(vtfd, VT_DISALLOCATE, vtnum);
51:     exit(0);
52: }
```

# CHAPTER 20

# The Linux Console

The Linux console normally imitates a serial terminal. By writing special character sequences to the console device, you control all aspects of the screen presentation. You will usually use S-Lang, curses, or some other screen-drawing library to draw to the screen; they use these escape sequences. The console can also be read and modified through an alternative full-screen interface, which is particularly useful for some specialized programs.

DOS programmers introduced for the first time to Linux programming often are dismayed to find that writing characters to the screen is not a simple matter of initializing a pointer to the address of the screen in memory and writing blindly through it. Some complain loudly about this "backwards" system that forces them to pretend that they are writing to a serial terminal, writing **escape sequences** in between the characters that are written to the screen to control cursor movement, color, screen clearing, and so on.

There are several good reasons to treat the console as a fancy serial terminal. Not the least is that when the program *is* being run on a serial terminal, it still works. More important—in these Internet-conscious times—the program runs correctly across networks and—in these GUI-conscious times—the program runs correctly in a terminal emulator window under X or any other GUI. Furthermore, programs that are run remotely, either via a network or a serial connection, display properly on your console.

Furthermore, you will find that the escape codes are a reasonable low-level interface to the screen, and they are a good base on which to build higher-level primitives, such as S-Lang, documented in Chapter 22, and curses, documented in *Programming with curses* [Strang, 1991A]. This is no accident; serial terminals are a venerable technology, fine-tuned over the years in response to programmers' real needs. The Linux console is based on the most popular family of serial terminals, the descendents of the DEC VT100.

Most escape sequences use the ANSI escape character, which has no convenient printed representation. We follow the termcap and terminfo libraries in using ^[ to denote the ANSI escape character; be aware when reading them that they sometimes refer to the same character as \E. As elsewhere in this book, as well as in termcap and terminfo, ^C indicates the Control-C character.

# 20.1 Capability Databases

The actions controlled by these escape sequences are often called **capabilities**. Some escape sequences are shared among many terminals, and many of those sequences are specified in the ANSI X3.64-1979 standard. Nearly all color-capable terminals use the same sequences to choose colors to display. However, many terminals have wildly different escape sequences. For instance, on a Wyse 30 terminal, pressing F1 sends the sequence ^A@\r, whereas pressing F1 on your Linux console sends the sequence ^[[[A. Similarly, to move the cursor up on a Wyse 30, you send it a ^K character; to move the cursor up on the Linux console, send the ^[[A sequence. To write a program that can work on either terminal, you clearly need a way to abstract these differences, which would allow you to program with the capabilities rather than the raw character sequences.

The most common programming library that provides this abstraction is called **curses**,[1] documented in *Programming with curses* [Strang, 1991A]. It has two important conceptual levels. The first level provides functions that (generally speaking) send one escape sequence to accomplish one action, such as move the cursor up, move it down, scroll the screen, and so on. The second level provides a concept of "windows": independent screen areas that can be manipulated separately, with curses quietly figuring out the shortest character sequences to send to effect the changes you request.

---

1. The curses library is defined by X/Open. The implementation included in Linux is currently base-level conformant with X/Open XSI Curses.

The curses library determines which sequences to send to the terminal by consulting a database that, for each terminal, maps capability names to the strings that need to be sent.

Linux, like all modern Unix systems, provides two databases that describe terminals in terms of the capabilities they possess and which escape sequences map to which capabilities. The older database is called **termcap** (short for **terminal capabilities**) and is kept in one large ASCII flat file called /etc/termcap. This file has become unwieldy; it has grown to approximately half a megabyte. The newer database is called **terminfo** (short for **terminal information**) and is kept in many binary files, one per terminal, normally in subdirectories of the /usr/lib/terminfo directory.

Within each database, the capability information for each terminal is indexed by one or more unique names. Both databases use the same name for the same terminal. For instance, the Linux console is called linux in both termcap and terminfo. You tell programs which terminal entry to use by setting the TERM environment variable. When writing programs that use termcap and terminfo, you rarely need to look at the TERM environment variable; usually, the low-level libraries for accessing the termcap or terminfo databases will automatically take care of that.

However, if you wish to do Linux-specific optimizations, especially if you want to use some of Linux's unusual capabilities that are not described in the capability databases, you can check the TERM environment variable with code like this:

```
if (!strcmp("linux", getenv("TERM"))) {
    /* should be a Linux console */
} else {
    /* handle as a normal serial terminal */
}
```

Also, if you wish to write programs in programming languages without easy access to curses or some other terminal abstraction library, you may find it convenient to use this documentation.

Of course, that your terminal type is linux does not guarantee that your program is running on a local terminal. If the terminal type is linux, you know you have access to the escape sequences documented in this chapter, but you do not know if you have access to the vcs devices (documented later in this chapter) or `ioctl()`s. POSIX specifies a `ttyname()` function that you can use to find the name of the device file for the controlling terminal. On a Linux system, the virtual consoles are named /dev/tty*n* for *n* between 1 and 63 (/dev/tty0 is always the current console).

Complete documentation for the termcap and terminfo systems is available in *termcap & terminfo* [Strang, 1991B]. Eric Raymond currently maintains the termcap and terminfo databases, which he makes available via the Web at http://www.ccil.org/~esr/terminfo/ The source code to ncurses (new curses, the implementation of curses used on Linux) includes an introduction to curses programming in the misc/ncurses-intro.html file.

Instead of curses, we document S-Lang, an easier-to-use terminal abstraction library, in Chapter 22. It uses the same termcap and terminfo databases as curses. We cover S-Lang instead of ncurses because S-Lang is smaller and easier to use for many tasks, and ncurses is adequately covered elsewhere.

# 20.2 Glyphs, Characters, and Maps

When you write a character to any terminal, several steps of translation may happen. The value written to the terminal is the character number, or character code. That character code is not enough to determine what to display on the screen, however. The shape depends on what font is being used. The character code 97 may be printed as an a in a font designed for rendering Latin-based languages, but might be rendered as an α in a font designed for rendering Greek or mathematics. The shape that is displayed is called a **glyph**. The translation from character codes to glyphs is called a **map**.

## 20.3 Linux Console Capabilities

The Linux console,[2] like most terminals, is **modal**: Its response to data depends on what mode it is in. By default, it prints on the screen the characters you send to it unless it receives an escape or control character. A **control character** simply causes some control action to be taken, but the next character is read normally; there is no change in processing mode. An **escape character** signals the beginning of an escape sequence and changes the processing mode to escape mode.

For example, consider the following C string:

```
"this is a line\na \033[1mbold\033[0m word\n"
```

The console processes the string in the following sequence:

1. Starting from the current cursor position, the console prints the words "this is a line".

2. It encounters the linefeed (\n) control character, so (because Linux and Unix traditionally operate in a mode in which a linefeed signals a carriage return, as well) it moves the cursor to the beginning of the next line, scrolling the whole display up one line if the cursor was already on the bottom line.

3. It displays the string "a " at the beginning of that line.

4. It encounters the escape character, "\033", and moves into escape mode.

5. It reads the "[" character, and moves into **Command Sequence Introduction** (CSI) mode.

6. In CSI mode, it reads a series of ASCII-coded decimal numbers separated by ";", which are called parameters, until a letter is encountered. The letter determines what action to take, modified by the data in the parameters. In this case, there is one parameter, "1", and the letter "m"

---

2. This description owes a considerable amount of organization to an excellent usenet post to the comp.os.linux.announce newsgroup by Peter Jones on September 30, 1995.

means that the parameter is used to determine **character rendition**; the "1" sets the bold attribute on.

7. It prints the string "bold" in a bold rendition.

8. Another character rendition sequence follows, which resets all attributes to their default, so it prints " word" in a normal rendition.

9. Finally, it encounters and processes another newline.

So, assuming that the cursor was at the beginning of a line to start with, the output from the entire string will look something like this:

```
this is a line
a bold word
```

## 20.3.1 Control Characters

The console reads control characters immediately, acts on them, and then continues to read characters in normal mode.

In termcap and terminfo files and documentation, control characters are represented by ^c. We use that convention often in this book, because it will be more generally useful to you than octal C escape sequences. To find the numeric value of a control character, some systems provide a CTRL() macro in <termios.h>, but it is not standard on all systems. Instead, we provide our own version, CTRLCHAR():

```
#define CTRLCHAR(ch) ((ch)&0x1F)
```

It is used like this:

```
if (c == CTRL('C')) {
    /* control-C was pressed */
}
```

The control characters understood by the Linux console are described in Table 20.1. The ^? character is actually '?'+0100, not '?'-0100, so it is not really a control-question-mark, but ^? is the standard name for it anyway. Its value is 0177 (octal), 127 (decimal), 7F (hexadecimal). You will not be

**Table 20.1** Console Control Characters

| Control Character | ASCII Name | Description |
|---|---|---|
| ^G | BEL | Sounds a tone |
| ^H | BS | Moves cursor to previous character without overwriting it if the cursor is not in the first column already |
| ^I | HT | Horizontal tab; moves cursor to next tab stop |
| ^J | LF | Line feed; moves cursor to next line, scrolls scrolling region if already at the bottom of the scrolling region |
| ^K | VT | Vertical tab; treated like a line feed |
| ^L | FF | Form feed; treated like a line feed |
| ^M | CR | Carriage return; moves cursor to beginning of current line |
| ^N | SO | Shift out; use alternate (G1) character set to display glyphs, display glyphs for control characters |
| ^O | SI | Shift in; use normal (G0) character set to display glyphs, do not display glyphs for control characters |
| ^X | CAN | Cancels any escape sequence in progress |
| ^Z | SUB | Cancels any escape sequence in progress |
| ^[ | ESC | ESCape; begins an escape sequence |
| ^? | DEL | Ignored |
| ALT-^[ | n/a | Introduces a command sequence, described later |

able to use the CTRL macro just described to test for it. Instead, use the numeric value 127.

Note that the effect of some of these codes will depend on the tty settings. Although the console itself is precisely documented here, the tty settings may alter what characters are sent. For instance, sending a ^J (LF) usually causes the tty layer to also send a ^M (CR), and ^? (DEL) can be set to send ^H (BS) instead.

The ALT-^[ character is not an ASCII character at all. It is an ESC character with the eighth bit set—ASCII specifies only 7-bit characters. You can use it as a shortcut for entering the CSI sequence, but we recommend that you avoid it because it requires an 8-bit-clean communications link, which might keep your program from running remotely on another Linux system connected, perhaps, by a serial link that transmits only seven bits out of every byte.

**Table 20.2** Console Control Sequences

| Escape Sequence | Description |
|---|---|
| ^[M | Moves cursor up one line in current column, back-scrolling screen if necessary (reverse line feed) |
| ^[D | Moves cursor down one line in current column, scrolling screen if necessary (line feed) |
| ^[E | Carriage return and line feed |
| ^[H | Sets tab stop in current column |
| ^[7 | Stores cursor position and attributes |
| ^[8 | Restores cursor position and attributes |
| ^[> | Puts keypad in numeric mode (normal) |
| ^[= | Puts keypad in **application mode** (act like DEC VT102 function keys) |
| ^[c | Resets every terminal setting that can be set through control characters and escape sequences |
| ^[Z | Requests terminal ID. Response is ^[[?6c, saying that the console faithfully emulates a DEC VT102 (it includes a large superset of the DEC VT102's capabilities) |

For more information on the ASCII characters, see the ascii(7) online manual page. Similarly, the iso_8859_1(7) manual page covers the 8-bit ISO Latin 1 character set (more properly, ISO 8859 Latin Alphabet number 1); this newer standard is becoming the de facto replacement for ASCII, which is now officially called ISO 646-IRV.

## 20.3.2 Escape Sequences

There are several distinct types of escape sequences. The simplest type of escape sequence consists of the escape character (^[) followed by a single command character. (Although the escape character is represented in C strings as \033, it is represented as ^[ in termcap and terminfo files and documentation.) Five of those single command characters preface more complex escape sequences called **command sequences,** and the rest cause the console to take simple actions and immediately leave escape mode. The simple escape sequences are documented in Table 20.2

Storing and restoring the cursor position (^[7 and ^[8) are not done on a stack; if you do two stores in a row, the second stored position overwrites the first stored position. Conversely, after storing the cursor position once, you can restore it as many times as you wish. Each time, the cursor will revert to the same location. When you restore the cursor position, you also restore character rendition attributes, current character set, and character set definitions, all described later in this chapter.

Cursor position is given in terms of a **character cell address**, an *x,y* pair of numbers that names one position on the screen. Character cell addresses on most terminals, including the Linux console, do not follow standard computer-science practice of counting from zero. The upper-left character on the screen is the **origin** and is addressed as character cell 1,1.

Note that control characters may be included in the middle of an escape sequence. For example, ^[^G8 will first beep and then restore the cursor position and attributes. The sequence ^[^X8 will simply print an 8.

### 20.3.3 Testing Sequences

To test most sequences, you merely need to log into a virtual console and run `cat`. Type the sequences you wish to test, and watch the results. For ^[, press the Escape key.

Terminal responses to commands such as the ^[Z terminal identification command or the `CSIn` command documented later show up as escape sequences that disappear in terminal handling. In cases in which you wish to see such a response, you can simply run

```
cat > /tmp/somefile
```

Then type the commands, followed by a return and a ^D. Use less, vi, Emacs, or some other program that can handle arbitrary characters to read `/tmp/somefile`, where you will find the responses directly following the sequences you typed.

**Table 20.3** Complex Console Escape Sequences

| Escape Sequence | Description |
|---|---|
| ^[[ | Begins a CSI sequence (ALT-^[ is a synonym for this) |
| ^[] | Begins a palette-setting sequence |
| ^[% | Begins a UTF (UTF-8 wide-character Unicode) sequence |
| ^[( | Chooses font mapping for G0 character set |
| ^[) | Chooses font mapping for G1 character set |
| ^[#8 | **DEC private** test sequence; fills screen with E characters |

## 20.3.4 Complex Escape Sequences

Five two-character escape sequences are really prefixes to longer, more-complex escape sequences, as shown in Table 20.3. We describe each of these sequences, in turn.

CSI sequences have three or four parts.

1. ^[[ starts a CSI sequence, putting the terminal in CSI mode.

2. For the h and l sequences only, you can include a ? character to allow you to set or clear **DEC Private modes** (see page 398).

3. You may provide up to 16 parameters. Parameters are decimal numbers separated by ; characters. 1;23;45 is a list of three parameters: 1, 23, and 45. (If the ; parameter separator is found after 16 parameters have already been read, the CSI sequence is terminated immediately and the terminal goes into normal mode, printing the rest of the sequence.)

4. A **command character** terminates the sequence and determines how to interpret the parameters the terminal has already encountered.

The parameters are usually referred to as *par1* through *par16*. If you do not set a parameter explicitly, its value is automatically set to 0 or 1, depending on what makes the most sense. The CSI command characters are documented in Table 20.4.

Several sequences take arguments describing colors; they all use the same mapping from numbers to colors, documented in Table 20.5. Sequences

**Table 20.4**  CSI Sequences

| Char | Description | |
| --- | --- | --- |
| h | Sets mode; see page 398 | |
| l | Clears mode; see page 398 | |
| n | *par1*=5 | Status report: Terminal responds with ^[[0n, which means "OK" |
| | *par1*=6 | Cursor position report: Terminal responds with ^[[*x;y*R, where *y* is relative to the origin rather than the region if origin mode is selected (see Table 20.9) |
| G or ' | Sets cursor horizontal position to column *par1* | |
| A | Moves cursor vertical position up by *par1* rows | |
| B or e | Moves cursor vertical position down by *par1* rows | |
| C or a | Moves cursor horizontal position right by *par1* columns | |
| D | Moves cursor horizontal position left by *par1* columns | |
| E | Moves cursor to beginning of line and down *par1* rows (1 by default) | |
| F | Moves cursor to beginning of line and up *par1* rows (1 by default) | |
| d | Sets cursor vertical position to row *par1* | |
| H or f | Sets cursor vertical position to row *par1* and horizontal position to column *par2* (both default to zero, moving the cursor to the origin) | |
| J | *par1*=0 | Clears from cursor to end of display |
| | *par1*=1 | Clears from origin to cursor |
| | *par1*=2 | Clears entire display |
| K | *par1*=0 | Clears from cursor to end of line |
| | *par1*=1 | Clears from start of line to cursor |
| | *par1*=2 | Clears entire line |
| L | Inserts *par1* lines above the current line | |
| M | Deletes *par1* lines, starting with the current line | |
| P | Deletes *par1* characters at the current position, shifting the rest of the line left | |
| c | Responds with ^[[?6c (synonym for ^[Z) | |
| g | *par1*=0 | Clears tab in current column (default) |
| | *par1*=3 | Clears all tabs |
| m | Character rendition sequence; see Table 20.7 | |
| q | Turns keyboard LED *par1* on and others off (0 turns all off) | |
| r | Sets scrolling region (applied only in DEC origin mode; see page 398): | |
| | *par1* | First line of region, must be between 1 (default) and *par2*-1 |
| | *par2* | Last line of region, must be between *par1*+1 and bottom line (default) |
| s | Stores cursor position and attributes (synonym for ^[7) | |
| u | Restores cursor position and attributes (synonym for ^[8) | |
| X | Erases up to *par1* characters, up to the end of the current line | |
| @ | Erases up to *par1* characters, up to the end of the current line | |
| ] | setterm sequences; see Table 20.10 | |

**Table 20.5** Color Codes

| N | Color | N | Bright Color |
|---|-------|---|--------------|
| 0 | Black | 8 | Dark gray |
| 1 | Red | 9 | Bright red |
| 2 | Green | 10 | Bright green |
| 3 | Brown | 11 | Yellow |
| 4 | Blue | 12 | Bright blue |
| 5 | Magenta | 13 | Bright magenta |
| 6 | Cyan | 14 | Bright cyan |
| 7 | Gray | 15 | White |

**Table 20.6** Color Palette Components

| Digit Number | Defines |
|--------------|---------|
| 1 | Palette entry to redefine |
| 2*16+3 | Value of red component of palette entry |
| 4*16+5 | Value of green component of palette entry |
| 6*16+7 | Value of blue component of palette entry |

that describe background colors accept only color numbers between 0 and 7; sequences that describe foreground colors accept numbers between 8 and 15 that describe bold or bright colors.

These colors are actually offsets into a table—the color names in the table describe the default colors stored at those offsets. However, you can change those colors with a palette-setting sequence; the ^[]P sequence is used to set an individual palette entry, and the ^[]R sequence will reset the palette to the system default palette. Palette entries are defined by seven hexadecimal digits that follow ^[]P, as documented in Table 20.6. So for each palette entry, you can provide a 24-bit color definition with eight bits for each color.

The character rendition sequences denoted by the CSI m command may have up to 16 parameters, documented in Table 20.7, in any order. They are applied to the terminal in the order in which they are given, so if 0 to set the default rendition is followed by 1 to set bold, the result will be a bold— but not blinking, reverse video, or underlined—character, regardless of the previous rendition settings.

Related somewhat to the character rendition sequences are the mode sequences. There are two types of modes: ANSI modes and DEC private modes. The CSI h sequence sets ANSI modes, documented in Table 20.8,

**Table 20.7**  Character Rendition Parameters

| par | Description |
|-----|-------------|
| 0 | Default rendition: normal intensity, no underline, not reverse video, no blinking, and the default color scheme (white on black unless set otherwise by the setterm store sequence ^[[]8) |
| 1 | Bold intensity |
| 2 | Dim intensity |
| 4 | Enables underline |
| 5 | Enables blink |
| 7 | Enables reverse video |
| 10 | Selects primary font (ISO latin 1), does not display control characters, unsets bit 8 on output |
| 11 | Selects alternate font (IBM Codepage 437), displays control characters as graphics, unsets bit 8 on output |
| 12 | Selects alternate font (IBM Codepage 437), displays control characters as graphics, leaves bit 8 set on output |
| 21 22 | Normal intensity |
| 24 | Disables underline |
| 25 | Disables blink |
| 27 | Disables reverse video |
| 30 – 37 | Sets foreground color to par \| \| 30; see Table 20.5 |
| 38 | Enables underline and uses default foreground color |
| 39 | Disables underline and uses default foreground color |
| 40 – 47 | Sets background color to par \| \| 40; see Table 20.5 |
| 49 | Uses default background color |

**Table 20.8**  ANSI Modes

| par | Description |
|-----|-------------|
| 3 | Displays control characters |
| 4 | Insert mode |
| 20 | CRLF mode (produces a carriage return when a linefeed is received) |

and the CSI l sequence clears them. More than one parameter can be included in a sequence. The CSI ?h sequence sets DEC private modes, documented in Table 20.9, and the CSI ?l sequence clears them. Again, more than one parameter can be included.

The setterm sequences are a set of CSI sequences with the command character ]. They are documented in Table 20.10.

**Table 20.9**   DEC Private Modes

| par | Description |
|-----|-------------|
| 1 | Cursor keys as **application keys**; in application mode, they are prefixed with ^[0 instead of the usual ^[[ |
| 3 | Unimplemented; may switch between 80- and 132-column mode in the future |
| 5 | Sets entire screen in inverse video |
| 6 | Sets DEC origin mode, in which scrolling regions are honored, and goes to the origin (of the current scrolling region, if any) |
| 7 | Sets autowrap mode (on by default), in which characters that would go beyond the screen cause an automatic CRLF. When autowrap mode is turned off, extra characters over-write the right-most character on the current line |
| 8 | Sets keyboard auto-repeat mode (on by default) |
| 9 | Mouse reporting mode 1 (support may be provided by an external program) |
| 25 | Makes cursor visible (on by default) |
| 1000 | Mouse reporting mode 2 (support may be provided by an external program) |

**Table 20.10**   Console setterm Sequences

| par | Description |
|-----|-------------|
| 1 | Sets color to use to represent **underline** attribute to *par2* |
| 2 | Sets color to use to represent **dim** attribute to *par2* |
| 8 | Stores current setterm attributes as the defaults, making them the default character rendition attributes |
| 9 | Sets screen-blank interval to *par2* minutes, but no more than 60 minutes. *par2* set to 0 disables screen-blank |
| 10 | Sets the console bell frequency to *par2* Hz or to the default pitch if *par2* is unspecified |
| 11 | Sets the console bell duration to *par2* milliseconds if *par2* is specified and is less than 2000. If *par2* is not specified, resets the duration to the default |
| 12 | If console *par2* is allocated, makes console *par2* active (see Chapter 19) |
| 13 | Unblanks the screen |
| 14 | Sets VESA power-down interval to *par2* minutes, but no more than 60 minutes. *par2* set to 0 disables VESA power down |

There is more to conversing with the console than telling it what to display; you also must recognize key sequences and know which keys they are attached to—and although some of them are specified in the terminfo database, others are not. To make life even more interesting, the keyboard

**Table 20.11**  Function-Key Encodings

| Key Sequence | Key(s) |
|---|---|
| ^[[[A | F1 |
| ^[[[B | F2 |
| ^[[[C | F3 |
| ^[[[D | F4 |
| ^[[[E | F5 |
| ^[[17~ | F6 |
| ^[[18~ | F7 |
| ^[[19~ | F8 |
| ^[[20~ | F9 |
| ^[[21~ | F10 |
| ^[[23~ | F11, Shift-F1, Shift-F11 |
| ^[[24~ | F12, Shift-F2, Shift-F11 |
| ^[[25~ | Shift-F3 |
| ^[[26~ | Shift-F4 |
| ^[[28~ | Shift-F5 |
| ^[[29~ | Shift-F6 |
| ^[[31~ | Shift-F7 |
| ^[[32~ | Shift-F8 |
| ^[[33~ | Shift-F9 |
| ^[[34~ | Shift-F10 |
| ^[[[A | Up arrow |
| ^[[[D | Left arrow |
| ^[[[B | Down arrow |
| ^[[[C | Right arrow |
| ^[[1~ | Home |
| ^[[2~ | Insert |
| ^[[3~ | Delete |
| ^[[4~ | End |
| ^[[5~ | Page Up |
| ^[[6~ | Page Down |

is modal.  In **application mode,** the cursor keys produce different codes. As shown in Table 20.9, they are prefixed with ^[0 instead of ^[[. This is to support legacy applications that assume that they are talking to DEC terminals.

The key sequences are documented in Table 20.11. Note that the function-key numbering has gaps and that it is designed so that people without F11 and F12 keys are not handicapped.

# 20.4 Direct Screen Writing

There are some cases in which being able to write characters to the screen is simply insufficient, partially because it is impossible to determine the current state of the screen. Although standard Unix practice is to ignore the state of the screen—to set it up as you need it, make changes to it as you have changes to make, and to redraw it completely any time the user requests it (usually by pressing ^L)—you may have other applications in mind.

In particular, screen capture and restore programs and functions need access to the current contents of the screen. Linux provides this through two interfaces. One provides only the text contents of the screen, and one contains attributes (color and so forth), as well.

The simple text device is called **vcs**, which presumably stands for **virtual console screen**.[3] The /dev/vcs0 device when read produces the contents of the current virtual console as it is being viewed at the time it is read. If the screen is currently scrolled back (the Control-PageUp and Control-PageDown keys are set up to control console scrolling by default), /dev/vcs0 contains the scrolled-back contents that are being viewed. The rest of the vcs devices, /dev/vcs*n*, each represent the current state of the virtual console *n*, normally accessed through /dev/tty*n*.

When you read /dev/vcs*, you are given no indication of new lines or of console size other than an EOF at the end of the screen. If you read 2,000 bytes and then receive an EOF, there is no indication whether the screen is 80 columns and 25 lines or 40 columns and 50 lines. No newline characters are produced to mark the ends of lines, and every empty character cell, whether or not it was ever written to, is denoted by a space character. There are several popular screen configurations, and there is no guarantee that each of them has a unique number of lines and columns. The vcs device provides an easy way for a savvy sysadmin or developer to see what is on any virtual console, but it is not very useful from a programmer's standpoint, at least alone.

---

3. This section belongs logically to Chapter 19 because it is related to virtual consoles, but it belongs in this chapter in a practical sense—you would not know to look in Chapter 19 unless you did not need to read this book in the first place.

One useful way to use vcs is from within X. XFree86, by default, starts the X server on the first free virtual console, not on the console that the program was started from. If you start XFree86 from virtual console 1, you do not need to change back to virtual console 1 to see the detection messages that XFree86 left on the screen; bring up a terminal window the same size as the console (normally 80 columns by 25 lines), become superuser (in order to gain access to the vcs device), and run `cat /dev/vcs1`. The contents of the first virtual console will fill your terminal window.

In order to write reliable programs, however, you need some basic knowledge about the state of the screen that a **vcs** device does not provide:

- Colors

- Other attributes (such as blinking)

- Current cursor position

- Screen configuration (number of rows and columns)

The **vcsa** device (which presumably stands for **virtual console screen with attributes**) provides all this. The first four bytes of /dev/vcsa*n* (for the same *n* as vcs devices) contain a header that gives the current cursor position and screen configuration. The first byte contains the number of rows, the second the number of columns, the third the cursor's current column, and the fourth the cursor's current row. The rest of the file contains alternating bytes that represent the text and text attribute bytes of the console in question.

So, if you need to know only the size of the console and its textual contents, you can read the first two bytes of the appropriate vcsa device and from then on use only the vcs device. If you want to set the current cursor position, write to the second and third bytes of the vcsa device (the first two bytes are read-only, so the first two characters are placeholders; we prefer to use spaces or some other similar character to make this more obvious). As an example, to move the cursor on the fourth virtual console to the seventh row and the nineteenth column:

```
echo n e '..\023\007' > /dev/vcsa4
```

**Table 20.12** Attributes

| Bit(s) | Effect |
|--------|------------|
| 7 | Blink |
| 6-4 | Background |
| 3 | Bold |
| 2-0 | Foreground |

The n keeps echo from adding a newline character to the end, and the e makes it interpret escape codes, so that \nnn is interpreted as octal character nnn.

The attributes and character contents are represented as alternating bytes, the first containing the character and the second containing the attributes to apply to the character. The attribute byte is normally defined like the attribute byte used on VGA hardware. Other kinds of hardware, including the TGA cards used on many Linux/Alpha machines and the SPARC console driver, emulate the VGA attribute handling. On video hardware without color support but with underline support, it can be read slightly differently; it is designed in such a way that you can pretend that it is all VGA hardware, and all other hardware will behave somewhat reasonably.

For each attribute byte, the bits are interpreted as documented in Table 20.12. That is the VGA representation; some color hardware replaces blink by a bright background. The monochrome representation uses bit 0 of the foreground color to indicate underline.

Part 4

# Development
# Libraries

# CHAPTER 21

# String Matching

There is more to comparing strings than `strcmp()` or even `strncmp()`. Linux provides several general string matching functions that will make your programming tasks simpler. We start with the simple tasks and then cover the more complex ones.

## 21.1  Globbing Arbitrary Strings

Chapter 11 explains how to glob file names using the `glob()` function, but people used to globbing capabilities sometimes wish to apply them to other sorts of strings. The `fnmatch()` function allows you to apply globbing rules to arbitrary strings.

```
#include <fnmatch.h>

int fnmatch(const char *pattern, const char *string, int flags);
```

The pattern is a standard glob expression with four special characters, modified by the `flags` argument.

*       Matches any string, including an empty one.

?       Matches exactly one character, any character.

[       Starts a list of characters to match, or, if the next character is ^, a list of characters not to match. The whole list will match, or not match, a single character. The list is terminated by a ].

Causes the next character to be interpreted literally instead of as a special character.

The `flags` argument affects some details of the glob, and is mostly there to be useful for globbing against file names. If you are not globbing file names, you will probably want to set `flags` to `0`.

FNM_NOESCAPE
Treat \ as an ordinary character, not a special character.

FNM_PATHNAME
Do not match / characters in `string` with a *, ?, or even a [/] sequence in `pattern`; match it only with a literal, non-special /.

FNM_PERIOD
A leading . character in `pattern` will match a . character in `string` only if it is the first character in `string` or if FNM_PATHNAME is set and the . character in `string` directly follows a \.

`fnmatch()` returns 0 if the pattern matches the string, `FNM_NOMATCH` if the pattern does not match the string, or some other unspecified value if an error occurs.

## 21.2 Regular Expressions

Regular expressions, as used in `sed`, `awk`, `grep`, `vi`, and countless other Unix programs through the years, have become a major part of the Unix programming environment. They are also available for use within C programs. This section explains how to use them and then presents a simple file parser using these functions.

Regular expressions have two flavors: **basic regular expressions** (BREs) and **extended regular expressions** (EREs). They correspond (roughly) to the `grep` and `egrep` commands. Both forms of regular expressions are explained in the grep man page, in the POSIX.2 standard [IEEE, 1993], in *A Practical Guide to Linux* [Sobell, 1997], and in other places, so we will not describe their syntax here, only the function interface that allows you to use regular expressions from within your programs.

POSIX specifies four functions to provide regular expression handling.

```
#include <regex.h>

int regcomp(regex_t *preg, const char *regex, int cflags);
int regexec(const regex_t *preg, const char *string, size_t nmatch,
            regmatch_t pmatch[], int eflags);
void regfree(regex_t *preg);
size_t regerror(int errcode, const regex_t *preg, char *errbuf,
                size_t errbuf_size);
```

Before you can compare a string to a regular expression, you need to **compile** it with the regcomp() function. The regex_t *preg holds all the state for the regular expression. You need one regex_t for each regular expression that you wish to have available concurrently. The regex_t structure has only one member on which you should rely: re_nsub, which specifies the number of parenthesized subexpressions in the regular expression. Consider the rest of the structure opaque.

The cflags argument determines many things about how the regular expression regex is interpreted. It may be 0 or it may be the logical OR of any of the following four items.

REG_EXTENDED

> If set, use extended regular expression syntax instead of basic regular expression syntax.

REG_ICASE

> If set, do not differentiate between upper and lower case.

REG_NOSUB

> If set, do not keep track of substrings. The regexec() function will then ignore the nmatch and pmatch arguments.

REG_NEWLINE

> If REG_NEWLINE is not set, the newline character is treated essentially the same as any other character. The ^ and $ characters match only the beginning and end of the entire string, not adjacent newline characters. If REG_NEWLINE is set, you get the same behavior you do with grep, sed, and other standard system tools.

A typical invocation looks like this:

```
if (regcomp(&p, "(^(.*[^\])#.*$)|(^[^#]+$)",
            REG_EXTENDED|REG_NEWLINE)) {
   /* error */
}
```

This extended regular expression finds lines of a file that are not commented out, or that are, at most, partially commented out, by # characters not prefixed with \ characters. This kind of regular expression might be useful as part of a simple parser for an application's configuration file.

Even if you are compiling an expression that you know is good, you should still check for errors. regcomp() returns 0 for a successful compilation, and a non-0 error code for an error. Most errors involve invalid regular expressions of one sort or another, but another possible error is running out of memory. See page 412 for a description of the regerror() function.

```
#include <regex.h>

int regexec(const regex_t *preg, const chat *string, size_t nmatch,
            regmatch_t pmatch[], int eflags);
```

The regexec() function tests a string against a compiled regular expression. The eflags argument may be 0, or it may be the logical OR of any of the following symbols.

REG_NOTBOL

> If set, the first character of the string will not match a ^ character. Any character following a newline character will still match ^ as long as REG_NEWLINE was set in the call to regcomp().

REG_NOTEOL

> If set, the final character of the string will not match a $ character. Any character preceding a newline character will still match $ as long as REG_NEWLINE was set in the call to regcomp().

The regmatch_t structure is used to represent the location of subexpressions in the regular expression.

```
#include <regex.h>

typedef struct {
    regoff_t rm_so;  /* byte index within string of start of match */
    regoff_t rm_eo;  /* byte index within string of end of match */
} regmatch_t;
```

The structures are filled in in the order they are expressed in the regular expression, and subexpressions that do not match have a value of -1 in their rm_so member. In C code, pmatch[*i*] is equivalent to the replacement expression \\*i+1* in sed or awk; pmatch[0] is equivalent to \\1, and so on. In the sample regular expression given in the regcomp() example, there are three subexpressions: The first is an entire line containing both text and a comment character, the second is the text preceding the comment character, and the third is an entire line containing no comment character. For a line with a comment character at the beginning, the second and third elements of pmatch[] will be -1; for a line with a comment character at the beginning, the first and second will be -1; and for a line with no comment characters, the second and third will be -1.

This code matches against a regular expression with subexpressions, and prints out all the subexpressions that match.

```
#include <regex.h>
regmatch_t *pmatch;

pmatch = alloca(sizeof(regmatch_t) * p.re_nsub);
if (!pmatch) {
    perror("alloca");
}
if (regexec(&p, string, p.re_nsub, pmatch, 0)) {
    printf("match failed for string %s\n", string);
} else {
    /* match succeeded */
    for (int i=0, i < p.re_nsub, i++) {
        /* print the matching portion(s) of the string */
        if (pmatch[i].rm_so != -1) {
            char *submatch;
            size_t matchlen = pmatch[i].rm_eo - pmatch[i].rm_so;
            submatch = malloc(matchlen+1);
```

```
        strncpy(submatch, string+pmatch[i].rm_so, matchlen);
        printf("match %i: %s\n", i, submatch);
        free (submatch);
    }
  }
}
```

Whenever you are done with a compiled regular expression, you need to free it to avoid a memory leak. You must use the regfree() function to free it, not the free() function.

```
#include <regex.h>

void regfree(regex_t *preg);
```

The POSIX.2 standard does not specify whether you need to use regfree() each time you call regcomp() or only after the final time you call regcomp(), if you call regcomp() multiple times on one regex_t structure. Therefore, to be as safe as possible on all platforms present and future, we suggest that you regfree() your regex_t structures between uses to avoid memory leaks.

Whenever you get a non-0 return code from regcomp() or regexec(), the regerror() function can provide a detailed message explaining what went wrong. It writes as much as possible of an error message into a buffer and returns the size of the total message. Because you do not know beforehand how big the error message might be, you first ask for its size, then allocate the buffer, and then use the buffer, as demonstrated in our sample code below. Because that kind of error handling gets old fast, and because you will need to include that error handling code at least twice (once after regcomp() and once after regexec()), we recommend that you write your own wrapper around regerror().

```
#include <regex.h>

size_t regerror(int errcode, const regex_t *preg, char *errbuf,
            size_t errbuf_size);
```

We suggest a wrapper something like this:

```
void do_regerror(int errcode, const regex_t *preg) {
   char *errbuf;
   size_t errbuf_size;

   errbuf_size = regerror(errcode, &preg, NULL, 0)
   errbuf = alloca(errbuf_size);
   if (!errbuf) {
      perror("alloca");
      return;
   }
   regerror(errcode, &preg, errbuf, errbuf_size);
   fprintf(stderr, "%s\n", errbuf);
}
```

Use your judgment about how to report the error, of course.

# CHAPTER 22

# Terminal Handling with S-Lang

The S-Lang library, written by John E. Davis, provides mid-level access to terminals. It encapsulates all the low-level terminal handling through a set of routines that allow direct access to the video terminal and automatically handle scrolling and color. Although little direct support for windows is present, and no widgets (or controls) are available in the S-Lang library, S-Lang provides a suitable base for such services.[1]

S-Lang is also available under DOS, which makes it attractive for applications that need to be built for both Unix and DOS platforms. John E. Davis based his jed editor on S-Lang, allowing it to work on a wide variety of platforms, including DOS.

S-Lang's terminal handling abilities fall into two categories. First, it provides a set of functions for reading keystrokes from the terminal in a controlled manner. Second, it provides routines for full-screen output to the terminal. These routines hide many terminal capabilities from the programmer but still take advantage of each terminal's abilities.[2] This chapter discusses how to use S-Lang in each of these capacities and ends with an example program that uses both.

---

1. One of the authors of this book has written a higher-level windowing toolkit based on S-Lang. It is available from ftp://ftp.redhat.com/pub/redhat/code/newt
2. As described by the terminfo database.

# 22.1   Input Handling

Terminal input handling is one of the least portable subsytems in the Unix world. BSD sgtty, System V termio, and POSIX termios have all been widely used. The S-Lang library hides this complexity through a few functions designed to make keyboard handling more straightforward and portable.

Writing a program to read a character at a time from the terminal and print each character onto its own line is fairly straightforward:

```
 1: /* slecho.c - Simple demonstration of SLANG input handling */
 2: #include <ctype.h>
 3: #include <slang/slang.h>
 4: #include <stdio.h>
 5:
 6: int main(void) {
 7:     char ch = '\0';
 8:
 9:     /*
10:         Start SLANG tty handling, with:
11:         -1 default interrupt character (normally, Ctrl-C)
12:          0 no flow control, allowing all characters (except
13:            interrupt) to pass through to the program
14:          1 enable OPOST output processing of escape sequences
15:     */
16:     SLang_init_tty(-1, 0, 1);
17:
18:     while (ch != 'q') {
19:         ch = SLang_getkey();
20:         printf("read: %c 0x%x\n", isprint(ch) ? ch : ' ', ch);
21:     }
22:
23:     SLang_reset_tty();
24:
25:     return 0;
26: }
```

This program assumes that /usr/include/slang contains all the S-Lang header files. If this is not the case for your system, you will need to change the code (and all other examples in this chapter) appropriately. When you compile and link this sample program, be sure to add `-lslang` to the link command so that the S-Lang functions will be found by the linker.

### 22.1.1 Initializing S-Lang Input Handling

Before any other input handling functions will work, the terminal must be placed in the state S-Lang expects through the `SLang_init_tty()` function:

```
int SLang_init_tty(int abort_char, int flow_ctrl, int opost);
```

The first parameter to `SLang_init_tty()` is an abort character to use. If -1 is passed, the current tty interrupt character (usually, Ctrl-C) is retained; otherwise the interrupt character is set to the value passed. Whenever the abort character is entered on the terminal, the kernel sends a `SIGINT` to the process, which normally terminates the application. Chapter 13 discusses how to handle signals such as `SIGINT`.

The next parameter turns flow control on and off. Terminal-level flow control allows the user to pause output to the terminal to prevent scrolling and then restart it. Normally, Ctrl-S is used to suspend terminal output and Ctrl-Q enables it. Although this feature is convenient for some line-oriented utilities, programs that take advantage of S-Lang are normally screen oriented, so it may not be necessary. S-Lang allows applications to turn off this capability, which allows the program to use the Stop and Start keystrokes for other commands. To enable flow control, pass a non-0 value as the second parameter to `SLang_init_tty()`.

The final parameter enables output post-processing on the terminal. All the kernel's post-processing mechanisms are enabled if the final parameter is non-0. See page 299 for information on output processing.

### 22.1.2 Restoring the Terminal State

Once the terminal state has been modified by `SLang_init_tty()`, the program must explicitly restore the terminal to its original state before exiting. If you do not do this, the terminal will be extremely difficult to use after your program exits. `SLang_reset_tty()` does not take any arguments, nor does it return one.

If you are writing a program that should suspend properly (normally when the user presses Ctrl-Z), this function will also need to be called when SIGTSTP is received. For more information on handling SIGTSTP properly, see Chapter 14.

When you are developing programs with S-Lang, the program will likely crash more than once during your development, leaving your terminal in a nonstandard state. You can easily fix this by running the command stty sane.

### 22.1.3 Reading Characters from the Terminal

Once the terminal has been initialized properly, reading single keystrokes is straightforward. The function SLang_getkey() returns a single character from the terminal. Note that does not mean it returns a single keystroke—in Unix, many keystrokes return multiple characters. For example, on a VT100 terminal (as well as on many other terminals, including the Linux console) pressing F1 sends four characters to the screen—ESC [ [ A (try running slecho and pressing F1 to see what characters it received). Those multiple-character sequences can be mapped to keystrokes via the terminfo database [Strang, 1991B].

SLang_getkey() waits for a character to be present before returning. It will wait indefinitely. If an error occurs, the function returns 0xFFFF rather than a valid character.[3]

### 22.1.4 Checking for Input with SLang_input_pending()

In many cases, you want to check for available characters without blocking. This is handy whenever a program needs to do background processing while polling the user for input (this is especially popular in video games). SLang_input_pending() is defined as follows.

```
int SLang_input_pending(int timeout);
```

SLang_input_pending() returns true if characters become available within n tenths of seconds. It returns as soon as the characters are available; it returns

---

3. An error occurs if a signal is received while S-Lang is waiting for a keystroke.

false if no characters become available within the timeout period. If a timeout period of 0 is given, `SLang_input_pending()` tells whether characters are currently available.

This behavior is easy to see. Just replace the test on the while loop in slecho.c with

```
while (ch != 'q' && SLang_input_pending(20))
```

The program will now wait a maximum of two seconds for more input. Once two seconds pass without any input, it will exit.

## 22.2 Output Handling

Internally, S-Lang's terminal output functions are divided into two sets: terminal handling functions (the `SLtt` family) and higher-level screen management functions (the `SLsmg` family).

The `SLtt` function family works directly with the terminal; it includes functions that map closely with capabilities defined in the terminal database. It also includes routines for defining foreground and background color pairs and turning the cursor on and off. Only a few of these functions are normally used by application programmers; the rest are called internally by S-Lang.

The `SLsmg` family provides a higher-level abstraction of the display terminal. Although these functions use the `SLtt` functions for terminal handling, they provide a much more powerful interface for application developers. These functions include string output, line drawing, and screen-querying functions. For performance reasons, these routines write to an internal buffer rather than directly to the terminal. When the application instructs S-Lang to update the physical terminal, S-Lang compares the new display to the original one and optimizes the output sequence appropriately.

## 22.2.1 Initializing Screen Management

Before using S-Lang's terminal output functions, a program must tell S-Lang to look up the current terminal (as determined by the TERM environment variable) in the terminal database. This is done by calling

```
void SLtt_get_terminfo(void);
```

One of the primary functions of SLtt_get_terminfo() is to set the physical size of the screen to the size listed in the terminal database. The number of rows and columns on the terminal are stored in SLtt_Screen_Rows and SLtt_Screen_Cols, respectively. Although the terminal database is often correct, resizeable terminals (such as xterms) are popular these days, and once they are resized from the defaults, the terminal database no longer contains the correct size for the terminal. To compensate for this, S-Lang allows programs to reset the values of SLtt_Screen_Rows and SLtt_Screen_Cols after the call to SLtt_get_terminfo(). Under Linux, the current terminal size is always available through the TIOCGWINSZ ioctl, which is discussed in detail on page 295.

Initializing the S-Lang's screen management layer is straightforward: simply call

```
void SLsmg_init_smg(void);
SLsmg_init_smg()
```

## 22.2.2 Updating the Display

Before the results of a sequence of SLsmg routines gets reflected on the physical terminal, you must call the SLsmg_refresh() function. This function does not take any arguments or return a value, but it does update the physical terminal with the results of any screen drawing that has been done since the previous time it was called.

## 22.2.3 Moving the Cursor

As in most programs, the terminal cursor is used by S-Lang as both the default location for text output and a cue for the user.  S-Lang programs can move the cursor with the following code:

```
extern void SLsmg_gotorc (int row, int column);
```

Note that the upper-left corner of the screen is (0, 0) and the bottom-right corner is (SLtt_Screen_Rows - 1, SLtt_Screen_Cols - 1).

## 22.2.4 Finishing Screen Management

When a program that uses SLsmg has finished, it needs to tell S-Lang it is done, allowing S-Lang to free buffers and restore the terminal state. Before doing this, it is a good idea to move the cursor to the bottom of the screen and refresh the display to make sure all output has been shown to the user.

## 22.2.5 Skeleton Screen Management

Here is a program that initializes S-Lang's screen management abilities and then closes them.  Although it certainly does not do much, it does illustrate the basics of using S-Lang's SLsmg functionality.

```
 1: /* slinit.c - Initialize SLsmg layer, and shut it down */
 2:
 3: #include <slang/slang.h>
 4: #include <stdio.h>
 5: #include <sys/ioctl.h>
 6: #include <termios.h>
 7:
 8: int main(void) {
 9:     struct winsize ws;
10:
11:     /* get the size of the terminal connected to stdout */
12:     if (ioctl(1, TIOCGWINSZ, &ws)) {
13:         perror("failed to get window size");
14:         return 1;
15:     }
```

```
16:
17:     SLtt_get_terminfo();
18:
19:     SLtt_Screen_Rows = ws.ws_row;
20:     SLtt_Screen_Cols = ws.ws_col;
21:
22:     SLsmg_init_smg();
23:
24:     /* heart of the program goes here */
25:
26:     SLsmg_gotorc(SLtt_Screen_Rows - 1, 0);
27:     SLsmg_refresh();
28:     SLsmg_reset_smg();
29:     SLang_reset_tty();
30:
31:     return 0;
32: }
```

## 22.2.6 Switching Character Sets

Most modern terminals (including the VT100, which the Linux console
closely emulates) support at least two character sets. The primary one is
usually ISO-8859-1 or something similiar; the second is used primarily for
line-drawing characters. S-Lang allows you to choose which character set
is used for drawing characters.

```
void SLsmg_set_char_set(int useAlternate)
```

When SLsmg_set_char_set() is called with a non-0 argument, new characters
written to the display are mapped through the alternate character set.
Calling SLsmg_set_char_set() with 0 as its parameter disables this mapping,
allowing characters to appear normally.

S-Lang defines a set of symbolic names for the commonly used line-
drawing characters contained in the alternate character set. Table 22.1
shows the available line-drawing characters and S-Lang's name for each.

**Table 22.1** Line Characters

| Glyph | Symbolic Constant |
|:-----:|-------------------|
| −     | SLSMG_HLINE_CHAR  |
| \|    | SLSMG_VLINE_CHAR  |
| ┌     | SLSMG_ULCORN_CHAR |
| ┐     | SLSMG_URCORN_CHAR |
| └     | SLSMG_LLCORN_CHAR |
| ┘     | SLSMG_LRCORN_CHAR |
| ┤     | SLSMG_RTEE_CHAR   |
| ├     | SLSMG_LTEE_CHAR   |
| ┬     | SLSMG_UTEE_CHAR   |
| ┴     | SLSMG_DTEE_CHAR   |
| +     | SLSMG_PLUS_CHAR   |

## 22.2.7 Writing to the Screen

Although there are a number of ways to write strings to the screen under
S-Lang, they all look about the same. Here is the entire set of functions:

```
void SLsmg_write_char(char ch);
void SLsmg_write_string(char * str);
void SLsmg_write_nchars(char * chars, int length);
void SLsmg_write_nstring(char * str, int length);
void SLsmg_printf(char * format, ...);
void SLsmg_vprintf(char * format, va_list args);
void SLsmg_write_wrapped_string(char * str, int row, int column,
                                int height, int width, int fill);
```

All of these functions, except SLsmg_write_wrapped_string(), write the requested string into the screen buffer[4] at the current cursor location using
the current color and character set. They all have different ways of decid-
ing what string to write, however. After the information has been written,
the cursor is advanced to the end of the area affected, just as on a normal terminal. Any strings that extend past the right side of the screen are
truncated rather than wrapped. Although this is different from normal
terminal output, it is reasonable for most full-screen applications, in which
wrapped text has an adverse effect on the screen's layout.

---

4. Remember, the physical terminal is updated only by SLsmg_refresh().

`void SLsmg_write_char()`

> Of all the screen output functions, this one is the simplest. It writes the character passed to the current cursor position and advances the cursor.

`SLsmg_write_string()`

> The string that is passed to the function is written to the screen.

`SLsmg_write_nchars()`

> The `length` characters pointed to by `chars` are written to the screen. `NULL` termination is ignored—a `'\0'` will be written if one is found, and the routine will continue past the end of the string.

`SLsmg_write_nstring()`

> At most `length` characters from `str` are written to the screen. If `str` is shorter than `length` characters, the remainder of the space will be filled with blank characters.

`SLsmg_printf()`

> As the name implies, this routine acts like the standard `printf()` function, formatting the first argument, with the remainder of the arguments used as parameters for the formatting. The formatted string is then written to the screen.

`SLsmg_vprintf()`

> Like the standard `vfprintf()` function, this routine expects a `va_arg` argument, which it uses to format the first parameter. The formatted string is then displayed.

`SLsmg_write_wrapped_string()`

> Although S-Lang truncates strings rather than wrap them, it does provide a simple function for writing strings wrapped to an arbitrary rectangle on the screen. `SLsmg_write_wrapped_string()` writes `str` to the rectangle that begins at `row` and `column` of size `height` and `width`.
>
> Although this routine does wrap on word boundaries, a `\n` in the string forces it to go to the next line. If final parameter `fill` is non-0, every line is filled to the full width of the rectangle, with spaces used for padding where necessary.

## 22.2.8 Drawing Lines and Boxes

Although SLsmg_set_char_set() provides all the functionality needed to draw simple line graphics on a terminal, S-Lang provides some shortcut functions that are easier to use.

```
void SLsmg_draw_hline(int row);
void SLsmg_draw_vline(int column);
void SLsmg_draw_box(int row, int column, int height, int width);
```

The SLsmg_draw_hline() function draws a single horizontal line at row row; SLsmg_draw_vline() draws a single vertical line at column col.

SLsmg_draw_box() draws a box starting at row and col that extends for height rows and width columns. SLsmg_draw_box() is similiar to a combination of SLsmg_draw_hline() and SLsmg_draw_vline(), but it gets the corners right, as well.

Here is an example program that draws a screen containing the normal character set and the alternate character set. It also demonstrates a simple use of SLsmg_draw_box().

```
 1: /* slcharset.c - S-Lang program to show normal and alternate
 2:    character sets */
 3: #include <slang/slang.h>
 4: #include <stdio.h>
 5: #include <sys/ioctl.h>
 6: #include <termios.h>
 7:
 8: /* displays a table containing 256 characters in a single character
 9:    set, starting a column col.  The 'label' is displayed over the
10:    table, and the alternate character set is displayed iff
11:    isAlternate is nonzero */
12: static void drawCharSet(int col, int isAlternate, char * label) {
13:     int i, j;
14:     int n = 0;
15:
16:     /* center the label */
17:     SLsmg_gotorc(0, col + 2);
18:     SLsmg_write_string(label);
19:
20:
```

```
21:        /* draw the horizontal legend */
22:        SLsmg_gotorc(2, col + 4);
23:        SLsmg_write_string("0 1 2 3 4 5 6 7 8 9 A B C D E F");
24:
25:        /* set the character set to use */
26:        SLsmg_set_char_set(isAlternate);
27:
28:        /* this iterates over the 4 most significant bits */
29:        for (i = 0; i < 16; i++) {
30:            SLsmg_gotorc(3 + i, 2 + col);
31:            SLsmg_write_char(i < 10 ? i + '0' : (i - 10) + 'A');
32:
33:            /* this iterates over the 4 least significant bits */
34:            for (j = 0; j < 16; j++) {
35:                SLsmg_gotorc(3 + i, col + 4 + (j * 2));
36:                SLsmg_write_char(n++);
37:            }
38:        }
39:
40:        SLsmg_set_char_set(0);
41: }
42:
43: int main(void) {
44:        struct winsize ws;
45:
46:        /* get the size of the terminal connected to stdout */
47:        if (ioctl(1, TIOCGWINSZ, &ws)) {
48:            perror("failed to get window size");
49:            return 1;
50:        }
51:
52:        SLtt_get_terminfo();
53:
54:        SLtt_Screen_Rows = ws.ws_row;
55:        SLtt_Screen_Cols = ws.ws_col;
56:
57:        SLsmg_init_smg();
58:        SLang_init_tty(-1, 0, 1);
59:
60:        drawCharSet(0, 0, "Normal Character Set");
61:        drawCharSet(40, 1, "Alternate Character Set");
```

```
62:
63:      SLsmg_refresh();
64:      SLang_getkey();
65:
66:      SLsmg_gotorc(SLtt_Screen_Rows - 1, 0);
67:      SLsmg_refresh();
68:      SLsmg_reset_smg();
69:      SLang_reset_tty();
70:
71:      return 0;
72: }
```

### 22.2.9 Using Color

S-Lang makes it easy to add color to an application. It allows the user to use a palette of 256 entries[5], each defining a foreground and background color. Most applications use a palette entry for one type of rendered object, such as window frame or listbox entry. A palette's colors are set through SLtt_set_color().

```
void SLtt_set_color(int entry, char * name, char * fg, char * bg);
```

The first parameter specifies the palette entry being modified. The name parameter is currently ignored and should be passed as NULL. The final two entries name the new foreground and background colors for that palette entry. Table 22.2 lists the colors S-Lang supports; the fg and bg should both be strings containing the name of the color to use. All the colors on the left side of the table may be used for the foreground or background color. However, the colors on the right side should be used only for foreground colors. Using them for background colors will give unpredictable results.[6]

Writes to the screen are done using the current palette entry, which is set by the SLsmg_set_color() function.

```
void SLsmg_set_color(int entry);
```

---

5. This number could be increased in the future, but it is doubtful such a change will ever be necessary.
6. Results might include blinking text on some systems.

**Table 22.2** S-Lang Colors

| Foreground or Background | Foreground |
|---|---|
| black | gray |
| red | brightred |
| green | brightgreen |
| brown | yellow |
| blue | brightblue |
| magenta | brightmagenta |
| cyan | brightcyan |
| lightgray | white |

This sets the current palette entry to the specified entry. The colors specified by this entry are used for future screen writes.

Although an application may use the color-related functions on any terminal type, a number of factors control whether colors are displayed. The SLtt_Use_Ansi_Colors global variable controls whether colors are displayed. If it is set to 0, no colors are used. Any other value allows colors to be displayed.

SLtt_get_terminfo() tries to guess whether color should be enabled on the current terminal. Unfortunately, many termcap and terminfo databases are incomplete in this regard. If the COLORTERM environment variable is set, S-Lang sets SLtt_Use_Ansi_Colors no matter what the terminal database indicates.

Most applications that provide color support also provide a command-line option to allow users to selectively enable color support. When the option is used, the application explicitly sets SLtt_Use_Ansi_Colors.

# CHAPTER 23

# The Database Library

Applications commonly wish to store some form of binary data in a file. Storing such data for efficient retrieval is tricky and error prone. The **Berkely db library** provides a uniform interface to hashed files, btree indexing, and simple record-number-oriented files.

There are two versions of the db library, version 1 and version 2. Version 1 is licensed under the BSD license mentioned on page 16; version 2 is under a more restrictive license that more closely resembles the GPL license discussed on page 15. The two versions have completely incompatible APIs, and we discuss version 1 here because of its looser licensing restrictions. Version 1 of the db library is available at ftp://ftp.cs.berkeley.edu/ucb/4bsd/db.tar.gz, and is standard with most major Linux distributions.

## 23.1  Overview

The db library provides access to indexed files through a pseudo-object-oriented approach. A single function, dbopen(), opens all three types of files. It returns a pointer to a DB structure that includes pointers to functions for the rest of the database operations. The DB structure looks like this:

```
#include <db.h>

typedef struct __db {
    DBTYPE type;
    int (*close)(struct __db *);
    int (*del)(const struct __db *, const DBT *, u_int);
    int (*get)(const struct __db *, const DBT *, DBT *, u_int);
```

```
    int (*put)(const struct __db *, DBT *, const DBT *, u_int);
    int (*seq)(const struct __db *, DBT *, DBT *, u_int);
    int (*sync)(const struct __db *, u_int);
    int (*fd) (const struct __db *));
    void *internal;
} DB;
```

We discuss the individual elements of this structure later in this chapter; the important thing to notice is the collection of function pointers included in DB. Every operation on an open db file is done through those function pointers.

Three types of databases are provided by db: hash tables, btrees, and simple record-number-oriented access. Both hash tables and btrees provide efficient indexing of large amounts of data; the two data structures have different trade-offs in their time and complexity measures, and these trade-offs influence which is a better choice for a given application [Cormen, 1992].

The simpler record-oriented indexing provides a one-to-one mapping between the $n$ records in the database and the integers $1...n$. When record number $i$ is removed, records $i+1...n$ are renumbered to $i...n-1$.

We discuss the basic db interface without discussing any of the specialized interfaces for the three methods. For full details on db, we recommend reading the following man pages: db(3), recno(3), hash(3), and btree(3).

All of the data types and function prototypes for db are in the ⟨db.h⟩ header file, which must be included in code that makes use of db.

All of the database types are treated as key/value pairs. Hashed, btree, and record-numbered database files allow arbitrary values, and both hashed and btree databases allow arbitrary keys. Record-oriented databases restrict the keys to integers as mentioned earlier.

Both keys and values are represented by a DBT[1] record, which is defined as follows:

---

1. DBT stands for **database thang**.

```
#include <db.h>

typedef struct {
    void    *data;      /* data element */
    size_t  size;       /* size of data element, in bytes */
} DBT;
```

The `data` element points to the actual data and `size` tells how many bytes `data` points to.

# 23.2  Basic Operations

## 23.2.1  Opening a db File

The `dbopen()` library function is used to open db files.

```
#include <db.h>

DB * dbopen(const char * filename, int flags, int mode, DBTYPE type,
          const void * openinfo);
```

The first argument is the name of the file to use for the database.[2] The `flags` and `mode` are the same as those passed to the `open()` system call, as discussed on pages 152–154. `O_WRONLY` may not be used as the access mode, however. The `type` argument specifies what type of file is being opened and must be one of `DB_HASH`, `DB_BTREE`, or `DB_RECNO`. The final parameter points to a structure that provides tuning parameters for this database file and depends on the `type` of database that is used. We will always set this to `NULL`, which tells db to use reasonable defaults.

If the file is successfully opened, a pointer to a `DB` is returned. If an error occurs, `NULL` is returned and `errno` is set to indicate the error.

---

2. Unlike some database libraries that use multiple files, commonly ending with `.pag` and `.dir`, the Berkeley db library normally uses only a single file.

## 23.2.2 Closing a Database

Database files are closed through the close member of DB, which looks like this:

```
int close(const DB * db);
```

The close() function returns 0 on success, and non-0 if it fails, which can occur if the database's buffers cannot be flushed for any reason. Here is an example program that opens a database file in the current directory and immediately closes it.

```
 1: /* dbsimple.c -- simple db example */
 2:
 3: /* this program opens a database, and then closes it immediately */
 4:
 5: #include <db.h>
 6: #include <errno.h>
 7: #include <fcntl.h>
 8: #include <stdio.h>
 9:
10: int main(void) {
11:     DB * db;
12:
13:     db = dbopen("test.db", O_RDWR | O_CREAT, 0666, DB_HASH, NULL);
14:     if (!db) {
15:         perror("dbopen");
16:         return 1;
17:     }
18:
19:     db->close(db);
20:
21:     return 0;
22: }
```

### 23.2.3 Obtaining the File Descriptor

A major shortcoming of db files is their lack of support for concurrent access. They make no attempt to lock databases, leaving that to the application. To make locking a little easier, they do provide a file descriptor that can be used for locking purposes.

```
int fd(DB * db);
```

The fd element points to a function that returns a file descriptor associated with the database. It is not guaranteed to be the only file descriptor db is using or even to be used by db at all. It is guaranteed to refer to a file unique for the database being accessed and that the file descriptor returned for a given database file will always reference the same file (there is a one-to-one correspondence between the file the file descriptor refers to and the file name passed to dbopen()). That guarantee is good enough to allow locking.

Most applications that need to lock a db file lock the entire file and allow only one writing process to have access at a time, but the allow multiple readers. See Chapter 12 for more information on file locking.

### 23.2.4 Syncing the Database

The db layer caches data in RAM to provide faster database access, and the Linux kernel caches disk writes for low-latency write() calls. An application can ensure the on-disk database is consistent with the buffered structures by syncing the database. When a database is synced, db flushes all its internal buffers and calls fsync() on the file descriptor. Syncing a db is nearly identical to closing one.

```
int sync(const DB * db, unsigned int flags);
```

The flags argument is 0 for DB_HASH and DB_BTREE files. For DB_RECNO files, it may be R_RECNOSYNC, which syncs only the underlying btree file for the database rather than the overlying file.[3] See the recno(3) man page for details.

---

3. DB_RECNO databases actually consist of two database files, one of which is a DB_BTREE database. This does not matter when you are using a DB_RECNO database, though.

## 23.3 Reading Records

There are two ways to read records from the database: looking up a record by its key, and reading sequential key/value pairs. The db library maps the file into memory[4] and returns information from the file to the application as pointers into the memory-mapped region. Because of this, it is a bad idea to modify the data returned from db functions; instead, make a local copy and modify it. One advantage of db's use of memory maps is that the data it returns does not need to be freed by the application.

## 23.4 Reading Records Sequentially

All the records in a database may be read through the seq function pointed to by the DB structure.

```
int seq(const DB * db, DBT * key, DBT * value, unsigned int flags);
```

The structures pointed to by key and value are set to reference the new record. The db library keeps track of the current record through an internal cursor. The cursor is moved only by the seq function. Every time seq returns a record, the cursor is moved to that record.

The flags parameters determine which record is returned and must be one of the following:

R_CURSOR      The record whose key is the same as key is returned.[5] If the database is of type DB_BTREE, the record with the smallest key greater than or equal to the requested key is returned, allowing efficient range searches.

R_FIRST       The first record in the database is returned.

R_NEXT        The record after the cursor is returned.

---

4. See Chapter 12 for information on memory maps.
5. This differs from the get function we are about to mention in that it moves the position of the cursor.

R_LAST           The last record in the database is returned (for DB_RECNO and
                 DB_BTREE databases only).

R_PREV           The record before the cursor is returned (for DB_RECNO and
                 DB_BTREE databases only).

The R_LAST and R_PREV parameters are not available for hashed databases
because hash databases are not ordered. Although *previous* could be defined as the opposite of *next*, traversing a hash table backward is no better
than traversing it forward, so the db designers did not allow it.

### 23.4.1 Reading a Particular Record

Looking up an entry by its key is usually done through the get function of
the DB structure (though seq could be used instead).

```
int get(const DB * db, const DBT * key, DBT * value, unsigned int flags);
```

If the key exists in the database, value is set to point to the value associated
with it and 0 is returned. If the record does not exist, 1 is returned; if an
error occurs, -1 is returned and errno is set.

The flags parameter is unused and should be set to 0 for compatibility with
future versions of db.

# 23.5   Modifying the Database

There are two operations that modify db databases: adding records and
removing records. Updating records is done in the same manner as adding
records.

## 23.5.1 Adding Records

New and updated records are recorded in the database through the DB structure's put function.

```
int put(const DB * db, const DBT * key, const DBT * value,
        unsigned int flags);
```

The key is the index value that can later be used to retrieve the information referenced by value. The put function overwrites any other record in the database whose key is key unless the flags argument is R_NOOVERWRITE.

If the new record is successfully stored, put returns 0. If another record with this key exists and R_NOOVERWRITE was specified, put returns 1. If any other error occurs, -1 is returned and errno is set appropriately.

## 23.5.2 Removing Records

There are two ways to remove records from the database. Usually, records are removed by specifying the key whose record should be removed. Alternatively, the record currently referenced by the cursor may be removed. In either case, the DB structure's del member references the function that is used.

```
int del(DB * db, const DBT * key, unsigned int flags);
```

If flags is R_CURSOR, the record currently referenced by the cursor is removed and the cursor's position is undefined. If flags is 0, the record whose key is key is removed.

If the specified key does not exist in the database, del returns 1. If any other error occurs, -1 is returned and errno is set. If the specified record is successfully removed, 0 is returned.

## 23.6 Example

To help make all of this more concrete, here is a sample application that makes use of most of db's features. It is intended as a simple phone database, although it can be used to store any simple name/value pairs. It stores its database in the user's home directory as .phonedb.

The -a flag adds an entry to the database. If -f is specified, any existing entry is overwritten with the new data. The next parameter is the key value to use and the last parameter is the data (usually, a phone number).

The -q flag queries the database for a particular key, which should be the only other parameter specified. Entries are removed from the database through the -d flag, which takes the key value to remove as the only other parameter.

If -l is specified, all the key/value pairs in the database are listed.

Here is an example of using phones:

```
$ ./phones -a Erik 374-5876
$ ./phones -a Michael 642-4235
$ ./phones -a Larry 527-7976
$ ./phones -a Barbara 227-2272
$ ./phones -q Larry
Larry 527-7976
$ ./phones -l
Larry 527-7976
Erik 374-5876
Michael 642-4235
Barbara 227-2272
$ ./phones -d Michael
$ ./phones -l
Larry 527-7976
Erik 374-5876
Barbara 227-2272
```

Although this program does something quite useful, it is only about 250 lines of source code and is well suited to managing large numbers of key/value pairs.

```
1: /* phones.c -- simple phone database to illustrate Berkeley db */
2:
3: /* This implements a very simple phone database. Full usage
4:    information is given in the text. */
5:
6: #include <alloca.h>
7: #include <db.h>
8: #include <errno.h>
9: #include <fcntl.h>
10: #include <stdio.h>
11: #include <stdlib.h>
12: #include <string.h>
13: #include <unistd.h>
14:
15: void usage(void) {
16:     fprintf(stderr, "usage: phones -a [-f] <name> <phone>\n");
17:     fprintf(stderr, "              -d <name>\n");
18:     fprintf(stderr, "              -q <name>\n");
19:     fprintf(stderr, "              -l\n");
20:     exit(1);
21: }
22:
23: /* Opens the database $HOME/.phonedb. If writeable is nonzero,
24:    the database is opened for updating. If writeable is 0, the
25:    database is opened read-only. An appropriate lock is put on
26:    the database in either case. */
27: DB * openDatabase(int writeable) {
28:     DB * db;
29:     char * filename;
30:     int flags;
31:     struct flock lock;
32:
33:     /* Set up a lock on the entire file (l_len = 0 means
34:        lock the whole file) */
35:     lock.l_whence = SEEK_SET;
36:     lock.l_start = 0;
37:     lock.l_len = 0;
38:
39:     /* Set the open and lock modes */
40:     if (writeable) {
41:         flags = O_CREAT | O_RDWR;
```

```
42:         lock.l_type = F_WRLCK;
43:     } else {
44:         flags = O_RDONLY;
45:         lock.l_type = F_RDLCK;
46:     }
47:
48:     filename = alloca(strlen(getenv("HOME")) + 20);
49:     strcpy(filename, getenv("HOME"));
50:     strcat(filename, "/.phonedb");
51:
52:     db = dbopen(filename, flags, 0666, DB_HASH, NULL);
53:     if (!db) {
54:         fprintf(stderr, "failed to open %s: %s\n", filename,
55:                 strerror(errno));
56:         return NULL;
57:     }
58:
59:     /* Now that the database is open, lock it */
60:     if (fcntl(db->fd(db), F_SETLK, &lock)) {
61:         if (errno == EAGAIN)
62:             fprintf(stderr, "the phone database is already "
63:                             "locked\n");
64:         else
65:             fprintf(stderr, "failed to lock database: %s\n",
66:                             strerror(errno));
67:         return NULL;
68:     }
69:
70:     return db;
71: }
72:
73: /* add a new record to the database; this parses the
74:    command-line arguments directly */
75: int addRecord(int argc, char ** argv) {
76:     DB * db;
77:     char * name, * phone;
78:     DBT key, value;
79:     int rc = 0;
80:     int overwrite = 0;
81:
82:     /* check for our parameters; -f means overwrite an
```

```
 83:        existing entry, and the name and phone number should
 84:        be all that remains */
 85:     if (!argc) usage();
 86:     if (!strcmp(argv[0], "-f")) {
 87:         overwrite = 1;
 88:         argc--, argv++;
 89:     }
 90:
 91:     if (argc != 2) usage();
 92:
 93:     name = argv[0];
 94:     phone = argv[1];
 95:
 96:     /* open the database for writing */
 97:     if (!(db = openDatabase(1))) return 1;
 98:
 99:     key.data = name;
100:     /* the +1 writes the trailing '\0' to the file */
101:     key.size = strlen(name) + 1;
102:
103:     /* if we shouldn't overwrite an existing entry, check
104:        to see if this name is already used */
105:     if (!overwrite) {
106:         rc = db->get(db, &key, &value, 0);
107:         if (rc == -1) {
108:             fprintf(stderr, "get failed: %s\n", strerror(errno));
109:             rc = 1;
110:         } else if (!rc) {
111:             fprintf(stderr, "%s already listed as %s\n", name,
112:                     (char *) value.data);
113:             rc = 1;
114:         } else {
115:             rc = 0 ;
116:         }
117:     }
118:
119:     /* if everything has worked so far, update the database */
120:     if (!rc) {
121:         value.data = phone;
122:         value.size = strlen(phone) + 1;
123:
```

```
124:            if (db->put(db, &key, &value, 0)) {
125:                fprintf(stderr, "put failed: %s\n", strerror(errno));
126:                rc = 1;
127:            }
128:        }
129:
130:    db->close(db);
131:
132:    return rc;
133: }
134:
135: /* looks up a name, and prints the phone number associated
136:    with it; parses the command line directly */
137: int queryRecord(int argc, char ** argv) {
138:     DB * db;
139:     DBT key, value;
140:     int rc;
141:
142:     /* only one argument is expected, a name to look up */
143:     if (argc != 1) usage();
144:
145:     /* open the database for reading */
146:     if (!(db = openDatabase(0))) return 1;
147:
148:     /* set up the key to look up */
149:     key.data = argv[0];
150:     key.size = strlen(argv[0]) + 1;
151:
152:     rc = db->get(db, &key, &value, 0);
153:     if (rc == -1) {
154:         fprintf(stderr, "get failed: %s\n", strerror(errno));
155:         rc = 1;
156:     } else if (rc) {
157:         fprintf(stderr, "%s is not listed\n", argv[0]);
158:         rc = 1;
159:     } else {
160:         printf("%s %s\n", argv[0], (char *) value.data);
161:         rc = 0;
162:     }
163:
164:     db->close(db);
```

```
165:
166:     return rc;
167: }
168:
169: /* delete the specified record; the name is passed as a
170:    command-line argument */
171: int delRecord(int argc, char ** argv) {
172:     DB * db;
173:     DBT key;
174:     int rc;
175:
176:     /* only a single argument is expected */
177:     if (argc != 1) usage();
178:
179:     /* open the database for updating */
180:     if (!(db = openDatabase(1))) return 1;
181:
182:     /* set up the key */
183:     key.data = argv[0];
184:     key.size = strlen(argv[0]) + 1;
185:
186:     rc = db->del(db, &key, 0);
187:     if (rc == -1) {
188:         fprintf(stderr, "del failed: %s\n", strerror(errno));
189:         rc = 1;
190:     } else if (rc) {
191:         fprintf(stderr, "%s is not listed\n", argv[0]);
192:         rc = 1;
193:     }
194:
195:     db->close(db);
196:
197:     return rc;
198: }
199:
200: /* lists all of the records in the database */
201: int listRecords(void) {
202:     DB * db;
203:     DBT key, value;
204:     int rc;
205:     int flags = R_FIRST;
```

```
206:
207:     /* open the database read-only */
208:     if (!(db = openDatabase(0))) return 1;
209:
210:     /* iterate over all of the records */
211:     while (!(rc = db->seq(db, &key, &value, flags))) {
212:         flags = R_NEXT;
213:         printf("%s %s\n", (char *) key.data, (char *) value.data);
214:     }
215:
216:     if (rc == -1) {
217:         fprintf(stderr, "seq failed: %s\n", strerror(errno));
218:         rc = 1;
219:     } else {
220:         rc = 0;
221:     }
222:
223:     db->close(db);
224:
225:     return rc;
226: }
227:
228: int main(int argc, char ** argv) {
229:     if (argc == 1) usage();
230:
231:     /* look for a mode flag, and call the appropriate function
232:        with the remainder of the arguments */
233:     if (!strcmp(argv[1], "-a"))
234:         return addRecord(argc - 2, argv + 2);
235:     else if (!strcmp(argv[1], "-q"))
236:         return queryRecord(argc - 2, argv + 2);
237:     else if (!strcmp(argv[1], "-d"))
238:         return delRecord(argc - 2, argv + 2);
239:     else if (!strcmp(argv[1], "-l")) {
240:         if (argc != 2) usage();
241:         return listRecords();
242:     }
243:
244:     usage();  /* did not recognize any options */
245:     return 0; /* doesn't get here due to usage() */
246: }
```

# CHAPTER 24

# Parsing Command-Line Options

Most Linux programs allow the user to specify command-line options. Such options perform a wide variety of functions but are fairly uniform in their syntax. **Short options** consist of a - character followed by a single alphanumeric character. **Long options**, common in GNU utilities, consist of two - characters followed by a string made up of letters, numbers, and hyphens. Either type of option may be followed by an argument. A space separates a short option from its arguments; either a space or an = separates a long option from an argument.

There are many ways of parsing command-line options. The most popular method is parsing the `argv` array by hand. The `getopt()` and `getopt_long()` library functions provide some assistance for option parsing. `getopt()` is provided by many Unix implementations, but it supports only short options. The `getopt_long()` function is available on Linux and allows automated parsing of both short and long options.

A library called popt exists specifically for option parsing. It includes a number of advantages over the `getopt()` functions.

- It does not make use of global variables, which allows it to be used when multiple passes are needed to parse `argv`.

- It can parse an arbitrary array of `argv`-style elements. This allows popt to be used for parsing command-line-style strings from any source.

- It provides a standard method of option aliasing. Programs that use popt can easily allow users to add new command-line options, which

**445**

are defined as combinations of already-existing options. This allows the user to define new, complex behaviors or change the default behaviors of existing options.

Like `getopt_long()`, the popt library supports short and long style options.

The popt library is highly portable and should work on any POSIX platform. The latest version is always available from ftp://ftp.redhat.com/pub/redhat/code/popt/

It may be redistributed under either the GNU General Public License or the GNU Library General Public License, at the distributor's discretion.

# 24.1   Basic popt Usage

## 24.1.1 The Option Table

Applications provide popt with information on their command-line options through an array of `struct poptOption` structures.

```
#include <popt.h>

struct poptOption {
    const char * longName;  /* may be NULL */
    char shortName;         /* may be '\0' */
    int argInfo;
    void * arg;             /* depends on argInfo */
    int val;                /* 0 means do not return, just update flag */
};
```

Each member of the table defines a single option that may be passed to the program. Long and short options are considered a single option that may occur in two different forms. The first two members, `longName` and `shortName`, define the names of the option; the first is a long name, and the latter is a single character.

**Table 24.1**  popt Argument Types

| Value | Description | arg **Type** |
|---|---|---|
| POPT_ARG_NONE | No argument is expected | int |
| POPT_ARG_STRING | No type checking should be performed | char * |
| POPT_ARG_INT | An integer argument is expected | int |
| POPT_ARG_LONG | A long integer is expected | long |

The argInfo member tells popt what type of argument is expected after the argument. If no option is expected, POPT_ARG_NONE should be used. The rest of the valid values are summarized in Table 24.1.[1]

The next element, arg, allows popt to automatically update program variables when the option is used. If arg is NULL, it is ignored and popt takes no special action. Otherwise, it should point to a variable of the type indicated in the right-most column of Table 24.1.

If the option takes no argument (argInfo is POPT_ARG_NONE), the variable pointed to by arg is set to 1 when the option is used. If the option does take an argument, the variable that arg points to is updated to reflect the value of the argument. Any string is acceptable for POPT_ARG_STRING arguments, but POPT_ARG_INT and POPT_ARG_LONG arguments are converted to the appropriate type, and an error is returned if the conversion fails.

The final option, val, is the value popt's parsing function should return when the option is encountered. If it is 0, the parsing function parses the next command-line argument rather than return.

The final structure in the table should have all the pointer values set to NULL and all the arithmetic values set to 0, marking the end of the table.

---

1. getopt() connoisseurs will note that argInfo is the only field of struct poptOption that is not directly analogous to a field in the getopt_long() argument table. The similarity between the two allows for easy transitions from getopt_long() to popt.

## 24.1.2 Creating a Context

popt can interleave the parsing of multiple command-line sets. It allows this by keeping all the state information for a particular set of command-line arguments in a `poptContext` data structure, an opaque type that should not be modified outside the popt library.

New popt contexts are created by `poptGetContext()`.

```
#include <popt.h>

poptContext poptGetContext(char * name, int argc, char ** argv,
                          struct poptOption * options, int flags);
```

The first parameter, `name`, is used only for alias handling (discussed later). It should be the name of the application whose options are being parsed, or should be `NULL` if no option aliasing is desired. The next two arguments specify the command-line arguments to parse. These are generally passed to `poptGetContext()` exactly as they were passed to the program's `main()` function. The `options` parameter points to the table of command-line options, which was described in the previous section. The final parameter, `flags`, is not currently used but should always be specified as 0 for compatibility with future versions of the popt library.

A `poptContext` keeps track of which options have already been parsed and which remain, among other things. If a program wishes to restart option processing of a set of arguments, it can reset the `poptContext` by passing the context as the sole argument to `poptResetContext()`.

When argument processing is complete, the process should free the `poptContext` as it contains dynamically allocated components. The `poptFreeContext()` function takes a `poptContext` as its sole argument and frees the resources the context is using.

Here are the prototypes of both `poptResetContext()` and `poptFreeContext()`.

```
#include <popt.h>

void poptFreeContext(poptContext con);
void poptResetContext(poptContext con);
```

## 24.1.3 Parsing the Command Line

After an application has created a poptContext, it may begin parsing arguments. The poptGetNextOpt() performs the actual argument parsing.

```
#include <popt.h>

int poptGetNextOpt(poptContext con);
```

Taking the context as its sole argument, this function parses the next command-line argument found. After finding the next argument in the option table, the function fills in the object pointed to by the option table entry's arg pointer if it is not NULL. If the val entry for the option is non-0, the function then returns that value. Otherwise, poptGetNextOpt() continues on to the next argument.

poptGetNextOpt() returns -1 when the final argument has been parsed, and other negative values when errors occur. This makes it a good idea to keep the val elements in the options table greater than 0.

If all of the command-line options are handled through arg pointers, command-line parsing is reduced to the following line of code:

```
rc = poptGetNextOpt(poptcon);
```

Many applications require more complex command-line parsing than this, however, and use the following structure.

```
while ((rc = poptGetNextOpt(poptcon)) > 0) {
    switch (rc) {
        /* specific arguments are handled here */
    }
}
```

When returned options are handled, the application needs to know the value of any arguments that were specified after the option. There are two ways to discover them. One is to ask popt to fill in a variable with the value of the option through the option table's arg elements. The other is to use poptGetOptArg().

```
#include <popt.h>

char * poptGetOptArg(poptContext con);
```

This function returns the argument given for the final option returned by
poptGetNextOpt(), or it returns NULL if no argument was specified.

### 24.1.4 Leftover Arguments

Many applications take an arbitrary number of command-line arguments,
such as a list of file names. When popt encounters an argument that does
not begin with a -, it assumes it is such an argument and adds it to a list
of leftover arguments. Three functions allow applications to access such
arguments:

```
char * poptGetArg(poptContext con);
```
> This function returns the next leftover argument and marks it as
> processed.

```
char * poptPeekArg(poptContext con);
```
> The next leftover argument is returned but not marked as processed.
> This allows an application to look ahead into the argument list,
> without modifying the list.

```
char ** poptGetArgs(poptContext con);
```
> All the leftover arguments are returned in a manner identical to argv.
> The final element in the returned array points to NULL, indicating the
> end of the arguments.

## 24.2 Error Handling

All of the popt functions that can return errors return integers. When an
error occurs, a negative error code is returned. Table 24.2 summarizes the
error codes that occur. Here is a more detailed discussion of each error.

**Table 24.2** popt Errors

| Error | Description |
|---|---|
| POPT_ERROR_NOARG | An argument is missing for an option. |
| POPT_ERROR_BADOPT | An option's argument could not be parsed. |
| POPT_ERROR_OPTSTOODEEP | Option aliasing is nested too deeply. |
| POPT_ERROR_BADQUOTE | Quotations do not match. |
| POPT_ERROR_BADNUMBER | An option could not be converted to a number. |
| POPT_ERROR_OVERFLOW | A given number was too big or too small. |

POPT_ERROR_NOARG

> An option that requires an argument was specified on the command line, but no argument was given. This can be returned only by poptGetNextOpt().

POPT_ERROR_BADOPT

> An option was specified in argv but is not in the option table. This error can be returned only from poptGetNextOpt().

POPT_ERROR_OPTSTOODEEP

> A set of option aliases is nested too deeply. Currently, popt follows options only 10 levels to prevent infinite recursion. Only poptGet-NextOpt() can return this error.

POPT_ERROR_BADQUOTE

> A parsed string has a quotation mismatch (such as a single quotation mark). poptParseArgvString(), poptReadConfigFile(), or poptReadDefaultConfig() can return this error.

POPT_ERROR_BADNUMBER

> A conversion from a string to a number (int or long) failed due to the string containing nonnumeric characters. This occurs when poptGetNextOpt() is processing an argument of type POPT_ARG_INT or POPT_ARG_LONG.

POPT_ERROR_OVERFLOW

> A string-to-number conversion failed because the number was too large or too small. Like POPT_ERROR_BADNUMBER, this error can occur only when poptGetNextOpt() is processing an argument of type POPT_ARG_INT or POPT_ARG_LONG.

POPT_ERROR_ERRNO
> A system call returned with an error, and `errno` still contains the error from the system call. Both `poptReadConfigFile()` and `poptRead-DefaultConfig()` can return this error.

Two functions are available to make it easy for applications to provide good error messages.

`const char * poptStrerror(const int error);`
> This function takes a popt error code and returns a string describing the error, just as with the standard `strerror()` function.

`char * poptBadOption(poptContext con, int flags);`
> If an error occurred during `poptGetNextOpt()`, this function returns the option that caused the error. If the `flags` argument is set to `POPT_BADOPTION_NOALIAS`, the outermost option is returned. Otherwise, `flags` should be 0, and the option that is returned may have been specified through an alias.

These two functions make popt error handling trivial for most applications. When an error is detected from most of the functions, an error message is printed along with the error string from `poptStrerror()`. When an error occurs during argument parsing, code similar to the following displays a useful error message.

```
fprintf(stderr, "%s: %s\n",
        poptBadOption(optCon, POPT_BADOPTION_NOALIAS),
        poptStrerror(rc));
```

# 24.3   Option Aliasing

One of the primary benefits of using popt over `getopt()` is the ability to use option aliasing. This lets the user specify options that popt expands into other options when they are specified. If the standard grep program made use of popt, users could add a `--text` option that expanded to `-i -n -E -2` to let them more easily find information in text files.

## 24.3.1 Specifying Aliases

Aliases are normally specified in two places: /etc/popt and the .popt file in the user's home directory (found through the HOME environment variable). Both files have the same format, an arbitrary number of lines formatted like this:

```
appname alias newoption expansion
```

The *appname* is the name of the application, which must be the same as the name parameter passed to poptGetContext(). This allows each file to specify aliases for multiple programs. The alias keyword specifies that an alias is being defined; currently popt configuration files support only aliases, but other abilities may be added in the future. The next option is the option that should be aliased, and it may be either a short or a long option. The rest of the line specifies the expansion for the alias. It is parsed similarly to a shell command, which allows \, ", and ' to be used for quoting. If a backslash is the final character on a line, the next line in the file is assumed to be a logical continuation of the line containing the backslash, just as in shell.

The following entry would add a --text option to the grep command, as suggested at the beginning of this section.

```
grep alias --text -i -n -E -2
```

## 24.3.2 Enabling Aliases

An application must enable alias expansion for a poptContext before calling poptGetNextArg() for the first time. There are three functions that define aliases for a context.

```
int poptReadDefaultConfig(poptContext con, int flags);
```
This function reads aliases from /etc/popt and the .popt file in the user's home directory. Currently, flags should be NULL, as it is provided only for future expansion.

```
int poptReadConfigFile(poptContext con, char * fn);
```
> The file specified by fn is opened and parsed as a popt configuration file. This allows programs to use program-specific configuration files.

```
int poptAddAlias(poptContext con, struct poptAlias alias, int flags);
```
> Occasionally, processes want to specify aliases without having to read them from a configuration file. This function adds a new alias to a context. The flags argument should be 0, as it is currently reserved for future expansion. The new alias is specified as a struct poptAlias, which is defined as:

```
struct poptAlias {
    char * longName;            /* may be NULL */
    char shortName;             /* may be '\0' */
    int argc;
    char ** argv;               /* must be free()able */
};
```

> The first two elements, longName and shortName, specify the option that is aliased. The final two, argc and argv, define the expansion to use when the aliases option is encountered.

# 24.4  Parsing Argument Strings

Although popt is usually used for parsing arguments already divided into an argv-style array, some programs need to parse strings that are formatted identically to command lines. To facilitate this, popt provides a function that parses a string into an array of string, using rules similiar to normal shell parsing.

```
#include <popt.h>

int poptParseArgvString(char * s, int * argcPtr, char *** argvPtr);
```

The string s is parsed into an argv-style array. The integer pointed to by the second parameter, argcPtr, contains the number of elements parsed, and the pointer pointed to by the final parameter is set to point to the newly created array. The array is dynamically allocated and should be `free()`ed when the application is finished with it.

The `argvPtr` created by `poptParseArgvString()` is suitable to pass directly to `poptGetContext()`.

## 24.5 Handling Extra Arguments

Some applications implement the equivalent of option aliasing but need to do so through special logic. The `poptStuffArgs()` function allows an application to insert new arguments into the current `poptContext`.

```
#include <popt.h>

int poptStuffArgs(poptContext con, char ** argv);
```

The passed `argv` must have a `NULL` pointer as its final element. When `poptGetNextOpt()` is next called, the "stuffed" arguments are the first to be parsed. popt returns to the normal arguments once all the stuffed arguments have been exhausted.

## 24.6 Sample Application

Robin, the sample application on pages 274–281 of Chapter 15, uses popt for its argument parsing. It provides a good example of how the popt library is generally used.

RPM, a popular Linux package management program, makes heavy use of popt's features. Many of its command-line arguments are implemented through popt aliases, which makes RPM an excellent example of how to take advantage of the popt library. For more information on RPM, see http://www.rpm.org

# CHAPTER 25

# Dynamic Loading at Run Time

Loading shared objects at run time can be a useful way to structure your applications. Done right, it can make your applications extensible, and it also forces you to partition your code into logically separate modules, which is a useful coding discipline.

Many Unix applications, particularly large ones, are mostly implemented by separate blocks of code, often called **plugins** or **modules**. In some cases, they are implemented as completely different programs, which communicate with the application's core code via pipes or some other form of interprocess communication (IPC). In other cases, they are implemented as shared objects.

These shared objects may be standard object files or they may be built like standard shared libraries (see Chapter 7), but they are used in a completely different way. The linker is never told about the shared objects, and they do not even need to exist when the application is linked. They do not need to be installed on the system in the same way most shared libraries do. The symbol names they use do not need to be unique; in fact, they usually are not unique. Different shared objects written for the same interface usually use entry points with the same names. With normal shared libraries, this would be a disaster; with shared objects dynamically loaded at run time, it is the obvious thing to do.

Perhaps the most common use of run-time-loaded shared objects is to create an interface to some generic type of capability that might have many different implementations. For instance, consider saving a graphics file. An application might have one internal format for managing its graphics, but there are a lot of file formats in which it might want to save graphics, and more are created on an irregular basis [Murray, 1996]. A generic interface for saving a graphics file that is exported to shared objects loaded at run time allows programmers to add new graphics file formats to the application without recompiling the application. If the interface is well documented, it is even possible for third parties who do not have the application's source code to add new graphics file formats.

A similar use is **framework** code that provides only an interface, not an implementation. For example, the PAM (Pluggable Authentication Modules) framework provides a general interface to challenge-response authentication methods, such as usernames and passwords. All the authentication is done by modules, and the choice of which authentication modules to use with which application is done at run time, not compile time, by consulting configuration files. The interface is well defined and stable, and new modules can be dropped into place and used at any time without recompiling either the framework or the application. The framework is loaded as a shared library, and code in that shared library loads and unloads the modules that provide the authentication methods.

# 25.1 The dl Interface

Dynamic loading consists of opening a library, looking up any number of symbols, handling any errors that occur, and closing the library. All the dynamic loading functions are declared in one header file, `<dlfcn.h>`.

The `dlerror()` function returns a string describing the most recent error that occurred in one of the other three dynamic loading functions.

```
const char * dlerror (void);
```

Each time it returns a value, it clears the error condition. Until another error condition is created, it will continue to return `NULL` instead of a string. The reason for this unusual behavior is detailed in the description of the `dlsym()` function.

The `dlopen()` function opens a library. This involves finding the library file, opening the file, and doing some preliminary processing. Environment variables and the options passed to `dlopen()` determine the details.

```
void * dlopen (const char *filename, int flag);
```

If filename is an absolute path (that is, it begins with a / character), dlopen() does not need to search for the library. This is the usual way to use dlopen() from within application code. If filename is a simple file name, dlopen() searches for the filename library in these places:

- A colon-separated set of directories specified in the environment variable LD_ELF_LIBRARY_PATH, or, if LD_ELF_LIBRARY_PATH does not exist, in LD_LIBRARY_PATH.

- The libraries specified in the file /etc/ld.so.cache. That file is generated by the ldconfig program, which lists every library it finds in a directory listed in /etc/ld.so.conf at the time that it is run.

- /usr/lib

- /lib

If filename is NULL, dlopen() opens an instance of the current executable. This is useful only in rare cases. dlopen() returns NULL on failure.

Finding the files is the easy part of dlopen()'s job; resolving the symbols is more complex. There are two fundamentally different types of symbol resolution, immediate and lazy. Immediate resolution causes dlopen() to resolve all the unresolved symbols before it returns; lazy resolution means that symbol resolution occurs on demand.

If most of the symbols will end up being resolved in the end, it is more efficient to perform immediate resolution. However, for libraries with many unresolved symbols, the time spent resolving the symbols may be noticeable; if this significantly affects your user interface, you may prefer lazy resolution. The difference in overall efficiency is not significant.

While developing and debugging, you will almost always want to use immediate resolution. If your shared objects have unresolvable symbols, you want to know about it immediately, not when your program crashes in the middle of seemingly unrelated code. Lazy resolution will be a source of hard-to-reproduce bugs if you do not test your shared objects with immediate resolution first.

This is especially true if you have shared objects that depend on other shared objects to supply some of their symbols. If shared object A depends on a symbol *b* in shared object B, and B is loaded after A, lazy resolution of *b* will succeed if it happens after B is loaded, but it will fail before B is loaded. Developing your code with immediate resolution enabled will help you catch this type of bug before it causes problems.

This implies that you should always load modules in reverse order of their dependencies: If A depends on B for some of its symbols, you should load B before you load A, and you should unload A before you unload B. Fortunately, most applications of dynamically loaded shared objects have no dependencies.

By default, the symbols in a shared object are not exported and so will not be used to resolve symbols in other shared objects. They will be available only for you to look up and use, as will be described in the next section. However, you may choose to export all the symbols in a shared object to all other shared objects; they will be available to all subsequently loaded shared objects.

All of this is controlled by the flags argument. It must be set to RTLD_LAZY for lazy resolution or RTLD_NOW for immediate resolution. Either of these may be OR'ed with RTLD_GLOBAL in order to export its symbols to other modules.

If the shared object exports a routine named _init, that routine is run before dlopen() returns.

The dlopen() function returns a **handle** to the shared object it has opened. This is an opaque object handle that you should use only as an argument to subsequent dlsym() and dlclose() function calls. If a shared object is opened multiple times, dlopen() returns the same handle each time, and each call increments a reference count.

The dlsym() function looks up a symbol in a library:

```
void * dlsym (void *handle, char *symbol);
```

The `handle` must be a handle returned by `dlopen()`, and `symbol` is a NULL-terminated string naming the symbol you wish to look up. `dlsym()` returns the address of the symbol that you specified, or it returns NULL if a fatal error occurs. In cases in which you know that NULL is not the correct address of the symbol (such as looking up the address of a function), you can test for errors by checking to see if it returned NULL. However, in the more general case, some symbols may be zero-valued and be equal to NULL. In those cases, you need to see if `dlerror()` returns an error. Since `dlerror()` will return an error only once and then revert to returning NULL, you should use code like this:

```
/* clear any error condition that has not been read yet */
dlerror();
p = dlsym(handle, this_symbol);
if ((error = dlerror()) != NULL) {
   /* error handling */
}
```

Since `dlsym()` returns a `void *`, you will need to use casts to make the C compiler stop complaining. When you store the pointer that `dlsym()` returns, store it in a variable of the type that you want to use, and make your cast when you call `dlsym()`. Do not store the result in a `void *` variable; you would have to cast it every time you use it.

The `dlclose()` function closes a library.

```
void * dlclose (void *handle);
```

`dlclose()` checks the reference count that was incremented on each duplicate `dlopen()` call, and if is zero, it closes the library. This reference count allows libraries to use `dlopen()` and `dlclose()` on arbitrary objects without worrying that the code that called it has already opened any of those objects.

## 25.1.1 Example

In Chapter 7, we presented an example of using a normal shared library. The shared library that we built, libhello.so, can also be loaded at run time. The loadhello program loads libhello.so dynamically and calls the `print_hello` function it loads from the library.

Here is loadhello.c:

```
1: /* usehello.c -- explicitly loads print_hello() function from libhello.so */
2: #include <dlfcn.h>
3: #include <stdio.h>
4: #include <stdlib.h>
5:
6: typedef void (*hello_function)(void);
7:
8: int main (void) {
9:     void *library;
10:    hello_function hello;
11:    const char *error;
12:
13:    library = dlopen("libhello.so", RTLD_LAZY);
14:    if (library == NULL) {
15:        fprintf(stderr, "Could not open libhello.so: %s\n", dlerror());
16:        exit(1);
17:    }
18:
19:    /* while in this case we know that the print_hello symbol
20:     * should never be null, that is not true for looking up
21:     * arbitrary symbols.  So we demonstrate checking dlerror()'s
22:     * return code instead of dlsym()'s.
23:     */
24:    dlerror();
25:    hello = dlsym(library, "print_hello");
26:    error = dlerror();
27:    if (error) {
28:        fprintf(stderr, "Could not find print_hello: %s\n", error);
29:        exit(1);
30:    }
31:
32:    (*hello)();
33:    dlclose(library);
34:    return 0;
35: }
```

# Names and the User Databases

Linux's security model uses numbers to identify users and groups, but people prefer names. The names are stored, along with other important information, in two system databases.

## 26.1   ID-to-Name Translation

When you type `ls -l` to list the contents of the current directory, the third and fourth columns give the user ID and group ID that owns each file. It looks like this:

```
drwxrwxr-x   5 christid christid   1024 Aug 15 02:30 christid
drwxr-xr-x  73 johnsonm root       4096 Jan 18 12:48 johnsonm
drwxr-xr-x  25 kim      root       2048 Jan 12 21:13 kim
drwxrwsr-x   2 tytso    tytso      1024 Jan 30  1996 tytso
```

But the kernel does not store the string `christid` anywhere; the ls program is translating from kernel-supplied numbers to names. It gets numbers from the `stat()` system call and looks up the names in two system databases. These are normally kept in the /etc/passwd and /etc/group files, although on some systems the information is stored somewhere on the network or in other, less standard, file locations. As a programmer, you do not have to worry about where the information is stored; generic functions are provided in the C library that read configuration files to determine where the information is stored, fetch the information, and return it to you transparently.

To demonstrate what ls gets from the kernel, run `ls -ln`:

```
drwxrwxr-x   5 500     500         1024 Aug 15 02:30 christid
drwxr-xr-x  73 100       0         4096 Jan 18 12:48 johnsonm
drwxr-xr-x  25 101       0         2048 Jan 12 21:13 kim
drwxrwsr-x   2 1008    1008        1024 Jan 30  1996 tytso
```

The structure that represents entries in /etc/passwd (or equivalent databases for a system) is contained in ⟨pwd.h⟩.

```
struct passwd {
    char *pw_name;          /*  Username        */
    char *pw_passwd;        /*  Password        */
    __uid_t pw_uid;         /*  User ID         */
    __gid_t pw_gid;         /*  Group ID        */
    char *pw_gecos;         /*  Real name       */
    char *pw_dir;           /*  Home directory  */
    char *pw_shell;         /*  Shell program   */
};
```

- `pw_name` is the **unique** username.

- `pw_passwd` may be the encrypted password or something else related to authentication. This is system-dependent.

- `pw_uid` is the (usually unique) number that the kernel uses to identify the user.

- `pw_gid` is the primary group that the kernel associates with the user.

- `pw_gecos` is a system-dependent field that stores information about the user. This generally includes the user's real name; on many systems, it is a comma-separated list of fields that includes home and office phone numbers.

- `pw_dir` is the home directory associated with the user. Normal login sessions start with this directory as the current directory.

- `pw_shell` is the shell that is started on normal logins for the user. This is usually something like /bin/bash, /bin/tcsh, /bin/zsh, and so on. However, entries used for other purposes may have other shells. /bin/false is used for passwd entries that should not be used for logins. Specialized shells are often used for purposes beyond the scope of this book.

The structure that represents entries in /etc/group (again, or equivalent databases) is contained in <grp.h>:

```
struct group {
  char *gr_name;          /*  Group name    */
  char *gr_passwd;        /*  Password      */
  __gid_t gr_gid;         /*  Group ID      */
  char **gr_mem;          /*  Member list   */
};
```

- gr_name is the unique name of the group.

- gr_passwd is the (usually unused) password. The same caveats apply to this field as to pw_passwd, only more so.

- gr_gid is the (usually unique) number the kernel uses to identify the group.

- gr_mem is a comma-separated list of group members. This is a list of usernames that are assigned to this group on a secondary basis (see Chapter 9).

There are two common reasons to access the system identification databases: if the kernel gives you a number and you want a name, or if someone or some program gives you a name and you need to give the kernel a number. There are two functions that look up numeric IDs, getpwuid() and getgrgid(), which take an integer ID and return a pointer to a structure containing information from the relevant system database. Similarly, there are two functions that look up names, getpwnam() and getgrnam(), and they return the same two structures. Here is a summary:

|        | User Database | Group Database |
|--------|---------------|----------------|
| Number | getpwuid()    | getgrgid()     |
| Name   | getpwnam()    | getgrnam()     |

All of these functions return pointers to structures. The structures are static structures that are overwritten the next time the function is called, so if you need to keep a structure around for any reason, you need to make a copy of it.

The four functions above are essentially shortcuts providing the most commonly needed functions for accessing the system databases. Lower-level functions called getpwent() and getgrent() iterate over the lines in the databases rather than search for some record in particular. Each time you call one of these functions, it reads another entry from the relevant system database and returns it. When you are finished reading the entries in, call endpwent() or endgrent() to close the relevant file.

As an example, here is getpwuid() written in terms of getpwent():

```
struct passwd *getpwuid(uid_t uid) {
   struct passwd *pw;

   while (pw = getpwent()) {
      if (!pw)
         /* error occurred;
          * fall through to error processing */
         break;
      if (pw->pw_uid == uid) {
         endpwent();
         return (pw);
      }
   }
   endpwent();
   return NULL;
}
```

## 26.1.1 Example: The id Command

The id command uses many of these functions and provides some excellent examples of how to work with them. It also uses some of the kernel features described in Chapter 9.

```
1: /* id.c -- implements simple version of id command */
2: #include <grp.h>
3: #include <pwd.h>
4: #include <sys/types.h>
```

```
 5: #include <stdlib.h>
 6: #include <stdio.h>
 7: #include <string.h>
 8: #include <unistd.h>
 9:
10: void usage(int die, char *error) {
11:     fprintf(stderr, "Usage: id [<username>]\n");
12:     if (error) fprintf(stderr, "%s\n", error);
13:     if (die) exit(die);
14: }
15:
16: void die(char *error) {
17:     if (error) fprintf(stderr, "%s\n", error);
18:     exit(3);
19: }
20:
21: int main(int argc, char *argv[]) {
22:     struct passwd *pw;
23:     struct group  *gp;
24:     int     current_user = 0;
25:     uid_t   id;
26:     int i;
27:
28:     if (argc > 2)
29:         usage(1, NULL);
30:
31:     if (argc == 1) {
32:         id = getuid();
33:         current_user = 1;
34:         if (!(pw = getpwuid(id)))
35:             usage(1, "Username does not exist");
36:     } else {
37:         if (!(pw = getpwnam(argv[1])))
38:             usage(1, "Username does not exist");
39:         id = pw->pw_uid;
40:     }
41:
42:     printf("uid=%d(%s)", id, pw->pw_name);
43:     if (gp = getgrgid(pw->pw_gid))
44:         printf(" gid=%d(%s)", pw->pw_gid, gp->gr_name);
45:
```

```
46:    if (current_user) {
47:        gid_t *gid_list;
48:        int    gid_size;
49:
50:        if (getuid() != geteuid()) {
51:            id = geteuid();
52:            if (!(pw = getpwuid(id)))
53:                usage(1, "Username does not exist");
54:            printf(" euid=%d(%s)", id, pw->pw_name);
55:        }
56:
57:        if (getgid() != getegid()) {
58:            id = getegid();
59:            if (!(gp = getgrgid(id)))
60:                usage(1, "Group does not exist");
61:            printf(" egid=%d(%s)", id, gp->gr_name);
62:        }
63:
64:        /* use getgroups interface to get current groups */
65:        gid_size = getgroups(0, NULL);
66:        if (gid_size) {
67:            gid_list = malloc(gid_size * sizeof(gid_t));
68:            getgroups(gid_size, gid_list);
69:
70:            for (i = 0; i < gid_size; i++) {
71:                if (!(gp = getgrgid(gid_list[i])))
72:                    die("Group does not exist");
73:                printf("%s%d(%s)", (i == 0) ? " groups=" : ",",
74:                                    gp->gr_gid, gp->gr_name);
75:            }
76:
77:            free(gid_list);
78:        }
79:    } else {
80:        /* get list of groups from group database */
81:        i = 0;
82:        while (gp = getgrent()) {
83:            char *c = *(gp->gr_mem);
84:
85:            while (c && *c) {
86:                if (!strncmp(c, pw->pw_name, 16)) {
```

```
 87:                     printf("%s%d(%s)", (i++ == 0) ? " groups=" : ",",
 88:                                     gp->gr_gid, gp->gr_name);
 89:                 c = NULL;
 90:             } else {
 91:                 c++;
 92:             }
 93:         }
 94:     }
 95:     endgrent();
 96:  }
 97:
 98:  printf("\n");
 99:  exit(0);
100: }
101:
```

The argument-handling code that starts on line 28 calls a few important functions.  When called with no command-line arguments, id looks up information based on what user ran it and reports on that.  getuid() is documented in Chapter 9; it returns the user ID of the process that calls it. getpwuid() then looks up the password file entry for that user ID. If id is given a username as a command-line argument, it instead looks up the entry based on the name that it is given, regardless of the ID of the user that runs it.

The id program first prints the user's numeric ID and name. The password file includes the name of the user's primary group.  If that group exists in the group file, id prints its number and name.

Chapter 9 documents all the different forms of IDs that the kernel uses. id needs to use geteuid() and getegid() to check the effective uid and gid and print them if they differ from the real uid and gid. Again, we look up password and group structures by numeric ID.

Finally, id needs to print out all the supplementary groups.  This is a little tricky because there are two ways to determine the list of supplementary groups.  If a user is running id with no arguments, then id will use the getgroups() function to determine what groups the user is a member of. Otherwise, it will get a list of groups out of the group database.

Using getgroups() is preferable because it lists the groups that the current process belongs to rather than the groups that the user would belong to if he logged in at that moment. That is, if the user has already logged in and been assigned a set of supplementary groups and then the group database is changed, getgroups() will get the set of groups that apply to that login process; examining the group database will get the set of groups that will be applied to the user's *next* login session.

As documented in Chapter 9, the getgroups() function has an unusual (but convenient) usage: Call it once with 0 size and an ignored pointer (which can, as here, be NULL) and it returns the number of data items it wants to return. So then id allocates the exact right size list and calls getgroups() again, this time with the correct size and a list capable of holding the information it wants.

Next, id iterates over the list, getting the entries it wants from the group database. Note that this is different from using the group database to get the list of groups to which a user belongs. In this case, id is using the group database only to map group numbers to group names. A more efficient interface would use getgrent() to iterate over the group database and look up entries in the list, rather than the other way around; that is left as an easy exercise. Remember to use endgrent() when you are done. Not doing so will leave a file handle open, and may cause later code to fail if that code assumes (reasonably enough) that getgrent() starts with the first entry.

Note that there is no guarantee that the entries in the list returned by getgroups() will be sorted in the same order that they appear in the group database, although it is often the case that they are.

If the user provided a username as a command-line argument, id needs to iterate over the group file, looking for groups in which the provided username is specified. Remember to call endgrent() to clean up after yourself!

# 26.2 Modifying the System Databases

The C library provides two functions for modifying the system databases, one for each database. However, they generally work only on systems that use the standard files and often damage systems that use alternate databases; the interfaces were not coded with the new systems in mind. Some systems, particularly ones that are part of networks, use multiple databases, with some users in some databases and other users in other databases. The current C library interface is fine for looking up users, but for modifying user information, it has a tendency to put all the modified entries in one particular database rather than in the database in which they were originally found.

Recently, two interfaces have been written to deal with this problem. Two types of information have traditionally been stored in the system databases: information about users and authentication information. Many current systems separate the two types of information in some way. The interfaces here are not included with some older Linux distributions as of this writing. They are, however, freely redistributable, so you can require them for any application you write.

## 26.2.1 Pluggable Authentication Modules

Pluggable Authentication Modules, or PAM, is a specification and library specifically for configuring authentication on a system. The library provides a standard and relatively simple interface for changing authentication information (such as a user's password), as well as for doing authentication itself. The Linux-PAM implementation[1] includes full documentation on how to program to the PAM interface.

PAM is a standard interface that is being implemented on nearly all versions of Unix and is already available on several. It is a portable interface, so we recommend that you authenticate users using PAM. If you need to port code written to the PAM standard to an operating system that does not support PAM, the port will be trivial. However, because PAM is a somewhat rigid standard, it can be less easy to port applications that do not support PAM to a system that does use PAM.

---

1. http://www.kernel.org/pub/linux/libs/pam/index.html

## 26.2.2 Password Database Library

Although PAM nicely handles authentication information, it is not designed to handle any other form of user information. For that, the pwdb[2] library was designed. In particular, it remembers whence it retrieved user information and updates user information in the correct database. pwdb was designed and written by members of the team that implemented Linux-PAM to solve problems that PAM was not designed to solve but that kept surfacing. Like Linux-PAM, the pwdb distribution includes programming information.

---

2. http://www.redhat.com/linux-info/pwdb/

# Appendices

# Direct Access to I/O Ports

Low-level programmers often need to talk directly to the hardware. Linux provides application programmers with minimal but useful access to hardware.

As a general rule, application-level (or even system-level) programs ought not to directly manipulate hardware on a Linux system. The relatively consistent abstract interface that the kernel provides to application and system programmers should not be abandoned lightly. Before you abandon it, you want to consider what it would take to write your code in a way that maintains the abstraction, generally by creating a device driver, a part of the kernel. Several resources are available that cover Linux kernel programming, including *Linux Kernel Internals* [Beck, 1996] and the *Linux Kernel Hackers' Guide*.[1]

That disclaimer made, it is not very difficult to access I/O ports from a user-level program. There are two completely different ways to access the ports, and each has its advantages.

## A.1 Almost Portable I/O Port Access

The first (and slower) way to do I/O port access preserves some of the kernel/user abstraction. The /dev/port device can easily be used to do some I/O port access. For instance, if you have a device attached to a parallel port and that device does not talk over the parallel port in the

---

1. http://www.redhat.com:8080/

same way as a parallel printer, the easiest way to control it might be a simple program that writes to /dev/port. Consider a mythical garage door opener remote control[2] that is activated by an approximately one-second strobe on the parallel port served by the /dev/lp1 device. The following **shell script**, run as root, would do the trick.

```
#!/bin/sh
# toggle-garage-door - activates garage door remote control
# 890 is the decimal address of /dev/lp1's control port
# (0x378 + 2)
echo -e '\001' | dd of=/dev/port bs=1 count=1 skip=890
sleep 1
echo -e '\000' | dd of=/dev/port bs=1 count=1 skip=890
```

That code sets bit 1 of the control port. One second later, it resets it.[3] It is equivalent to the following C code, which you may find more comprehensible even though it is longer:

```
#include <sys/types.h>
#include <sys/stat.h>
#include <fcntl.h>
#include <unistd.h>

int main(void) {
  unsigned char command;
  int fd;

  fd = open("/dev/port", O_WRONLY, 0);

  command = 0x01;
  lseek(fd, 0x378 + 2, SEEK_SET);
  write(fd, &command, 1);

  sleep(1);

  command = 0x00;
```

---

2. If you have a garage door opener remote control hooked up to your computer, you are braver than either of the authors.

3. We do not recommend writing device drivers as shell scripts. We just wish to point out that device drivers are not necessarily magic, incomprehensible kernel code. The source code for device drivers in the kernel is much more readable than that shell script.

```
lseek(fd, 0x378 + 2, SEEK_SET);
write(fd, &command, 1);

return 0;
}
```

# A.2   Direct I/O Port Access

It is possible to execute I/O instructions from user-mode programs. However, by default, doing so will cause a segmentation fault. You must first enable I/O port access; then you can execute I/O instructions.[4] What you would like to do is something more like this:

```
#define control(port) (port + 2)
#define LP_PSTROBE 0x01
...
outb(LP_PSTROBE, control(0x378));
sleep(1);
outb(0, control(0x378));
```

But you need to get permission to call `outb()`. There are two ways to get that permission: `ioperm()` and `iopl()`.

## A.2.1  The Safe Way

A program running with superuser privileges can separately enable and disable access to each I/O port in the range 0–0x3ff. For example, to allow access to the three ports starting with 0x378 (the ports used to access /dev/lp1), use

```
ioperm(0x378, 3, 1);
```

If you need to access only port 0x37a, you can instead use

```
ioperm(0x37a, 1, 1);
```

---

4. Yes, this description is rather Intel-specific. However, other Linux platforms, even those with CPUs that do not have I/O instructions, provide the same functions.

The `ioperm()` function is used to allow and deny access to ports between 0 and 0x3ff.[5] It takes three arguments:

- The first port of the range

- The number of ports in the range

- 1 to allow access to ports in that range; 0 to deny access

`ioperm()` returns 0 on success and -1 on error.

## A.2.2 The Dangerous Way

A program running with superuser privileges can enable *all* I/O port access at once with a single call:

```
iopl(3);
```

This moves the process into "I/O protection level 3," which does two things: It allows the process all access to the I/O bus, and it allows the process to disable and enable interrupts with `cli()` and `sti()`, respectively. If you do use `iopl()`, make sure that you never call `cli()`—doing so will crash symmetric multi-processing (SMP) systems.[6] In general, use `ioperm()` if possible, and use `iopl()` only if you need to access ports higher than 0x3ff.

---

5. The upper limit is 0x3ff because on Linux/i386, access rights for the first 0x400 ports are stored in the task structure. Storing access rights for all the ports in each task structure would use a disproportionately large amount of memory (8KB per process), and most ports that can be usefully accessed from user-level programs are low ones.

6. Do not call `sti()`, either—but it probably will not hurt anything.

# ladsh *Source Code*

```
 1: /* ladsh4.c -- job control */
 2:
 3: #include <ctype.h>
 4: #include <errno.h>
 5: #include <fcntl.h>
 6: #include <glob.h>
 7: #include <signal.h>
 8: #include <stdio.h>
 9: #include <stdlib.h>
10: #include <string.h>
11: #include <sys/ioctl.h>
12: #include <sys/wait.h>
13: #include <unistd.h>
14:
15: #define MAX_COMMAND_LEN 250       /* max length of a single command
16:                                      string */
17: #define JOB_STATUS_FORMAT "[%d] %-22s %.40s\n"
18:
19: enum redirectionType { REDIRECT_INPUT, REDIRECT_OVERWRITE, REDIRECT_APPEND };
20:
21: struct jobSet {
22:     struct job * head;        /* head of list of running jobs */
23:     struct job * fg;          /* current foreground job */
24: };
25:
26: struct redirectionSpecifier {
27:     enum redirectionType type;  /* type of redirection */
28:     int fd;                   /* file descriptor being redirected */
29:     char * filename;          /* file to redirect fd to */
30: };
31:
32: struct childProgram {
```

```
33:      pid_t pid;              /* 0 if exited */
34:      char ** argv;           /* program name and arguments */
35:      int numRedirections;    /* elements in redirection array */
36:      struct redirectionSpecifier * redirections;  /* I/O redirections */
37:      glob_t globResult;      /* result of parameter globbing */
38:      int freeGlob;           /* should we globfree(&globResult)? */
39:      int isStopped;          /* is the program currently running? */
40: };
41:
42: struct job {
43:      int jobId;              /* job number */
44:      int numProgs;           /* total number of programs in job */
45:      int runningProgs;       /* number of programs running */
46:      char * text;            /* name of job */
47:      char * cmdBuf;          /* buffer various argv's point into */
48:      pid_t pgrp;             /* process group ID for the job */
49:      struct childProgram * progs; /* array of programs in job */
50:      struct job * next;      /* to track background commands */
51:      int stoppedProgs;       /* number of programs alive, but stopped */
52: };
53:
54: void freeJob(struct job * cmd) {
55:      int i;
56:
57:      for (i = 0; i < cmd->numProgs; i++) {
58:          free(cmd->progs[i].argv);
59:          if (cmd->progs[i].redirections) free(cmd->progs[i].redirections);
60:          globfree(&cmd->progs[i].globResult);
61:      }
62:      free(cmd->progs);
63:      if (cmd->text) free(cmd->text);
64:      free(cmd->cmdBuf);
65: }
66:
67: int getCommand(FILE * source, char * command) {
68:      if (source == stdin) {
69:          printf("# ");
70:          fflush(stdout);
71:      }
72:
73:      if (!fgets(command, MAX_COMMAND_LEN, source)) {
```

```
 74:          if (source == stdin) printf("\n");
 75:          return 1;
 76:      }
 77:
 78:      /* remove trailing newline */
 79:      command[strlen(command) - 1] = '\0';
 80:
 81:      return 0;
 82: }
 83:
 84: void globLastArgument(struct childProgram * prog, int * argcPtr,
 85:                          int * argcAllocedPtr) {
 86:      int argc = *argcPtr;
 87:      int argcAlloced = *argcAllocedPtr;
 88:      int rc;
 89:      int flags;
 90:      int i;
 91:      char * src, * dst;
 92:
 93:      if (argc > 1) {             /* cmd->globResult is already initialized */
 94:          flags = GLOB_APPEND;
 95:          i = prog->globResult.gl_pathc;
 96:      } else {
 97:          prog->freeGlob = 1;
 98:          flags = 0;
 99:          i = 0;
100:      }
101:
102:      rc = glob(prog->argv[argc - 1], flags, NULL, &prog->globResult);
103:      if (rc == GLOB_NOSPACE) {
104:          fprintf(stderr, "out of space during glob operation\n");
105:          return;
106:      } else if (rc == GLOB_NOMATCH ||
107:                  (!rc && (prog->globResult.gl_pathc - i) == 1 &&
108:                  !strcmp(prog->argv[argc - 1],
109:                      prog->globResult.gl_pathv[i]))) {
110:          /* we need to remove whatever \ quoting is still present */
111:          src = dst = prog->argv[argc - 1];
112:          while (*src) {
113:              if (*src != '\\') *dst++ = *src;
114:              src++;
```

```
115:            }
116:            *dst = '\0';
117:        } else if (!rc) {
118:            argcAlloced += (prog->globResult.gl_pathc - i);
119:            prog->argv = realloc(prog->argv, argcAlloced * sizeof(*prog->argv));
120:            memcpy(prog->argv + (argc - 1), prog->globResult.gl_pathv + i,
121:                    sizeof(*(prog->argv)) * (prog->globResult.gl_pathc - i));
122:            argc += (prog->globResult.gl_pathc - i - 1);
123:        }
124:
125:    *argcAllocedPtr = argcAlloced;
126:    *argcPtr = argc;
127: }
128:
129: /* Return cmd->numProgs as 0 if no command is present (e.g. an empty
130:    line). If a valid command is found, commandPtr is set to point to
131:    the beginning of the next command (if the original command had more
132:    then one job associated with it) or NULL if no more commands are
133:    present. */
134: int parseCommand(char ** commandPtr, struct job * job, int * isBg) {
135:    char * command;
136:    char * returnCommand = NULL;
137:    char * src, * buf, * chptr;
138:    int argc = 0;
139:    int done = 0;
140:    int argvAlloced;
141:    int i;
142:    char quote = '\0';
143:    int count;
144:    struct childProgram * prog;
145:
146:    /* skip leading white space */
147:    while (**commandPtr && isspace(**commandPtr)) (*commandPtr)++;
148:
149:    /* this handles empty lines */
150:    if (!**commandPtr) {
151:        job->numProgs = 0;
152:        *commandPtr = NULL;
153:        return 0;
154:    }
155:
```

```
156:        *isBg = 0;
157:        job->numProgs = 1;
158:        job->progs = malloc(sizeof(*job->progs));
159:
160:        /* We set the argv elements to point inside of this string. The
161:           memory is freed by freeJob().
162:
163:           Getting clean memory relieves us of the task of NULL
164:           terminating things and makes the rest of this look a bit
165:           cleaner (though it is, admittedly, a tad less efficient) */
166:        job->cmdBuf = command = calloc(1, strlen(*commandPtr) + 1);
167:        job->text = NULL;
168:
169:        prog = job->progs;
170:        prog->numRedirections = 0;
171:        prog->redirections = NULL;
172:        prog->freeGlob = 0;
173:        prog->isStopped = 0;
174:
175:        argvAlloced = 5;
176:        prog->argv = malloc(sizeof(*prog->argv) * argvAlloced);
177:        prog->argv[0] = job->cmdBuf;
178:
179:        buf = command;
180:        src = *commandPtr;
181:        while (*src && !done) {
182:            if (quote == *src) {
183:                quote = '\0';
184:            } else if (quote) {
185:                if (*src == '\\') {
186:                    src++;
187:                    if (!*src) {
188:                        fprintf(stderr, "character expected after \\\n");
189:                        freeJob(job);
190:                        return 1;
191:                    }
192:
193:                    /* in shell, "\'" should yield \' */
194:                    if (*src != quote) *buf++ = '\\';
195:                } else if (*src == '*' || *src == '?' || *src == '[' ||
196:                        *src == ']')
```

```
197:                        *buf++ = '\\';
198:                    *buf++ = *src;
199:                } else if (isspace(*src)) {
200:                    if (*prog->argv[argc]) {
201:                        buf++, argc++;
202:                        /* +1 here leaves room for the NULL which ends argv */
203:                        if ((argc + 1) == argvAlloced) {
204:                            argvAlloced += 5;
205:                            prog->argv = realloc(prog->argv,
206:                                        sizeof(*prog->argv) * argvAlloced);
207:                        }
208:                        prog->argv[argc] = buf;
209:
210:                        globLastArgument(prog, &argc, &argvAlloced);
211:                    }
212:                } else switch (*src) {
213:                  case '"':
214:                  case '\'':
215:                    quote = *src;
216:                    break;
217:
218:                  case '#':                        /* comment */
219:                    done = 1;
220:                    break;
221:
222:                  case '>':                        /* redirections */
223:                  case '<':
224:                    i = prog->numRedirections++;
225:                    prog->redirections = realloc(prog->redirections,
226:                                sizeof(*prog->redirections) * (i + 1));
227:
228:                    prog->redirections[i].fd = -1;
229:                    if (buf != prog->argv[argc]) {
230:                        /* the stuff before this character may be the file number
231:                            being redirected */
232:                        prog->redirections[i].fd = strtol(prog->argv[argc], &chptr, 10);
233:
234:                        if (*chptr && *prog->argv[argc]) {
235:                            buf++, argc++;
236:                            globLastArgument(prog, &argc, &argvAlloced);
237:                        }
```

```
238:                }
239:
240:                if (prog->redirections[i].fd == -1) {
241:                    if (*src == '>')
242:                        prog->redirections[i].fd = 1;
243:                    else
244:                        prog->redirections[i].fd = 0;
245:                }
246:
247:                if (*src++ == '>') {
248:                    if (*src == '>')
249:                        prog->redirections[i].type = REDIRECT_APPEND, src++;
250:                    else
251:                        prog->redirections[i].type = REDIRECT_OVERWRITE;
252:                } else {
253:                    prog->redirections[i].type = REDIRECT_INPUT;
254:                }
255:
256:                /* This isn't POSIX sh compliant. Oh well. */
257:                chptr = src;
258:                while (isspace(*chptr)) chptr++;
259:
260:                if (!*chptr) {
261:                    fprintf(stderr, "file name expected after %c\n", *src);
262:                    freeJob(job);
263:                    return 1;
264:                }
265:
266:                prog->redirections[i].filename = buf;
267:                while (*chptr && !isspace(*chptr))
268:                    *buf++ = *chptr++;
269:
270:                src = chptr - 1;              /* we src++ later */
271:                prog->argv[argc] = ++buf;
272:                break;
273:
274:            case '|':                        /* pipe */
275:                /* finish this command */
276:                if (*prog->argv[argc]) argc++;
277:                if (!argc) {
278:                    fprintf(stderr, "empty command in pipe\n");
```

```
279:                    freeJob(job);
280:                    return 1;
281:                }
282:            prog->argv[argc] = NULL;
283:
284:            /* and start the next */
285:            job->numProgs++;
286:            job->progs = realloc(job->progs,
287:                            sizeof(*job->progs) * job->numProgs);
288:            prog = job->progs + (job->numProgs - 1);
289:            prog->numRedirections = 0;
290:            prog->redirections = NULL;
291:            prog->freeGlob = 0;
292:            argc = 0;
293:
294:            argvAlloced = 5;
295:            prog->argv = malloc(sizeof(*prog->argv) * argvAlloced);
296:            prog->argv[0] = ++buf;
297:
298:            src++;
299:            while (*src && isspace(*src)) src++;
300:
301:            if (!*src) {
302:                fprintf(stderr, "empty command in pipe\n");
303:                return 1;
304:            }
305:            src--;              /* we'll ++ it at the end of the loop */
306:
307:            break;
308:
309:        case '&':                       /* background */
310:          *isBg = 1;
311:        case ';':                       /* multiple commands */
312:          done = 1;
313:          returnCommand = *commandPtr + (src - *commandPtr) + 1;
314:          break;
315:
316:        case '\\':
317:          src++;
318:          if (!*src) {
319:              freeJob(job);
```

```
320:                         fprintf(stderr, "character expected after \\\n");
321:                         return 1;
322:                     }
323:                 if (*src == '*' || *src == '[' || *src == ']' || *src == '?')
324:                     *buf++ = '\\';
325:                 /* fallthrough */
326:             default:
327:                 *buf++ = *src;
328:             }
329:
330:         src++;
331:     }
332:
333:     if (*prog->argv[argc]) {
334:         argc++;
335:         globLastArgument(prog, &argc, &argvAlloced);
336:     }
337:     if (!argc) {
338:         freeJob(job);
339:         return 0;
340:     }
341:     prog->argv[argc] = NULL;
342:
343:     if (!returnCommand) {
344:         job->text = malloc(strlen(*commandPtr) + 1);
345:         strcpy(job->text, *commandPtr);
346:     } else {
347:         /* This leaves any trailing spaces, which is a bit sloppy */
348:
349:         count = returnCommand - *commandPtr;
350:         job->text = malloc(count + 1);
351:         strncpy(job->text, *commandPtr, count);
352:         job->text[count] = '\0';
353:     }
354:
355:     *commandPtr = returnCommand;
356:
357:     return 0;
358: }
359:
360: int setupRedirections(struct childProgram * prog) {
```

```
361:        int i;
362:        int openfd;
363:        int mode;
364:        struct redirectionSpecifier * redir = prog->redirections;
365:
366:        for (i = 0; i < prog->numRedirections; i++, redir++) {
367:            switch (redir->type) {
368:              case REDIRECT_INPUT:
369:                mode = O_RDONLY;
370:                break;
371:              case REDIRECT_OVERWRITE:
372:                mode = O_RDWR | O_CREAT | O_TRUNC;
373:                break;
374:              case REDIRECT_APPEND:
375:                mode = O_RDWR | O_CREAT | O_APPEND;
376:                break;
377:            }
378:
379:            openfd = open(redir->filename, mode, 0666);
380:            if (openfd < 0) {
381:                /* this could get lost if stderr has been redirected, but
382:                   bash and ash both lose it as well (though zsh doesn't!) */
383:                fprintf(stderr, "error opening %s: %s\n", redir->filename,
384:                            strerror(errno));
385:                return 1;
386:            }
387:
388:            if (openfd != redir->fd) {
389:                dup2(openfd, redir->fd);
390:                close(openfd);
391:            }
392:        }
393:
394:        return 0;
395: }
396:
397: int runCommand(struct job newJob, struct jobSet * jobList,
398:                int inBg) {
399:        struct job * job;
400:        char * newdir, * buf;
401:        int i, len;
```

```
402:     int nextin, nextout;
403:     int pipefds[2];              /* pipefd[0] is for reading */
404:     char * statusString;
405:     int jobNum;
406:
407:     /* handle built-ins here -- we don't fork() so we can't background
408:        these very easily */
409:     if (!strcmp(newJob.progs[0].argv[0], "exit")) {
410:         /* this should return a real exit code */
411:         exit(0);
412:     } else if (!strcmp(newJob.progs[0].argv[0], "pwd")) {
413:         len = 50;
414:         buf = malloc(len);
415:         while (!getcwd(buf, len)) {
416:             len += 50;
417:             buf = realloc(buf, len);
418:         }
419:         printf("%s\n", buf);
420:         free(buf);
421:         return 0;
422:     } else if (!strcmp(newJob.progs[0].argv[0], "cd")) {
423:         if (!newJob.progs[0].argv[1] == 1)
424:             newdir = getenv("HOME");
425:         else
426:             newdir = newJob.progs[0].argv[1];
427:         if (chdir(newdir))
428:             printf("failed to change current directory: %s\n",
429:                     strerror(errno));
430:         return 0;
431:     } else if (!strcmp(newJob.progs[0].argv[0], "jobs")) {
432:         for (job = jobList->head; job; job = job->next) {
433:             if (job->runningProgs == job->stoppedProgs)
434:                 statusString = "Stopped";
435:             else
436:                 statusString = "Running";
437:
438:             printf(JOB_STATUS_FORMAT, job->jobId, statusString,
439:                     job->text);
440:         }
441:         return 0;
442:     } else if (!strcmp(newJob.progs[0].argv[0], "fg") ||
```

```
443:                      !strcmp(newJob.progs[0].argv[0], "bg")) {
444:          if (!newJob.progs[0].argv[1] || newJob.progs[0].argv[2]) {
445:              fprintf(stderr, "%s: exactly one argument is expected\n",
446:                      newJob.progs[0].argv[0]);
447:              return 1;
448:          }
449:
450:          if (sscanf(newJob.progs[0].argv[1], "%%%d", &jobNum) != 1) {
451:              fprintf(stderr, "%s: bad argument '%s'\n",
452:                      newJob.progs[0].argv[0], newJob.progs[0].argv[1]);
453:              return 1;
454:          }
455:
456:          for (job = jobList->head; job; job = job->next)
457:              if (job->jobId == jobNum) break;
458:
459:          if (!job) {
460:              fprintf(stderr, "%s: unknown job %d\n",
461:                      newJob.progs[0].argv[0], jobNum);
462:              return 1;
463:          }
464:
465:          if (*newJob.progs[0].argv[0] == 'f') {
466:              /* Make this job the foreground job */
467:
468:              if (tcsetpgrp(0, job->pgrp))
469:                  perror("tcsetpgrp");
470:              jobList->fg = job;
471:          }
472:
473:          /* Restart the processes in the job */
474:          for (i = 0; i < job->numProgs; i++)
475:              job->progs[i].isStopped = 0;
476:
477:          kill(-job->pgrp, SIGCONT);
478:
479:          job->stoppedProgs = 0;
480:
481:          return 0;
482:      }
483:
```

```
484:    nextin = 0, nextout = 1;
485:    for (i = 0; i < newJob.numProgs; i++) {
486:        if ((i + 1) < newJob.numProgs) {
487:            pipe(pipefds);
488:            nextout = pipefds[1];
489:        } else {
490:            nextout = 1;
491:        }
492:
493:        if (!(newJob.progs[i].pid = fork())) {
494:            signal(SIGTTOU, SIG_DFL);
495:
496:            if (nextin != 0) {
497:                dup2(nextin, 0);
498:                close(nextin);
499:            }
500:
501:            if (nextout != 1) {
502:                dup2(nextout, 1);
503:                close(nextout);
504:            }
505:
506:            /* explicit redirections override pipes */
507:            setupRedirections(newJob.progs + i);
508:
509:            execvp(newJob.progs[i].argv[0], newJob.progs[i].argv);
510:            fprintf(stderr, "exec() of %s failed: %s\n",
511:                    newJob.progs[i].argv[0],
512:                    strerror(errno));
513:            exit(1);
514:        }
515:
516:        /* put our child in the process group whose leader is the
517:           first process in this pipe */
518:        setpgid(newJob.progs[i].pid, newJob.progs[0].pid);
519:
520:        if (nextin != 0) close(nextin);
521:        if (nextout != 1) close(nextout);
522:
523:        /* If there isn't another process, nextin is garbage
524:           but it doesn't matter */
```

```
525:            nextin = pipefds[0];
526:        }
527:
528:    newJob.pgrp = newJob.progs[0].pid;
529:
530:    /* find the ID for the job to use */
531:    newJob.jobId = 1;
532:    for (job = jobList->head; job; job = job->next)
533:        if (job->jobId >= newJob.jobId)
534:            newJob.jobId = job->jobId + 1;
535:
536:    /* add the job to the list of running jobs */
537:    if (!jobList->head) {
538:        job = jobList->head = malloc(sizeof(*job));
539:    } else {
540:        for (job = jobList->head; job->next; job = job->next);
541:        job->next = malloc(sizeof(*job));
542:        job = job->next;
543:    }
544:
545:    *job = newJob;
546:    job->next = NULL;
547:    job->runningProgs = job->numProgs;
548:    job->stoppedProgs = 0;
549:
550:    if (inBg) {
551:        /* we don't wait for background jobs to return -- append it
552:            to the list of backgrounded jobs and leave it alone */
553:
554:        printf("[%d] %d\n", job->jobId,
555:                newJob.progs[newJob.numProgs - 1].pid);
556:    } else {
557:        jobList->fg = job;
558:
559:        /* move the new process group into the foreground */
560:
561:        if (tcsetpgrp(0, newJob.pgrp))
562:            perror("tcsetpgrp");
563:    }
564:
565:    return 0;
```

```
566: }
567:
568: void removeJob(struct jobSet * jobList, struct job * job) {
569:     struct job * prevJob;
570:
571:     freeJob(job);
572:     if (job == jobList->head) {
573:         jobList->head = job->next;
574:     } else {
575:         prevJob = jobList->head;
576:         while (prevJob->next != job) prevJob = prevJob->next;
577:         prevJob->next = job->next;
578:     }
579:
580:     free(job);
581: }
582:
583: /* Checks to see if any background processes have exited -- if they
584:    have, figure out why and see if a job has completed */
585: void checkJobs(struct jobSet * jobList) {
586:     struct job * job;
587:     pid_t childpid;
588:     int status;
589:     int progNum;
590:
591:     while ((childpid = waitpid(-1, &status, WNOHANG | WUNTRACED)) > 0) {
592:         for (job = jobList->head; job; job = job->next) {
593:             progNum = 0;
594:             while (progNum < job->numProgs &&
595:                         job->progs[progNum].pid != childpid)
596:                 progNum++;
597:             if (progNum < job->numProgs) break;
598:         }
599:
600:         if (WIFEXITED(status) || WIFSIGNALED(status)) {
601:             /* child exited */
602:             job->runningProgs--;
603:             job->progs[progNum].pid = 0;
604:
605:             if (!job->runningProgs) {
606:                 printf(JOB_STATUS_FORMAT, job->jobId, "Done", job->text);
```

```
607:                    removeJob(jobList, job);
608:                }
609:            } else {
610:                /* child stopped */
611:                job->stoppedProgs++;
612:                job->progs[progNum].isStopped = 1;
613:
614:                if (job->stoppedProgs == job->numProgs) {
615:                    printf(JOB_STATUS_FORMAT, job->jobId, "Stopped", job->text);
616:                }
617:            }
618:        }
619:
620:    if (childpid == -1 && errno != ECHILD)
621:        perror("waitpid");
622: }
623:
624: int main(int argc, char ** argv) {
625:     char command[MAX_COMMAND_LEN + 1];
626:     char * nextCommand = NULL;
627:     struct jobSet jobList = { NULL, NULL };
628:     struct job newJob;
629:     FILE * input = stdin;
630:     int i;
631:     int status;
632:     int inBg;
633:
634:     if (argc > 2) {
635:         fprintf(stderr, "unexpected arguments; usage: ladsh1 "
636:                         "<commands>\n");
637:         exit(1);
638:     } else if (argc == 2) {
639:         input = fopen(argv[1], "r");
640:         if (!input) {
641:             perror("fopen");
642:             exit(1);
643:         }
644:     }
645:
646:     /* don't pay any attention to this signal; it just confuses
647:        things and isn't really meant for shells anyway */
```

```
648:        signal(SIGTTOU, SIG_IGN);
649:
650:        while (1) {
651:            if (!jobList.fg) {
652:                /* no job is in the foreground */
653:
654:                /* see if any background processes have exited */
655:                checkJobs(&jobList);
656:
657:                if (!nextCommand) {
658:                    if (getCommand(input, command)) break;
659:                    nextCommand = command;
660:                }
661:
662:                if (!parseCommand(&nextCommand, &newJob, &inBg) &&
663:                                    newJob.numProgs) {
664:                    runCommand(newJob, &jobList, inBg);
665:                }
666:            } else {
667:                /* a job is running in the foreground; wait for it */
668:                i = 0;
669:                while (!jobList.fg->progs[i].pid ||
670:                        jobList.fg->progs[i].isStopped) i++;
671:
672:                waitpid(jobList.fg->progs[i].pid, &status, WUNTRACED);
673:
674:                if (WIFEXITED(status) || WIFSIGNALED(status)) {
675:                    /* the child exited */
676:                    jobList.fg->runningProgs--;
677:                    jobList.fg->progs[i].pid = 0;
678:
679:                    if (!jobList.fg->runningProgs) {
680:                        /* child exited */
681:
682:                        removeJob(&jobList, jobList.fg);
683:                        jobList.fg = NULL;
684:
685:                        /* move the shell to the foreground */
686:                        if (tcsetpgrp(0, getpid()))
687:                            perror("tcsetpgrp");
688:                    }
```

```
689:                  } else {
690:                      /* the child was stopped */
691:                      jobList.fg->stoppedProgs++;
692:                      jobList.fg->progs[i].isStopped = 1;
693:
694:                      if (jobList.fg->stoppedProgs == jobList.fg->runningProgs) {
695:                          printf("\n" JOB_STATUS_FORMAT, jobList.fg->jobId,
696:                                  "Stopped", jobList.fg->text);
697:                          jobList.fg = NULL;
698:                      }
699:                  }
700:
701:              if (!jobList.fg) {
702:                  /* move the shell to the foreground */
703:                  if (tcsetpgrp(0, getpid()))
704:                      perror("tcsetpgrp");
705:              }
706:          }
707:      }
708:
709:      return 0;
710: }
```

# *The GNU Licenses*

## C.1   The GNU General Public License

GNU GENERAL PUBLIC LICENSE
Version 2, June 1991

Copyright © 1989, 1991   Free Software Foundation, Inc.
675 Mass Ave, Cambridge, MA 02139, USA

Everyone is permitted to copy and distribute verbatim copies of this license document, but changing it is not allowed.

Preamble

The licenses for most software are designed to take away your freedom to share and change it. By contrast, the GNU General Public License is intended to guarantee your freedom to share and change free software—to make sure the software is free for all its users. This General Public License applies to most of the Free Software Foundation's software and to any other program whose authors commit to using it. (Some other Free Software Foundation software is covered by the GNU Library General Public License instead.) You can apply it to your programs, too.

When we speak of free software, we are referring to freedom, not price. Our General Public Licenses are designed to make sure that you have the freedom to distribute copies of free software (and charge for this service if you wish), that you receive source code or can get it if you want it, that you can change the software or use pieces of it in new free programs; and that you know you can do these things.

To protect your rights, we need to make restrictions that forbid anyone to deny you these rights or to ask you to surrender the rights. These restrictions translate to certain responsibilities for you if you distribute copies of the software, or if you modify it.

For example, if you distribute copies of such a program, whether gratis or for a fee, you must give the recipients all the rights that you have. You must make sure that they, too, receive or can get the source code. And you must show them these terms so they know their rights.

**497**

We protect your rights with two steps: (1) copyright the software, and (2) offer you this license which gives you legal permission to copy, distribute and/or modify the software.

Also, for each author's protection and ours, we want to make certain that everyone understands that there is no warranty for this free software. If the software is modified by someone else and passed on, we want its recipients to know that what they have is not the original, so that any problems introduced by others will not reflect on the original authors' reputations.

Finally, any free program is threatened constantly by software patents. We wish to avoid the danger that redistributors of a free program will individually obtain patent licenses, in effect making the program proprietary. To prevent this, we have made it clear that any patent must be licensed for everyone's free use or not licensed at all.

The precise terms and conditions for copying, distribution and modification follow.

GNU GENERAL PUBLIC LICENSE
TERMS AND CONDITIONS FOR COPYING,
DISTRIBUTION AND MODIFICATION

0. This License applies to any program or other work which contains a notice placed by the copyright holder saying it may be distributed under the terms of this General Public License. The "Program", below, refers to any such program or work, and a "work based on the Program" means either the Program or any derivative work under copyright law: that is to say, a work containing the Program or a portion of it, either verbatim or with modifications and/or translated into another language. (Hereinafter, translation is included without limitation in the term "modification".) Each licensee is addressed as "you".

Activities other than copying, distribution and modification are not covered by this License; they are outside its scope. The act of running the Program is not restricted, and the output from the Program is covered only if its contents constitute a work based on the Program (independent of having been made by running the Program). Whether that is true depends on what the Program does.

1. You may copy and distribute verbatim copies of the Program's source code as you receive it, in any medium, provided that you conspicuously and appropriately publish on each copy an appropriate copyright notice and disclaimer of warranty; keep intact all the notices that refer to this License and to the absence of any warranty; and give any other recipients of the Program a copy of this License along with the Program.

You may charge a fee for the physical act of transferring a copy, and you may at your option offer warranty protection in exchange for a fee.

2. You may modify your copy or copies of the Program or any portion of it, thus forming a work based on the Program, and copy and distribute such modifications or work under the terms of Section 1 above, provided that you also meet all of these conditions:

   a) You must cause the modified files to carry prominent notices stating that you changed the files and the date of any change.

   b) You must cause any work that you distribute or publish, that in whole or in part contains or is derived from the Program or any part thereof, to be licensed as a whole at no charge to all third parties under the terms of this License.

   c) If the modified program normally reads commands interactively when run, you must cause it, when started running for such interactive use in the most ordinary way, to print or display an announcement including an appropriate copyright notice and a notice that there is no warranty (or else, saying that you provide a warranty) and that users may redistribute the program under these conditions, and telling the user how to view a copy of this License. (Exception: if the Program itself is interactive but does not normally print such an announcement, your work based on the Program is not required to print an announcement.)

These requirements apply to the modified work as a whole. If identifiable sections of that work are not derived from the Program, and can be reasonably considered independent and separate works in themselves, then this License, and its terms, do not apply to those sections when you distribute them as separate works. But when you distribute the same sections as part of a whole which is a work based on the Program, the distribution of the whole must be on the terms of this License, whose permissions for other licensees extend to the entire whole, and thus to each and every part regardless of who wrote it.

Thus, it is not the intent of this section to claim rights or contest your rights to work written entirely by you; rather, the intent is to exercise the right to control the distribution of derivative or collective works based on the Program.

In addition, mere aggregation of another work not based on the Program with the Program (or with a work based on the Program) on a volume of a storage or distribution medium does not bring the other work under the scope of this License.

3. You may copy and distribute the Program (or a work based on it, under Section 2) in object code or executable form under the terms of Sections 1 and 2 above provided that you also do one of the following:

a) Accompany it with the complete corresponding machine-readable source code, which must be distributed under the terms of Sections 1 and 2 above on a medium customarily used for software interchange; or,

b) Accompany it with a written offer, valid for at least three years, to give any third party, for a charge no more than your cost of physically performing source distribution, a complete machine-readable copy of the corresponding source code, to be distributed under the terms of Sections 1 and 2 above on a medium customarily used for software interchange; or,

c) Accompany it with the information you received as to the offer to distribute corresponding source code. (This alternative is allowed only for noncommercial distribution and only if you received the program in object code or executable form with such an offer, in accord with Subsection b above.)

The source code for a work means the preferred form of the work for making modifications to it. For an executable work, complete source code means all the source code for all modules it contains, plus any associated interface definition files, plus the scripts used to control compilation and installation of the executable.

However, as a special exception, the source code distributed need not include anything that is normally distributed (in either source or binary form) with the major components (compiler, kernel, and so on) of the operating system on which the executable runs, unless that component itself accompanies the executable.

If distribution of executable or object code is made by offering access to copy from a designated place, then offering equivalent access to copy the source code from the same place counts as distribution of the source code, even though third parties are not compelled to copy the source along with the object code.

4.  You may not copy, modify, sublicense, or distribute the Program except as expressly provided under this License.  Any attempt otherwise to copy, modify, sublicense or distribute the Program is void, and will automatically terminate your rights under this License.  However, parties who have received copies, or rights, from you under this License will not have their licenses terminated so long as such parties remain in full compliance.

5.  You are not required to accept this License, since you have not signed it. However, nothing else grants you permission to modify or distribute the Program or its derivative works.  These actions are prohibited by law if you do not accept this License. Therefore, by modifying or distributing the Program (or any work based on the Program), you indicate your acceptance of this License to do so, and all its terms and conditions for copying, distributing or modifying the Program or works based on it.

6.  Each time you redistribute the Program (or any work based on the Program), the recipient automatically receives a license from the original licensor to copy, distribute or modify the Program subject to these terms and conditions.  You may not impose any further restrictions on the recipients' exercise of the rights granted herein.  You are not responsible for enforcing compliance by third parties to this License.

7.  If, as a consequence of a court judgment or allegation of patent infringement or for any other reason (not limited to patent issues), conditions are imposed on you (whether by court order, agreement or otherwise) that contradict the conditions of this License, they do not excuse you from the conditions of this License.  If you cannot distribute so as to satisfy simultaneously your obligations under this License and any other pertinent obligations, then as a consequence you may not distribute the Program at all.  For example, if a patent license would not permit royalty-free redistribution of the Program by all those who receive copies directly or indirectly through you, then the only way you could satisfy both it and this License would be to refrain entirely from distribution of the Program.

If any portion of this section is held invalid or unenforceable under any particular circumstance, the balance of the section is intended to apply and the section as a whole is intended to apply in other circumstances.

It is not the purpose of this section to induce you to infringe any patents or other property right claims or to contest validity of any such claims; this section has the sole purpose of protecting the integrity of the free software distribution system, which is implemented by public license practices. Many people have made generous contributions to the wide range of software distributed through that system in reliance on consistent application of that system; it is up to the author/donor to decide if he or she is willing to distribute software through any other system and a licensee cannot impose that choice.

This section is intended to make thoroughly clear what is believed to be a consequence of the rest of this License.

8. If the distribution and/or use of the Program is restricted in certain countries either by patents or by copyrighted interfaces, the original copyright holder who places the Program under this License may add an explicit geographical distribution limitation excluding those countries, so that distribution is permitted only in or among countries not thus excluded. In such case, this License incorporates the limitation as if written in the body of this License.

9. The Free Software Foundation may publish revised and/or new versions of the General Public License from time to time. Such new versions will be similar in spirit to the present version, but may differ in detail to address new problems or concerns.

Each version is given a distinguishing version number. If the Program specifies a version number of this License which applies to it and "any later version", you have the option of following the terms and conditions either of that version or of any later version published by the Free Software Foundation. If the Program does not specify a version number of this License, you may choose any version ever published by the Free Software Foundation.

10. If you wish to incorporate parts of the Program into other free programs whose distribution conditions are different, write to the author to ask for permission. For software which is copyrighted by the Free Software Foundation, write to the Free Software Foundation; we sometimes make exceptions for this. Our decision will be guided by the two goals of preserving the free status of all derivatives of our free software and of promoting the sharing and reuse of software generally.

NO WARRANTY

11. BECAUSE THE PROGRAM IS LICENSED FREE OF CHARGE, THERE IS NO WARRANTY FOR THE PROGRAM, TO THE EXTENT PERMITTED BY APPLICABLE LAW. EXCEPT WHEN OTHERWISE STATED IN WRITING THE COPYRIGHT HOLDERS AND/OR OTHER PARTIES PROVIDE THE PROGRAM "AS IS" WITHOUT WARRANTY OF ANY KIND, EITHER EXPRESSED OR IMPLIED, INCLUDING, BUT NOT LIMITED TO, THE IMPLIED WARRANTIES OF MERCHANTABILITY AND FITNESS FOR A PARTICULAR PURPOSE. THE ENTIRE RISK AS TO THE QUALITY AND PERFORMANCE OF THE PROGRAM IS WITH YOU. SHOULD THE PROGRAM PROVE DEFECTIVE, YOU ASSUME THE COST OF ALL NECESSARY SERVICING, REPAIR OR CORRECTION.

12. IN NO EVENT UNLESS REQUIRED BY APPLICABLE LAW OR AGREED TO IN WRITING WILL ANY COPYRIGHT HOLDER, OR ANY OTHER PARTY WHO MAY MODIFY AND/OR REDISTRIBUTE THE PROGRAM AS PERMITTED ABOVE, BE LIABLE TO YOU FOR DAMAGES, INCLUDING ANY GENERAL, SPECIAL, INCIDENTAL OR CONSEQUENTIAL DAMAGES ARISING OUT OF THE USE OR INABILITY TO USE THE PROGRAM (INCLUDING BUT NOT LIMITED TO LOSS OF DATA OR DATA BEING RENDERED INACCURATE OR LOSSES SUSTAINED BY YOU OR THIRD PARTIES OR A FAILURE OF THE PROGRAM TO OPERATE WITH ANY OTHER PROGRAMS), EVEN IF SUCH HOLDER OR OTHER PARTY HAS BEEN ADVISED OF THE POSSIBILITY OF SUCH DAMAGES.

END OF TERMS AND CONDITIONS

Appendix: How to Apply These Terms to Your New Programs

If you develop a new program, and you want it to be of the greatest possible use to the public, the best way to achieve this is to make it free software which everyone can redistribute and change under these terms.

To do so, attach the following notices to the program. It is safest to attach them to the start of each source file to most effectively convey the exclusion of warranty; and each file should have at least the "copyright" line and a pointer to where the full notice is found.

```
<one line to give the program's name and a brief idea of what it does.>
Copyright (C) 19yy  <name of author>

This program is free software; you can redistribute it and/or modify
it under the terms of the GNU General Public License as published by
the Free Software Foundation; either version 2 of the License, or
(at your option) any later version.

This program is distributed in the hope that it will be useful,
but WITHOUT ANY WARRANTY; without even the implied warranty of
MERCHANTABILITY or FITNESS FOR A PARTICULAR PURPOSE.  See the
GNU General Public License for more details.

You should have received a copy of the GNU General Public License
along with this program; if not, write to the Free Software
Foundation, Inc., 675 Mass Ave, Cambridge, MA 02139, USA.
```

Also add information on how to contact you by electronic and paper mail.

If the program is interactive, make it output a short notice like this when it starts in an interactive mode:

```
Gnomovision version 69, Copyright (C) 19yy name of author
Gnomovision comes with ABSOLUTELY NO WARRANTY; for details type 'show w'.
This is free software, and you are welcome to redistribute it
under certain conditions; type 'show c' for details.
```

The hypothetical commands 'show w' and 'show c' should show the appropriate parts of the General Public License. Of course, the commands you use may be called something other than 'show w' and 'show c'; they could even be mouse-clicks or menu items—whatever suits your program.

You should also get your employer (if you work as a programmer) or your school, if any, to sign a "copyright disclaimer" for the program, if necessary. Here is a sample; alter the names:

```
Yoyodyne, Inc., hereby disclaims all copyright interest in the program
'Gnomovision' (which makes passes at compilers) written by James Hacker.

<signature of Ty Coon>, 1 April 1989
Ty Coon, President of Vice
```

This General Public License does not permit incorporating your program into proprietary programs. If your program is a subroutine library, you may consider it more
useful to permit linking proprietary applications with the library. If this is what you
want to do, use the GNU Library General Public License instead of this License.

## C.2  The GNU Library General Public License

GNU LIBRARY GENERAL PUBLIC LICENSE
Version 2, June 1991

Copyright © 1991   Free Software Foundation, Inc.
675 Mass Ave, Cambridge, MA 02139, USA

Everyone is permitted to copy and distribute verbatim copies of this license document, but changing it is not allowed.

[This is the first released version of the library GPL. It is numbered 2 because it goes with version 2 of the ordinary GPL.]

Preamble

The licenses for most software are designed to take away your freedom to share and change it.  By contrast, the GNU General Public Licenses are intended to guarantee your freedom to share and change free software—to make sure the software is free for all its users.

This license, the Library General Public License, applies to some specially designated Free Software Foundation software, and to any other libraries whose authors decide to use it. You can use it for your libraries, too.

When we speak of free software, we are referring to freedom, not price. Our General Public Licenses are designed to make sure that you have the freedom to distribute copies of free software (and charge for this service if you wish), that you receive source code or can get it if you want it, that you can change the software or use pieces of it in new free programs; and that you know you can do these things.

To protect your rights, we need to make restrictions that forbid anyone to deny you these rights or to ask you to surrender the rights. These restrictions translate to certain responsibilities for you if you distribute copies of the library, or if you modify it.

For example, if you distribute copies of the library, whether gratis or for a fee, you must give the recipients all the rights that we gave you. You must make sure that they, too, receive or can get the source code.  If you link a program with the library, you must provide complete object files to the recipients so that they can relink them with the library, after making changes to the library and recompiling it.  And you must show them these terms so they know their rights.

Our method of protecting your rights has two steps:  (1) copyright the library, and (2) offer you this license which gives you legal permission to copy, distribute and/or modify the library.

Also, for each distributor's protection, we want to make certain that everyone understands that there is no warranty for this free library. If the library is modified by someone else and passed on, we want its recipients to know that what they have is not the original version, so that any problems introduced by others will not reflect on the original authors' reputations.

Finally, any free program is threatened constantly by software patents. We wish to avoid the danger that companies distributing free software will individually obtain patent licenses, thus in effect transforming the program into proprietary software. To prevent this, we have made it clear that any patent must be licensed for everyone's free use or not licensed at all.

Most GNU software, including some libraries, is covered by the ordinary GNU General Public License, which was designed for utility programs. This license, the GNU Library General Public License, applies to certain designated libraries. This license is quite different from the ordinary one; be sure to read it in full, and don't assume that anything in it is the same as in the ordinary license.

The reason we have a separate public license for some libraries is that they blur the distinction we usually make between modifying or adding to a program and simply using it. Linking a program with a library, without changing the library, is in some sense simply using the library, and is analogous to running a utility program or application program. However, in a textual and legal sense, the linked executable is a combined work, a derivative of the original library, and the ordinary General Public License treats it as such.

Because of this blurred distinction, using the ordinary General Public License for libraries did not effectively promote software sharing, because most developers did not use the libraries. We concluded that weaker conditions might promote sharing better.

However, unrestricted linking of non-free programs would deprive the users of those programs of all benefit from the free status of the libraries themselves. This Library General Public License is intended to permit developers of non-free programs to use free libraries, while preserving your freedom as a user of such programs to change the free libraries that are incorporated in them. (We have not seen how to achieve this as regards changes in header files, but we have achieved it as regards changes in the actual functions of the Library.) The hope is that this will lead to faster development of free libraries.

The precise terms and conditions for copying, distribution and modification follow. Pay close attention to the difference between a "work based on the library" and a "work that uses the library". The former contains code derived from the library, while the latter only works together with the library.

Note that it is possible for a library to be covered by the ordinary General Public License rather than by this special one.

GNU LIBRARY GENERAL PUBLIC LICENSE
TERMS AND CONDITIONS FOR COPYING,
DISTRIBUTION AND MODIFICATION

0.  This License Agreement applies to any software library which contains a notice placed by the copyright holder or other authorized party saying it may be distributed under the terms of this Library General Public License (also called "this License"). Each licensee is addressed as "you".

A "library" means a collection of software functions and/or data prepared so as to be conveniently linked with application programs (which use some of those functions and data) to form executables.

The "Library", below, refers to any such software library or work which has been distributed under these terms. A "work based on the Library" means either the Library or any derivative work under copyright law: that is to say, a work containing the Library or a portion of it, either verbatim or with modifications and/or translated straightforwardly into another language. (Hereinafter, translation is included without limitation in the term "modification".)

"Source code" for a work means the preferred form of the work for making modifications to it. For a library, complete source code means all the source code for all modules it contains, plus any associated interface definition files, plus the scripts used to control compilation and installation of the library.

Activities other than copying, distribution and modification are not covered by this License; they are outside its scope. The act of running a program using the Library is not restricted, and output from such a program is covered only if its contents constitute a work based on the Library (independent of the use of the Library in a tool for writing it). Whether that is true depends on what the Library does and what the program that uses the Library does.

1.  You may copy and distribute verbatim copies of the Library's complete source code as you receive it, in any medium, provided that you conspicuously and appropriately publish on each copy an appropriate copyright notice and disclaimer of warranty; keep intact all the notices that refer to this License and to the absence of any warranty; and distribute a copy of this License along with the Library.

You may charge a fee for the physical act of transferring a copy, and you may at your option offer warranty protection in exchange for a fee.

2.  You may modify your copy or copies of the Library or any portion of it, thus forming a work based on the Library, and copy and distribute such modifications or work under the terms of Section 1 above, provided that you also meet all of these conditions:

a)   The modified work must itself be a software library.

b)   You must cause the files modified to carry prominent notices stating that you changed the files and the date of any change.

c)   You must cause the whole of the work to be licensed at no charge to all third parties under the terms of this License.

d)   If a facility in the modified Library refers to a function or a table of data to be supplied by an application program that uses the facility, other than as an argument passed when the facility is invoked, then you must make a good faith effort to ensure that, in the event an application does not supply such function or table, the facility still operates, and performs whatever part of its purpose remains meaningful.

(For example, a function in a library to compute square roots has a purpose that is entirely well-defined independent of the application. Therefore, Subsection 2d requires that any application-supplied function or table used by this function must be optional: if the application does not supply it, the square root function must still compute square roots.)

These requirements apply to the modified work as a whole. If identifiable sections of that work are not derived from the Library, and can be reasonably considered independent and separate works in themselves, then this License, and its terms, do not apply to those sections when you distribute them as separate works. But when you distribute the same sections as part of a whole which is a work based on the Library, the distribution of the whole must be on the terms of this License, whose permissions for other licensees extend to the entire whole, and thus to each and every part regardless of who wrote it.

Thus, it is not the intent of this section to claim rights or contest your rights to work written entirely by you; rather, the intent is to exercise the right to control the distribution of derivative or collective works based on the Library.

In addition, mere aggregation of another work not based on the Library with the Library (or with a work based on the Library) on a volume of a storage or distribution medium does not bring the other work under the scope of this License.

3.   You may opt to apply the terms of the ordinary GNU General Public License instead of this License to a given copy of the Library. To do this, you must alter all the notices that refer to this License, so that they refer to the ordinary GNU General Public License, version 2, instead of to this License. (If a newer version than version 2 of the ordinary GNU General Public License has appeared, then you can specify that version instead if you wish.) Do not make any other change in these notices.

Once this change is made in a given copy, it is irreversible for that copy, so the ordinary GNU General Public License applies to all subsequent copies and derivative works made from that copy.

This option is useful when you wish to copy part of the code of the Library into a program that is not a library.

4.  You may copy and distribute the Library (or a portion or derivative of it, under Section 2) in object code or executable form under the terms of Sections 1 and 2 above provided that you accompany it with the complete corresponding machine-readable source code, which must be distributed under the terms of Sections 1 and 2 above on a medium customarily used for software interchange.

    If distribution of object code is made by offering access to copy from a designated place, then offering equivalent access to copy the source code from the same place satisfies the requirement to distribute the source code, even though third parties are not compelled to copy the source along with the object code.

5.  A program that contains no derivative of any portion of the Library, but is designed to work with the Library by being compiled or linked with it, is called a "work that uses the Library". Such a work, in isolation, is not a derivative work of the Library, and therefore falls outside the scope of this License.

    However, linking a "work that uses the Library" with the Library creates an executable that is a derivative of the Library (because it contains portions of the Library), rather than a "work that uses the library". The executable is therefore covered by this License. Section 6 states terms for distribution of such executables.

    When a "work that uses the Library" uses material from a header file that is part of the Library, the object code for the work may be a derivative work of the Library even though the source code is not. Whether this is true is especially significant if the work can be linked without the Library, or if the work is itself a library. The threshold for this to be true is not precisely defined by law.

    If such an object file uses only numerical parameters, data structure layouts and accessors, and small macros and small inline functions (ten lines or less in length), then the use of the object file is unrestricted, regardless of whether it is legally a derivative work. (Executables containing this object code plus portions of the Library will still fall under Section 6.)

    Otherwise, if the work is a derivative of the Library, you may distribute the object code for the work under the terms of Section 6. Any executables containing that work also fall under Section 6, whether or not they are linked directly with the Library itself.

6.  As an exception to the Sections above, you may also compile or link a "work that uses the Library" with the Library to produce a work containing portions of the Library, and distribute that work under terms of your choice, provided that the terms permit modification of the work for the customer's own use and reverse engineering for debugging such modifications.

    You must give prominent notice with each copy of the work that the Library is used in it and that the Library and its use are covered by this License. You must supply a copy of this License. If the work during execution displays copyright notices, you must include the copyright notice for the Library among them, as well as a reference directing the user to the copy of this License. Also, you must do one of these things:

a)   Accompany the work with the complete corresponding machine-readable source code for the Library including whatever changes were used in the work (which must be distributed under Sections 1 and 2 above); and, if the work is an executable linked with the Library, with the complete machine-readable "work that uses the Library", as object code and/or source code, so that the user can modify the Library and then relink to produce a modified executable containing the modified Library. (It is understood that the user who changes the contents of definitions files in the Library will not necessarily be able to recompile the application to use the modified definitions.)

b)   Accompany the work with a written offer, valid for at least three years, to give the same user the materials specified in Subsection 6a, above, for a charge no more than the cost of performing this distribution.

c)   If distribution of the work is made by offering access to copy from a designated place, offer equivalent access to copy the above specified materials from the same place.

d)   Verify that the user has already received a copy of these materials or that you have already sent this user a copy.

For an executable, the required form of the "work that uses the Library" must include any data and utility programs needed for reproducing the executable from it. However, as a special exception, the source code distributed need not include anything that is normally distributed (in either source or binary form) with the major components (compiler, kernel, and so on) of the operating system on which the executable runs, unless that component itself accompanies the executable.

It may happen that this requirement contradicts the license restrictions of other proprietary libraries that do not normally accompany the operating system. Such a contradiction means you cannot use both them and the Library together in an executable that you distribute.

7.   You may place library facilities that are a work based on the Library side-by-side in a single library together with other library facilities not covered by this License, and distribute such a combined library, provided that the separate distribution of the work based on the Library and of the other library facilities is otherwise permitted, and provided that you do these two things:

a) Accompany the combined library with a copy of the same work based on the Library, uncombined with any other library facilities. This must be distributed under the terms of the Sections above.

b) Give prominent notice with the combined library of the fact that part of it is a work based on the Library, and explaining where to find the accompanying uncombined form of the same work.

8. You may not copy, modify, sublicense, link with, or distribute the Library except as expressly provided under this License. Any attempt otherwise to copy, modify, sublicense, link with, or distribute the Library is void, and will automatically terminate your rights under this License. However, parties who have received copies, or rights, from you under this License will not have their licenses terminated so long as such parties remain in full compliance.

9. You are not required to accept this License, since you have not signed it. However, nothing else grants you permission to modify or distribute the Library or its derivative works. These actions are prohibited by law if you do not accept this License. Therefore, by modifying or distributing the Library (or any work based on the Library), you indicate your acceptance of this License to do so, and all its terms and conditions for copying, distributing or modifying the Library or works based on it.

10. Each time you redistribute the Library (or any work based on the Library), the recipient automatically receives a license from the original licensor to copy, distribute, link with or modify the Library subject to these terms and conditions. You may not impose any further restrictions on the recipients' exercise of the rights granted herein. You are not responsible for enforcing compliance by third parties to this License.

11. If, as a consequence of a court judgment or allegation of patent infringement or for any other reason (not limited to patent issues), conditions are imposed on you (whether by court order, agreement or otherwise) that contradict the conditions of this License, they do not excuse you from the conditions of this License. If you cannot distribute so as to satisfy simultaneously your obligations under this License and any other pertinent obligations, then as a consequence you may not distribute the Library at all. For example, if a patent license would not permit royalty-free redistribution of the Library by all those who receive copies directly or indirectly through you, then the only way you could satisfy both it and this License would be to refrain entirely from distribution of the Library.

If any portion of this section is held invalid or unenforceable under any particular circumstance, the balance of the section is intended to apply, and the section as a whole is intended to apply in other circumstances.

It is not the purpose of this section to induce you to infringe any patents or other property right claims or to contest validity of any such claims; this section has the sole purpose of protecting the integrity of the free software distribution system which is implemented by public license practices. Many people have made generous contributions to the wide range of software distributed through that system in reliance on consistent application of that system; it is up to the author/donor to decide if he or she is willing to distribute software through any other system and a licensee cannot impose that choice.

This section is intended to make thoroughly clear what is believed to be a consequence of the rest of this License.

12. If the distribution and/or use of the Library is restricted in certain countries either by patents or by copyrighted interfaces, the original copyright holder who places the Library under this License may add an explicit geographical distribution limitation excluding those countries, so that distribution is permitted only in or among countries not thus excluded. In such case, this License incorporates the limitation as if written in the body of this License.

13. The Free Software Foundation may publish revised and/or new versions of the Library General Public License from time to time. Such new versions will be similar in spirit to the present version, but may differ in detail to address new problems or concerns.

    Each version is given a distinguishing version number. If the Library specifies a version number of this License which applies to it and "any later version", you have the option of following the terms and conditions either of that version or of any later version published by the Free Software Foundation. If the Library does not specify a license version number, you may choose any version ever published by the Free Software Foundation.

14. If you wish to incorporate parts of the Library into other free programs whose distribution conditions are incompatible with these, write to the author to ask for permission. For software which is copyrighted by the Free Software Foundation, write to the Free Software Foundation; we sometimes make exceptions for this. Our decision will be guided by the two goals of preserving the free status of all derivatives of our free software and of promoting the sharing and reuse of software generally.

NO WARRANTY

15. BECAUSE THE LIBRARY IS LICENSED FREE OF CHARGE, THERE IS NO WARRANTY FOR THE LIBRARY, TO THE EXTENT PERMITTED BY APPLICABLE LAW. EXCEPT WHEN OTHERWISE STATED IN WRITING THE COPYRIGHT HOLDERS AND/OR OTHER PARTIES PROVIDE THE LIBRARY "AS IS" WITHOUT WARRANTY OF ANY KIND, EITHER EXPRESSED OR IMPLIED, INCLUDING, BUT NOT LIMITED TO, THE IMPLIED WARRANTIES OF MERCHANTABILITY AND FITNESS FOR A PARTICULAR PURPOSE. THE ENTIRE RISK AS TO THE QUALITY AND PERFORMANCE OF THE LIBRARY IS WITH YOU. SHOULD THE LIBRARY PROVE DEFECTIVE, YOU ASSUME THE COST OF ALL NECESSARY SERVICING, REPAIR OR CORRECTION.

16. IN NO EVENT UNLESS REQUIRED BY APPLICABLE LAW OR AGREED TO IN WRITING WILL ANY COPYRIGHT HOLDER, OR ANY OTHER PARTY WHO MAY MODIFY AND/OR REDISTRIBUTE THE LIBRARY AS PERMITTED ABOVE, BE LIABLE TO YOU FOR DAMAGES, INCLUDING ANY GENERAL, SPECIAL, INCIDENTAL OR CONSEQUENTIAL DAMAGES ARISING OUT OF THE USE OR INABILITY TO USE THE LIBRARY (INCLUDING BUT NOT LIMITED TO LOSS OF DATA OR DATA BEING RENDERED INACCURATE OR LOSSES SUSTAINED BY YOU OR THIRD PARTIES OR A FAILURE OF THE LIBRARY TO OPERATE WITH ANY OTHER SOFTWARE), EVEN IF SUCH HOLDER OR OTHER PARTY HAS BEEN ADVISED OF THE POSSIBILITY OF SUCH DAMAGES.

END OF TERMS AND CONDITIONS

Appendix: How to Apply These Terms to Your New Libraries

If you develop a new library, and you want it to be of the greatest possible use to the public, we recommend making it free software that everyone can redistribute and change. You can do so by permitting redistribution under these terms (or, alternatively, under the terms of the ordinary General Public License).

To apply these terms, attach the following notices to the library. It is safest to attach them to the start of each source file to most effectively convey the exclusion of warranty; and each file should have at least the "copyright" line and a pointer to where the full notice is found.

```
<one line to give the library's name and a brief idea of what it does.>
Copyright (C) <year>  <name of author>

This library is free software; you can redistribute it and/or
modify it under the terms of the GNU Library General Public
License as published by the Free Software Foundation; either
version 2 of the License, or (at your option) any later version.

This library is distributed in the hope that it will be useful,
but WITHOUT ANY WARRANTY; without even the implied warranty of
MERCHANTABILITY or FITNESS FOR A PARTICULAR PURPOSE.  See the GNU
Library General Public License for more details.

You should have received a copy of the GNU Library General Public
License along with this library; if not, write to the Free
Software Foundation, Inc., 675 Mass Ave, Cambridge, MA 02139, USA.
```

Also add information on how to contact you by electronic and paper mail.

You should also get your employer (if you work as a programmer) or your school, if any, to sign a "copyright disclaimer" for the library, if necessary. Here is a sample; alter the names:

```
Yoyodyne, Inc., hereby disclaims all copyright interest in the
library 'Frob' (a library for tweaking knobs) written by James Random Hacker.

<signature of Ty Coon>, 1 April 1990
Ty Coon, President of Vice
```

That's all there is to it!

# Glossary

**advisory locking**   Locking that is not enforced: All processes that manipulate the locked files must explicitly check for the existence of locks.

**ar**   The archiving utility used most often to create libraries.

**big-endian**   Multibyte values stored with the *most* significant byte in the lowest memory address or first byte transmitted, followed by the remainder of the bytes in order of significance.

**blocked signals**   Signals a process is not prepared to accept.  Usually, signals are blocked for a short time while the process is performing a sensitive task.  When a signal is sent to a process that is blocking that signal, the signal remains pending until the process unblocks the signal.

**BRE**   Basic Regular Expression, the type of string matching expression used by the `grep` utility.

**break**   A long stream of 0 bits on a serial interface.

**capability**   Actions a terminal can take in response to received escape sequences.

**catching a signal**   Providing a function that gets executed when a particular signal is sent to the process.

**control character**   A character in a data stream that provides control information to the processing program but does not change the processing mode.

**copy-on-write**   Marking as read-only a page meant to be writeable and private to multiple processes, producing a writeable version for each process as each process tries to write to it.

**CSI**   Command Sequence Introduction; a character that initiates a relatively complex escape sequence.

**dangling link**   A symbolic link that references a nonexistent file.

**dotted-decimal notation**   Writing an IP address in the form *aaa.bbb.ccc.ddd*

**ELF**   Executable and Linking Format; a generic file format for various kinds of binary files, including object files, libraries, shared libraries, and executables.

**epoch**   A point from which time is measured. Linux, like all Unix systems, defines its epoch as midnight, January 1, 1970 UTC.

**ERE**   Extended Regular Expression, the type of string matching expression used by the `egrep` utility.

**escape character**   A character in a data stream that changes the data processing mode from *normal* mode to an *escape mode,* which usually involves reading some subsequent characters for control information.

**escape sequence**   A series of characters that is treated differently by the program reading it. The escape sequence often encodes control information in a stream of data.

**file mode**   A 16-bit value that specifies a file's type and access permissions.

**fsgid**   The group ID associated with a process that is used to verify permissions for file system accesses by that process.

**fsuid**   The user ID associated with a process that is used to verify permissions for file system accesses by that process.

**glob**   Expanding *, ?, and [] according to file-name matching rules.

**glyph**   The shape used to represent a character.

**init process**   The first process on a Linux system. It is the only process started by the kernel and is responsible for starting every other process on the system. When processes are orphaned, the init process becomes the parent of the orphaned process and is responsible for preventing that process from becoming a zombie.

**kernel mode**   The unlimited, privileged execution environment in which the kernel runs, protected from programs running in user mode.

**little-endian**   Multibyte values stored with the *least* significant byte in the lowest memory address or first byte transmitted, followed by the remainder of the bytes in order of significance.

**ln**   The linker that combines object files into an executable.

**locked memory**   A memory region that is never swapped.

**major fault**   A fault caused by a process accessing memory that is not currently available, which forces the kernel to access the disk.

**mandatory locking**   Locking that is enforced; for example, processes attempting to write to an area on which another process has placed a write lock block until the write lock is removed.

**minor fault**   A fault caused by a process accessing memory that is not currently available but that does not require a disk access for the kernel to satisfy.

**modal**   The method of control in which the response to input depends on the mode a program is in, which is generally determined by prior input.

**network byte order**   The order in which bytes in multibyte values are transmitted across a network. For TCP/IP, the network byte order is big-endian.

**origin**   The first character of the first row of a character-matrix display.

**orphan process**   A process whose parent has died.

**pending connections**   Socket connections made to addresses that have been `listen()`ed to but have not yet been `accept()`ed.

**pending signals**   Signals that have been sent to a process but have not yet been delivered.

**pid**   A positive integer associated with a process. A process's pid is not shared with any other process on the system.

**process group**   Set of processes logically related. Process groups are moved between a terminal's foreground and background through job control, most commonly by shells.

**reliable signals**   Signal implementations defined to allow consistent and correct signal handling.

**reserved ports**   The TCP port numbers from 0 to 1,024, which may be used only by processes running as root.

**resident set size**    Amount of RAM a process is currently using (swapped out portions of the process do not contribute to its resident set size).

**session**    Set of process groups running on a single terminal.

**shell**    Program whose primary purpose is to run other programs and perform job control; popular Linux shells include the Bourne again shell (bash) and the enhanced C-shell tcsh.

**system call**    The mechanism used by user-mode processes to request kernel-mode services.

**termcap**    Original terminal capabilities database.

**terminfo**    New, improved terminal capabilities database.

**tty**    Bit-stream-oriented terminal interface.

**unreliable signals**    Signal implementations that make consistant signal handling impossible.  Most unreliable signal implementations either deliver signals no matter what a process's execution state is, or they reset signal handlers to a default value when a signal is delivered.

**user mode**    The limited execution environment in which programs run.

**vcs**    Virtual console screen; a memory-oriented device for accessing and changing the contents of a virtual console.

**vcsa**    Virtual console screen with attributes; a memory-oriented device for accessing and changing the contents and attributes of a virtual console.

**zombie**    A process that has terminated, but whose parent has not collected its exit status, causing the terminated process to be left in the system's process table.

# Bibliography

[Albitz, 1996] Albitz, Paul and Liu, Cricket. *DNS and BIND (second edition)*. O'Reilly, 1996. ISBN 1-54592-236-0.

[Bach, 1986] Bach, Maurice J. *The Design of the UNIX Operating System*. Prentice-Hall, 1986. ISBN 0-13-201799-7.

[Beck, 1996] Beck, Michael; Bohme, Harold; Dziadzka, Mirko; Kunitz, Ulrich; Magnus, Robert; and Verworner, Dirk. *LINUX Kernel Internals*. Addison Wesley Longman, 1996. ISBN 0-201-87741-4.

[Butenhof, 1997] Butenhof, David R. *Programming with POSIX®Threads*. Addison Wesley Longman, 1997. ISBN 0-201-63392-2.

[Cameron, 1996] Cameron, Debra; Rosenblatt, Bill; and Raymond, Eric. *Learning GNU Emacs*. O'Reilly, 1996. ISBN 1-56592-152-6.

[CSRG, 1994a] Computer Systems Research Group, UC Berkeley. *4.4BSD Programmer's Reference Manual*. O'Reilly, 1994. ISBN 1-56592-078-3.

[CSRG, 1994b] Computer Systems Research Group, UC Berkeley. *4.4BSD Programmer's Supplementary Documents*. O'Reilly, 1994. ISBN 1-56592-079-1.

[CSRG, 1994c] Computer Systems Research Group, UC Berkeley. *4.4BSD User's Reference Manual*. O'Reilly, 1994. ISBN 1-56592-075-9.

[CSRG, 1994d] Computer Systems Research Group, UC Berkeley. *4.4BSD User's Supplementary Documents*. O'Reilly, 1994. ISBN 1-56592-076-7.

[CSRG, 1994e] Computer Systems Research Group, UC Berkeley. *4.4BSD System Manager's Manual*. O'Reilly, 1994. ISBN 1-56592-080-5.

[Cormen, 1992] Cormen, Thomas H.; Leiserson, Charles E; and Rivest, Ronald L. *Introduction to Algorithms*. McGraw Hill, 1992. ISBN 0-07-013143-0.

[Gallmeister, 1995] Gallmeister, Bill O. *POSIX.4: Programming for the Real World*. O'Reilly, 1995. ISBN 1-56592-074-0.

[Garfinkel, 1996] Garfinkel, Simson and Spafford, Gene. *Practical UNIX & Internet Security*. O'Reilly, 1996. ISBN 1-56592-148-8.

[Heckman, 1997] Heckman, Jessica P. *Linux in a Nutshell*. O'Reilly, 1997. ISBN 1-56592-167-4.

[IEEE, 1993] IEEE. *Portable Operating System Interface (POSIX) Part 2*. IEEE, 1993. ISBN 1-55937-255-9.

[Kernighan, 1988] Kernighan, Brian W. and Ritchie, Dennis M. *The C Programming Language (second edition)*. Prentice Hall, 1988. ISBN 0-13-110362-8.

[Koenig, 1989] Koenig, Andrew. *C Traps and Pitfalls*. Addison Wesley Longman, 1989. ISBN 0-201-17928-8.

[Lamb, 1990] Lamb, Linda. *Learning the vi Editor*. O'Reilly, 1990. ISBN 0-937175-67-6.

[Lehey, 1995] Lehey, Greg. *Porting UNIX Software*. O'Reilly, 1995. ISBN 1-56592-126-7.

[Loukides, 1997] Loukides, Mike and Oram, Andy. *Programming with GNU Software*. O'Reilly, 1997. ISBN 1-56592-112-7.

[Matthew, 1996] Matthew, Niel and Stones, Richard. *Beginning Linux Programming*. Wrox, 1996. ISBN 1-874416-68-0.

[McKusick, 1996] McKusick, Marshall Kirk; Bostic, Keith; Karels, Michael J.; Quarterman, John S. *The Design and Implementation of the 4.4BSD Operating System*. Addison Wesley Longman, 1996. ISBN 0-201-54979-4.

[Murray, 1996] Murray, James D. and van Ryper, William. *Encyclopedia of Graphics File Formats (second edition)*. O'Reilly, 1996. ISBN 1-56592-161-5.

[Newham, 1995] Newham, Cameron and Rosenblatt, Bill. *Learning the bash Shell*. O'Reilly, 1995. ISBN 1-56592-147-X.

[Nichols, 1996] Nichols, Bradford; Buttlar, Dick; and Proulx Farrell, Jacqueline. *Pthreads Programming*. O'Reilly, 1996. ISBN 1-56592-115-1.

[Nohr, 1994] Nohr, Mary Lou. *Understanding ELF Object Files and Debugging Tools*. Prentice-Hall, 1994. ISBN 0-13-091109-7.

[Oram, 1993] Oram, Andrew and Talbott, Steve. *Managing Projects with make*. O'Reilly, 1993. ISBN 0-93715-90-0.

[Oualline, 1993] Oualline, Steven. *Practical C Programming*. O'Reilly, 1993. ISBN 1-56592-03-5.

[Rubini, 1998] Rubini, Alessandro. *Linux Device Drivers*. O'Reilly, 1998. ISBN 1-56592-292-1.

[Salus, 1994] Salus, Peter H. *A Quarter Century of Unix*. Addison Wesley Longman, 1994. ISBN 0-201-54777-5.

[Schneier, 1996] Schneier, Bruce. *Applied Cryptography*. John Wiley, 1996. ISBN 0-471-11709-9.

[Sobell, 1997] Sobell, Mark G. *A Practical Guide to Linux*. Addison Wesley Longman, 1997. ISBN 0-201-89549-8.

[Stevens, 1990] Stevens, W. Richard. *UNIX Network Programming*. Prentice Hall, 1990. ISBN 0-13-949876-1.

[Stevens, 1992] Stevens, W. Richard. *Advanced Programming in the UNIX®Environment*. Addison Wesley Longman, 1992. ISBN 0-201-56317-7.

[Stevens, 1994] Stevens, W. Richard. *TCP/IP Illustrated, Volume 1: The Protocols*. Addison Wesley Longman, 1994. ISBN 0-201-63346-9.

[Strang, 1991A] Strang, John. *Programming with curses*. O'Reilly, 1991. ISBN 0-937175-02-1.

[Strang, 1991B] Strang, John; Mui, Linda; and O'Reilly, Tim. *termcap & terminfo*. O'Reilly, 1991. ISBN 0-937175-22-6.

[Summit, 1996] Summit, Steve. *C Programming FAQs: Frequently Asked Questions*. Addison Wesley Longman, 1996. ISBN 0-201-84519-9.

[Tranter, 1996] Tranter, Jeff. *Linux Multimedia Guide*. O'Reilly, 1996. ISBN 1-56592-219-0.

[Vahalia, 1997] Vahalia, Uresh. *UNIX Internals: The New Frontiers.* Prentice Hall, 1997. ISBN 0-13-101902-2.

[Welsh, 1996] Welsh, Matt and Kaufman, Lars. *Running Linux (second edition).* O'Reilly, 1996. ISBN 1-565-92151-8.

# *Index*

**525**